Web Enable Your Small Business

Check the Web for Updates

To check for updates or corrections relevant to this book and/or CD-ROM visit our updates page on the Web at **http://www.prima-tech.com/updates**.

Send Us Your Comments:

To comment on this book or any other PRIMA TECH title, visit our reader response page on the Web at **http://www.prima-tech.com/comments**.

How to Order:

For information on quantity discounts, contact the publisher: Prima Publishing, P.O. Box 1260BK, Rocklin, CA 95677-1260; (916) 787-7000. On your letterhead, include information concerning the intended use of the books and the number of books you want to purchase. For individual orders, turn to the back of this book for more information.

Web Enable Your Small Business

John W. Gosney

A DIVISION OF PRIMA PUBLISHING

© 2000 by Prima Publishing. All rights reserved. No part of this book may be reproduced or transmitted in any form or by any means, electronic or mechanical, including photocopying, recording, or by any information storage or retrieval system without written permission from Prima Publishing, except for the inclusion of brief quotations in a review.

A Division of Prima Publishing

Prima Publishing and colophon and In a Weekend and associated logos are registered trademarks of Prima Communications, Inc. PRIMA TECH is a trademark of Prima Communications, Inc., Roseville, California 95661.

Publisher: Stacy L. Hiquet
Marketing Manager: Judi Taylor Wade
Associate Marketing Manager: Jody Kennen
Managing Editor: Sandy Doell
Acquisitions Editor: Emi Nakamura
Project Editor: Cathleen D. Snyder
Technical Reviewer: André Paree-Huff
Copy Editor: Gabrielle Nemes
Interior Layout: Shawn Morningstar
Cover Design: Prima Design Team
Indexer: Sharon Hilgenberg
Proofreader: Kelli Crump

Microsoft, FrontPage, Internet Explorer, Access, and SQL are trademarks or registered trademarks of Microsoft Corporation. Netscape is a registered trademark of Netscape Communications Corporation. Netscape Navigator, Netscape Messenger, and Netscape Communicator are also trademarks of Netscape Communications Corporation. Paint Shop Pro is a trademark of Jasc Software, Inc. Macromedia and Flash are trademarks or registered trademarks of Macromedia, Inc. This book is not affiliated with, or sponsored or endorsed by Netscape or Microsoft.

Important: Prima Publishing cannot provide software support. Please contact the appropriate software manufacturer's technical support line or Web site for assistance.

Prima Publishing and the author have attempted throughout this book to distinguish proprietary trademarks from descriptive terms by following the capitalization style used by the manufacturer.

Information contained in this book has been obtained by Prima Publishing from sources believed to be reliable. However, because of the possibility of human or mechanical error by our sources, Prima Publishing, or others, the Publisher does not guarantee the accuracy, adequacy, or completeness of any information and is not responsible for any errors or omissions or the results obtained from use of such information. Readers should be particularly aware of the fact that the Internet is an ever-changing entity. Some facts may have changed since this book went to press.

ISBN: 0-7615-2972-1
Library of Congress Catalog Card Number: 00-104876
Printed in the United States of America
00 01 02 03 04 BB 10 9 8 7 6 5 4 3 2 1

To Tim Ross, one of the smartest men I've ever met, who I think still really likes me even though I drive a Chrysler.

And to Debby Ross, one of the most hilarious and caring persons I've ever met. I love you both very much!

CONTENTS AT A GLANCE

Introduction xvi

FRIDAY EVENING
What E-Commerce Means to Your Small Business 1

SATURDAY MORNING
Working with FrontPage 23

SATURDAY AFTERNOON
Advanced FrontPage Functionality 55

SATURDAY EVENING
Dynamic Webs: Processing Forms and Integrating Databases . . 115

SUNDAY MORNING
Adding FrontPage Spice: Form Validation, DHTML, and E-Mail . . 167

SUNDAY AFTERNOON
Examining a Web-Enabled Small Business Example:
BestPop CD Shop 189

SUNDAY EVENING
Publishing Your Web. 241

APPENDIX A
Finding a Web Hosting Service 263

APPENDIX B
Access Essentials. 269

APPENDIX C
What's On the CD-ROM?. 295

Glossary. 307

Index 313

CONTENTS

Introduction xvi

FRIDAY EVENING
What E-Commerce Means to Your Small Business 1

    E-Commerce Considerations 6
        Living on Web Time..7
        Enabling Data Using HTML 9
    Considering Web Site Design Essentials..11
    Knowing What You Want versus What You Need 14
    Gathering and Organizing Information 16
        Building a Web Site Framework..19
        Developing a Process Plan 20
    Using the Tools of the Trade: FrontPage and Access....................21
        Using FrontPage 21
        Using Access 22
    Session in Review 22

SATURDAY MORNING
Working with FrontPage 23

    Locating Personal Web Server on Your Computer........................25
    Installing Personal Web Server...27
        Verifying the PWS Installation...29

  Checking the Rest of Your Components 32
  Disabling the Windows Automatic Dial-Up Connection 33
 Take a Break! 36
 Exploring FrontPage 2000 36
 Creating Your First Web Page 39
  Placing and Formatting Text 39
  Inserting Graphics 41
  Working with FrontPage Components 47
  Saving Your Web Pages 51
 Session in Review 53

SATURDAY AFTERNOON
Advanced FrontPage Functionality 55

 Building a FrontPage Web 57
  Naming a FrontPage Web 58
  Adding New Pages to Your Web 61
  Understanding Where FrontPage
   Webs are Stored on Your Computer 63
  Using a Web Browser to Access Pages in Your Web 65
 Working with FrontPage Wizards and Themes 67
  Using the Corporate Presence Wizard 67
  Customizing Webs Created Using Wizards 71
 Adding Tables to Organize Your Information 75
  Formatting Tables 77
  Adding Text and Graphics to Your Tables 80
 Take a Break! 83

Working with Frames	83
Creating and Saving a Frames Page	85
Saving Frames Pages	87
Understanding Frames Page Mechanics	89
Customizing Frame Properties with FrontPage	93
Working with Forms in Your Web Pages	96
Form Element: One-Line Text Box	100
Form Element: Scrolling Text Box	100
Form Element: Check Box	101
Form Element: Radio Button	102
Form Element: Drop-Down Menu	103
Form Element: The Push Button	104
Adding Hyperlinks	106
Adding Text Hyperlinks to Your Pages	106
Testing Hyperlinks in a Browser	110
Adding Graphical Hyperlinks to Your Pages	111
Session in Review	113

SATURDAY EVENING
Dynamic Webs: Processing Forms and Integrating Databases..115

What's So Dynamic about Dynamic Webs?	118
Active Server Pages 101	118
Getting Your Web Ready for ASP	120
Processing Forms	121
Creating a Form-Processing Web Page	124
Take a Break!	133
The Background of Dynamic Webs	133
Using a Database	135
Organizing Your Business Process Flow	136
Preparing Your Access Database for the Web	142
Establishing a Data Source Name (DSN)	142
Creating Your First Database-Driven Web Page	146
Adding a Search Form	151
Take a Break!	157
Inserting Information: Advanced Database Integration	158
Inserting Information into a Database	158
Session in Review	164

SUNDAY MORNING
Adding FrontPage Spice: Form Validation, DHTML, and E-Mail. 167

Validating Forms 170
    Determining Required Form Fields 170
    Validating Other Form Elements....................................176
Take a Break!..178
Integrating E-Mail with FrontPage Webs.....................................178
Working with DHTML Effects..181
Adding a Search Feature to Your Web Site.................................184
Session in Review 188

SUNDAY AFTERNOON
Examining a Web-Enabled Small Business Example: BestPop CD Shop 189

History of BestPop CD Shop 192
    Investigating the Web Construction Options 193
    Considering the Web Design Firm Suggestions 194
    Building a Web Site on Their Own...196
Overview of the BestPop Web Site 197
    Looking at the BestPop Home Page Design 199
Examining the BestPop Database 201
Analyzing the location.htm Page 206
Analyzing the catalog_search.asp and search_results.asp Pages....210
Take a Break!..218
Analyzing the guestbook.asp and guestbook_confirm.htm Pages ..218
    Working with the guestbook.asp Page 218
    Understanding the guestbook_confirm.htm Page 223
Analyzing the mailing_list.asp
    and mailing_confirm.htm Pages..223
Analyzing the order.asp Page...225
Analyzing the place_order.asp Page..231
    Analyzing the insert_order.asp Page 236
Analyzing the order_status.htm and
    order_status_results.asp Pages 236
Wrapping up with the BestPop Web Site....................................238
Session in Review 239

SUNDAY EVENING
Publishing Your Web... 241

    Registering a Name for Your Web Site...243
        Using Register.com to Find a Domain Name 244
    Publishing Your Web with the FrontPage Server Extensions 247
        Editing Pages on the Web Server 250
        Selectively Publishing Web Pages...252
    Publishing Your Web without the FrontPage Server Extensions...253
        Publishing Your Web Using FrontPage 254
        Publishing Your Web Using the
            Windows 98 Web Publishing Wizard 255
    Take a Break!...256
    Promoting Your Small Business Web Site....................................256
    Performing Monetary Transactions on the Web 258
    Weekend Wrap-Up..260

APPENDIX A
Finding a Web Hosting Service 263

    A Sample Listing of Web Hosting Providers 267

APPENDIX B
Access Essentials.. 269

    Creating a Database 272
    Creating Tables in Design View..273
    Entering Data into a Table Using the Datasheet View 283
    Modifying a Table that Contains Data..284
        Inserting a New Field into an Existing Table 285
        Deleting a Field from an Existing Table 287
        Modifying a Field Data Type...288
    Using the Access Simple Query Wizard......................................290

APPENDIX C
What's On the CD-ROM?.............................. 295

    Running the CD..297
        Windows 95/98/NT4/2000/Me 297

The Prima License	298
The Prima User Interface	298
Resizing and Closing the User Interface	298
Using the Left Panel	299
Using the Right Panel	299
Command Buttons	300
Pop-Up Menu Options	300
The Software	301

Glossary **307**

Index **313**

ABOUT THE AUTHOR

John W. Gosney is currently Director of Technology Services for the Indiana University School of Dentistry, Indianapolis. He has also served as a technical writer and Web development consultant for a major pharmaceutical corporation. John has worked extensively with Microsoft applications and Web development tools for several years, and has experience with Allaire ColdFusion and other Web development technologies. He is the author of several books, ranging from test preparation guides to e-business titles. John is also an adjunct instructor for the Community College of Indiana.

John received his B.A. in Technical Writing and Psychobiology in 1992 from Purdue University. In 1996, he was awarded an M.A. in English from Butler University. When not working (which is rare these days), John enjoys spending as much time as he can with his family, rooting for his favorite teams (Pacers, Colts, and Boilermakers), and furthering his reputation as an expert in all things popular culture.

ACKNOWLEDGMENTS

I had the great fortune of working with some exceptionally talented, creative, energetic individuals during the process of writing this book.

Special thanks to Emi Nakamura for agreeing to hire me in the first place and for giving me the opportunity to see this idea to fruition. Thanks are also due to Cathleen Snyder for her outstanding editorial skill and great sense of humor. Not only is Cathleen a joy to work with, but the book's content has been immeasurably improved thanks to her involvement. I'd also like to thank Gabrielle Nemes for making the text easy to read and for having such a fine eye for the little details. Also, my thanks to André Paree-Huff, who verified the book's technical content.

Finally, extra special thanks to Melissa, Genna, and Jackson for all their love and support while I worked on this and other projects.

Introduction

You're interested in having a Web presence for your small business, but you're not sure if the time involved in developing and implementing a Web site is really worth the effort.

Think again.

E-commerce is becoming more pervasive by the day (did someone say minute?), and one major ingredient of a successful small business is a successful Web site. But you keep asking yourself, "Wait a minute. I only have a *small* business. What good is all this e-stuff to me?" The answer to this question lies in how Joe Consumer uses the Web as a first step in gathering information about services and products. Just like having an advertisement in the Yellow Pages, having a Web site for your small business is good exposure, if nothing else. Add to this the tremendous cost savings of e-commerce, as well as other Web-related functionality, and the benefits of a well-designed Web site become clear.

What This Book is About

You may be asking yourself another question: "OK, I'm thinking that a Web site could help my small business, but how can I possibly find the time and money to build one?" Well, I've got some great news for you. Using FrontPage and Access, you have all the tools you need to quickly

build a powerful, functional Web site for your small business. Better news still is that once your Web site is up and running, these applications make it very easy to maintain and update your site's content. *Web Enable Your Small Business in a Weekend* will take you through all the steps to develop, implement, and maintain your small business Web site. And yes, you really can learn to do it all in a weekend!

Who Should Read This Book?

If you've never touched a computer before, then you might want to give someone else the job of building your small business Web site. But, if you're the like millions of other computer users who use applications like Microsoft Word and Excel every day, and you're familiar with some basic Web terminology (you know how to use a Web browser such as Internet Explorer, and you're familiar with typical Web features such as e-mail and search engines), then you possess all the knowledge you need to construct a Web site for your small business.

Microsoft FrontPage and Access are as easy to learn as the other Office applications. (In fact, you might find them even easier to use than Excel. I know I do!) You don't need to be a programmer or have any interest in programming to read and benefit from this book. Moreover, this book is organized in a step-by-step, hands-on manner, so you'll have plenty of guidance along the way.

What You Need to Begin

To get the most out of this book, you'll need the following components installed on your computer:

- Microsoft Access 2000 (or Access 97).
- Microsoft FrontPage 2000 (or FrontPage 98).
- Microsoft Personal Web Server. I'll give details on how to find and install the Personal Web Server during Saturday morning's session; you'll find this helpful if you don't already have it running on your machine.

CAUTION While it is possible to use FrontPage 98 to complete the tasks in this book, you will encounter significant differences between FrontPage 98 and FrontPage 2000, due primarily to the fact that FP 2000 has many features not found in FrontPage 98. This will become very apparent in the Saturday Evening session, when you will learn how to integrate your Access databases with Web pages. So, if you are using FrontPage 98, proceed with some amount of caution, as not all of the examples presented in this book will function with the 98 version of the application.

How This Book is Organized

You really can build a Web site for your small business in a weekend. This book assumes that you don't have any Web development experience, so it's best to go through the information in the order it is presented. If you do have some experience in building Web pages, there is still plenty of small business-specific information within each section to make it worth your effort to read them.

- **Friday Evening: What E-Commerce Means to Your Small Business.** Before you even open FrontPage on your computer, there are some crucial e-commerce decisions you'll need to make about your small business Web site. This section will discuss these issues and ensure you have a solid foundation from which to begin designing your site.

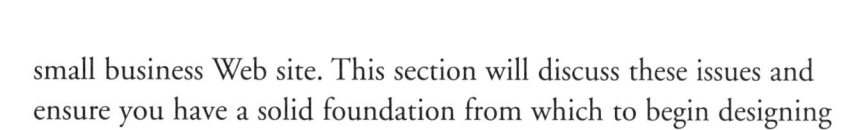

- **Saturday Morning: Working with FrontPage.** Although FrontPage shares many similarities with the other applications in the Office suite, there are some unique elements of how the program functions. In this section, you'll be introduced to the basics of FrontPage, including its user interface and special features. You'll also build your first Web page before lunch!

- **Saturday Afternoon: Advanced FrontPage Functionality.** After Saturday morning's session, you'll be amazed at how easy it is to build a Web page. In this section, you'll see how easy it is to implement powerful, advanced features into your site, and you'll learn to design forms to capture customer information

- **Saturday Evening: Dynamic Webs: Processing Forms and Integrating Databases.** Every functional small business Web site needs a database behind it for two reasons: to capture information submitted by the customer (such as product orders), and to present the customer with the latest information about the products and services of your small business. Before you turn in for the night, you'll have your Web pages writing information to, and reading information from, Access databases.

- **Sunday Morning: Adding FrontPage Spice: Form Validation, DHTML, and E-Mail.** By this point in the weekend, you'll have a working draft of your Web site. Now, take the time to add some pizzazz to your work by including e-mail features and form input validation in your Web pages.

- **Sunday Afternoon: Examining a Web-Enabled Small Business Example: BestPop CD Shop.** All Web developers learn from studying the efforts of others. Why should you be any different? After your Sunday lunch, I'll take you through a complete small business Web site, from the design framework to how it interacts with a database.

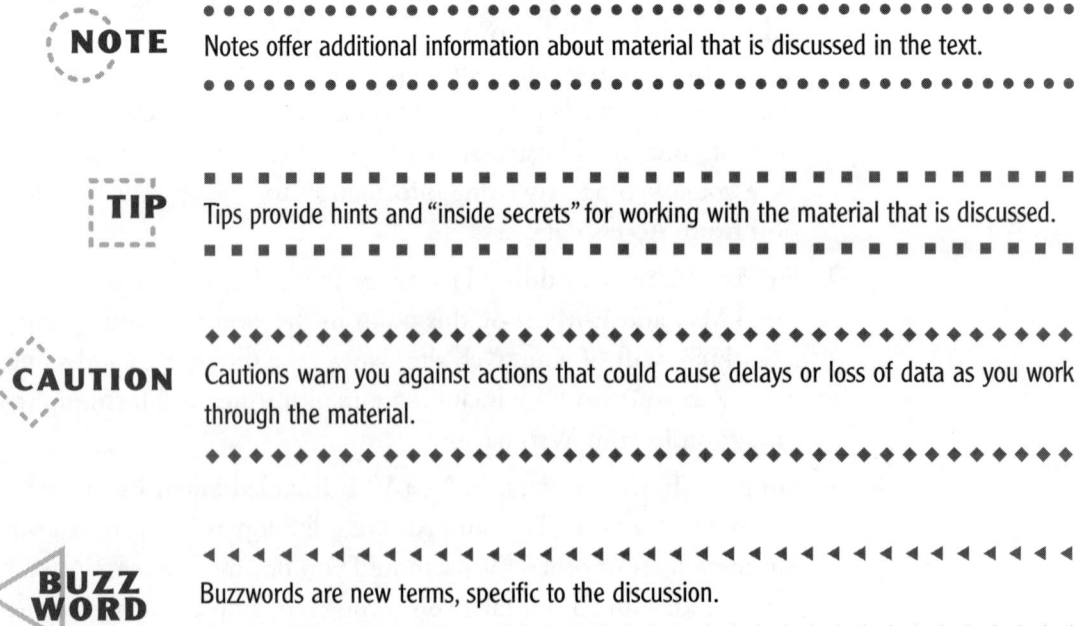

- **Sunday Evening: Publishing Your Web.** You have your site finished and now you're ready to post it to the Web for all your potential customers. In this last book section, I'll give you practical advice on how to shop around for the best method of placing your site on the Web. You'll also learn some tips about how to advertise your Web site and how to keep its content current after you have everything up and running.

The appendixes provide you with a list of Internet Service Providers that support the features necessary for publishing Web sites built with FrontPage and Access. I'll also give you a tour of what's included on the CD-ROM. Finally, you'll find a glossary of terms that clearly explains the (sometimes) confusing terms used in e-commerce and Web site development.

Special Features of This Book

NOTE Notes offer additional information about material that is discussed in the text.

TIP Tips provide hints and "inside secrets" for working with the material that is discussed.

CAUTION Cautions warn you against actions that could cause delays or loss of data as you work through the material.

BUZZ WORD Buzzwords are new terms, specific to the discussion.

Are You Ready?

You're one of the adventurous individuals who have made the exciting decision to start a small business. Now you want to take that small business into the 21st century with a well-designed, functional Web site. Get ready to have some fun; by Monday morning, you'll have a Web site. Let's get started!

FRIDAY EVENING

What E-Commerce Means to Your Small Business

- E-Commerce Considerations
- Considering Web Site Design Essentials
- Knowing What You Want versus What You Need
- Gathering and Organizing Information
- Using the Tools of the Trade: FrontPage and Access

Consider the following e-commerce example: A potential customer is interested in one of your company's products and decides to find out more about your product via your Web site. Moreover, pretend that this particular customer is somewhat of an insomniac and has decided to check out your Web site at 1:30 a.m. on a Thursday!

You've registered your Web site with various search engines, so the customer is able to quickly locate the address of your site by performing a Yahoo! search on your company's name. The customer clicks your company's name as it appears in the list of results generated by the search engine (see Figure 1.1), and is taken to your Web site's home page.

Registering your Web site with a search engine, not to mention establishing a specific domain name, are important first steps in publishing your completed Web site. These and related issues will be discussed in the Sunday Evening session, "Publishing Your Web."

A *home page* is the first page users see when visiting your Web site. Since this page is the first introduction to your site, it is crucial that it is well-designed and conveys all the required information about your company and its products and services.

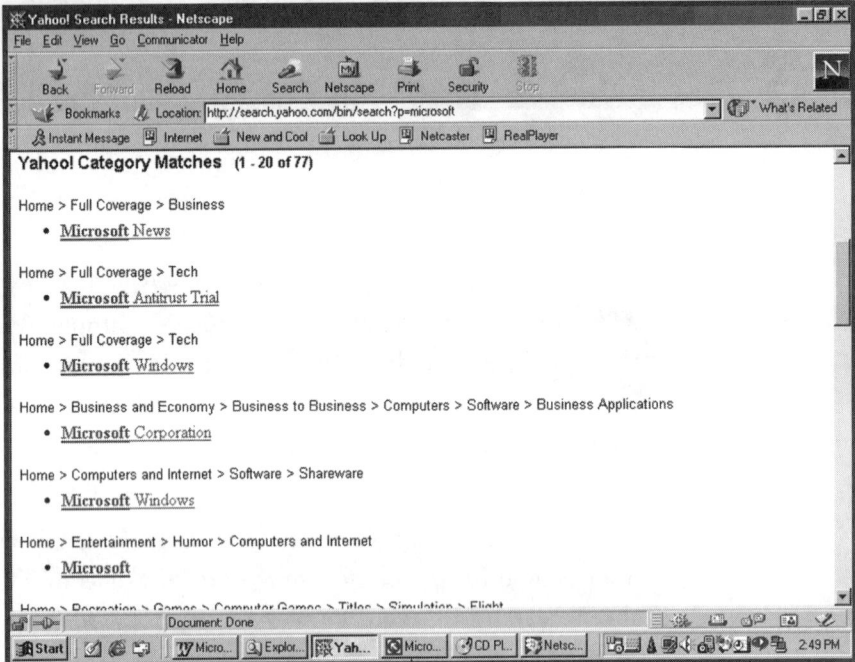

Figure 1.1

Results of a Yahoo! search on the term "microsoft"

Your Web site is exceptionally well-designed (of course!), so the customer is able to quickly find information about the product they are interested in buying. For this example, pretend that you have placed a picture of the product on your home page. When the customer clicks on the picture, a separate home page loads in his or her Web browser and displays information specific to the product.

After reading the information, the customer decides that yes, this is the desired product. Since your site is so well-designed, you have placed a quick order link on this information page. The customer clicks the link and is immediately taken to an order form on which the usual name, address, and billing information is completed.

The transaction for our sleepless customer is almost finished. After the customer completes the order information form and clicks the submit button, your site does a quick search of your product database to determine

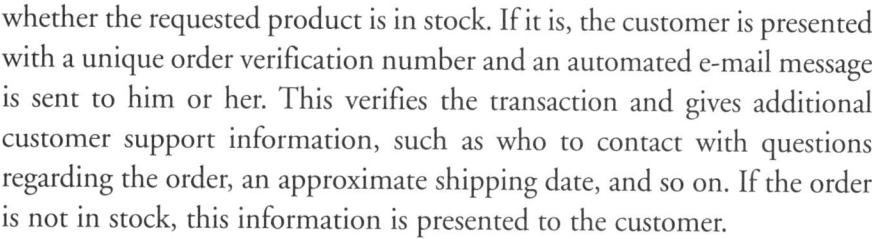

whether the requested product is in stock. If it is, the customer is presented with a unique order verification number and an automated e-mail message is sent to him or her. This verifies the transaction and gives additional customer support information, such as who to contact with questions regarding the order, an approximate shipping date, and so on. If the order is not in stock, this information is presented to the customer.

All in all, a fairly typical e-commerce transaction. What makes this so different from a traditional business transaction? Consider the following important details:

- Wal-Mart and 7-Eleven aside, it's a fairly good bet that the regular business hours for your small business do not include 1:30 a.m. on a Thursday morning. But with the "24/7" convenience of a Web site, your customers can gather information about your products—and order them—at any time of the day or night. This is a major benefit of the Web, and its importance should not be understated.

- Instead of requiring a customer to drive to the local mall, your company has an office in cyberspace. Like time convenience, this is also an important issue when you consider how your customers like to shop for products. Instead of packing the kids into the mini-van and battling traffic, your customers can quickly navigate to your Web site using search engines. Of course, if they already know your Web address, they can simply type it into their Web browser. With a few clicks of the mouse, they are inside your company's virtual office.

- Detailed information is immediately available to your customer about any product. How many times have you gone into a store and been frustrated with the well-meaning but misinformed teenager acting as your sales representative? By carefully writing and placing your product information online, you can rest assured that your customers have the most current, detailed information about your products. In addition, this information is presented to each and every customer in the same manner, free of potential false information resulting from the various knowledge levels and communication skills of sales representatives.

- Having your product information online and accessible through a database ensures that your customers are given the most accurate, up-to-the-minute inventory information. If a product is temporarily out of stock, your customer can be notified immediately, rather than waiting for a phone call informing them of their order status.

- Finally, through a well-designed Customer Relationship Management (CRM) strategy, you can keep your customers happy before, during, and after the sale. From an enticing, attractive Web site design to a clear, quick, secure order process, you can be certain that each visitor to your Web site is treated as the Most Important Customer. By sending post-sale e-mail messages to track order status and provide additional product information, you provide the accurate and invaluable impression that you care about your customers after the sale.

◄ ◄

Customer Relationship Management (CRM) is a catch-all term used to describe the entire sales process. From ensuring that your internal processes result in the most effective communication between related components of your company to presenting your customers with the easiest method of ordering a product, CRM is a critical ingredient in e-commerce.

◄ ◄

E-Commerce Considerations

As illustrated in the previous example, performing business transactions on the Web has many advantages over the traditional business model. From the tremendous convenience afforded by Web shopping to the instantaneous product information, e-commerce transactions can provide customers with a more enjoyable experience in many ways. You'll also retain effective control of your products, from the dissemination of product information to inventory control.

While all of this sounds very appealing (and arguably, it is), there are important issues you need to consider and understand before you begin to design your small business Web site.

Living on Web Time

As illustrated in the example, time is of special importance when dealing with the Web. Given the nearly instantaneous speed in which electronic transactions can occur, it is critical that your data (presented on your Web site or stored in your database) be able to respond to this speed. The traditional business model that allows for a given period of time between placing an order and processing the order simply does not exist on the Web.

In this example, when the customer completed the order form and clicked the submit button, various transactions occurred almost instantly.

- **The customer's information (name, address, and so on) was inserted into a database.** As with any business, you want to store customer information so that you can solicit this customer with information on additional products. Additionally, retaining customer information can help you target specific segments of the market as you gain a better understanding of who frequents your site based on specific criteria, such as age, level of income, gender, and geographic location.

- **The product ordered by the customer was checked against currently available inventory.** In a well-designed Web site like the one you will learn to build this weekend, the information presented on your Web pages is *dynamic* rather than *static*. As much as possible, product information presented on your pages should come from your database. By storing information in your database rather than directly on your page, you provide your customers with the most current information. For example, one of your Web pages could list the quantity of a given product that is currently available. This number would be read directly from your database and would be, therefore, always up to date.

▤▤▤▤▤▤▤▤▤▤▤▤▤▤▤▤▤▤▤▤▤▤▤▤▤
A *static* Web page is one where information presented on the page is scripted directly into the HTML code that makes up the page. In other words, the content does not change. On the other hand, the information presented on a *dynamic* Web page can potentially change each time a page is loaded, since the information is read from a data source (database).
▤▤▤▤▤▤▤▤▤▤▤▤▤▤▤▤▤▤▤▤▤▤▤▤▤

◆◆◆◆◆◆◆◆◆◆◆◆◆◆◆◆◆◆◆◆◆◆◆◆◆
It is essential that you keep the information in your databases current! If you are presenting current inventory information to your customers via your Web site and the information is read from a database, the database information must be up to date or you run the risk of having some very dissatisfied customers. You'll learn about this and other database issues in the Saturday Evening session, "Dynamic Webs: Processing Forms and Integrating Databases."
◆◆◆◆◆◆◆◆◆◆◆◆◆◆◆◆◆◆◆◆◆◆◆◆◆

- **Information relevant to the customer's order was stored in a database.** Once it has been confirmed that the product in question is available, specific details about the customer's order (type of product ordered, the quantity, billing information, and so on) are stored in a database.

- **E-mail messages about the order were automatically composed and distributed to the customer, as well as others.** Quality CRM demands that you provide immediate electronic confirmation of an order by sending an e-mail message to the customer that gives specific details about the order. Additionally, you may want to send messages about the order to specific individuals or groups within your organization, notifying them that an order has been placed. That way, they can begin processing the order.

All of the above tasks need to occur instantaneously (and for all intents and purpose, simultaneously). Your site should be designed to allow the smooth completion of each of these tasks and to complete them—literally—at the click of a button.

Enabling Data Using HTML

The importance of static versus dynamic Web pages is a distinction that cannot be overstated. In order for your Web site to be a true, accurate reflection of the most current information about your company and product, the Web pages need to have their HTML code built dynamically. That is, information must be retrieved from a database each time a customer loads your Web pages.

▶ BUZZ WORD

▶▶▶▶▶▶▶▶▶▶▶▶▶▶▶▶▶▶▶▶▶▶▶▶▶▶▶▶▶▶

HTML is short for Hypertext Markup Language. HTML is the coding structure used to build Web pages. Applications like FrontPage are WYSIWYG (what-you-see-is-what-you-get) HTML editors. By using a standard interface, the application automatically produces the HTML for you.

▶▶▶▶▶▶▶▶▶▶▶▶▶▶▶▶▶▶▶▶▶▶▶▶▶▶▶▶▶▶

NOTE The great benefit of using an application like FrontPage is that you don't have to worry about coding any of the HTML yourself; FrontPage does it for you. However, there are times when you'll want to tweak the HTML that is automatically generated by FrontPage, in order to add some increased functionality to your pages or customize them to fit your specific needs. Throughout this book, I'll highlight some of these instances when you'll want to get in and "mess around" with the actual HTML.

There is really no difference in the final structure of a static Web page when compared to a dynamic one—the resulting HTML will look the same in either case. However, with a dynamic Web page, you can give yourself lots of freedom when designing, since you don't have to anticipate what each individual customer will want to see.

What do I mean? Consider this example. Over the course of a specific day, 50 customers visit your Web site. Of these 50, 25 of them are returning customers. Since you've designed your site to accommodate visitor profiles, when these returning customers open your site, they see a personalized greeting at the top of the page, the date and time of their visit, and perhaps some information specific to their last order. Take a look at Figure 1.2 for an example of this customization feature in a dynamic Web site.

From this example, you can see the potential difficulty in trying to provide personalized information about a static Web page. As you sit down to build a page like this, imagine trying to anticipate not only which customers will visit your site, but the day and time they will visit, as well as information about their most recent order. Obviously, you couldn't build a static Web page to accomplish these tasks, as there is no way to accurately present the information for so many variables.

It is for this very reason that you need to build your Web pages dynamically—so that they are unique to each specific visitor. By basing the HTML code on which your page is constructed on information stored in a database, you can present unique information to each visitor.

Figure 1.2

At Amazon.com, returning customers are given a personalized greeting and recommendations for similar products that might interest them.

Considering Web Site Design Essentials

Although your data will potentially be unique to each visitor to your site, you'll still need a standardized template from which to work. A *template* is the basic shell of your Web pages. This shell will normally address the following design components:

- **A general navigation scheme.** Perhaps you will use drop-down menus like you see in most Windows applications (see Figure 1.3). This type of interface is a very intuitive, easy-to-use navigation scheme. Or maybe you plan to use frames to produce a table of contents that will remain visible to customers as they move through your site, as shown in Figure 1.4.

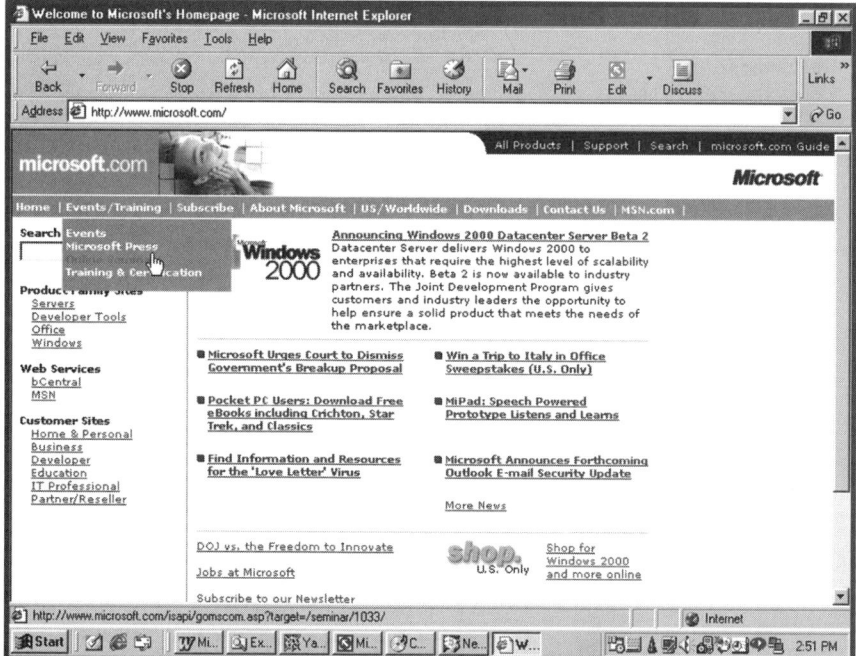

Figure 1.3

The Microsoft Web site uses a familiar, Windows-style menu interface.

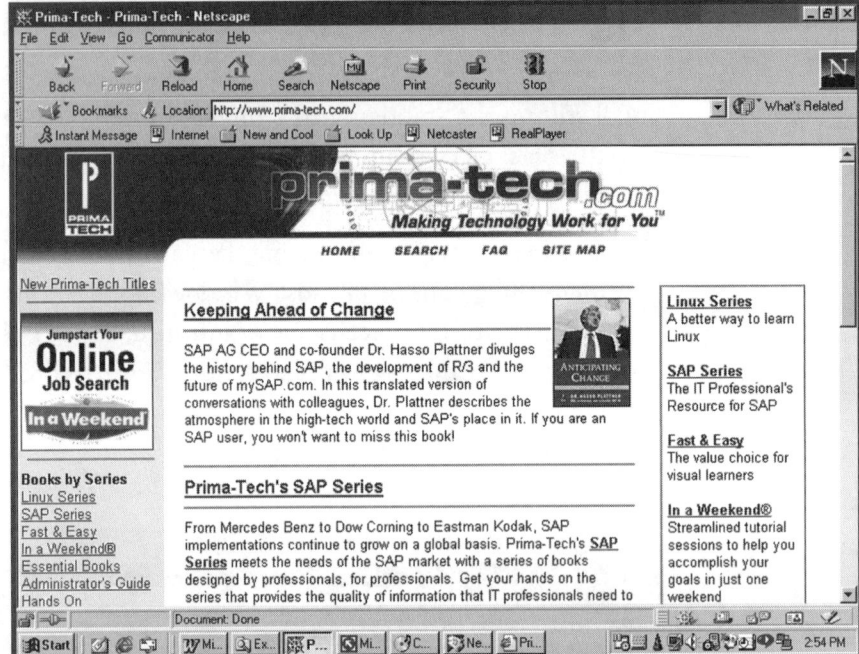

Figure 1.4

Prima-Tech.com uses frames to create a table of contents that is always visible to the user.

 As with all aspects of Web design, you need to be careful that what you design functions and looks roughly the same in different types of Web browsers. For example, try opening the Microsoft site in Netscape Navigator. You'll find that the drop-down menus shown in Figure 1.3 no longer function as they do when you view the site with Internet Explorer!

 Be careful when working with frames, because they have unique properties. If not designed properly, frames can lead to customer frustration.

FRIDAY EVENING What E-Commerce Means to Your Small Business

- **Special elements.** Along with a general navigation scheme, you'll also need to consider what types of special elements (including graphics, sound, and video) you might want to add to your site. While there are a number of plug-in applications that might make your content more exciting and dynamic, not all users will have the various plug-ins (or will want to take the time to download and install them). In addition, these types of special elements usually increase the amount of time it takes for your Web pages to load; you'll need to carefully consider how much value they add to your site compared to their size and download time.

BUZZ WORD

A *plug-in* is an application that runs inside your Web browser to increase the functionality of the content being displayed.

NOTE Most of the popular browser plug-ins are free. Many of them are included and preloaded with the most current versions of the more popular Web browsers (Netscape Navigator and Internet Explorer). You just need to consider whether the functionality afforded by these plug-ins is worth the possibly increased loading time of the Web pages that use them.

- **Design theme.** The most visually appealing, well-designed Web sites also have a common design theme. For example, specific text (such as topic headings) is the same color across pages. Graphics, links, or other items that provide customer interaction functionality are placed uniformly on each page. For example, the upper-right corner of every page might contain a link to your home page. Again, this is an important issue and should be considered when designing your shell, so each page will have a clean, uniform look.

Knowing What You Want versus What You Need

There's an old Rolling Stones song that says, "You can't always get what you want, but you get what you need." Certainly, an axiom to ponder, especially in Web site design.

What do I mean by this? Remember that your small business Web site should ultimately be a useful tool for your customers. That said, if your customers can't use your site (due to poor design, hyperlinks that point to nowhere, outdated information on your products, and so on), it goes without saying that your site—and potentially, your business—will not be successful.

Take a look at Figure 1.5 to see what is perhaps the most familiar Web page of all: the Yahoo! home page. Deceptively simple in design, Yahoo!'s layout provides visitors with a functional navigation scheme and limited use of graphics, thus ensuring that the page loads quickly even with the slowest connection speeds. Also, the layout allows the site content to be easily updated (for example, the In the News links) without having to redesign the site around the new content.

Yahoo! is a great example of form following function. The layout is simple and clean. Various areas of information, such as personal links, information categories, In the News links, and online shopping are neatly organized—and most importantly, all visible at one time.

TIP
To scroll, or not to scroll, that is the question. Well, it may be a question, but the answer is rather simple. As you start to imagine the look of your home page, think about what kind of information you are going to display. Ideally, on first loading your customers should not need to scroll down the page to view essential information. If they do, you run the risk of unintentionally hiding your information; your customers might not scroll down the page to view it. Worse still, they might not even know that the information is there. Good site organization—including an effective navigational design—can help remedy this problem.

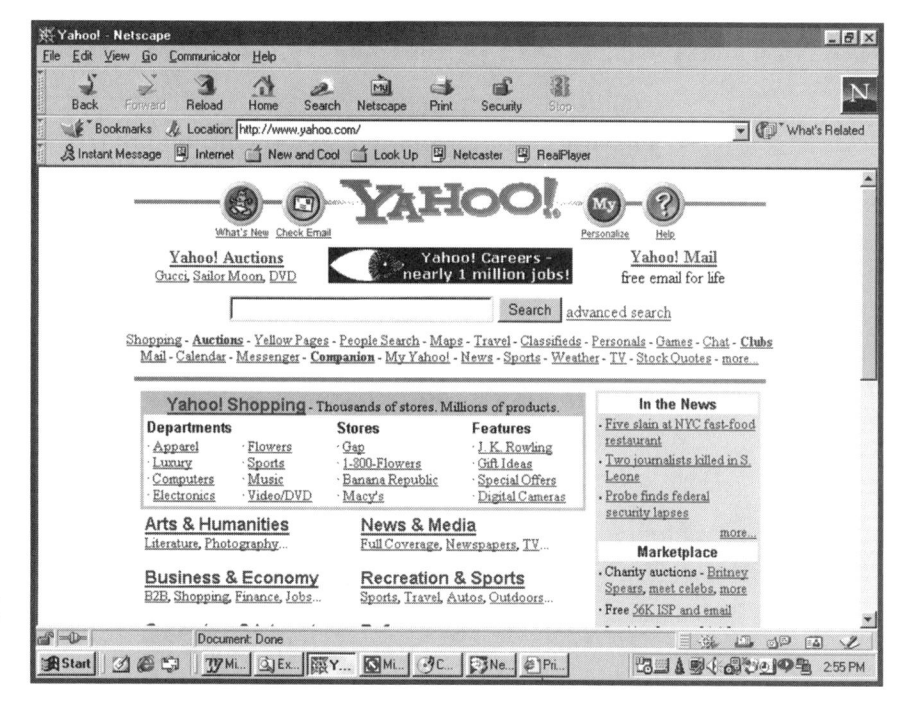

FRIDAY EVENING What E-Commerce Means to Your Small Business

Figure 1.5

Yahoo!'s tried and true design

The important lesson to take from this discussion is that, while having all the bells and whistles on your Web site can be fun, an overabundance of special elements can lead to confusion on the part of the customer. If a customer can't find product information because an animated graphic takes five minutes to load, he or she will look elsewhere; I guarantee it. When you retire this evening and dream about your soon-to-be small business Web site, remember this: Less really can be more.

> **TIP**
>
> Keeping in mind the concept of a simple, clean, functional Web site, you should also remember that despite advances in connection speeds (via cable modem lines and DSL, for example), the majority of your customers will likely be connecting to your Web site at 56K or less. While this represents a dramatic increase from the old days (i.e., 1994!) of connecting to the Web, it can still result in a slow-loading Web page, especially if the page is graphic and special-element intensive.

Gathering and Organizing Information

I've talked about the importance of good design and discussed such ideas as a navigational scheme, a design theme, and the use of special elements. But before you can start to build your Web site, you need to do some planning!

Remember back in high school or college when you had to write a term paper for class? How did you start the process? Well, if you were like me, you waited until the last minute, then sat down in front of your computer or word processor and just started flailing away at the keyboard. Unless you were a far more talented writer than I was, what you produced for your first draft probably wasn't the next Great American Novel.

Hopefully, you wrote your paper in a more organized fashion, rather than following that process. You planned what major topics you were going to discuss, where in the paper you were going to talk about them, and what the overall goal (or, to use English composition lingo, the *thesis*) of your paper was going to be.

Guess what? This type of logical, outline approach works extremely well when you are thinking about Web site design, too! In fact, you should consider it the essential first step in thinking about your Web site.

Ultimately, your small business Web site will be a reflection of your actual company processes. Particularly if you plan to allow orders to be placed on your site, you'll need to map out how your ordering process will work. In this way, you can effectively transform the ordering process to your Web site. As you try to transfer your company processes to your Web site, you might find that your existing processes are a little disorganized.

If this is the case, don't fret. As discussed at the start of this session, the world of e-commerce is different from traditional business models; the most notable exception is the speed at which electronic transactions can occur. You may find that your current company processes are too fragmented for proper transformation to an electronic setting.

FRIDAY EVENING What E-Commerce Means to Your Small Business

If this is indeed the case (and most likely it will be for at least one of your current processes), then planning becomes all the more important. While a complete description of how to organize your company processes is far beyond the scope of this book, there are some questions you can ask yourself to ensure that your site is well-organized. Again, try to keep the term paper approach in mind, as the organization concepts are quite similar.

- **What is the primary goal of your Web site?** Undoubtedly if this is a small business-oriented Web site, your goal is to sell your company's products or services. But this larger goal can be broken down into smaller sub-categories. Do you also want to talk about your company's history? Do you want to solicit for potential new employees? Do you want to provide links to potential business partners' Web sites? In other words, your overall goal can be composed of several, smaller goals.

- **What are the major topics of discussion on your Web site?** You also need to think about how you want to present the various components of your small business on your Web site. You should consider how these areas will fit together, providing the customer with the most logical, natural access from one area to another. For example, let's say you have an order form on your site. After the ordering process is complete and the customer has received verification of their order, what do you want the screen to display? Obviously, you don't want to suddenly leave the customer out in the cold with a message saying something like, "Thanks for your order; that's all we really wanted out of you." You need to *always* have a method, such as a good navigation scheme, so that your customer can move back and forth between areas of interest within your site. Keep the customer interested in all facets of your small business, even after they have completed their order.

- **Where in your small business Web site will you place specific information?** Your effective Web site should immerse the customer in your small business, not only to entice them to order your product or service, but also to generate interest in how your business can help them in the future and with potential secondary needs they might have right now. In order to get this connectivity working within your site, you'll need to consider what areas of your business are related and how you want to reflect these relationships. A good example of this concept is a link between your company profile and an online job application form. One page of your site might give details about your company history, your benefits to your employees, the city in which you are located, and perhaps your philanthropic activities. From this page, it would make good sense to have a link to another page where the visitor could complete an online application. The ability to quickly link related topics is one of the most powerful features of the Web, and you should take full advantage of it.

INTEGRATING DATABASES WITH WEB PAGES

Don't forget the database! As you plan your Web site, remember that you want to produce a dynamic site. To do so, you'll need to have a database sitting behind your site. This will ensure that as your pages load into your customers' browsers, the most current information you can provide is displayed, not only about your products and services, but about every facet of your business.

Database design is a huge topic and it is not my intention here to make you a professional database developer. But the basics are quite easy to understand and you can use them to your advantage when planning the database that will drive the content and function of your site.

Database design will be discussed during tomorrow evening's session, "Dynamic Webs: Processing Forms and Integrating Databases," and in Appendix B, "Access Essentials." For now, start thinking about the type of information you want to capture from your customers, such as general information about where they live, their order information, customer feedback information, and so on. In addition, think about what types of information you want to keep current for your customers, such as your company profile and current product inventory.

FRIDAY EVENING What E-Commerce Means to Your Small Business — 19

Building a Web Site Framework

You have a lot to think about in terms of planning your Web site, but it's important to note that you don't have to get it all right the first time. As your business grows and develops, so can your Web site.

For now, a good way to organize your information might be to draw a simple site map, illustrating the major organizational topics within your site and how each area might connect to other related areas. Using a simple drawing, you can plan your site's organizational structure. At this point, don't worry about being too inclusive with the details. Your site will grow as your business grows and you'll always get new ideas along the way. Take a look at Figure 1.6 for an example.

As you move through the discussion this weekend, you can refer back to this drawing as your Site Charter. While you don't have to illustrate every area of your small business in this drawing, you should at least try to list the major areas of interest.

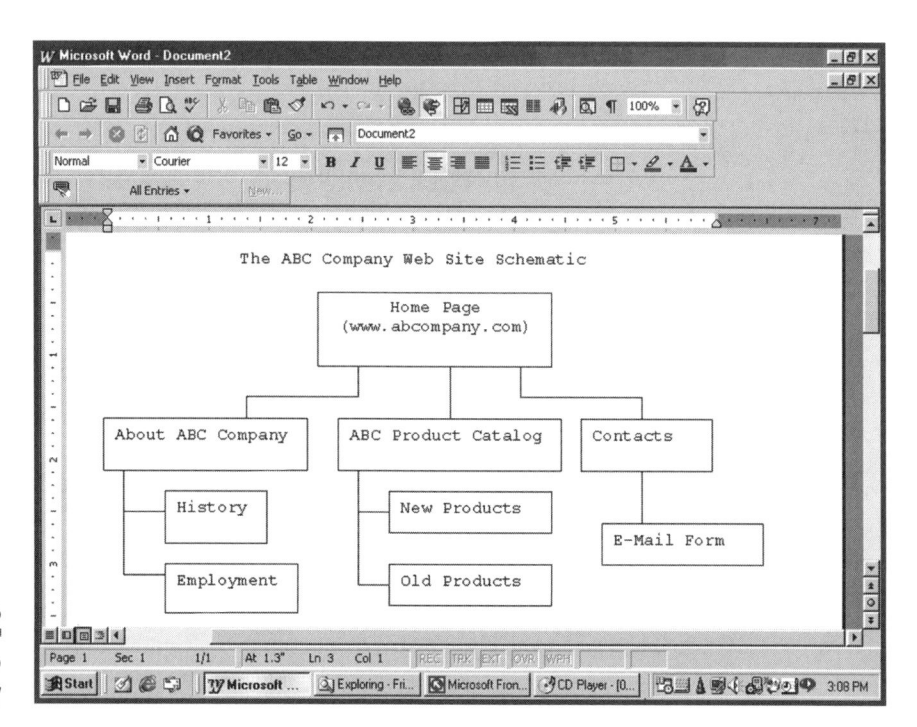

Figure 1.6

A simple site map for ABC Company

Developing a Process Plan

Just as you need to think about the actual framework of your site, you also need to consider how your Web site will fit into the day-to-day operations of your small business. A common error small business owners make as they move to e-commerce is not giving enough attention to the special demands a Web site places on their company. It is important to consider the following issues:

- **Keep the information on your site current.** I'm sure you've visited Web sites that have a "Last Updated" tag on them. Just how reassuring is it to see a tag that says, "Content last updated 1/1/98," when we are now in the early days of the new millenium? Not only is this unprofessional, but it can seriously limit your site's credibility and, by default, put a serious damper on your ability sell your products and services. If I haven't stressed it enough already, let me say it once again: Time is an entirely different animal on the Web. You'll need to develop a plan for updating your site content (including your product inventory) to ensure that it is current for each visiting customer.

- **Establish a process of change control.** I'm sure you've noticed how quickly technology changes. A product is barely out the door before a new version is being planned and released! While you certainly don't have to worry about upgrading your Web site's technical features on a monthly (or even yearly) basis, you should keep abreast of current advances in technology that might make your site run smoother and thus more effectively.

> **TIP** If your Internet Service Provider is worth the money you pay them to host your Web site, they'll do much of the research into new technologies for you. Keep in mind, however, that they may be hosting several hundred Web sites, so it will ultimately be your responsibility to ensure that your site still functions the way you intend as they make upgrades to their equipment. If you notice changes, especially errors, in your site's functioning, you should contact your ISP immediately.

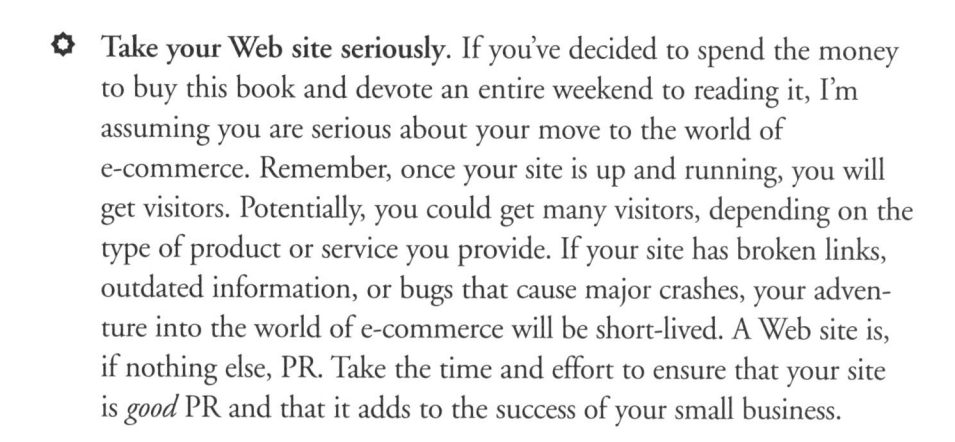

○ **Take your Web site seriously.** If you've decided to spend the money to buy this book and devote an entire weekend to reading it, I'm assuming you are serious about your move to the world of e-commerce. Remember, once your site is up and running, you will get visitors. Potentially, you could get many visitors, depending on the type of product or service you provide. If your site has broken links, outdated information, or bugs that cause major crashes, your adventure into the world of e-commerce will be short-lived. A Web site is, if nothing else, PR. Take the time and effort to ensure that your site is *good* PR and that it adds to the success of your small business.

Using the Tools of the Trade: FrontPage and Access

Before you hit the hay, let's take a quick look at the tools you'll use to build your small business Web site.

NOTE Although the material in this book is written to the Office 2000 versions of FrontPage and Access, you will still find the book useful if you are using older versions of these applications (specifically, FrontPage 98 and Access 97). Where appropriate, I will point out large differences between the versions of these applications.

Using FrontPage

FrontPage is easy to use. In fact, you might find it the easiest of all the Office applications to use and understand. While it does have a somewhat different user interface, you will also find the familiar menu options (such as File, Edit, and Help) on the menu bar.

In addition to the application, you will also need to use a Web server to test your pages as you develop them. Don't let this term throw you. Microsoft produces a really neat personal Web server (in fact, that is its name: Personal

Web Server) that might already be installed on your machine. The details of installing and using this important component will be covered in tomorrow morning's session, "Working with FrontPage."

> **BUZZ WORD**
>
> A ***Web server*** is a machine that distributes information (most notably Web pages) to your Web browser. The Internet and World Wide Web are comprised of literally thousands of interconnected Web servers, which in turn form the network that allows a student working on a computer in Kansas City to display information being "served" by a Web server located in Paris, France.

Using Access

Despite the daunting term "database application," Access is just as easy to learn and use as the other Office applications. While the field of database design and database theory is very complex, you don't have to worry about being intimidated by Access. I'll show you how easy it really is to develop a database structure that works logically with your Web site design. Plus, FrontPage has all kinds of database wizards that allow your Web pages to send information to, and read information from, an Access database—all without you having to write a line of programming code.

Session in Review

This evening you've learned some fundamental concepts of e-commerce and what you need to think about in terms of planning your small business Web site. The applications you'll use to create your site have been introduced and, hopefully, your confidence level at how easy (and fun) this stuff really is has been raised!

Tomorrow morning you'll jump straight into FrontPage. Before your lunch break, you'll have designed your first Web page. See you on the flip side!

SATURDAY MORNING

Working with FrontPage

- Locating Personal Web Server on Your Computer
- Installing Personal Web Server
- Exploring FrontPage 2000
- Creating Your First Web Page

Welcome to the beginning of your Web site creation adventure. After last night's session, you should have some idea of the general content you want to place on your site and how you might want to organize that content into specific categories.

If you are still unsure about all the organization stuff, that's okay too. This morning's session is designed to introduce you to FrontPage's general user interface and give you a chance to design your first Web page.

> **TIP**
>
> It really is okay if you don't have your entire Web site mapped out in your head. As you move through these early sessions, I will periodically remind you of important details relevant to planning and organizing your site. Of course, as you use FrontPage and as it becomes more familiar to you, you will begin to envision how your own Web site will look and function.

Locating Personal Web Server on Your Computer

Before diving into FrontPage, you must first install the Microsoft Personal Web Server, if it isn't already installed on your computer. Although you won't be using your own computer as the actual server for your small business Web site (that is the job of your Web Presence Provider, or

WPP), it is critical that you have Personal Web Server (PWS) up and running on your computer.

Why is this the case? In order to ensure that your site will function as intended once you publish it to the Web, you need to be able to test it in a true "development" environment. This very purpose is one of the functions of PWS; in short, it allows you to mimic the functionality of the Web on your own computer before you publish your site.

Also, since you will learn how to have your Web pages interact with a database, it is essential that you install PWS so that you can experiment and test this critical aspect of your functional small business Web site.

You might already have PWS installed on your computer. Take a look at the status area of your screen (the area of the Windows taskbar where the clock is located) and see if the PWS icon, shown in Figure 2.1, is there. If you don't see the PWS icon on your taskbar, then you'll need to install PWS now. Fortunately, installing PWS is easy, but first you need a copy. You can obtain your free copy of PWS using one of the following methods:

- **Install it from your Windows 98 CD-ROM.** If you are running Windows 98, a copy of PWS is available on the Windows 98 CD-ROM. Place the CD in your computer's CD-ROM drive, click the Windows Start button, and choose Run. In the Run dialog box, type **d:\add-ons\pws\setup.exe** (substituting the letter of your computer's CD-ROM drive for the letter "d"), then click OK.

- **Download it from Microsoft's Web site.** You can also download PWS from the Microsoft Web site (http://www.microsoft.com).

Figure 2.1

If you see this icon, PWS is already installed on your computer.

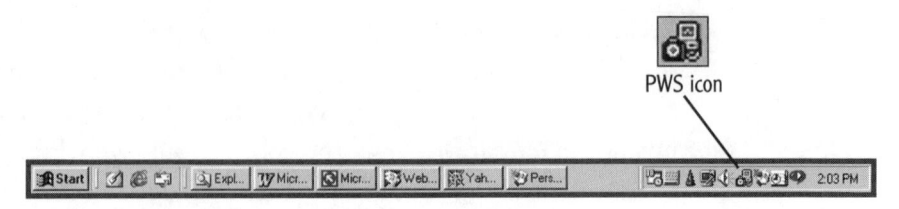

> **USING PWS WITHIN AN INTRANET**
>
> PWS is also used with company intranets so employees can use the features of the Web, such as hyperlinks, HTML, and file sharing, within a closed network, as opposed to having potentially sensitive company information available (and vulnerable) on the Web at large.
>
> An *intranet* is an "enclosed" version of the Internet (notice the structure of the word: "intra," meaning "within"). Companies often build their own intranets so they can feature the same flexibility and ease-of-use of the Web, while at the same time imposing strict security guidelines. Most often, intranets are not accessible by anyone outside the company.

Installing Personal Web Server

Once you have located a copy of PWS, it's time to install it. PWS is easy to install; simply follow these steps.

> **CAUTION** As with all program installations, it is a good idea to quit all other open applications before you begin.

1. When the PWS setup procedure begins, you will be presented with the Microsoft Personal Web Server Setup greeting, shown in Figure 2.2. Click Next when you are ready to proceed with the installation.

2. As shown in Figure 2.3, the next dialog box asks you if you want to add new components, remove installed components, or remove all installed components. Regardless of whether you have an earlier version of PWS installed on your machine, click Add/Remove.

Figure 2.2

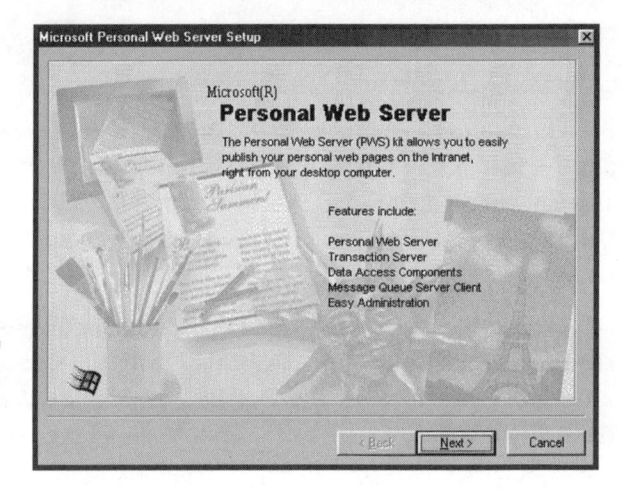

Welcome to the Microsoft Personal Web Server setup process!

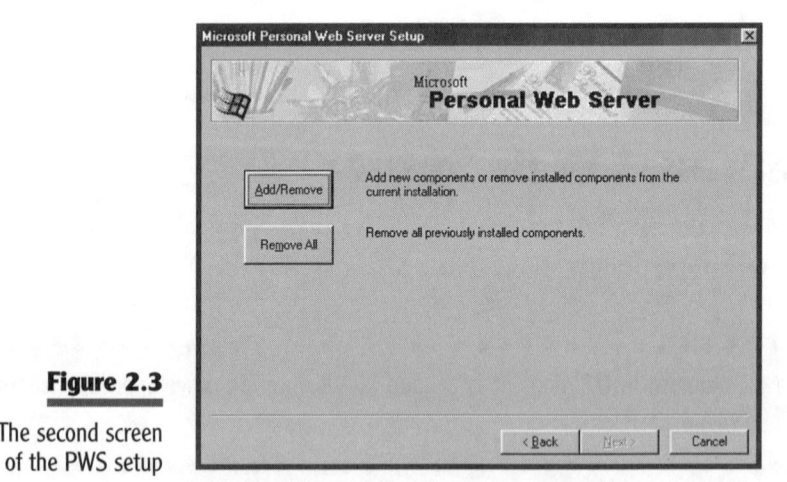

Figure 2.3

The second screen of the PWS setup

3. You are then presented with a list of components to install. Be sure that the following items are checked for installation, as shown in Figure 2.4:

- Common Program Files
- FrontPage 98 Server Extensions
- Microsoft Data Access Components 1.5
- Personal Web Server

SATURDAY MORNING Working with FrontPage   29

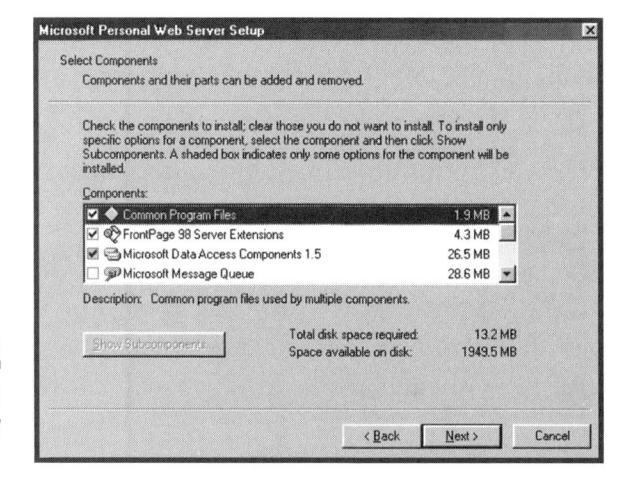

Figure 2.4

Be sure to select all the necessary components.

> **NOTE**
>
> Why not install all the options presented with PWS? Simply put, you don't need them for how you'll be using PWS. And, they will take up precious space on your computer.

4. Click Next. After a few moments, you will receive verification that PWS has been installed on your computer. You will also see a message instructing you to restart your machine so the new installation will function properly. Go ahead and restart your machine at this point.

> **TIP**
>
> If you installed PWS from your Windows 98 CD-ROM, be sure to leave the CD in your computer's CD-ROM drive as it restarts.

Verifying the PWS Installation

After your computer restarts, the PWS icon should appear in your Windows taskbar (in the status area of your screen).

Web Enable Your Small Business In a Weekend

Double-click the PWS icon to start Personal Web Manager and take a look at some of the important features supported by the program (see Figure 2.5).

There are several buttons presented in the left pane of the PWS window:

- **Main**. This option displays basic information about PWS. You can see the location of your home directory (in this case, it is the default C:\Webshare\wwwroot), and review important usage statistics, including the number of active connections and how many people have visited your site.

NOTE Although PWS will only be used in this book to test Web pages as they are developed, you can use it as a full-fledged Web server. For example, you might want to display this kind of statistical information in the context of a company intranet.

- **Publish**. This button calls up the Publishing Wizard, which is one way to Web enable your files. Although it is easy to use, this book focuses exclusively on the (also easy to use) Web publishing features of FrontPage.

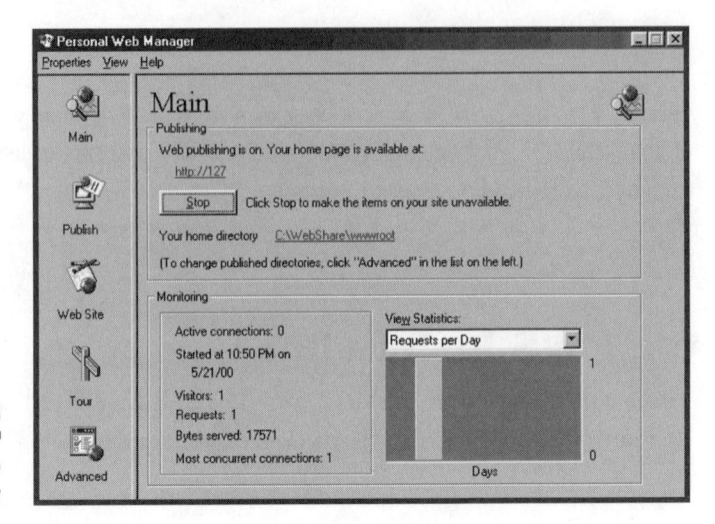

Figure 2.5

The Personal Web Manager window

SATURDAY MORNING Working with FrontPage 31

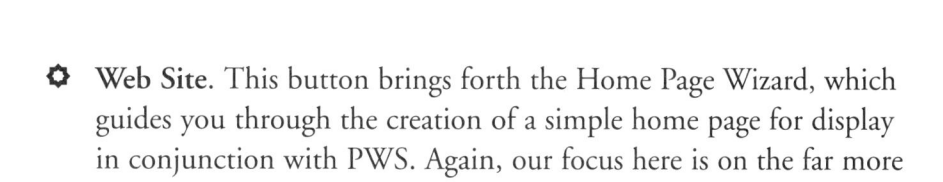

- **Web Site.** This button brings forth the Home Page Wizard, which guides you through the creation of a simple home page for display in conjunction with PWS. Again, our focus here is on the far more robust Web page creation tools available in FrontPage.
- **Tour.** This option provides a general overview of the features of PWS (see Figure 2.6). This is an excellent source of basic information about what a Web server is and how you can use PWS in conjunction with your Web design efforts. The opening screen of the tour includes the text, "Or, use PWS as a development staging platform before uploading your site to an Internet provider." That is exactly the reason you're installing PWS!
- **Advanced.** This option allows you to customize and edit specific directories. These issues won't be discussed in the context of this book.

You should recognize that the real benefit of installing and using PWS is that it allows you to test your Web pages before you upload them to your Internet Service Provider for actual placement on the World Wide Web. As you move through today's sessions, the power of PWS as a true staging platform will become even more apparent.

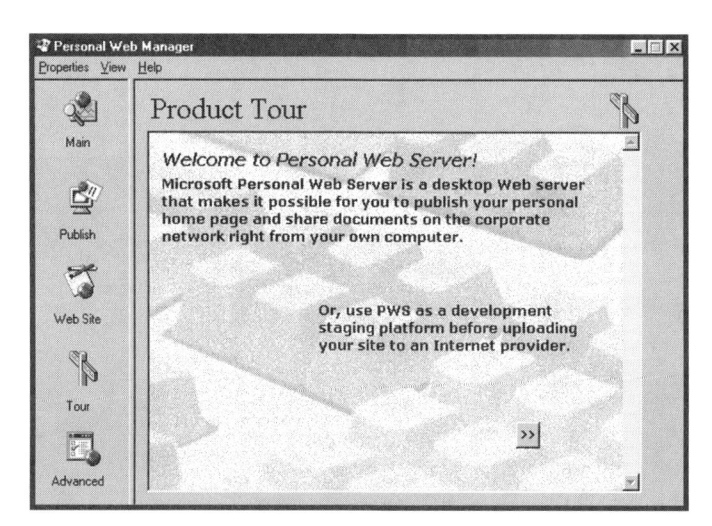

Figure 2.6

The PWS Product Tour page

Checking the Rest of Your Components

Before leaving the initial discussion of PWS, you should also make sure that you have the latest FrontPage 2000 server extensions installed. To verify the installation of the FrontPage 2000 server extensions, follow these steps:

1. Click the Start button, then choose Programs, Microsoft Office Tools, Server Extensions Administrator.

2. When the Microsoft Management Console window opens, expand the FrontPage Server Extensions folder, as shown in Figure 2.7.

3. Right-click the item listed under the FrontPage Server Extensions folder, and a shortcut menu will appear.

4. Choose Task/Upgrade Server Extensions. If you see "Check Server Extensions" in the shortcut menu, FrontPage 2000 server extensions have already been installed.

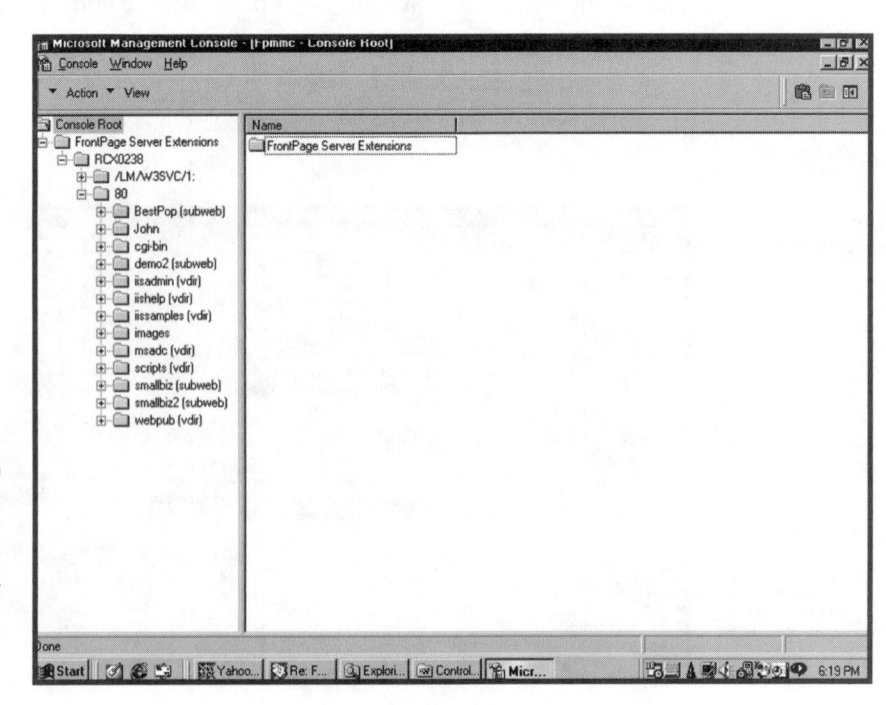

Figure 2.7

The Microsoft Management Console. Check here to see whether the latest PWS server extensions are installed.

Disabling the Windows Automatic Dial-Up Connection

Before beginning the actual FrontPage discussion, there is one additional housekeeping task to handle. Have you ever noticed that when you first start your Web browser, the Windows Dial-up Connection dialog box appears and your modem attempts to automatically connect to your default Internet Service Provider, as shown in Figure 2.8?

Since you'll be developing your Web site with Personal Web Server, there is no need for you to connect to the Internet. In this case, your service is your own machine!

The problem, however, is that when you try to open a Web served by your Personal Web Server, Windows automatically attempts to connect you to the Internet by dialing your default service provider. Unless you have a dedicated phone line (so you don't mind being online as you develop your Web site), you'll need to disable this auto-connect feature so you can stay offline and work exclusively within the realm of your own machine.

To disable the auto-connect feature, follow these steps:

1. Open the Windows Control Panel by clicking Start and choosing Settings, Control Panel (see Figure 2.9).
2. When the Control Panel opens, double-click the Internet Options icon. The Internet Properties dialog box appears.
3. Now click the Connections tab. Your screen should appear similar to Figure 2.8
4. Select Never Dial a Connection.
5. To complete this process, click Apply. Then click OK to close the Internet Properties dialog box.

Figure 2.8

The Windows Dial-up Connection dialog box

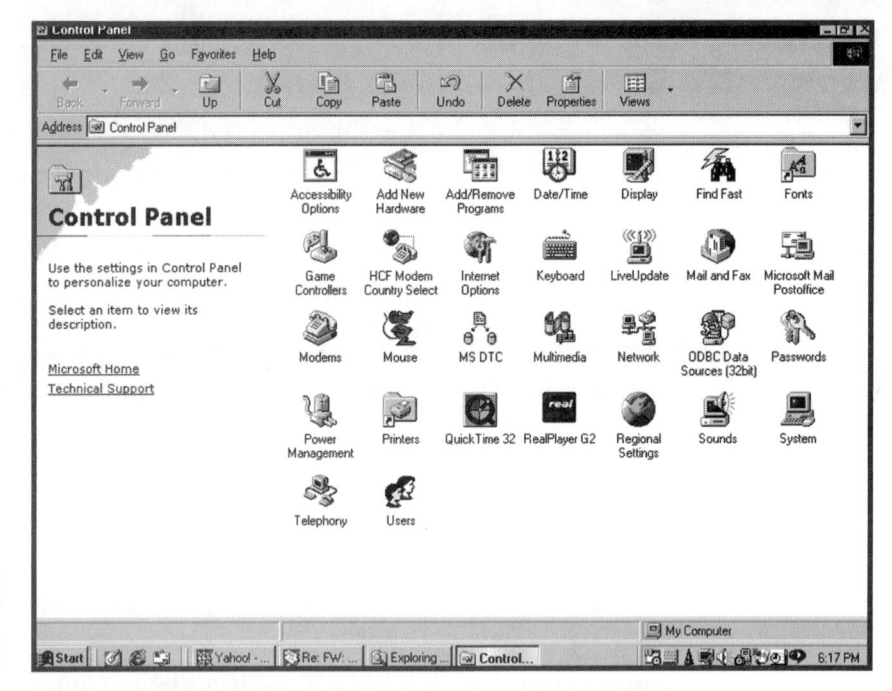

Figure 2.9

The Windows Control Panel

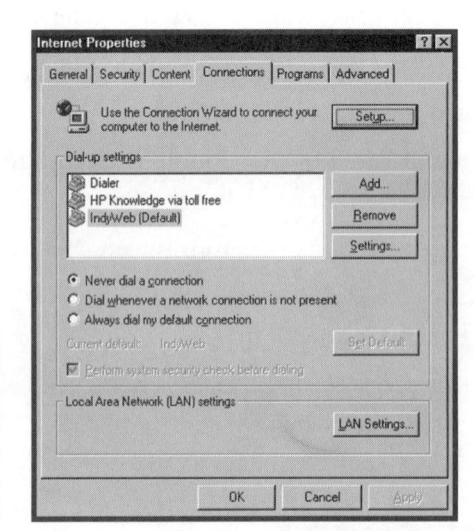

Figure 2.10

The Internet Properties dialog box with the Connections tab selected

SATURDAY MORNING Working with FrontPage   35

Now when you open your FrontPage Web sites that are "served up" by Personal Web Server, Windows won't attempt to connect you to the Web and you can work exclusively offline. This keeps your phone line open while you're developing your small business Web site!

CAUTION If you disable automatic dial-up networking connections, you'll need to manually select the connection you want to use for all Internet connections. You can do this by clicking the Start button, then choosing the service to which you want to connect, as shown in Figure 2.11.

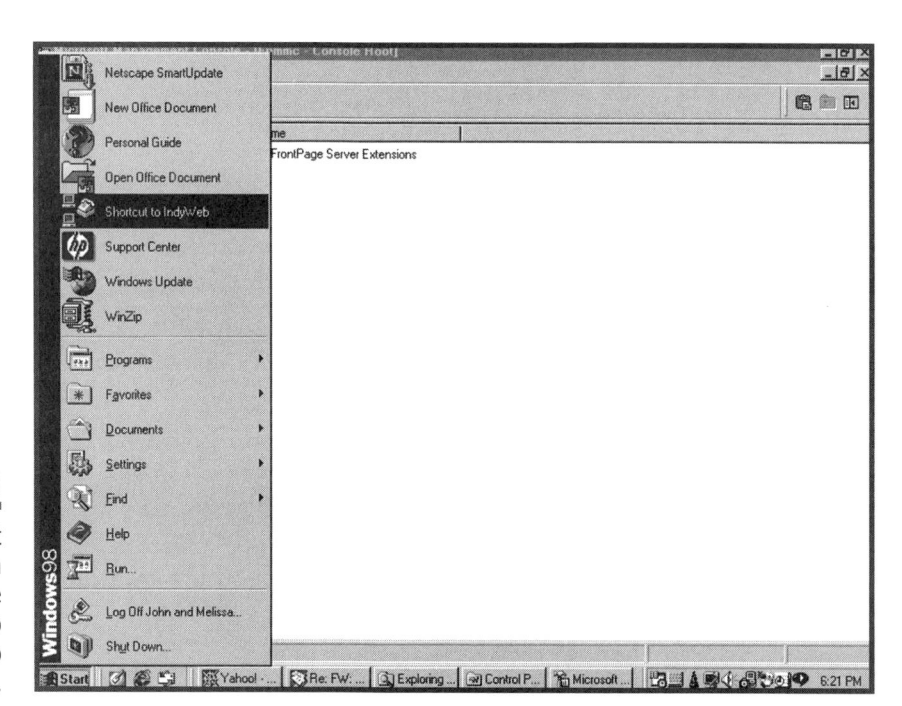

Figure 2.11

From the Start menu, you can manually select the service you want to use to connect to the Internet.

Take a Break!

You've done some technical groundwork in preparation for building your first Web page. Take a moment now for a break. When you get back, the FrontPage 2000 introduction will begin!

Exploring FrontPage 2000

Despite the enormous popularity of the Internet and World Wide Web, if I were a betting man, I would place my money on the belief that most people think that designing and implementing Web pages—let alone a complete small business Web site—is best left to the techno-geeks. Fortunately, this is not the case. In fact, this is about as far away from the truth as you can get. Since I don't consider myself a techno-geek, this had better be the case, right?

Microsoft has produced some intuitive, easy-to-use products that place a tremendous amount of computing power in the hands of the masses. FrontPage 2000 (along with Access and the rest of the Office suite) is one of those products.

Let's begin with the most basic of operations—starting FrontPage 2000. Click Start, then choose Programs, Microsoft FrontPage. After a few seconds, the application will start (see Figure 2.12). As with other Office applications, FrontPage's menu bar contains several menus that should be familiar to you (File, Edit, View, and so on).

When FrontPage opens, you are immediately placed in Page View. What are the different views, and what do they mean? Take another look at the left side of Figure 2.12. The various buttons running vertically (Page, Folders, Reports, and so on) represent the different FrontPage views.

- **Page View.** This is the default view when FrontPage starts. Similar to a blank Word document, Page View represents a blank Web page. You can think of the large white space as your Web canvas, onto which you can place form elements, text, and other Web elements.

SATURDAY MORNING Working with FrontPage

Figure 2.12

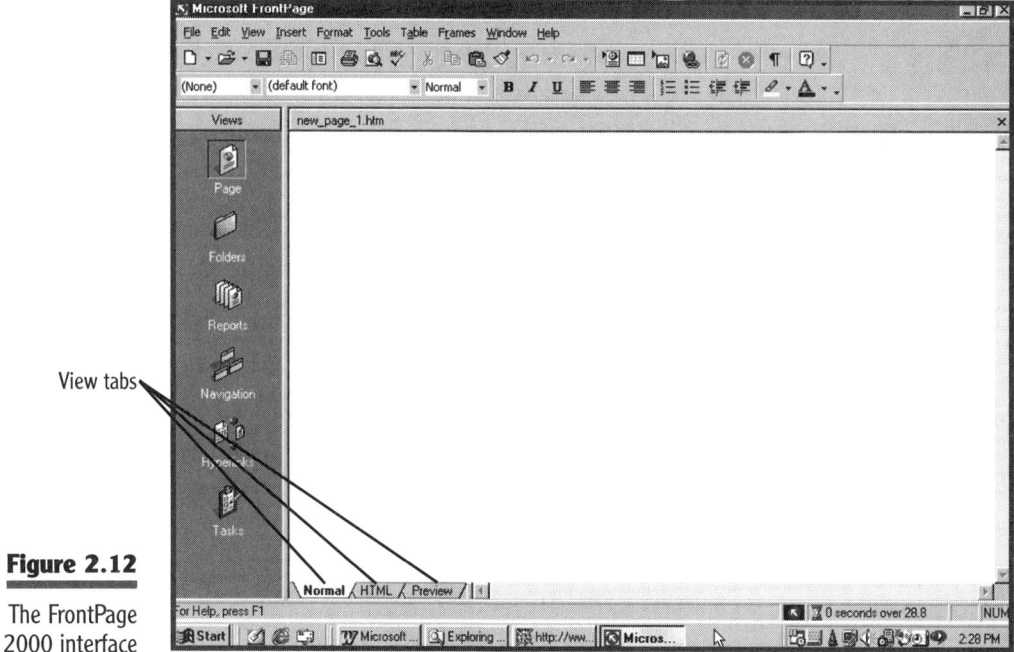

The FrontPage 2000 interface

There are three specific view tabs within Page View: Normal, HTML, and Preview. Just take note of them for now. They'll be discussed in more detail when you create your first Web page later this morning.

○ **Folders View.** As you create your small business Web site, you will organize your Web pages into folders. Folders View allows you to get a snapshot of your organization, including the file size of your various Web pages, the date they were last modified, and so on.

○ **Reporting View.** This view gives you more specific analysis of your Web site's content, from an administrative viewpoint. For example, from within Reporting View, you can take note of Web pages that don't have any hyperlinks to them or pages that are slow to load in a Web browser.

> **BUZZ WORD**
>
> ◀◀◀◀◀◀◀◀◀◀◀◀◀◀◀◀◀◀◀◀◀◀◀◀
> A *hyperlink* is a specially formatted element on a Web page that, when clicked, opens another page in the Web browser. In other words, it serves as a link to another page. Hyperlinks can be text as well as graphics.
> ◀◀◀◀◀◀◀◀◀◀◀◀◀◀◀◀◀◀◀◀◀◀◀◀

- **Navigation View.** This view allows you to quickly add navigation elements to the various Web pages within your site. While you won't learn a great deal about this view, you will see it demonstrated later this afternoon.

- **Hyperlinks View.** Just as you wouldn't think of taking a cross-country trip without a good map or atlas, you shouldn't have to design your Web site without a method of seeing its overall structure at a glance. With the Hyperlinks View, you can see all the various hyperlinks between your pages. This "picture" of your Web site is presented graphically, making it easy to see which pages link to other pages. You should use Hyperlinks View extensively as you check your site's construction, in order to verify that each page links where it should.

- **Tasks View.** Especially in a corporate environment, building a Web site is a team effort, as various individuals with different areas of expertise are called upon to design one or more features or areas. FrontPage is equipped to assign and track tasks to specific individuals, facilitating a team effort approach in building a Web site. Tasks View displays this information, showing at a glance to whom a specific task was assigned, its priority, and when it is due to be completed. Since you are flying solo (at least for this weekend!) in your Web development endeavors, Tasks View won't be discussed in this book.

Feeling a bit confused about all these views? Don't let the view conundrum concern you; the vast majority of the time, you'll be working exclusively in Page View. As a matter of fact, think of the other views as administrative views that are placed within FrontPage to help you quickly see the organizational structure of your site.

Creating Your First Web Page

Since you have FrontPage open, you might as well create your first Web page, right? Let's get to it!

In this exercise, you will construct a basic home page for your small business Web site. Don't worry if, after completing this morning's session, your work doesn't quite, ah, "make the grade." You'll have plenty of opportunity to revise and perfect throughout the weekend. The point of this morning's session is for you to get comfortable working within the FrontPage environment, as well as with the available tool sets for Web page creation.

Placing and Formatting Text

If you don't already have FrontPage running on your computer, go ahead and start it now so you can follow along with the discussion. Once you have started FrontPage, notice that the Formatting toolbar is very similar to the toolbar in other Office applications (see Figure 2.13).

> **TIP** Can't see the Formatting toolbar? It may be hidden. Select View, Toolbars to display a list of available toolbars. On the list that appears, make sure Formatting is selected.

To help you become familiar with formatting text in FrontPage, here's a simple formatting exercise.

1. The first text you need to create is the name of your company. To center the name of your company left-to-right on the page, click the Center button on the Formatting toolbar. The cursor moves to the center of the page.

Web Enable Your Small Business In a Weekend

Figure 2.13

The Formatting toolbar in FrontPage

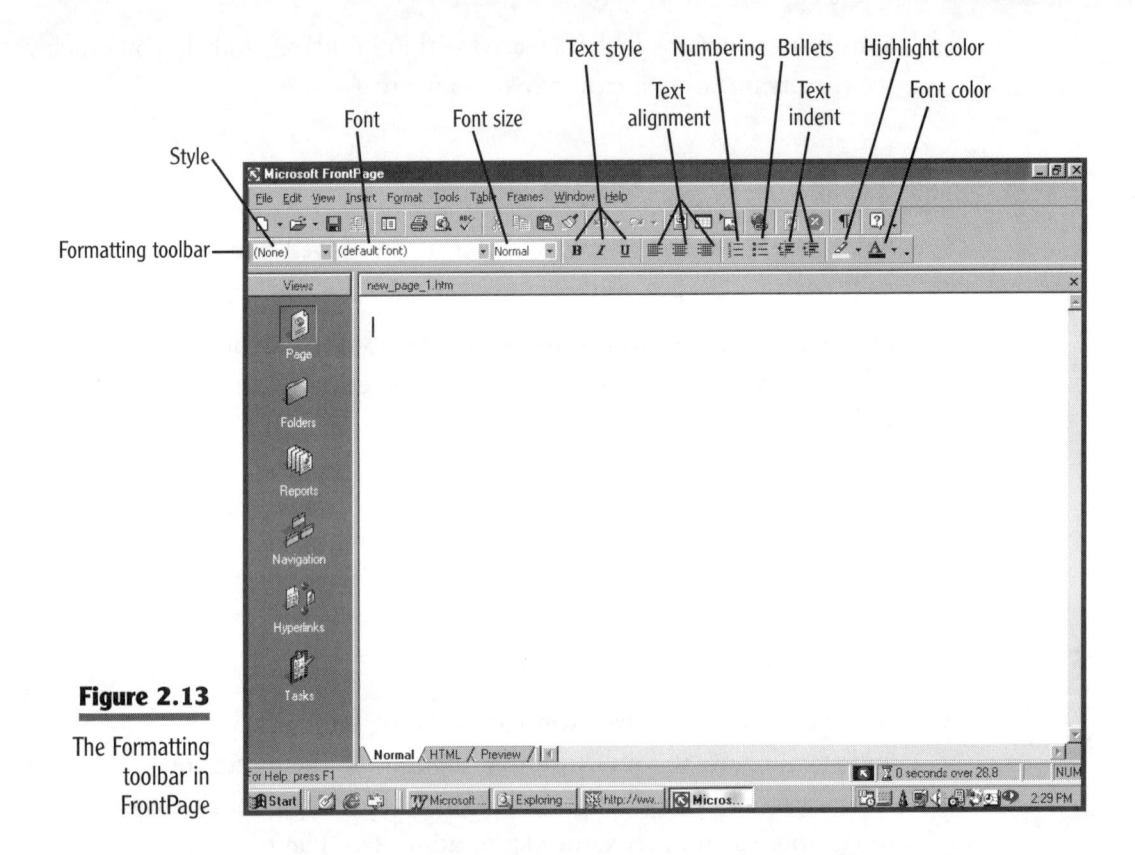

2. Now change the font and font size. From the Font drop-down menu, select a font that appeals to you. Then, from the Font Size drop-down menu, select 14 point as the font size that you want to use.

3. To add emphasis to your company name, click Bold. Then select a color for the text from the Font Color drop-down menu.

4. Now type the name of your company. Take some time to experiment with different fonts, sizes, and colors. See Figure 2.14 for an example of some simple formatting.

Got the idea about formatting text? If you've done any work within Microsoft Word (or any other word processing application), formatting text is probably second nature. Formatting in FrontPage is no different.

SATURDAY MORNING Working with FrontPage   41

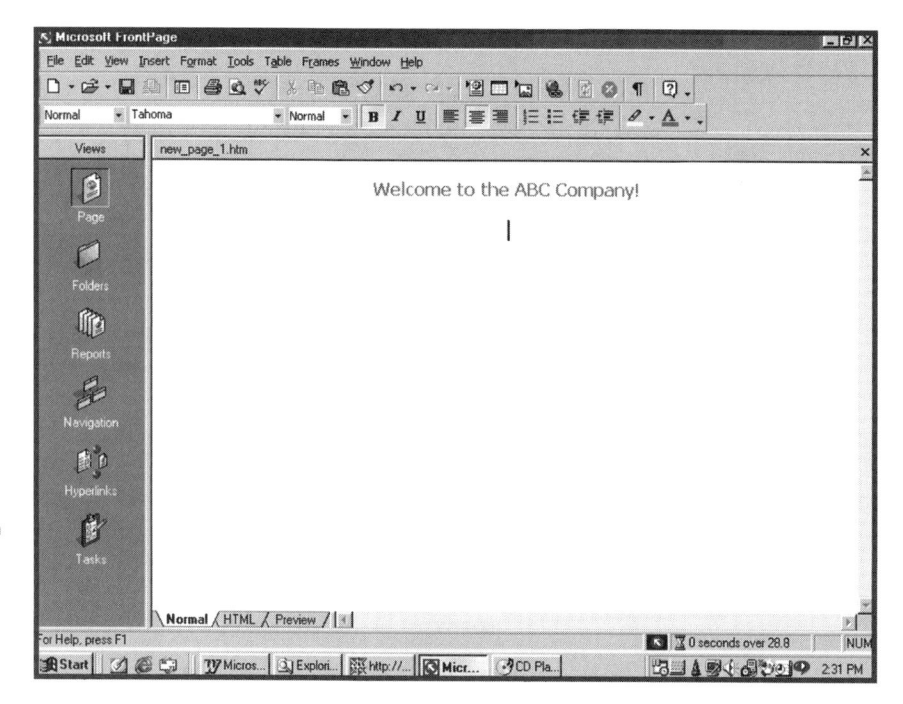

Figure 2.14

A simple formatting example. I've chosen Tahoma font, 14 point, bold, and centered.

Inserting Graphics

The most visually appealing Web sites are the ones that make good use of graphics. However, you must temper your desire to go wild with graphic placement, and keep the following tips in mind:

○ **Compared to text, graphics can take a long time to download.** You've probably surfed the Web and encountered a site that seemed to take forever to download to your browser, usually due to an excessive use of graphics. Keep this in mind when using graphics on your own site. If a site takes an excessively long time to load, visitors will move on. Don't let this happen to your small business Web site just because you've placed too many graphics on your pages.

○ **Be savvy when choosing graphics.** They can give your site either a very professional feel or, if chosen poorly, a very sloppy feel. More information about graphics will be discussed in tomorrow's sessions. Keep in mind the general tone you are attempting to set with your Web site when choosing graphics. For example, if your small business is a daycare center, it would be perfectly appropriate to have graphics of cartoon children or animals on your site. However, these types of graphics might set the wrong impression if your business is not a daycare. Choose wisely!

- **Don't frustrate yourself and waste valuable time by trying to design your own graphics.** This is perhaps the most important point, especially if you are not an artist. There are literally millions of graphics, ranging from static images to animated GIFs, available for your free use. Some of these can be found on your own computer in the form of clip art, while others can be downloaded from the Web. Take advantage of this valuable creative resource!

> **TIP**
> Be sure to see the enclosed CD-ROM for a variety of ready-to-use (and free!) graphics that you can incorporate into your Web pages.

> **CAUTION**
> All Web designers learn from studying the work of others. This is one of the great community aspects of the Web. However, if you plan to use a graphic or any Web element designed and programmed by someone else, be sure you have their permission to do so. Also, be sure to credit the designer as the creator of the work, if he or she requires it.

Now experiment with adding some graphics to your Web page. FrontPage has several options available for inserting graphics, so explore a few of them.

1. From the previous exercise, you should have the name of your company nicely formatted at the center of your page. If you don't,

SATURDAY MORNING Working with FrontPage 43

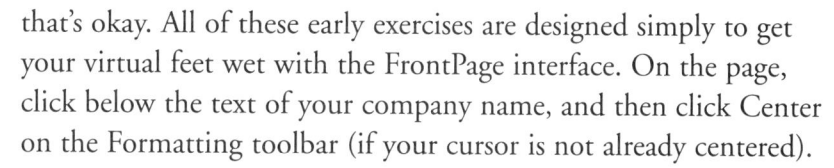

that's okay. All of these early exercises are designed simply to get your virtual feet wet with the FrontPage interface. On the page, click below the text of your company name, and then click Center on the Formatting toolbar (if your cursor is not already centered).

2. Click Insert, and move the mouse pointer to Picture (see Figure 2.15). You can insert a picture from Clip Art or from a file, and you can also insert video clips and sounds, which you'll learn about in tomorrow's sessions.

NOTE If you can't see all the available menu options, hold your mouse over the down arrow at the bottom of the menu and the rest of the menu options will be revealed.

3. Choose Clip Art. The Clip Art Gallery window appears (see Figure 2.16).

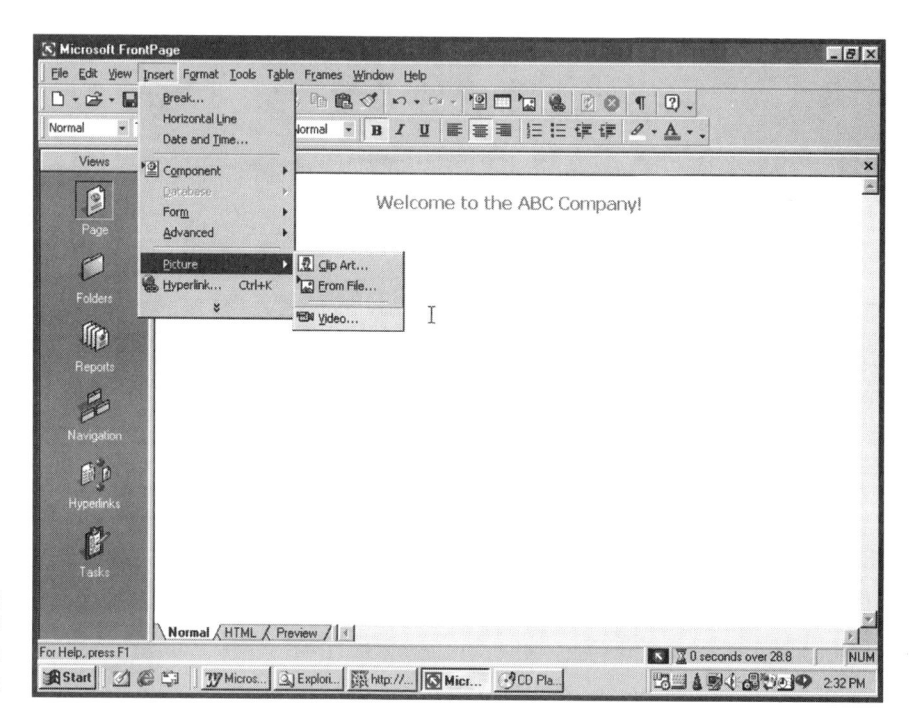

Figure 2.15

Adding graphics to your home page

> ### WORKING WITH CLIP ART
>
> Take a closer look at the Clip Art Gallery. Notice the three tabs: Pictures, Sounds, and Motion Clips. Multimedia aspects will be covered in tomorrow's sessions, so for now be sure the Pictures tab is selected.
>
> The Clip Art Gallery has a handy search feature that you can use to easily locate a specific type of graphic. Also, notice the two buttons at the top of the window: Import Clips and Clips Online. Import Clips allows you to insert graphics from your own Clip Art collection. This is useful for organizational purposes, so that you can keep all your graphics in one place. Clips Online is a special Microsoft service that lets you download new and interesting clip art directly into FrontPage. If you find yourself using clip art frequently, you should investigate Clips Online for the latest and greatest clip art!

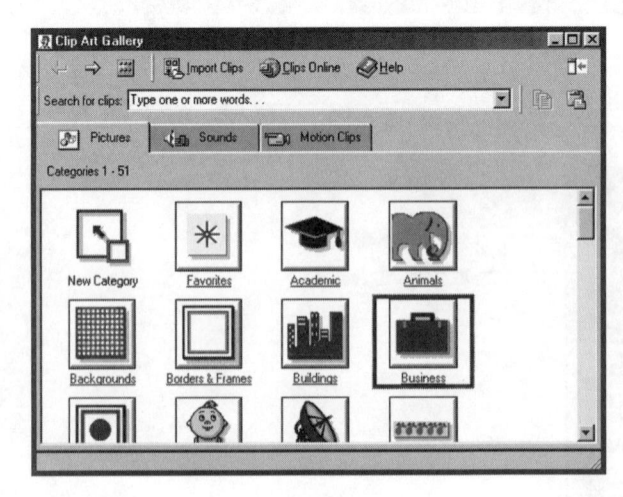

Figure 2.16

The Clip Art Gallery window allows you to insert graphics, video clips, and sounds into your Web pages.

4. With the Pictures tab selected, click the Business icon, which will display all current clip art on your machine in the Business category. Select a graphic that appeals to you. A shortcut menu will

appear (see Figure 2.17). The shortcut menu gives you different options for what you can do with the graphic.

5. The first button in the shortcut menu inserts the selected graphic directly onto your Web page. The second button opens a preview of the graphic, which is useful for seeing the entire graphic before it is inserted. For now, click the first button. The graphic appears on your Web page, as shown in Figure 2.18.

6. You can manipulate a graphic on your page in various ways. Click once on the graphic to select it. Handles appear around the graphic and the Picture toolbar appears at the bottom of the window, as shown in Figure 2.19.

7. Dragging any of the handles that surround the graphic changes the size and shape of the graphic. Keep in mind that dragging a corner handle proportionally modifies the size of the graphic, while dragging a side handle may distort the image. Take some time now to experiment with the Picture toolbar. Rest the mouse pointer on the various buttons in the Picture toolbar to display a ToolTip that lets you know what action each button executes. Experiment with some of the buttons in the Picture toolbar, paying close attention to how they affect your graphic.

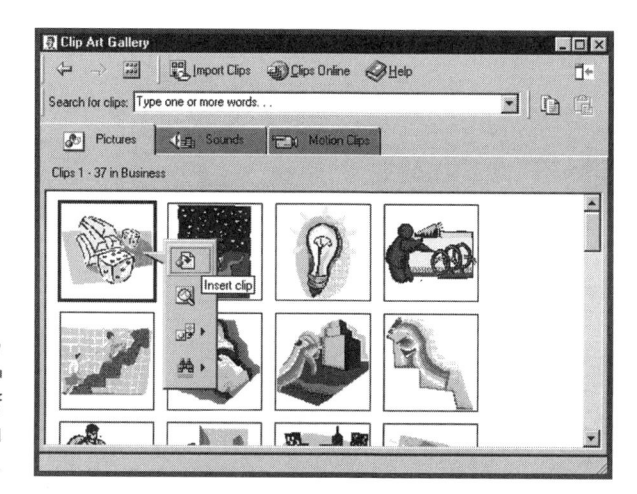

Figure 2.17

Selecting a piece of clip art gives you this shortcut menu.

Figure 2.18

A clip art graphic inserted onto your Web page

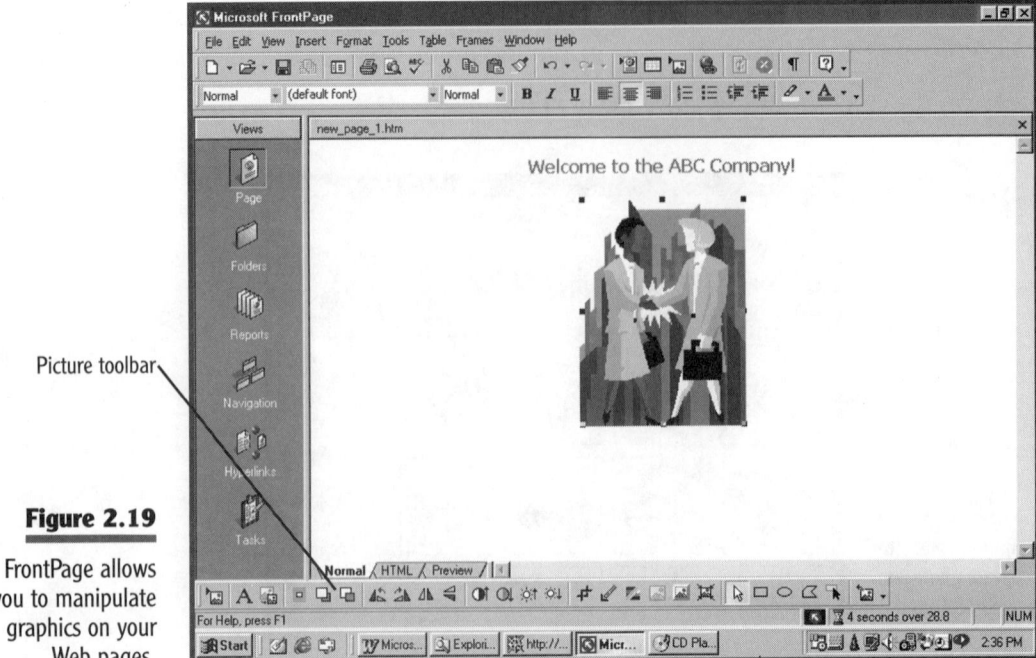

Figure 2.19

FrontPage allows you to manipulate graphics on your Web pages.

> **TIP**
>
> If the Picture toolbar disappears, you've probably deselected your graphic. Simply click once on the graphic to bring the Picture toolbar back to your screen.

Working with FrontPage Components

At this point in your initial Web page creation, you have inserted and formatted some text and placed a graphic or two on your page. Now, take a moment to investigate a unique feature of FrontPage as a Web development tool: the FrontPage Components.

You can use Components to easily include some of the more common functions found on well-designed Web pages, such as:

- **Hit counters.** Hit counters are used to visually track the number of visitors to your site. When it is well positioned, the hit counter can serve as a powerful PR tool, reflecting the popularity of your site by highlighting the number of visitors who have loaded your site into their browser.

- **Hover buttons.** Hover buttons allow special effects to occur when the user hovers his or her mouse pointer over a button. For example, you might place a hover button titled, "Song Excerpt." When the user hovers the mouse pointer over this particular button, a short excerpt of a song (which you have also inserted onto the Web page) begins to play.

- **Marquees.** Marquees allow text to scroll across an area of a page, much like the electronic marquee you might see at a professional sports arena. Within FrontPage, you can customize not only the text that appears in the marquee, but also the direction and speed at which the text scrolls.

- **Search forms.** Search forms are essential tools for any well-designed site, as they allow users to quickly locate a term (or terms).

You can view the various FrontPage Components by choosing Component from the Insert menu (see Figure 2.20).

Web Enable Your Small Business In a Weekend

Figure 2.20

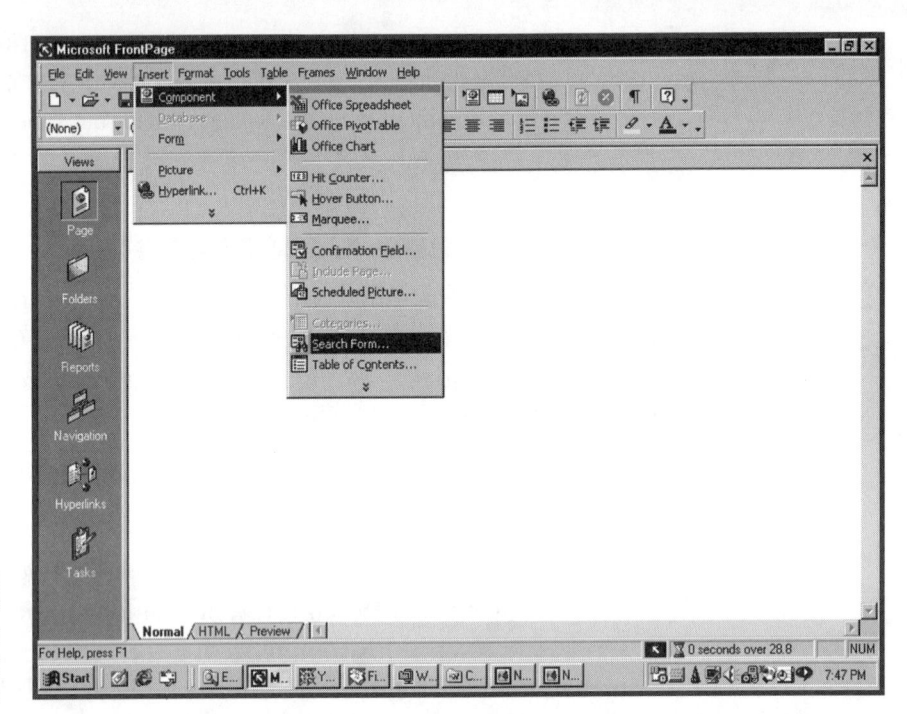

The FrontPage 2000 Component menu

> **NOTE**
>
> In Figure 2.20, you'll undoubtedly notice more component options than those described in the previous bulleted list. Although some additional components will be touched on throughout the weekend, you'll mostly learn about those four components.

Try inserting a FrontPage Component into your sample Web page. You can insert the Marquee component using these steps:

1. Click on the location on the Web page where you want the marquee to appear. For this example, click underneath the picture you inserted during the previous exercise.

2. From the Insert menu, choose Component, Marquee. The Marquee Properties dialog box appears (see Figure 2.21).

SATURDAY MORNING Working with FrontPage

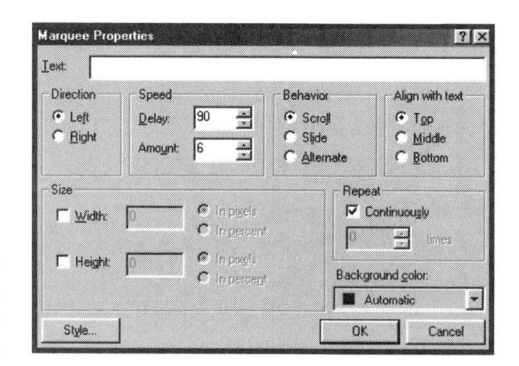

Figure 2.21

The Marquee Properties dialog box

3. Type some text into the Text field. Type a sentence or two, rather than just one word, so you can see the full marquee effect in action. Leave the other options as they are, and click OK. The text you typed in the Marquee Properties dialog box appears on the Web page. Once your page is published, you will see the marquee in action. Your Web page should now look something like Figure 2.22.

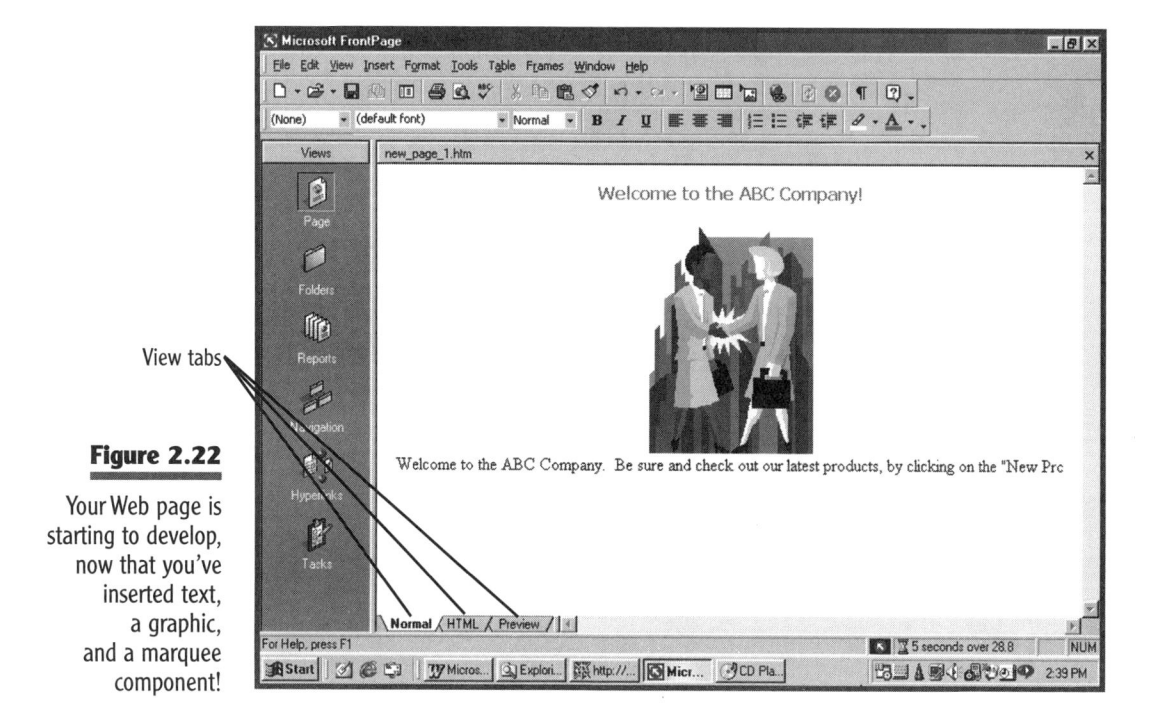

View tabs

Figure 2.22

Your Web page is starting to develop, now that you've inserted text, a graphic, and a marquee component!

4. Ready to see the marquee in action? Look at the bottom of the FrontPage window and notice the three view tabs: Normal, HTML, and Preview. Up to this point, you've been working in Normal view. Click the Preview tab to get a feel for how your page will look when it is live. Your marquee text scrolls across the page, as shown in Figure 2.23.

You should note that the preview might not be a completely accurate representation of how your page will look in an actual Web browser. Not all elements you insert into your Web pages are immediately visible using the Preview tab. Some elements, such as the hit counter, must first be published to be seen in action.

This is why the installation of Personal Web Server, which you completed this morning, is so crucial. It provides you with a complete development environment on your own computer so you can get an accurate picture of how your site will function when it is live on the Web.

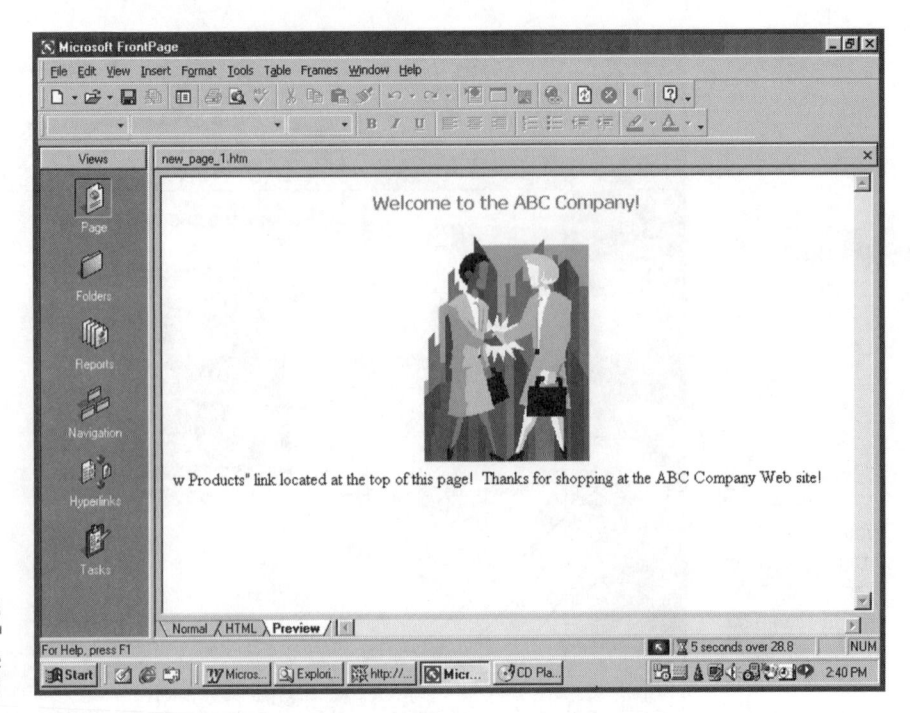

Figure 2.23

The marquee in action!

SATURDAY MORNING Working with FrontPage

> **NOTE**
> The HTML view tab displays the actual HTML code that is used to build your Web pages. Using HTML view, you can tweak the actual HTML code to your specifications. HTML view will be used in later sessions this weekend.

Saving Your Web Pages

You've done some significant Web page construction this morning. As with all work done on a computer, it is a good idea to frequently save your work. That said, go ahead and save your Web page now.

1. If you are still in Preview view from the previous exercise, click the Normal view tab.

2. From the File menu, choose Save As. The Save As dialog box appears, as shown in Figure 2.24. Notice the similarities to Save As dialog boxes in other Office applications.

3. Using the Save In drop-down menu, navigate to the folder where you'd like to save your Web page.

4. Next, in the File Name box, type a name for your Web page. Leave Save as Type set to Web Pages.

5. Click Save. If you have inserted graphics into your page, you'll also be presented with the Save Embedded Files dialog box, as shown in Figure 2.25. Click OK to save these embedded pictures along with your Web page.

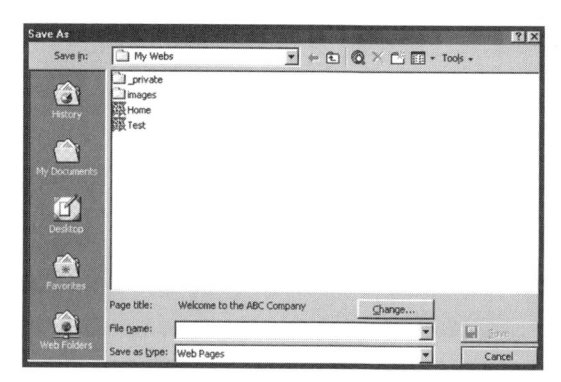

Figure 2.24

The FrontPage Save As dialog box

As soon as your page is saved, FrontPage displays the Folder List pane so that you can see where on your hard drive the page has been saved (see Figure 2.26).

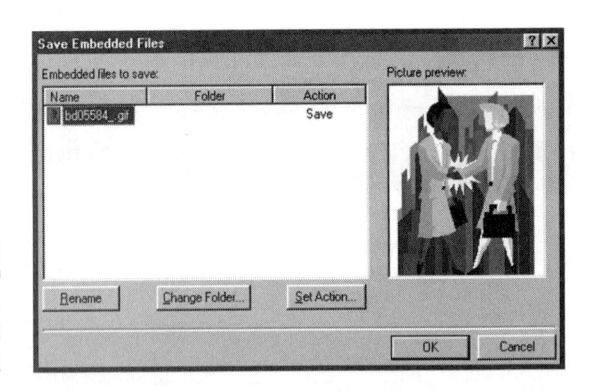

Figure 2.25

The Save Embedded Files dialog box

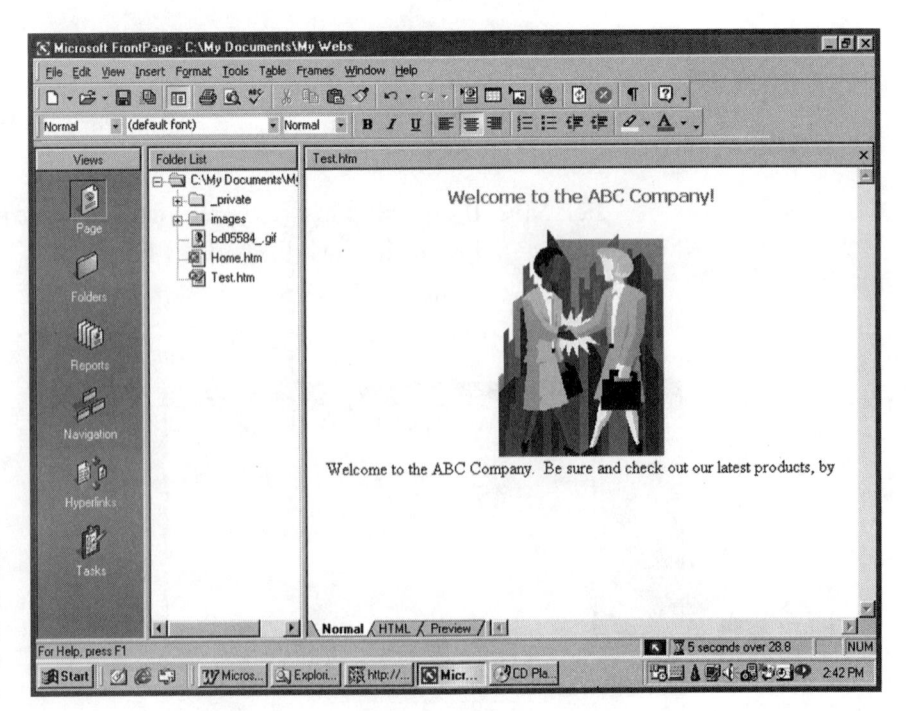

Figure 2.26

The Folder List pane displays the folder in which you are working.

Session in Review

I think it's time to grab some lunch. Before you head out, take a look at everything you've learned this morning:

- To begin the session, you installed Personal Web Server on your machine so you will have a complete development environment as you construct your Web site.
- Next, you took a tour of the FrontPage interface and learned about the general similarities and differences between it and the other applications in the Office suite.
- You also constructed a simple Web page and, in the process, learned some of the basics of working with FrontPage. You formatted some text, inserted graphics, and learned about the FrontPage Components, including how to insert a scrolling marquee onto your Web page.
- Finally, you saved your Web page in preparation for future work.

Whew! That's a lot of material for a Saturday morning—hope you had fun! After lunch, you'll build on what you've learned so far in Web page design by working with forms, frames, hyperlinks, and e-mail. You'll also begin organizing your Web site using Personal Web Server, as well as the different views talked about this morning.

SATURDAY AFTERNOON
Advanced FrontPage Functionality

- ✿ Building a FrontPage Web
- ✿ Working with FrontPage Wizards and Themes
- ✿ Adding Tables to Organize Your Information
- ✿ Working with Frames
- ✿ Working with Forms in Your Web Pages
- ✿ Adding Hyperlinks

This morning you created your first Web page and then used the traditional File, Save menu command to store your creation. While this is a great beginning, you need to think of your Web site as a collection of integrated, linked pages. In other words, all of your Web pages, as well as any included graphics, their supporting databases, and so on, must be organized in a coherent, logical fashion. This is the purpose of a FrontPage Web.

> **BUZZ WORD**
>
> ◄
> A *FrontPage Web* is, simply put, a folder for storing all of your Web pages and related elements. However, in addition to the usual Windows folders, other properties can be applied to a FrontPage Web. This allows the contents of the Web to be accessed (via a Web server such as Personal Web Server) using a browser.
> ◄

Building a FrontPage Web

You should think of building a Web as the first step in keeping everything organized from the very beginning. You'll begin your deeper exploration of FrontPage by first building a Web.

58   Web Enable Your Small Business In a Weekend

> **NOTE** If you've used FrontPage before and feel comfortable with the various features, such as inserting tables, creating forms, and working with frames, you can use this afternoon's session as a refresher course. This will prepare you to learn how to integrate your FrontPage Webs with Access databases in this evening's session.

Naming a FrontPage Web

If FrontPage isn't running on your machine, you should start it now. Once the application starts, follow these steps to create your first FrontPage Web:

1. From the File menu, choose New, Web, as shown in Figure 3.1. The New dialog box appears (see Figure 3.2).

2. For now, select Empty Web, but don't click OK just yet!

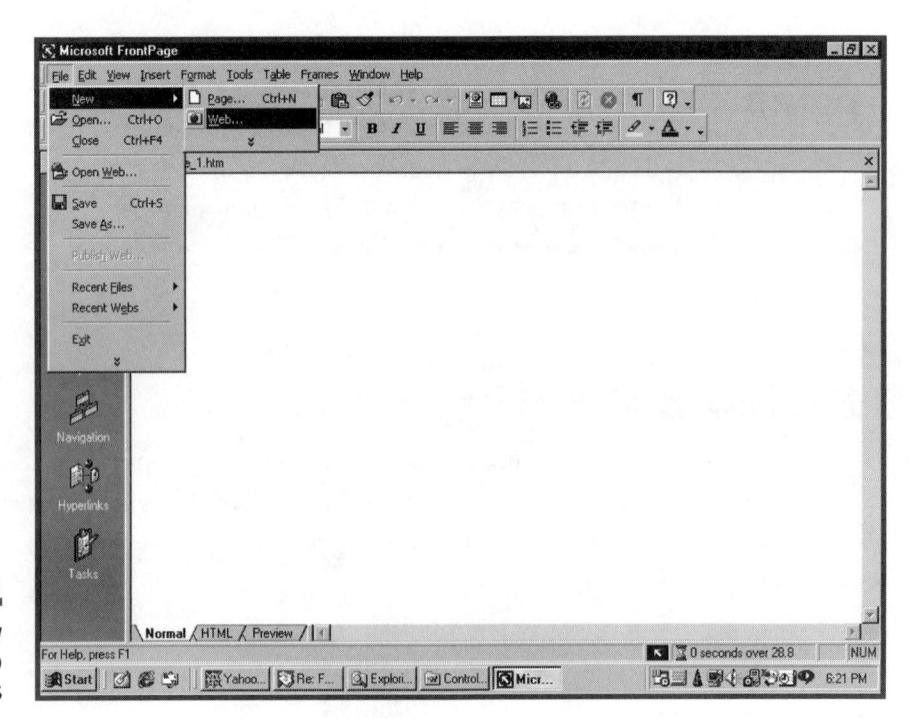

Figure 3.1

Beginning the new FrontPage Web creation process

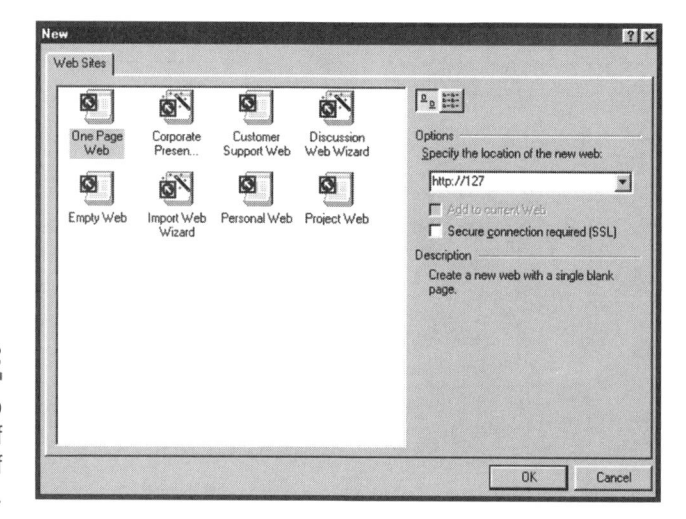

SATURDAY AFTERNOON Advanced FrontPage Functionality — 59

Figure 3.2

Select Empty Web and take note of the location of the new Web.

3. In Figure 3.2, take a look at the Specify the Location of the New Web drop-down menu. The options presented in this drop-down menu may differ depending on your machine, whether you are connected to a network, and whether you used a previous version of FrontPage on your machine before upgrading to FrontPage 2000. You'll want to create the Web in the home directory of Personal Web Server.

4. To determine the home directory of PWS, first click the Personal Web Server icon in your Windows taskbar. When Personal Web Manager begins, clear the Tip of the Day (if it displays), so that you can see the home page location, as shown in Figure 3.3.

5. Look in the Publishing section to see the location of your home page and home directory based on your specific machine setup. More information about both of these items will be discussed later in this afternoon's session. For now, make sure that the entry in the Specify the Location of the New Web box (shown in Figure 3.2), matches the URL of your home page displayed in the Publishing section (shown in Figure 3.3).

Figure 3.3

You can see the URL of Personal Web Server's home page, as well as your home directory, from Personal Web Manager's Main window.

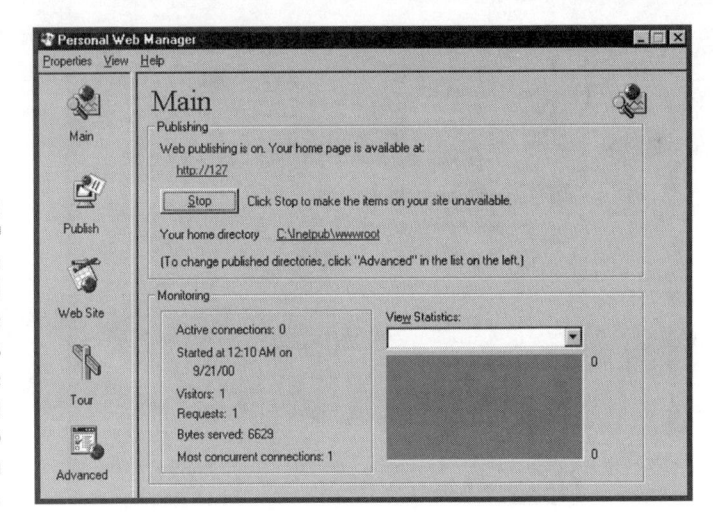

> **NOTE**
>
> Don't be concerned if the location of your home page differs from what is shown here. The actual name of the URL can vary, due to your own system specifications. The important thing is to simply note the URL that is displayed here, so you can be sure to key in the right address when you access pages "served" by PWS.

6. After you've selected your home page URL from the drop-down menu, add the following to the end of the home URL: **/smallbiz**. The New Web dialog box should now look like Figure 3.4.

7. Click OK. The Create New Web dialog box appears, displaying the location of your new Web as it is created (see Figure 3.5).

> **TIP**
>
> If, during this Web creation process, the Windows Dial-Up Connection dialog box pops up, you need to be sure you've turned off automatic dialing. See this morning's session, "Working with FrontPage" for more information about temporarily disabling this feature while you work with Personal Web Server on your machine.

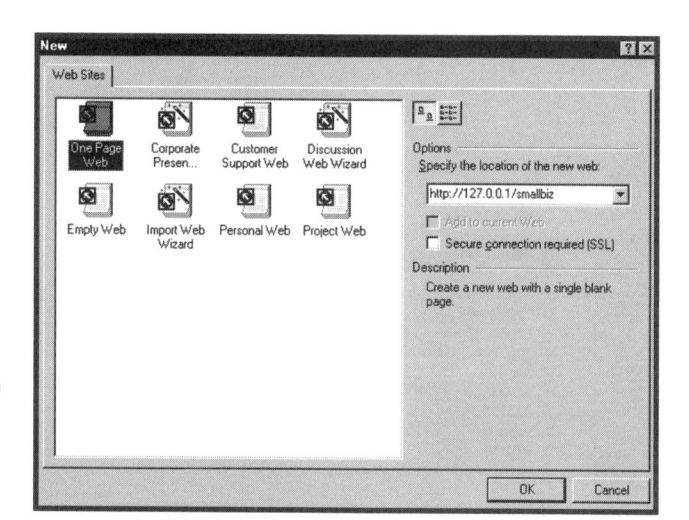

SATURDAY AFTERNOON Advanced FrontPage Functionality   **61**

Figure 3.4

Specifying the exact location of your new FrontPage Web

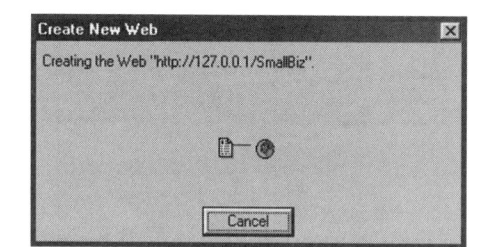

Figure 3.5

The Create New Web dialog box

Congratulations! You've just created your first FrontPage Web! You should now be looking at the FrontPage editor in Page View, and your new Web should appear in the Folder List pane, as shown in Figure 3.6.

Adding New Pages to Your Web

Now that you have a brand-new FrontPage Web, you need to add some Web pages! Adding a new Web page to a FrontPage Web is done exactly the same way as adding a new page to a folder.

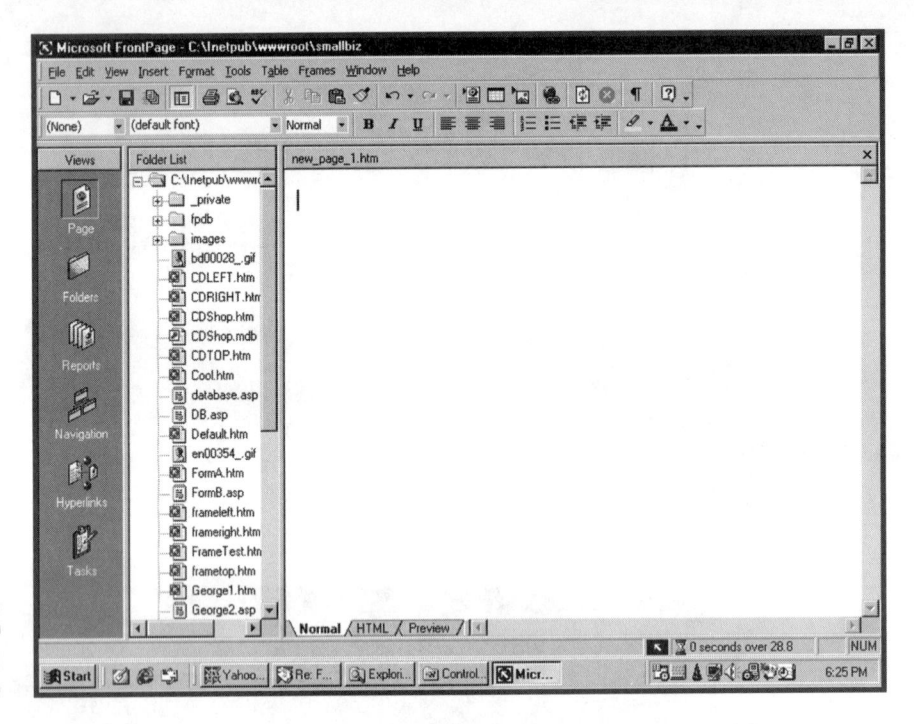

Figure 3.6

Your newly created FrontPage Web

When your new Web was created, a blank Web page was also created. To save this page into the Web, giving it a name in the process, follow these steps:

1. From the File menu, choose Save As. The Save As dialog box will appear, as shown in Figure 3.7.

2. In the File Name box, type **Home**. Notice the directory name in which you are saving this page; the Save In box should display your newly created Web.

3. Leave the Save as Type box set to the default Web Pages option.

4. Click Save. Your page is saved into your Web directory (smallbiz) with the name you specified (Home).

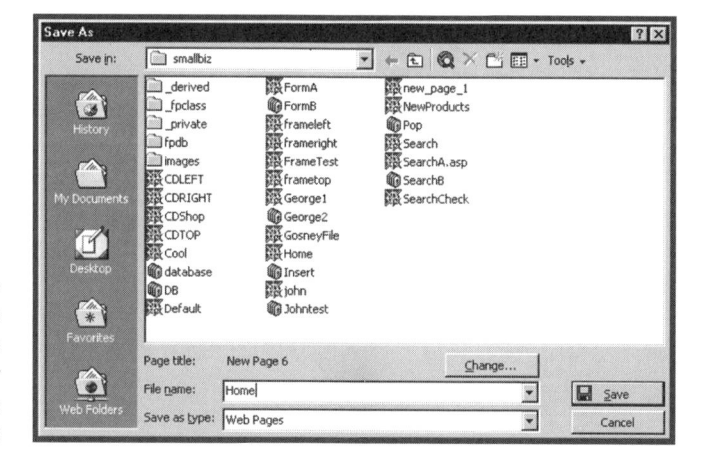

SATURDAY AFTERNOON Advanced FrontPage Functionality   63

Figure 3.7

Setting the parameters for saving a page into your Web

Understanding Where FrontPage Webs are Stored on Your Computer

Since you're using Personal Web Server to build and test your small business Web site, you need to know where on your computer Webs are stored.

1. Open Windows Explorer. To do so, click Start, then choose Programs, Windows Explorer.
2. Open the Wwwroot folder, located in the Webshare folder, as shown in Figure 3.8. The names of all FrontPage Webs you create are in the Wwwroot folder, and each Web is a folder.

If you are working in FrontPage and you want to open a Web, you can navigate to the Wwwroot folder from the Open File dialog box, as shown in Figure 3.9. Select a FrontPage Web and click Open. You are presented with a list of all items inside the Web (see Figure 3.10). Select a Web page, then click Open.

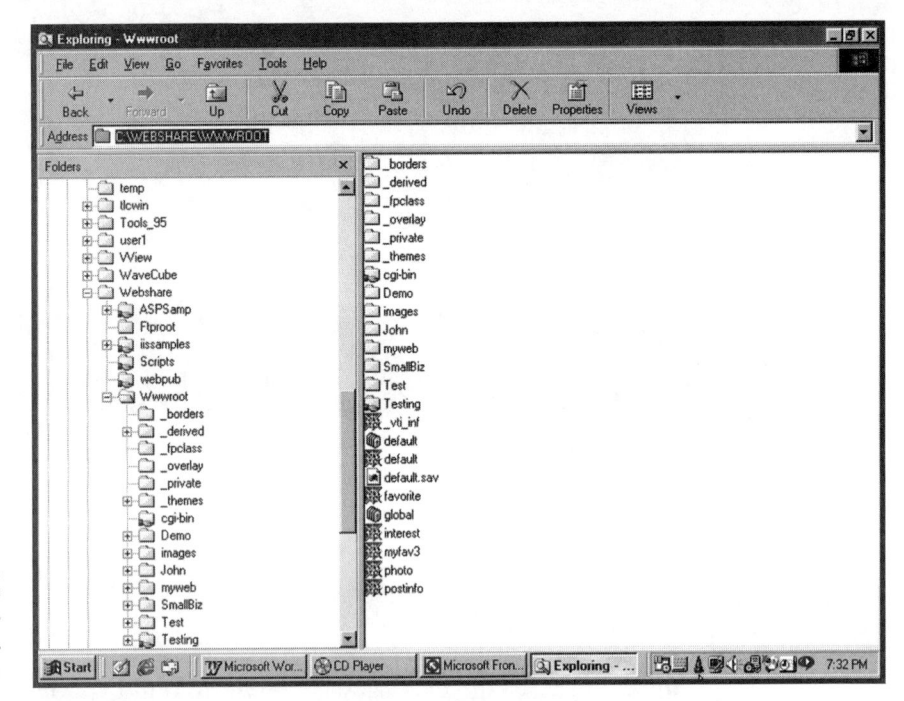

Figure 3.8

Do you see your SmallBiz folder in this list?

Figure 3.9

Opening a Web within FrontPage

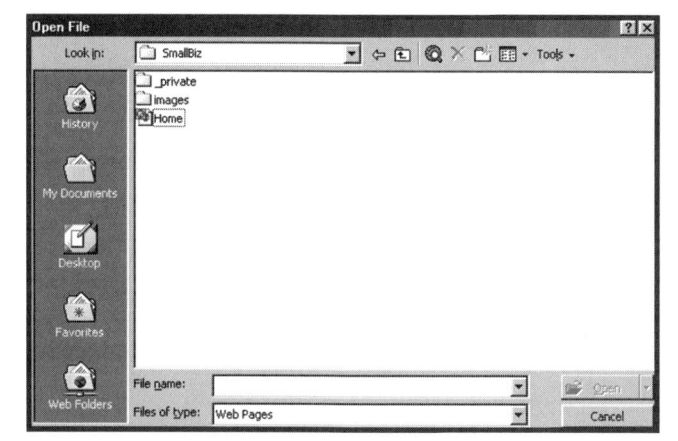

SATURDAY AFTERNOON Advanced FrontPage Functionality 65

Figure 3.10

Selecting an item within your FrontPage Web

Using a Web Browser to Access Pages in Your Web

As you may recall, the purpose of installing Personal Web Server this morning was to provide you with a complete, easy-to-use Web development environment on your own machine.

In order to see the power (and fun) of creating Webs and Web pages using this setup, load the home page you just created into your Web browser. Type your home page URL into the Location field of your browser, along with the path to your Web and the specific page. Personal Web Server will access the SmallBiz Web and display the Home.htm page created in the previous example (see Figure 3.11).

Not a very interesting page, is it? Don't despair—this exercise was important because you learned how to access your Web pages from a Web browser using Personal Web Server on your own machine.

Now that the (admittedly boring) mechanics of creating and accessing Webs are out of the way, you can move to the exciting and fun aspects of designing Web pages. Let's get started!

66 Web Enable Your Small Business In a Weekend

Your SmallBiz Web address

Figure 3.11

Your Home.htm page. Not very exciting yet!

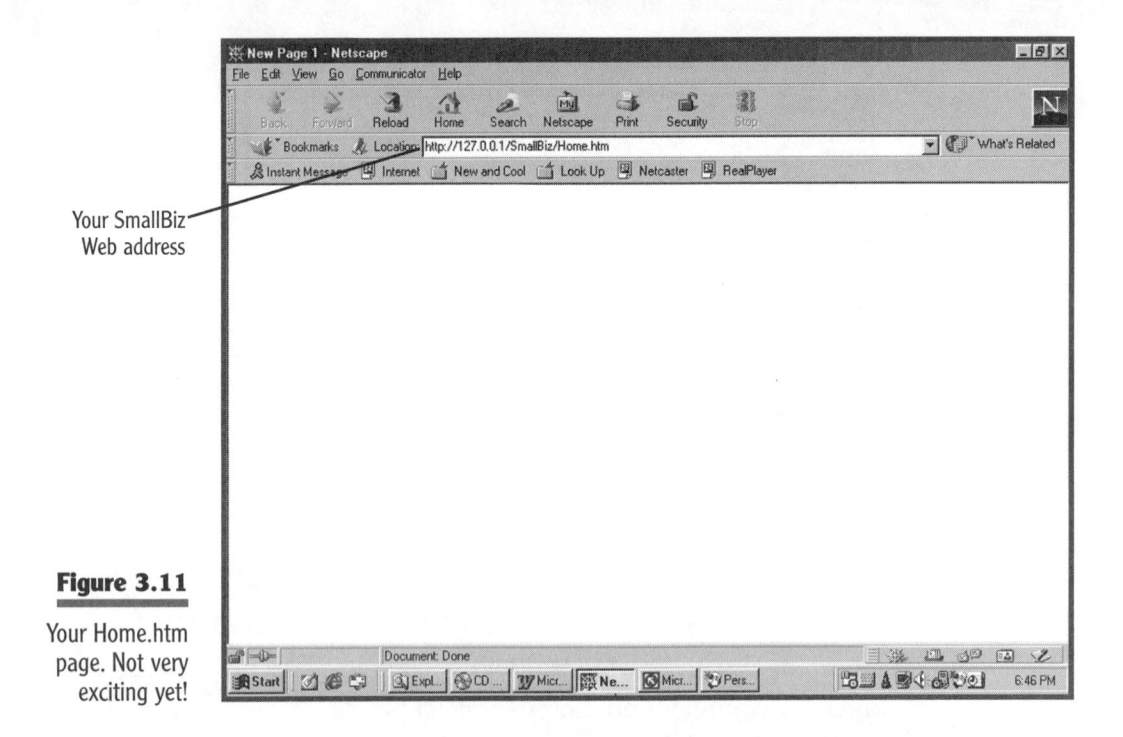

NETSCAPE NAVIGATOR OR INTERNET EXPLORER?

In case you haven't noticed, FrontPage 2000 is a Microsoft product. That said, you should be aware that while the application is extremely powerful and easy to use, the Web pages you develop within FrontPage are intended to be displayed using Microsoft's own Web browser, Internet Explorer.

This doesn't mean that Netscape Navigator won't display pages created in FrontPage. In fact, nothing could be further from the truth. However, be aware that some of the nifty effects you can add to your Web pages in FrontPage will only display if your visitors use Internet Explorer as their browser.

Fortunately, most of these features are simply window dressing. You don't have to be concerned that you'll lose major functionality if Netscape Navigator is the browser of choice for some of your customers. You can, for example, still database enable your Webs without worrying about this browser conundrum. I'll periodically point out those FrontPage features that are "Internet Explorer Only" in function.

Working with FrontPage Wizards and Themes

I admit it—I'm not the most graphically inclined person in the world. My father was a great artist and my sister can easily put pen to paper and draw whatever is in her head. But I missed out on the artistic gene. So it goes, I guess!

Whether you're like me or you're the next Rembrandt, FrontPage can help bring out your design talents. By utilizing the wizards and themes within FrontPage, you can quickly build a complete, attractive Web site.

> **CAUTION** If you just want a simple presence on the Web, then you might consider only using the FrontPage Wizards discussed in this section. You should also be aware that despite how easy it is to create Webs using the wizards, their functionality could be somewhat limited. So, take this section with a grain of salt, paying attention to the tools available to you. Realize, however, that greater functionality is in store for your small business Web site—especially this evening, when you'll learn how to database enable your Webs.

Using the Corporate Presence Wizard

Although you just created a new, blank Web (the SmallBiz Web that will be used for the remainder of this weekend), take a look at the Web creation wizards offered by FrontPage 2000.

In this exercise, you'll create another Web with the help of the Corporate Presence Wizard. The power of such a Web is somewhat limited, especially when compared to what you'll be learning tonight and tomorrow. But it's worth taking the time to experiment, so you can gain further insight into how FrontPage Webs are created, organized, and accessed.

1. From the File menu, choose New, Web. The New Web dialog box appears.
2. Click Corporate Presence Wizard.

3. Select the correct location in which to create this Web from the Specify the Location of the New Web drop-down menu. Select the home URL of your Personal Web Server and title this Web **/Demo**. Your New Web dialog box should now look like Figure 3.12.

4. Click OK. FrontPage begins to create your Web using the Corporate Presence Wizard (see Figure 3.13).

5. After a few moments, the first Corporate Presence Web Wizard dialog box appears, as shown in Figure 3.14. Read the information presented, then click Next.

6. The next dialog box asks you which features you want to include in this Web. For now, leave all of them selected, as shown in Figure 3.15. Then click Next.

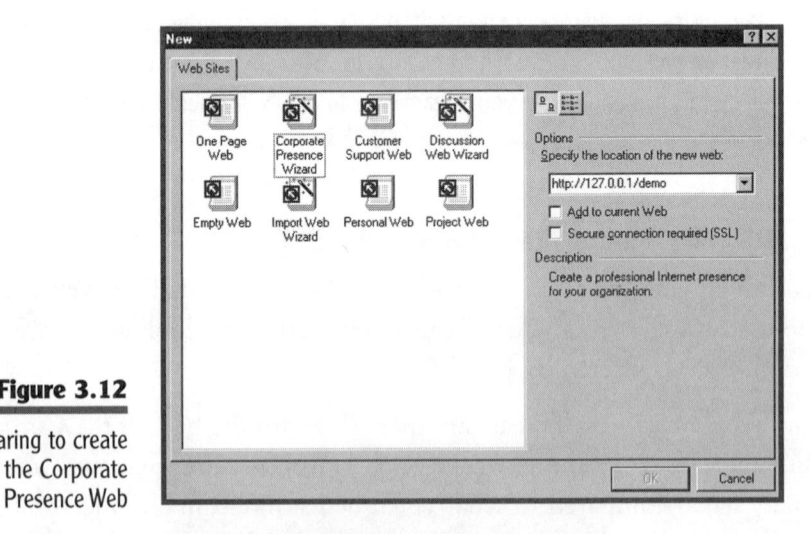

Figure 3.12

Preparing to create the Corporate Presence Web

Figure 3.13

Creating the Corporate Presence Web

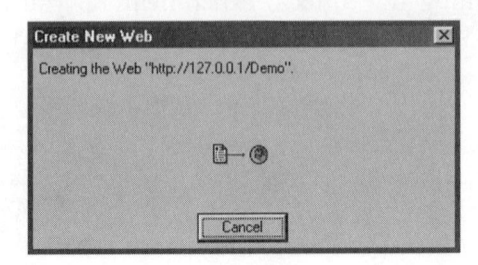

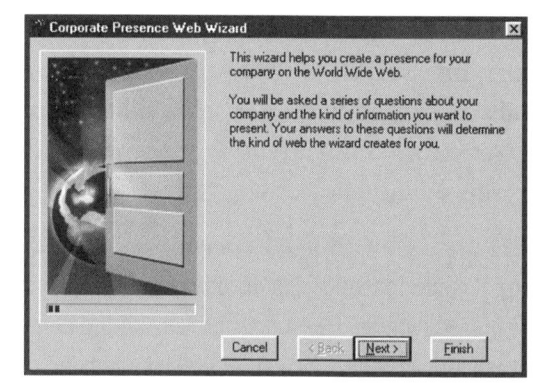

SATURDAY AFTERNOON Advanced FrontPage Functionality   69

Figure 3.14

Beginning the Corporate Presence Web Wizard

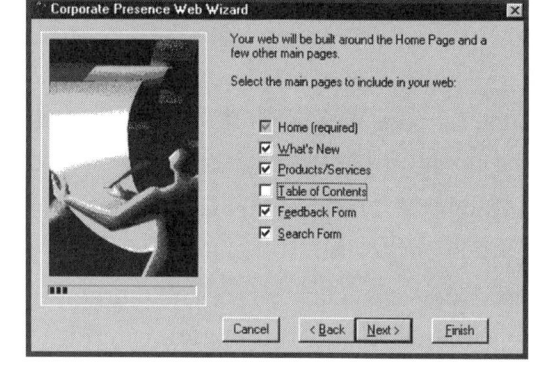

Figure 3.15

Selecting the main pages to include in your Web

7. The next dialog box asks you to select specific content options for your home page. Verify that Mission Statement and Contact Information are selected (see Figure 3.16).

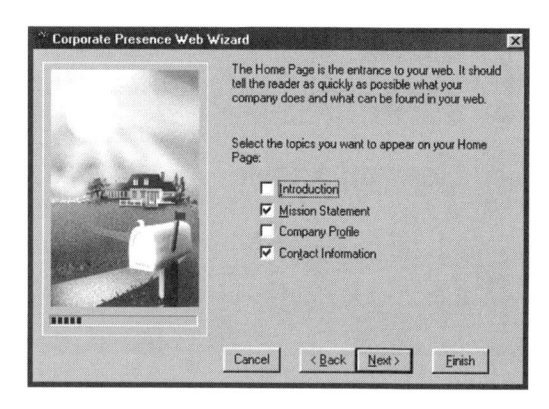

Figure 3.16

Determining content for your home page

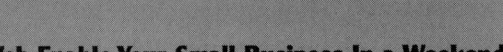

8. In the next several dialog boxes, you are asked to provide information concerning your What's New, Products and Services, and Table of Contents pages. You'll also see a few dialog boxes that ask you to enter contact information about your company. For this exercise, leave only the default choices selected.

> **NOTE** Feel free to change the information in the dialog boxes you encounter during the Wizard setup—you can't break anything. I've suggested leaving the default information only to speed up your investigation of this function, as you'll be moving on to bigger and better things later in this section and in this evening's session!

9. Eventually, you'll come to a dialog box asking you to choose a Web theme. Click Choose Web Theme. The Choose Theme dialog box appears, as shown in Figure 3.17.
10. Browse through the available themes until you find one that is appealing, then click OK.
11. In the next dialog box, click Next. The Corporate Presence Wizard has finally gathered all the information it needs to construct your Web.

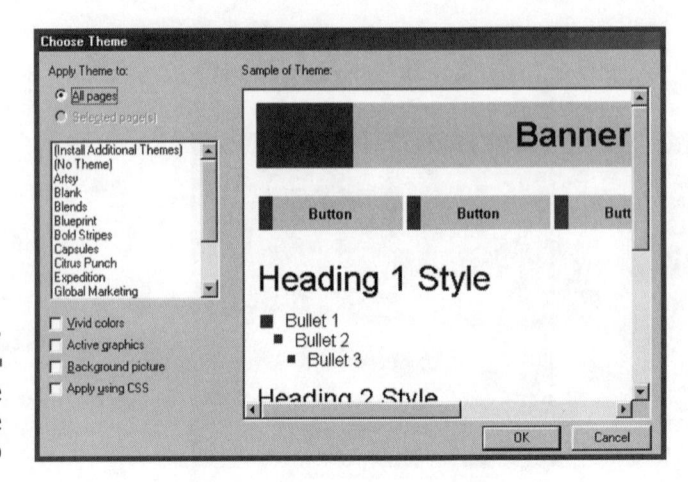

Figure 3.17

Choosing a theme for the Corporate Presence Web

SATURDAY AFTERNOON Advanced FrontPage Functionality

12. In the final dialog box, notice that the check box titled Show Tasks View after Web is Uploaded is checked (see Figure 3.18). Leave this box selected; after your Web is uploaded, FrontPage will remind you of additional tasks you'll need to complete.
13. Click Finish. FrontPage creates your Corporate Presence Web and, after a few moments, returns you to Tasks View (see Figure 3.19).

Customizing Webs Created Using Wizards

As you can see from the Tasks View, you still need to do some work to prepare your Corporate Presence Web. Select the first task in the list, Customize Home Page, and the Task Details dialog box appears (see Figure 3.20).

The Description area shows what needs to be done for this specific task (for example, "replace generic text with something more specific to your company"). For now, click Start Task. Page View appears, with the home page (Default.htm) of your Corporate Presence Web displayed, as shown in Figure 3.21.

Make some minor changes to the home page. For this example, you don't need to spend too much time customizing the content, but at least replace the text described in the Task Details dialog box. After you change the text, be sure to choose File, Save to ensure that your changes are recorded.

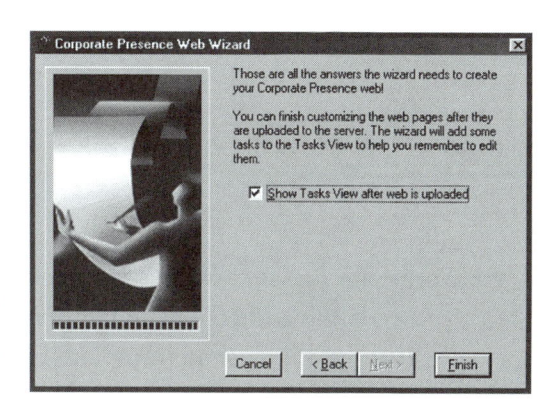

Figure 3.18

Finalizing the Web creation process

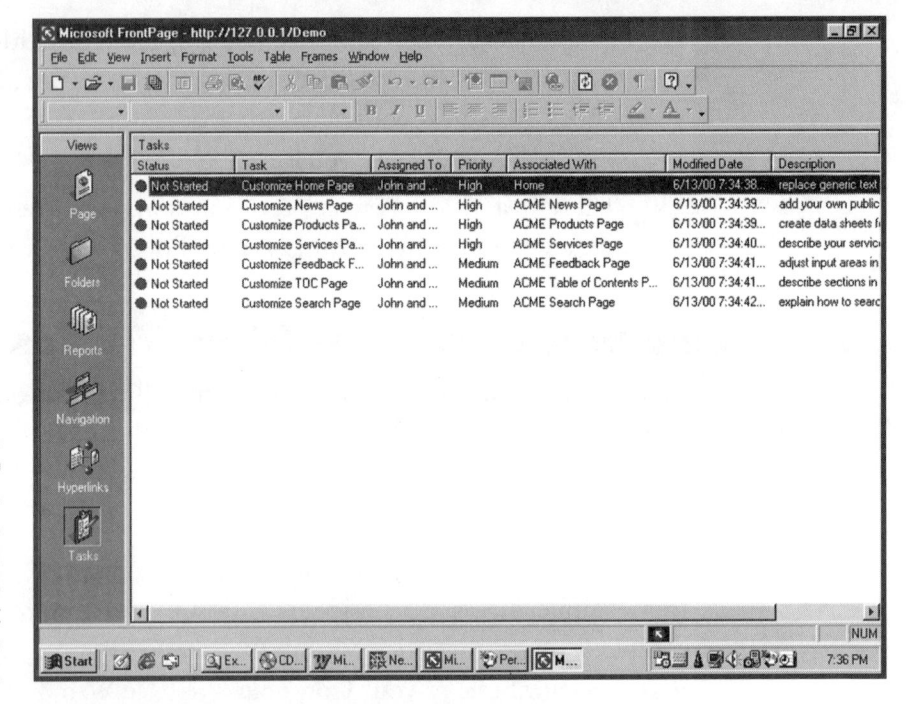

Figure 3.19

Your Corporate Presence Web is created, and FrontPage reminds you of important tasks that need to be completed.

Figure 3.20

Task Details provides more specific information about items that still need some work.

Now see what the Corporate Presence Web looks like in a Web browser. Start your browser and type the address of the Corporate Presence Web. When the page loads, it should look something like Figure 3.22. Notice that the links are active, so you can see how your entire site is organized.

SATURDAY AFTERNOON Advanced FrontPage Functionality 73

Name of displayed page

Address of the Corporate Presence Web

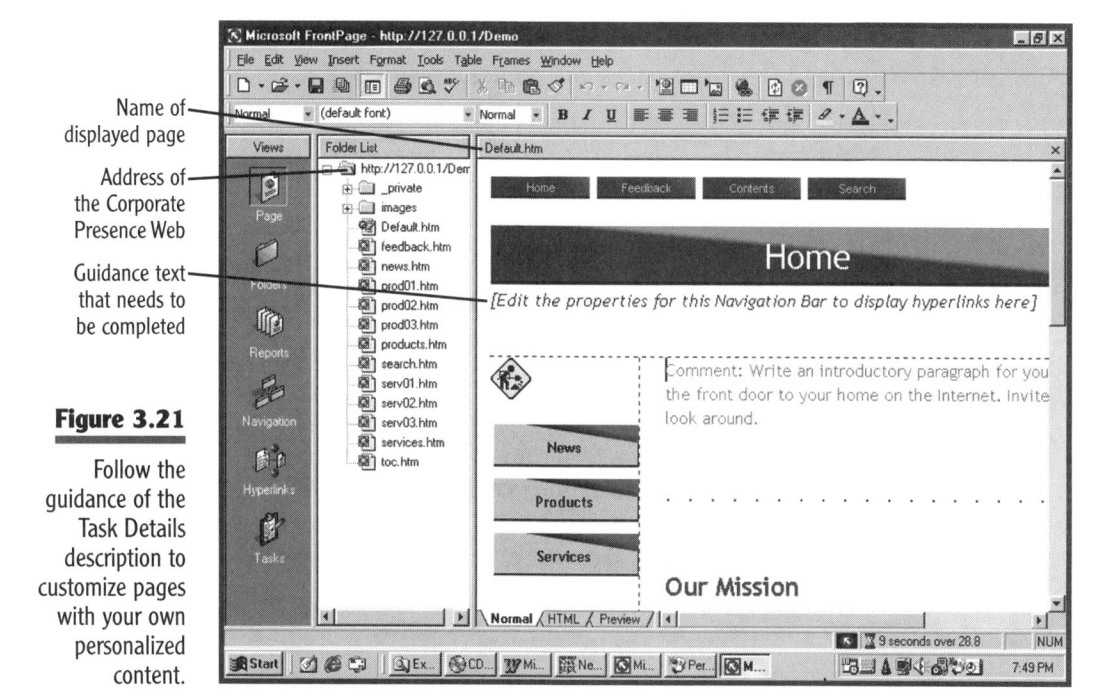

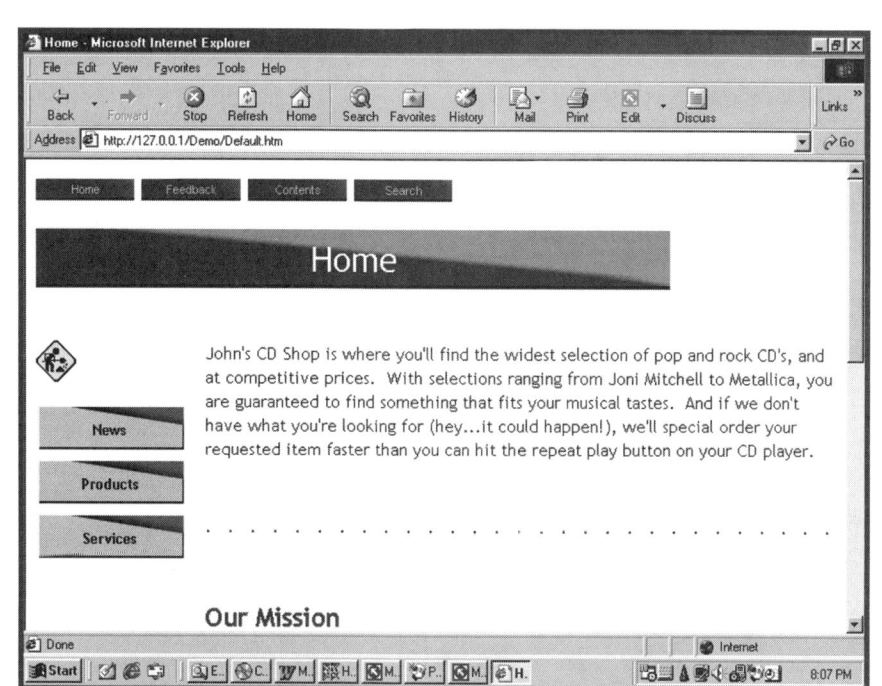

Guidance text that needs to be completed

Figure 3.21

Follow the guidance of the Task Details description to customize pages with your own personalized content.

Figure 3.22

The home page of your Corporate Presence Web site, with some customized text

If you'd like, take some time to go back into FrontPage and customize some of the other pages within the Corporate Presence Web. When you're finished experimenting, move on to a more detailed discussion of the various HTML design considerations, such as working with forms, tables, and frames.

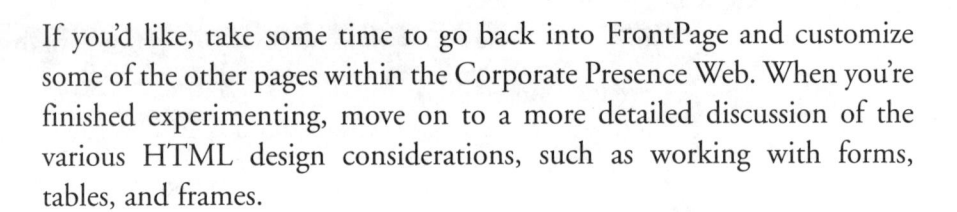

CUSTOMER RELATIONSHIP MANAGEMENT AND GOOD WEB DESIGN

Customer Relationship Management (CRM) is an important element in any e-commerce discussion. In essence, CRM involves ensuring that your Web site is an accurate, functional representation (and extension) of your business processes, both internal and external. The most successful e-commerce Web sites for businesses both large and small have carefully executed CRM strategies that give the customer a functional, easy-to-use interface for browsing and purchasing products and services via the Web. Think Amazon.com, and you can envision a well-designed CRM-enabled site.

A full discussion of CRM is beyond the scope of this book (although we'll talk more about it during tomorrow afternoon's session). However, an important element of CRM is the design of your Web interface. Keep the following CRM considerations in mind:

- **Keep your site product-oriented.** Always feature your products and services in a predominant manner. For example, instead of just having a hyperlink with text, place a picture of your product on the page and make the picture itself the link to more information.

- **Provide good site navigation.** Wherever possible, provide links back to the home page, a product order page, and other important customer contact information such as order history, profile, and so on.

- **Provide a personalized site experience.** Where appropriate, personalize your site using data gathered about your customers. You can then present specific information based on the customer's previous buying history and their profile information, such as their marital status, geographic location, and interests. You can do this by having your Web pages dynamically build from a database, which you'll learn how to do in this evening's session.

> - **Keep your customers informed.** From product announcements when your home page first loads, to post-order e-mails that let customers know their order was received and when it will arrive, keeping customers informed is a crucial element to the CRM strategy. If customers feel as if they are in control—with knowledge about their orders, profile, and your products and services—they will have a better experience with your site and will be more likely to return.
>
> Remember that the most important word in customer relationship management is *relationship.* If your customers feel that your site is personalized to their needs, and if they are presented with information quickly and efficiently and given a functional, easy-to-use order process, they will feel as if they are part of the entire e-commerce process. In turn, they will be more likely to return to your site in the future, and to recommend it to others.

Adding Tables to Organize Your Information

The greatest HTML tag ever invented? Well, maybe not quite that good, but you will quickly come to love—and hate—the <TABLE> tag. The good news is that FrontPage does most of the dirty work for you in designing and formatting tables. You'll spend more time being creative and deciding how to best present your content on your page.

The best way to learn tables is to just experiment. So, do a little table experimenting using these steps:

1. If it's not already open, open the Home.htm page within the SmallBiz Web. If you created the Corporate Presence Web, you may have two instances of FrontPage running. Look in your taskbar; if you see two Microsoft FrontPage icons, one of them is for the Corporate Presence Web and can be closed. If you closed your SmallBiz Web, open it by choosing File, Open from the FrontPage menu.

TIP

You can quickly access recently opened files and Webs by choosing File, Recent Files or File, Recent Webs.

2. From the Table menu, choose Insert, Table. The Insert Table dialog box appears.

3. Leave the default values in the Insert Table dialog box as they appear. Click OK to insert a table drawn to the parameters set in the Insert Table dialog box, 2 rows by 2 columns in this example (see Figure 3.23).

As you can see, using the Insert Table command isn't difficult. But FrontPage's table features don't stop with the simple Insert feature. Rather, you can format and design your tables—and insert graphics and text into the various table cells—to produce some really nice effects.

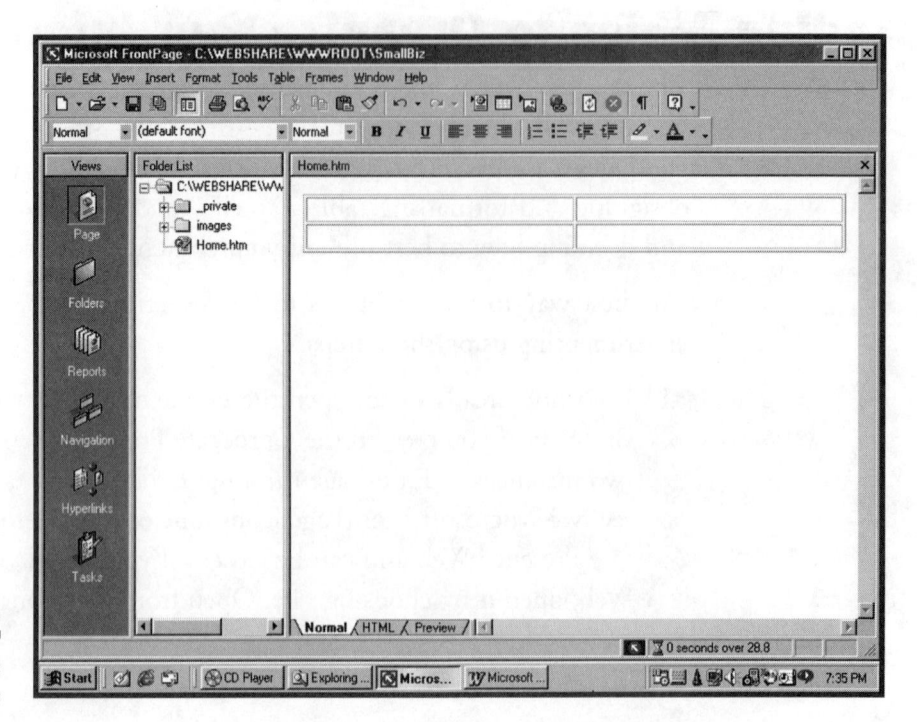

Figure 3.23

Creating a table in FrontPage

Formatting Tables

To access the table formatting features, click in any cell in your table. Then, from the Table menu, choose Properties, Table. The Table Properties dialog box appears, as shown in Figure 3.24.

Refer to Figure 3.24 as you examine the different sections of the Table Properties dialog box:

- **Layout.** This section allows you to set the alignment of the table cells, as well as cell padding and cell spacing. Changing the cell padding and spacing affects the look of your table. Compare the table in Figure 3.25, with cell padding and spacing set to 6, to the table in Figure 3.23, where the padding and spacing are set to the default values.
- **Borders.** This section lets you define both the size and color of your table borders.
- **Background.** This section allows you to select images and graphics to use as a background within your table. See Figure 3.26 for examples of two different table backgrounds.

In addition to controlling properties for the entire table, you can also set specific cell properties in the Cell Properties dialog box (see Figure 3.27). You'll notice that the features in the Cell Properties dialog box are similar

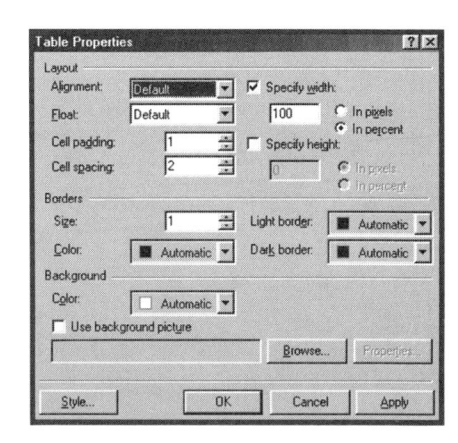

Figure 3.24

The Table Properties dialog box

Web Enable Your Small Business In a Weekend

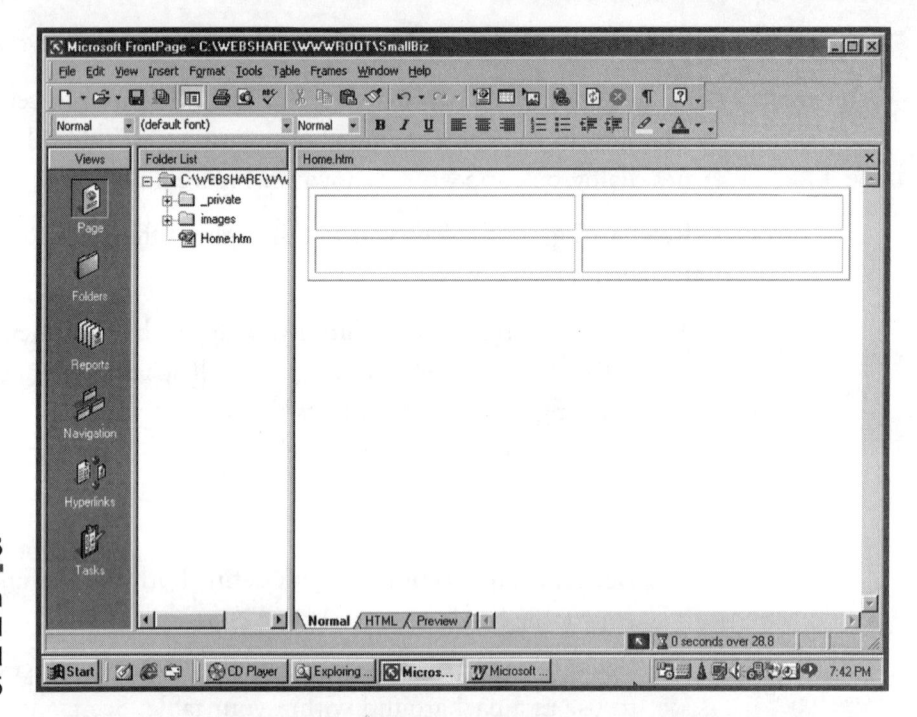

Figure 3.25

A two-column table with cell padding and spacing set to 6

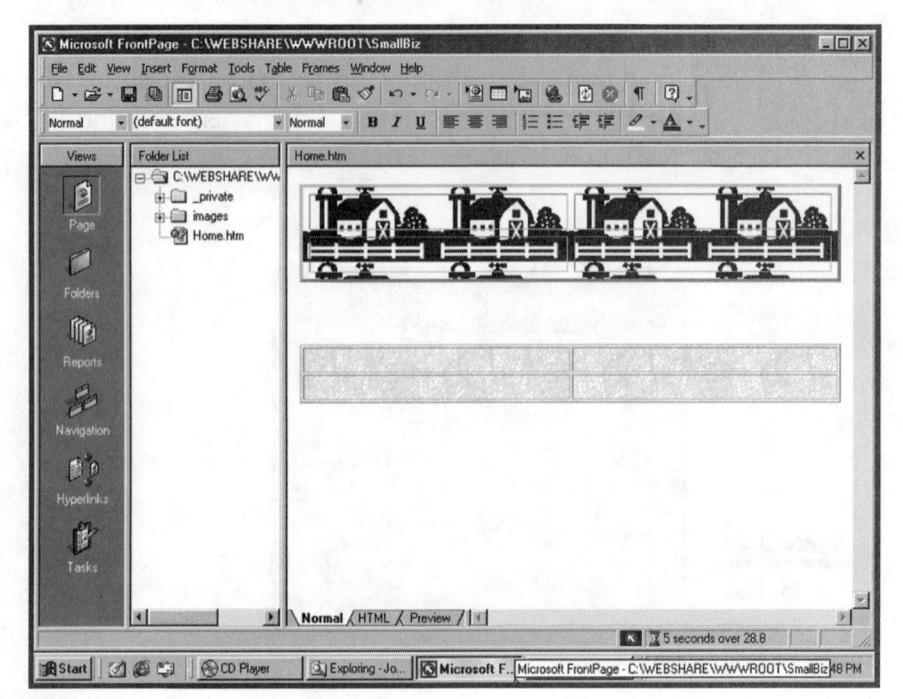

Figure 3.26

The first table uses a clip art graphic as a background image, while the second table uses a simple fill pattern.

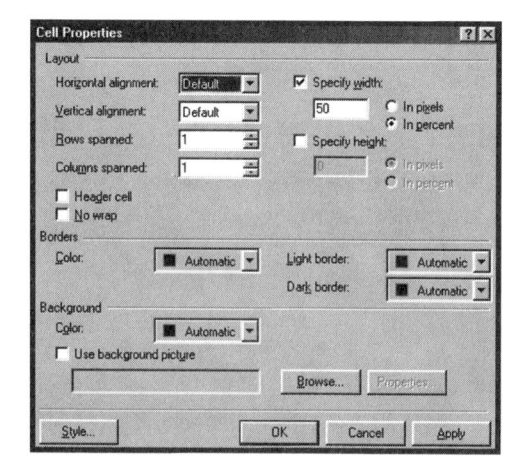

SATURDAY AFTERNOON Advanced FrontPage Functionality

Figure 3.27

The Cell Properties dialog box

to those in the Table Properties dialog box. You can access the Cell Properties dialog box from the Table menu by choosing Properties, Cell, or by right-clicking in the table cell you want to modify and then choosing Cell Properties from the resulting shortcut menu.

Of course, once you've inserted your table, you can edit it by adding or deleting rows, columns, and cells. To insert an element into your table, click in the table. From the Table menu, choose Insert, then choose Rows, Columns, or Cell. To delete an element, first select the element in the table. Then, from the Table menu, choose the Delete command.

> **TIP**
> You can also add a caption to your table by choosing Insert, Caption from the Table menu. This will place your cursor directly above the table, where you can add text.

Finally, you can also split and merge cells in a table, which produces some interesting table structures.

1. In the table you just created, select the first cell. You'll need to click in the cell, then, from the Table menu, choose Select, Cell. The cell will then be highlighted.

2. Next, right-click to open the shortcut menu and choose Split Cells. The Split Cells dialog box will appear.
3. Split the cell into four columns and click OK, as shown in Figure 3.28.
4. Select the upper-right cell, then choose Split Cells from the Table menu and split the cell into two rows. Your table should now look something like Figure 3.29.

> **TIP**
> In addition to splitting cells, you can also merge cells. To merge cells, select the cell elements you want to merge. Then, from the Table menu, choose Merge Cells.

Adding Text and Graphics to Your Tables

The table created thus far is very basic. This section will demonstrate how you can use a table as a powerful design element by spicing it up using text and graphics (see Figure 3.30).

> **CAUTION**
> Tables are no exception to the *test in different browsers* rule. You'll want to ensure that your tables and entire Web site, for that matter, look neat and well-designed in both Internet Explorer and Netscape Navigator (and in other browsers, too, if you have access to them).
>
> Netscape and IE can, and do, render tables differently. Sometimes the differences are so small they are unnoticeable; other times, it seems as if you've created two entirely different versions of your table! Test, test, test!

Figure 3.28

The Split Cells dialog box, with the instructions to split the cell into four columns

SATURDAY AFTERNOON Advanced FrontPage Functionality

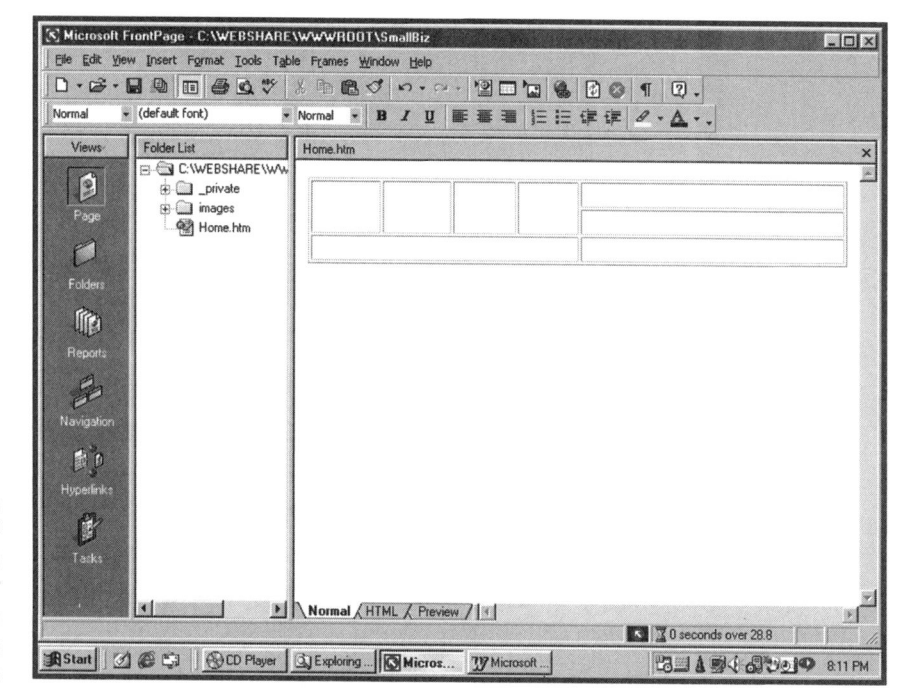

Figure 3.29

One cell has been split into four columns, with another cell split into two rows

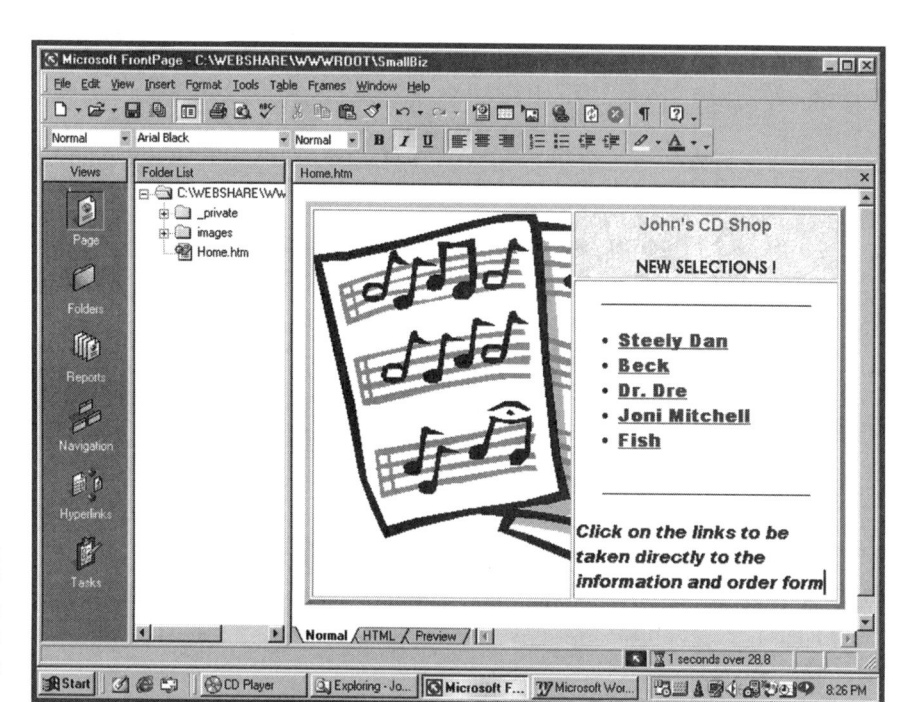

Figure 3.30

Simple table formatting can produce nice effects.

Try spicing up your table by adding a picture to one of the cells. Simply follow these steps:

1. First, remove the existing table. To do so, select the entire table, then choose Delete Cells from the Table menu. You table will be erased.

2. Now that you have a clean slate, you can create a new table. From the Table menu, choose Insert, Table. When the Insert Table dialog box appears, leave the number of rows set to one, but change the number of columns to two. Click OK, and the table appears.

3. Select the right cell, right-click, and choose Split Cells. From the Split Cells dialog box, divide the cell into two rows. The basic structure of the table is now defined.

4. Now, add a graphic to the left cell (the cell that hasn't been split). Click in the cell and then, from the Table menu, choose Properties, Cell (or, right-click in the selected cell and choose Cell Properties from the shortcut menu).

5. In the Background section of the Cell Properties dialog box, click Browse. The Select Background Picture dialog box appears, as shown in Figure 3.31.

6. Browse through the image files (if you have any) on your machine, or click Clip Art and find a graphic that appeals to you. Your

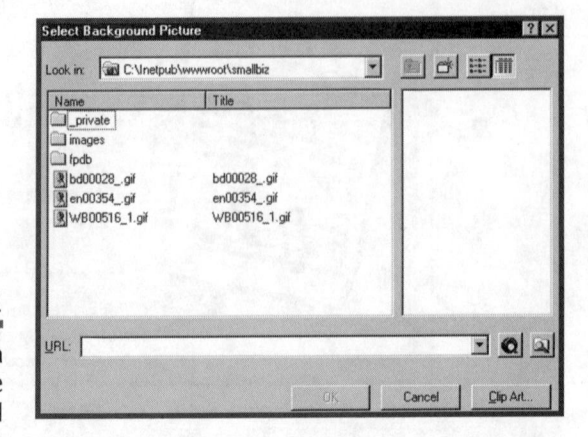

Figure 3.31

Selecting a background picture for a table cell

graphic will be inserted into the selected cell. In the example table in Figure 3.30, the music pages are simple clip art.

7. Finally, format the two cells on the right any way you want. In Figure 3.30, I've created an information table for the fictitious "John's CD Shop," listing new arrivals in the store.

NOTE In the example table, you may notice that the new release titles, such as Steely Dan and Beck, appear as possible hyperlinks. Well, they are! When the customer clicks on the artist name, they are taken directly to the information and order form, as noted in the text at the bottom-right of the table. You'll learn how to add hyperlinks to your pages later in this session.

Take some time now to play around with formatting your table. Try splitting and merging cells, adding and deleting elements, and formatting text and graphics. When you're finished, take a short break.

Take a Break!

You've been at it for a while now, learning how FrontPage Webs are organized, and experimenting with inserting and formatting tables. Take a short break now—grab a snack, check the score of the game, whatever. When you return, you'll be ready to jump into a discussion of Web page frames.

Working with Frames

You might not realize it, but a large percentage of the Web pages you visit in your browsing adventures through cyberspace use frames. What are frames? Take a look at Figure 3.32.

Web Enable Your Small Business In a Weekend

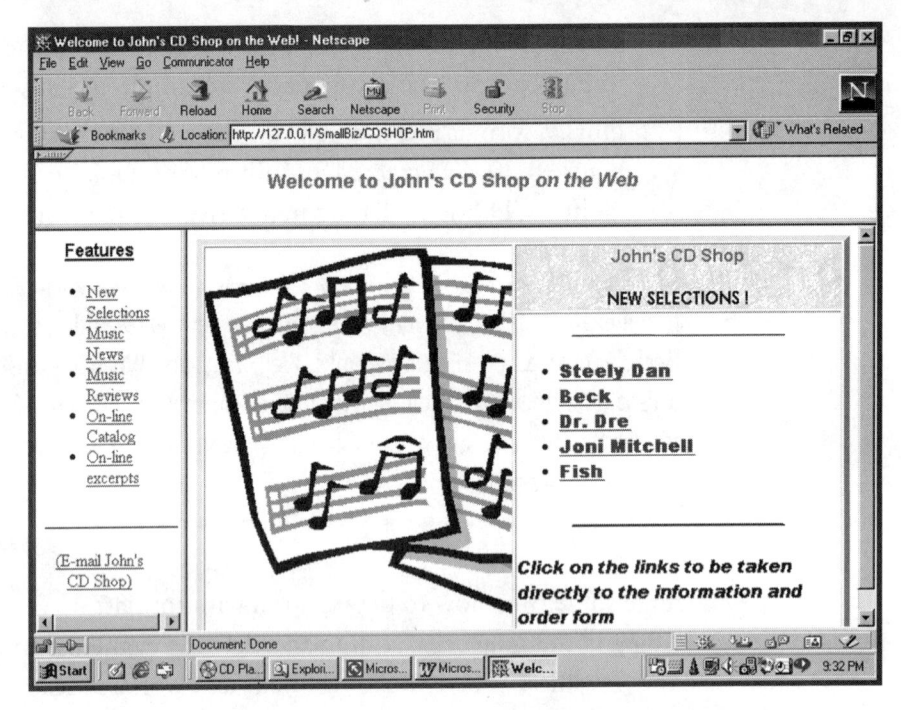

Figure 3.32

Frames provide an attractive, functional way of presenting your information.

Figure 3.32 includes some important characteristics:

- The top frame is used to display the name of the company—my fictitious "John's CD Shop." This company name frame always remains on the screen as information in the content frame scrolls up and under it.

- The left frame is used as a table of contents. From here, customers can quickly select an area of interest, such as New Selections or Music News. When they click on one of these selections (which are hyperlinks), the resulting information is displayed in the right, or *content*, frame.

- Finally, the content frame is used to display information based on which hyperlink the customer clicks in the table of contents (or left) frame. In Figure 3.32, the customer clicked on the New Selections link, resulting in the display of New Selections in the content frame.

SATURDAY AFTERNOON Advanced FrontPage Functionality

> **NOTE**
> You can probably safely assume that the vast majority of customers visiting your Web site will use at least version 4.0 or higher of the popular browsers, including the AOL browser. However, you may have customers who use older versions of Web browsers that are not able to display frames.
>
> What do you do so you don't lose these important customers? You need to provide an alternative to your frames page. Look for information on this a bit later in the, "Understanding Frames Page Mechanics" section.

Are frames easy to design? Yes, thanks to FrontPage and the frame-design features it provides. In the days before snazzy Web page editors like FrontPage, working with frames could get a bit complicated. The next discussion begins by walking you through the process of creating a Web page that uses frames. Although similar in most ways to creating a regular Web page, there are some important differences.

Creating and Saving a Frames Page

Start by creating and saving a frames page, using these steps:

1. From within your SmallBiz Web, choose File, New, Page. When the New Page dialog box appears, click the Frames Pages tab, as shown in Figure 3.33.

2. For this example, select the Banner and Contents layout, then click OK. You are presented with the basic structure of the frame. Notice that each frame is essentially three separate Web pages. FrontPage asks you if you want to create each frame from scratch or use an existing page (see Figure 3.34).

3. Click New Page in each frame. You are presented (in Page View) with three blank Web pages, each corresponding to a frame.

4. Notice the additional view tabs at the bottom of the screen. For now, take special notice of the No Frames tab. Remember your customers who don't have browsers capable of displaying frames? FrontPage has a built-in No Frames option so you can construct a no frames page to display to these customers (see Figure 3.35).

86 Web Enable Your Small Business In a Weekend

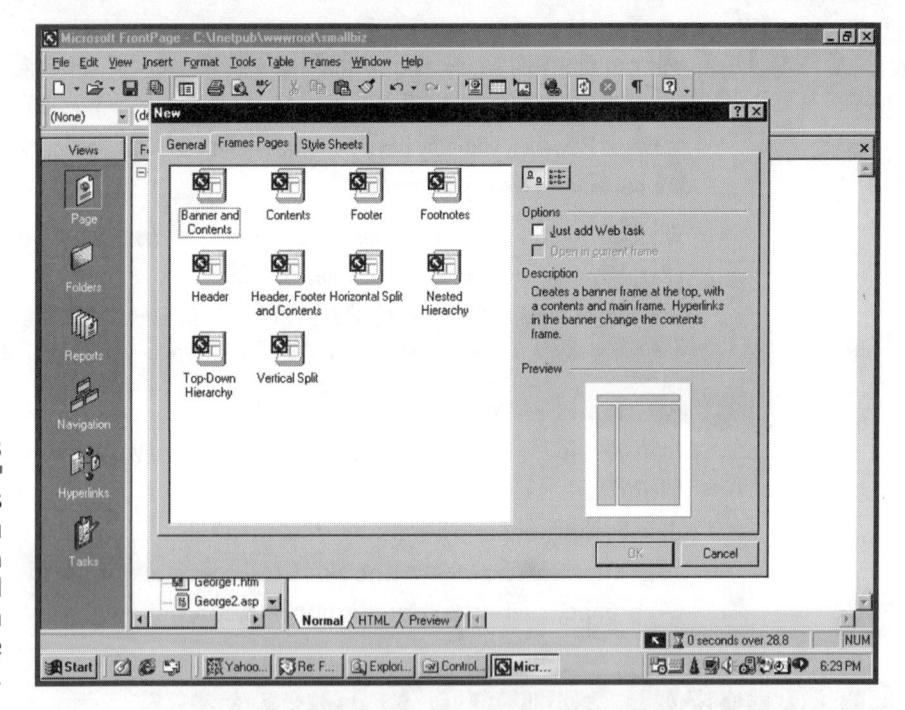

Figure 3.33

In the Frames Pages tab, you are provided a description and preview of each type of frame layout.

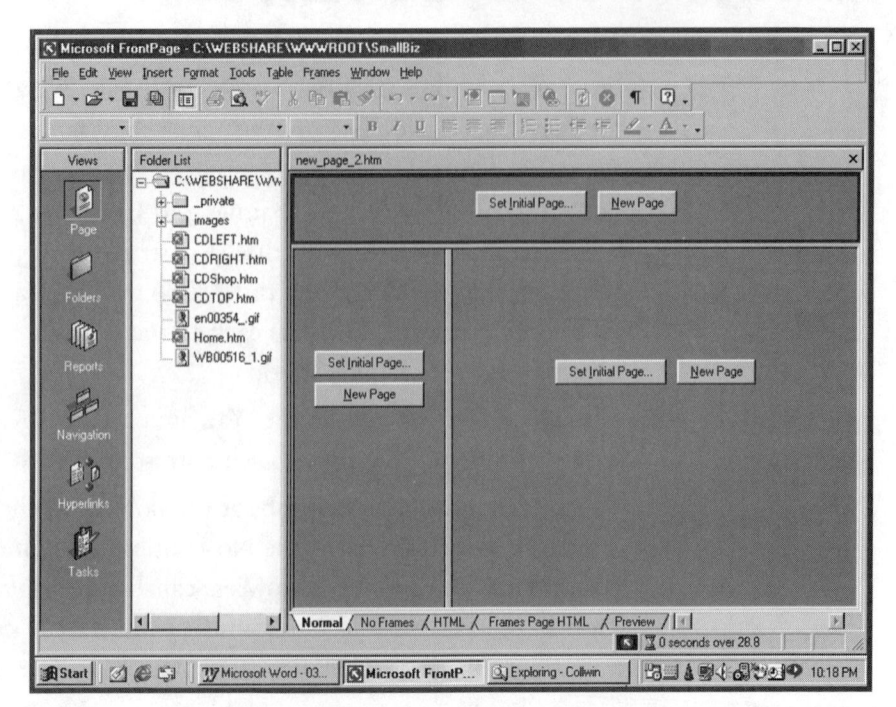

Figure 3.34

You can build your frames page from existing pages or create new pages from scratch.

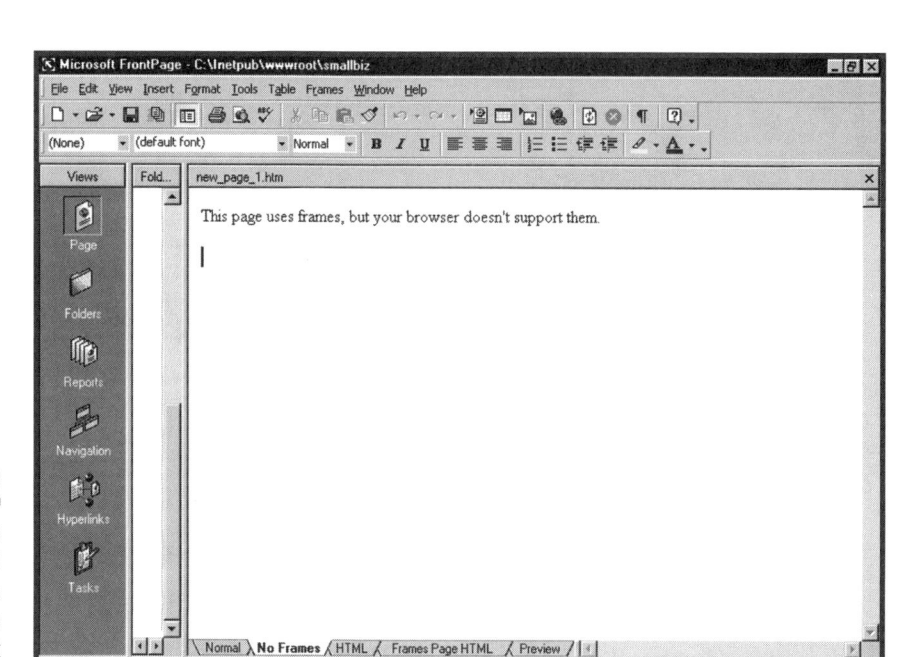

SATURDAY AFTERNOON Advanced FrontPage Functionality

Figure 3.35

Use this page to display special messages to customers who use older browsers that can't display frames pages.

Saving Frames Pages

Building and saving frames pages is similar to working with regular HTML pages in FrontPage, but with a few unique differences. Now that you have a structure for your frame page, you should immediately save it using these steps:

1. From the File menu, choose Save As. The Save As dialog box appears, as shown in Figure 3.36. Notice how the structure of your frames page is presented.

2. For this example, name the entire frames page FrameTest, then click Save.

3. You are now asked to save the table of contents frame. Remember that each frame is an individual Web page, so you have to save each one. Since your frames page consists of three Web pages, you'll

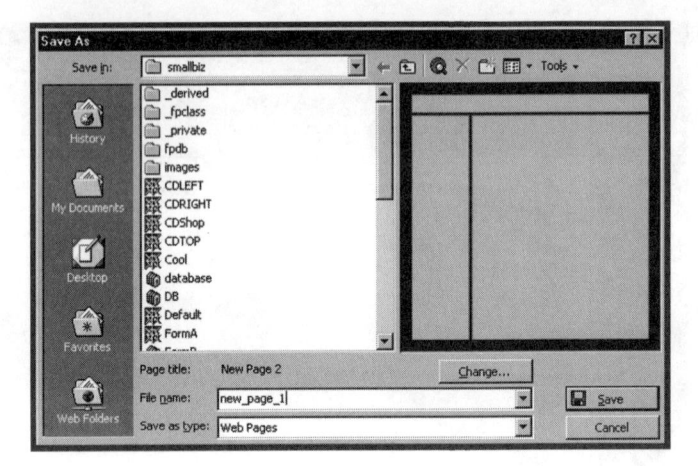

Figure 3.36

The file name you choose will be the name of the entire frames page.

need to save each one individually. In this example, use the name frameleft for the table of contents frame.

4. After you type a name for each frame, you will be taken to the next frame until all frames (or Web pages) are saved.

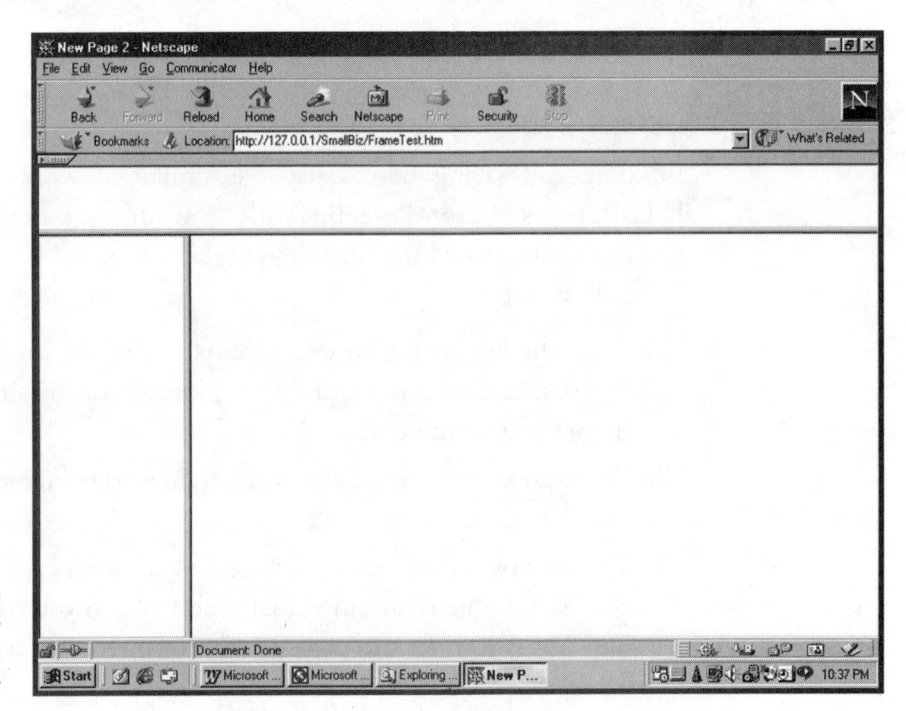

Figure 3.37

Displaying your empty frames page in a Web browser

Now you can see what your new frames page looks like in a Web browser (see Figure 3.37). Open your browser and type the URL for your Personal Web Server, followed by SmallBiz and the name of your frames page. The URL you type should look something like http://127.0.0.1/SmallBiz/FrameTest.htm.

Now that the structure of your frames page is saved and you've displayed it in a Web browser, it's time go back to FrontPage and explore the unique properties that make up a frames page.

Understanding Frames Page Mechanics

Even though you don't have the actual HTML code that supports your Web pages, you can examine how it works in relation to frames pages. This will make it easier for you to understand frames.

1. If you're still viewing the blank FrameTest.htm page in your browser, open the FrontPage window and, if necessary, navigate back to your SmallBiz Web. Then open the FrameTest.htm page. Your screen should look like Figure 3.38.

2. Click the Frames Page HTML tab at the bottom of the frames page. This will open the HTML code that comprises the FrameTest.htm page (see Figure 3.39).

NOTE When you first began the save process for your frames page, the first file name FrontPage asked you to provide was the name of the *container* page. In this example, you named it FrameTest.htm. The container page is, in essence, the structure of a frames page. It sets basic attributes of the page (the width of the scrollbars, the size of individual frames, and so on) and calls the actual Web pages that make up the frame. Remember that each frame is a separate Web page.

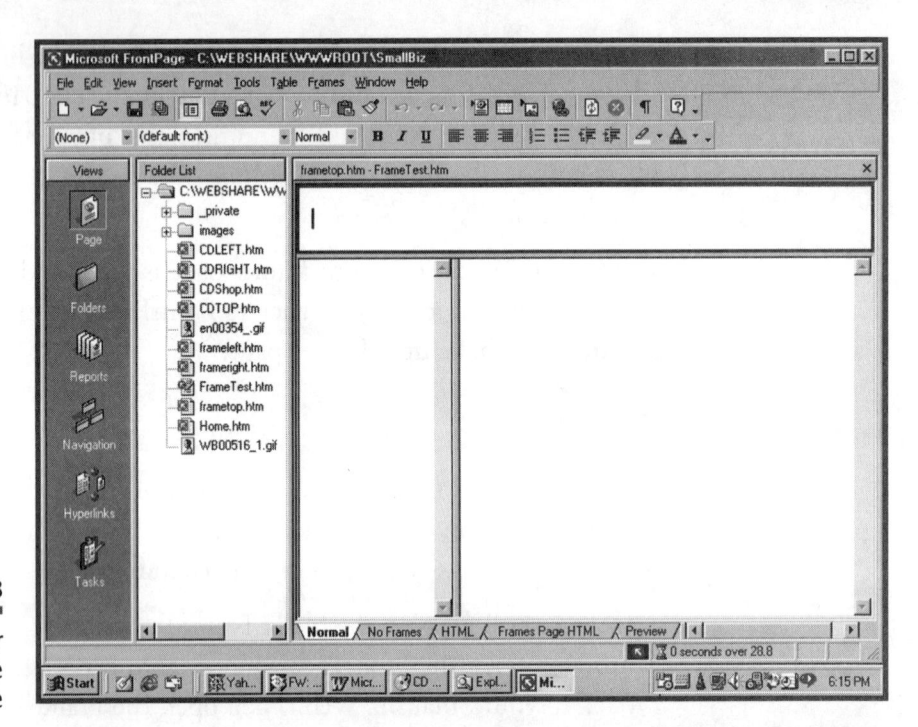

Figure 3.38

Viewing your new frames page in FrontPage

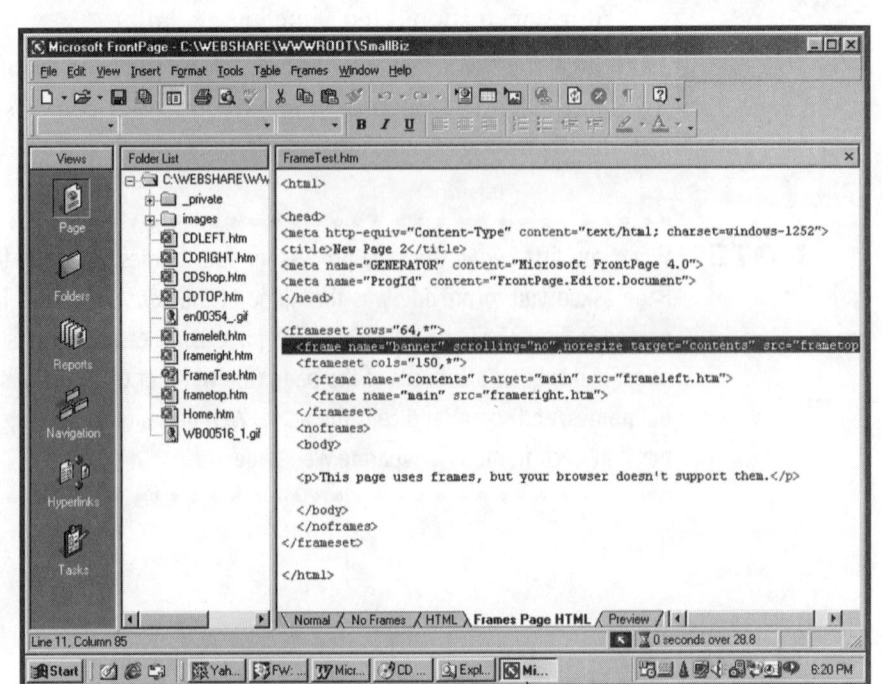

Figure 3.39

Using the Frames Page HTML tab, you can see exactly how your frames page is constructed with HTML code.

3. Examine the following code:

```
<frameset rows="64,*">
  <frame name="banner" scrolling="no" noresize
      target="contents"            src="frametop.htm">
  <frameset cols="150,*">
  <frame name="contents" target="main" src="frameleft.htm">
  <frame name="main" src="frameright.htm">
  </frameset>
  <noframes>
  <body>
  <p>This page uses frames, but your browser doesn't
      support them.</p>
  </body>
  </noframes>
</frameset>
```

Notice the three <frame name> tags: banner, contents, main. Also, notice the src (short for "source") of these three frame names (frametop.htm, frameleft.htm, and frameright.htm). Recall that when you were saving the frames, you were asked to provide a file name for each one. FrontPage correlated the names you provided with the frame structure name (banner, contents, and main). Table 3.1 displays how the file names you provided correlate to the frame structure names inserted by FrontPage.

Table 3.1 Description of Frame Structure

File Name Provided during the Save Process	Correlating FrontPage Frame Name
frametop.htm	banner
frameleft.htm	contents
frameright.htm	main

Next, notice the target component of each `<frame>` tag in the HTML excerpt. For example, take a closer look at this piece of HTML code:

```
<frame name="contents" target="main" src="frameleft.htm">
```

This tag refers to the table of contents frame (the left frame). The name of this frame is contents and the Web page represented by this frame is frameleft.htm. The target attribute refers to the frame to which hyperlinks will point. For example, if a hyperlink called New Products is placed in this frame, when the customer clicks on the link, the results of the hyperlink will be displayed in the content frame (the frameright.htm page).

> **NOTE** Hyperlinks in general, as well as using them in frames, will be discussed in the "Adding Hyperlinks" section, later in this session.

Finally, before leaving the HTML analysis of frames, look at the following code:

```
<noframes>
<body>
<p>This page uses frames, but your browser doesn't
    support them.</p>
</body>
</noframes>
```

Most of your customers will have browsers capable of displaying frames. However, for those who don't, the `<noframes>` tag displays the message: "This page uses frames, but your browser doesn't support them." You can change this message to display anything you want by clicking on the No Frames tab in FrontPage. You can then access and customize this no frame option.

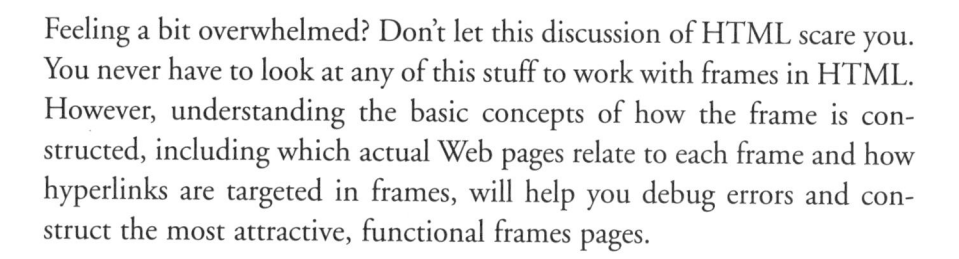

SATURDAY AFTERNOON Advanced FrontPage Functionality

Feeling a bit overwhelmed? Don't let this discussion of HTML scare you. You never have to look at any of this stuff to work with frames in HTML. However, understanding the basic concepts of how the frame is constructed, including which actual Web pages relate to each frame and how hyperlinks are targeted in frames, will help you debug errors and construct the most attractive, functional frames pages.

Customizing Frame Properties with FrontPage

As I said previously, you really don't have to worry about the relating HTML code to work with frames. In fact, you can set all the frame properties using the friendly FrontPage interface. This section will introduce some customization of frame properties. You'll see how changing values affects the appearance of frames.

1. If the Frames Page HTML tab is still selected, click the Normal tab. Right-click inside any of the three frames and, from the shortcut menu that appears, choose Frame Properties. The Frame Properties dialog box appears, as shown in Figure 3.40.

2. The Frame Properties dialog box in Figure 3.40 displays settings for the main frame, the frame associated with the file frameright.htm. You can set the size of a specific frame by manipulating the Frame Size and Margin attributes. Change the Frame Size Width to 125 and the Row Height to 8, and the frame will look similar to Figure 3.41 when it is displayed in a Web browser.

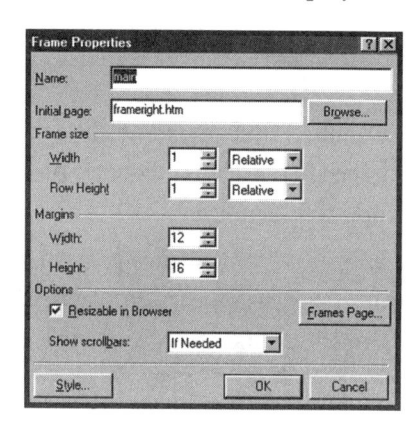

Figure 3.40

The Frame Properties dialog box

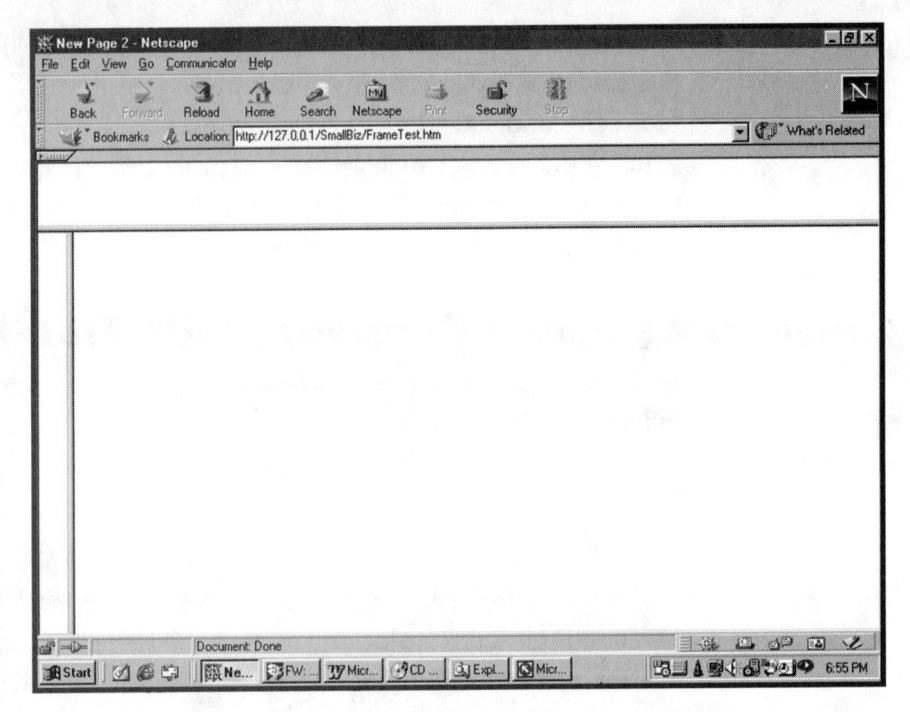

Figure 3.41

By changing the frame width, you change the appearance of not only the selected frame, but other frames as well.

3. Take some time to experiment with resizing the different frames, being sure to choose File, Save before viewing the frame in a browser, so that you can see the effects of your changes.

4. Click on the Frames Page button in the Frame Properties dialog box. The Page Properties dialog box appears, as shown in Figure 3.42. In this dialog box, you can manipulate specific features of the frames page.

5. Now click the Frames tab. The important element to recognize is the Show Borders check box. Clear the check box, then click OK to close the Page Properties dialog box.

6. Choose File, Save, then view your frames page in your browser. Although it is a frames page, it appears empty because Show Borders has been deselected, and it contains no content (see Figure 3.43).

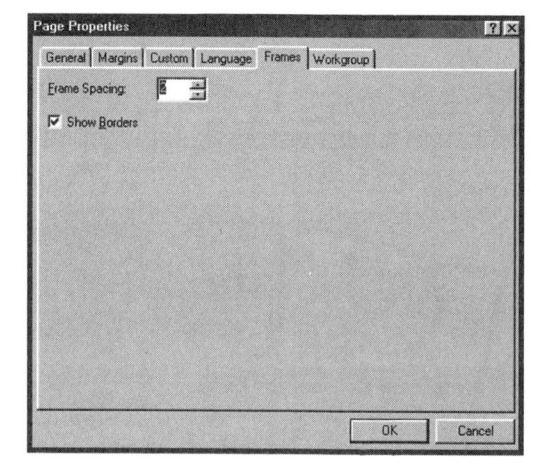

Figure 3.42

The Page Properties dialog box, with the Frames tab selected

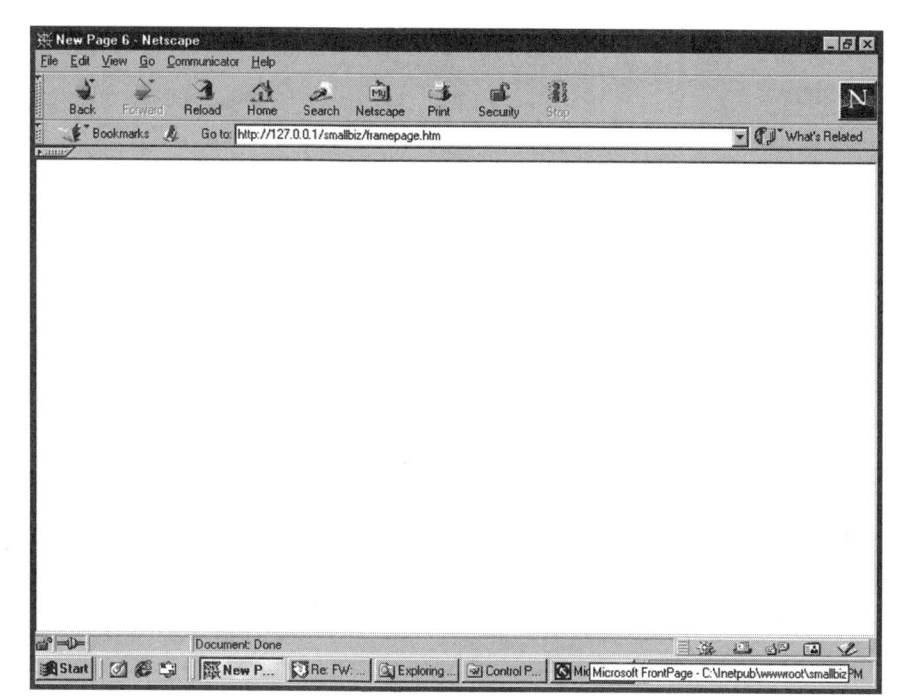

Figure 3.43

An "empty" frames page

Why would you want to turn off borders? Depending on the design of your page, not showing borders can give your frames page a cleaner look, since the lines (borders) that separate the frames are not viewable. See Figure 3.44 for another example of a frames page without borders.

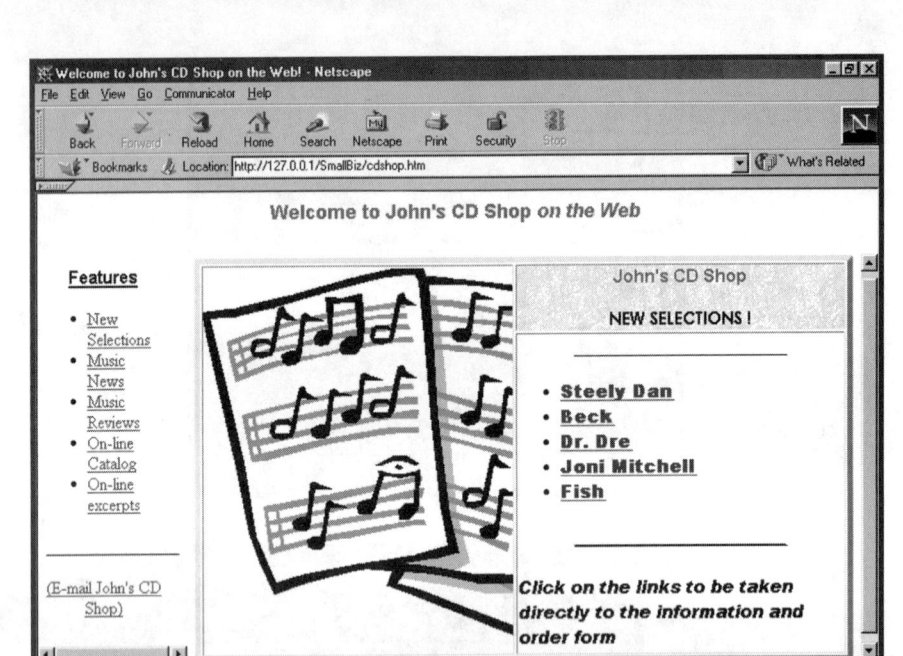

Figure 3.44

"John's CD Shop" with the borders turned off

Designing with frames is an important issue. In tomorrow's session, you will learn more about the different ways to customize and display frames. In addition to discussing issues such as frame border size and the inclusion of scroll bars, you'll also learn about adding sounds and graphics to your frames pages.

Feel free to play around a bit with customizing your frames page, perhaps adding a bit of content (including a table or two). Be sure to see how your changes display in your browser. When you're done experimenting, move on to the very important topic of using forms in your Web pages.

Working with Forms in Your Web Pages

Providing your customers with the ability to enter data into your Web pages, and having that data concurrently stored in a database so you can retrieve it later is one of the coolest features of the Web. With tools such as FrontPage, you don't have to know a single line of programming code to build a form and have it insert data into a database such as Access.

This section will discuss the more common form elements and their special properties. Even though storing form results in a database won't be discussed until this evening, you will, by the end of this section, know how construct and format a form so it is ready to capture important data, such as a customer's product orders!

Before beginning a discussion of form elements, you'll need to create a new page on which you can experiment with forms. Follow these steps:

1. From your SmallBiz Web, choose File, New.
2. When the New dialog box appears, select the default Normal Page.
3. When the page is created, immediately save it, giving it the file name of FormTest.

Now that you have a blank slate, it's time to start working with form elements! FrontPage makes it easy to access Form elements. From the Insert menu, choose Form. A list of all the available form elements appears.

So that you can see all the form elements in action, the next set of steps inserts one instance of every available form element into the FormTest.htm page.

1. To begin, choose Insert, Form and then click One-Line Text Box. This form element is inserted into your Web page.
2. Next, click below the Reset button on your Web page. Be sure your cursor is still within the dotted outline, then return to the Insert menu and choose the Scrolling Text Box form element.
3. Repeat Step 2 until you have added one instance of every available form element to your Web page. When you're finished, your page should look similar to Figure 3.45.

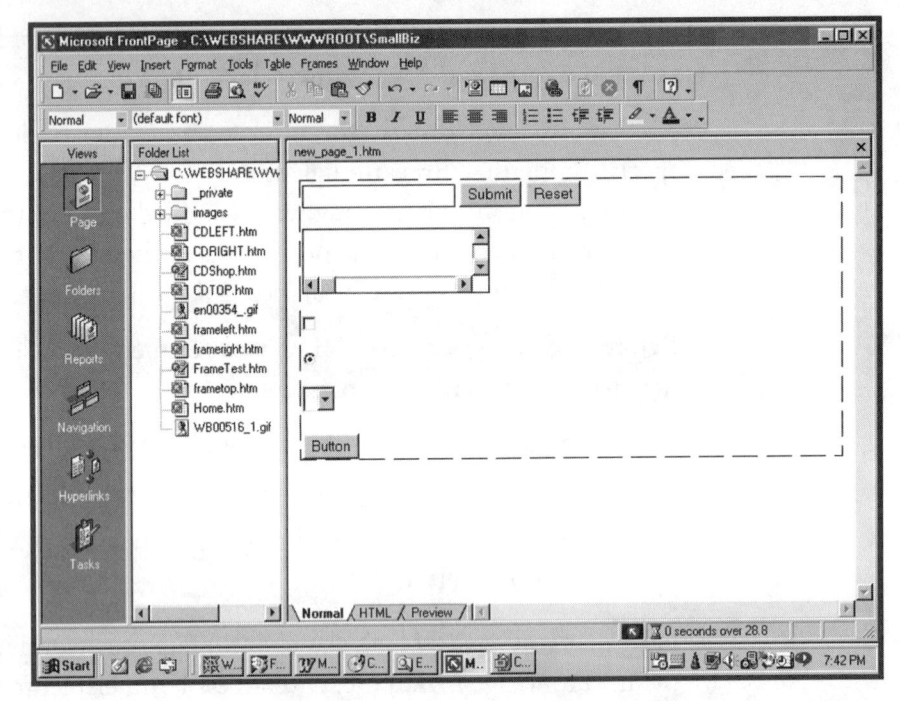

Figure 3.45

Your Web page, containing one instance of each of the available form elements

The dotted outline represents the area of your form. Any element you place within this area (not just form elements, but text and graphics, too) is subject to processing by the form when your customers click the Submit button.

In order for your form elements to be processed together, they need to be part of the same form. Although form processing is discussed in this evening's session, you should be aware that when your customers click the Submit button, each form is sent to an individual receiving (or processing) page. Therefore, if you have several form elements that you want processed together (for example, customer last name, first name, address, and telephone), all of these elements must be in the same form.

In Figure 3.45, you can tell that the form elements are all within the same form because the dotted outline surrounds the group of elements. In Figure 3.46, each form element is part of its own form; each element is surrounded by its own dotted outline.

SATURDAY AFTERNOON Advanced FrontPage Functionality   99

Figure 3.46

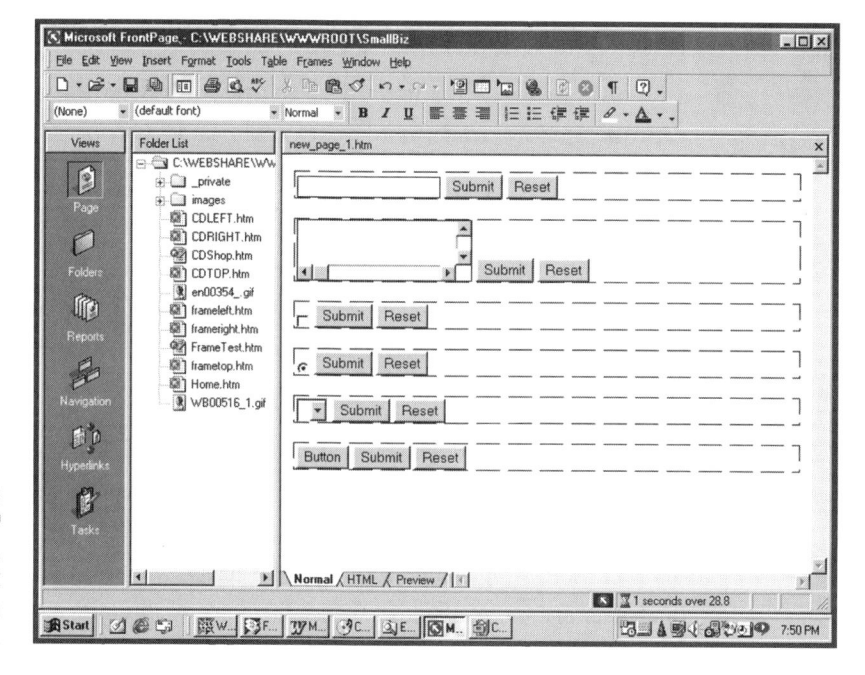

In this example, each form element is part of its own unique form.

> **NOTE**
>
> There is nothing wrong with having multiple forms on one Web page. In fact, in some instances this is a good thing. You might want some information to be processed by one page (such as customer mailing information) and other form information (such as a product catalog page) to be processed when a separate submit button is clicked. These are important elements of Web page design and are particularly critical when keeping CRM strategies in mind.

In the following sections, you'll learn more about each of the form elements you've inserted into the FormTest.htm page.

> **TIP**
>
> Nearly all form elements have some type of form validation. Form validation occurs when the user is required to enter a value, or enter a value within a specific range, before the form can be processed. You'll learn more about form validation in tomorrow morning's session.

Form Element: One-Line Text Box

The one-line text box is used in a variety of situations where you need to capture a short amount of text, such as a customer's name, address, or phone number. Double-click inside a text box element to display its Text Box Properties dialog box (see Figure 3.47).

The major properties of a one-line text box include the name of the text box, an initial, default value (the value that is inserted into the text box when the page first loads), and the maximum number of characters that can be typed in the box.

> **NOTE** Don't confuse a one-line text box with a scrolling text box. A one-line text box is literally that: one line of space for the entry of data. A scrolling text box has (among other things) a word-wrap feature so that as the customer types information, the text wraps to another line (or, *scrolls* down, hence the name of this form element).

Form Element: Scrolling Text Box

The scrolling text box allows your customers to enter more lengthy information than the one-line text box. As its name suggests, the scrolling text box allows the entry of multiple lines of text. The text can be set to wrap to the next line when it reaches the text box border. Double-click inside the scrolling text box element to view the Scrolling Text Box Properties dialog box, as shown in Figure 3.48.

Figure 3.47

The Text Box Properties dialog box

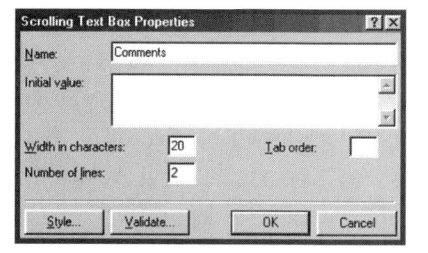

Figure 3.48

The Scrolling Text Box Properties dialog box

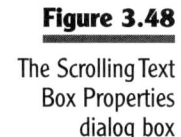

Similar to the one-line text box, the scrolling text box properties include values for name and initial value. However, this form element includes the ability to set the Width in Characters and Number of Lines properties.

Form Element: Check Box

The check box element provides the user with an easy way of marking a selection. Think of the check box as it relates to a written questionnaire where you are asked to "check all categories that apply." Similarly, you will see check box elements used in this way on Web forms, where the designer of the Web page might want visitors to select all elements that apply to their situation. Double-click the check box element to display the Check Box Properties dialog box (see Figure 3.49).

As with other form elements discussed so far, the check box element requires that a name and value be set. The value of a check box is what is passed to the processing form page, if the check box is selected. Notice the Initial State value. When set to Checked, the specific check box is selected when the user first loads the form page into their browser.

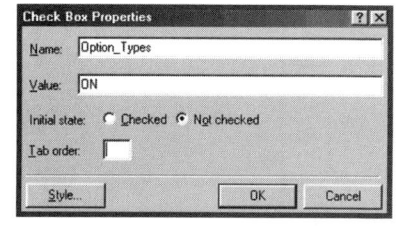

Figure 3.49

The Check Box Properties dialog box

CAUTION If a check box is not checked, then it does not pass as a form element to the processing page. This can lead to errors if you are not careful with your design, as the Web page processing the form results will look for a form element (in this case, the "unchecked" check box) that doesn't exist. You'll learn more about avoiding these errors in form processing in both tonight's and tomorrow's sessions.

Form Element: Radio Button

The radio button element is similar in some ways to the check box. However, there are important distinctions. The most notable difference is that check box elements can stand alone as individual elements. Radio buttons, on the other hand, are placed on Web pages in groups. The general concept here is that you use radio buttons when you only want users to select a single option; conversely, use check boxes when you want users to click all that apply. Double-click the radio button to display the Radio Button Properties dialog box (see Figure 3.50).

You should notice the Group Name attribute in the Radio Button Properties dialog box. This control is used to define the group of radio buttons from which the user can select only one choice. For example, let's say that you have a used car lot and you are building a Web site for your business. You want to provide your customers a way of searching for a specific color of vehicle. You place a group of radio buttons on your Web page. For the Group Name attribute, you define this as "Color" and similarly do this for each radio button in the group. Then, for the value of each radio button, you set it to a specific color (see Table 3.2).

Figure 3.50

The Radio Button Properties dialog box

SATURDAY AFTERNOON Advanced FrontPage Functionality

TABLE 3.2	RADIO BUTTON DESCRIPTIONS	
Radio Button	**Group Name**	**Value**
1	Color	Red
2	Color	Blue
3	Color	White
4	Color	Black
5	Color	Green

Form Element: Drop-Down Menu

You can use the drop-down menu form element to save space and provide users with an easy way of selecting specific types of information. As usual, double-click the element to display the Drop-Down Menu Properties dialog box (see Figure 3.51).

Just like other elements, you are asked to provide a name for the drop-down menu. You must then provide the choices that will appear in the menu.

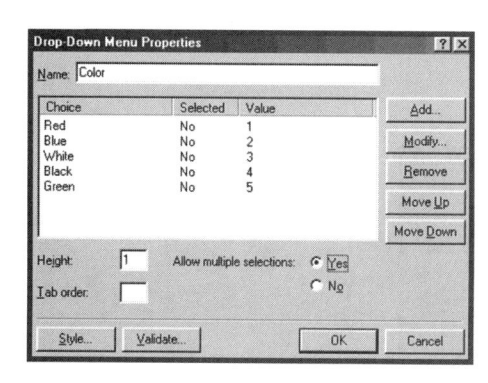

Figure 3.51

The Drop-Down Menu Properties dialog box

In Figure 3.51, I have mimicked the functionality of placing five check boxes (corresponding to the car color example) by combining these options in a drop-down menu. Notice that the Allow Multiple Selections option is selected. The Height property is set to 5, which causes the drop-down menu to be five lines in height, thus allowing all choices to be visible on the page.

NOTE If you set the Allow Multiple Selections option to No, then the user is only allowed to select one value from the drop-down menu. The drop-down menu then mimics the function of a group of radio buttons, although in a way that takes up less screen real estate. This presents one "group" of radio buttons (in this case, car color), but only one choice is allowed for processing.

Click Add to add individual choices to the drop-down menu. The Add Choice dialog box appears, as shown in Figure 3.52.

In the Choice field, enter the name of the option you wish to present (such as green, red, or blue). If you want to pass a value for each option, select Specify Value and then type the desired value into the Specify Value box.

Form Element: The Push Button

Certainly, the most popular and widely-used push button is the submit button, used on every form to send information entered into the form to a processing page.

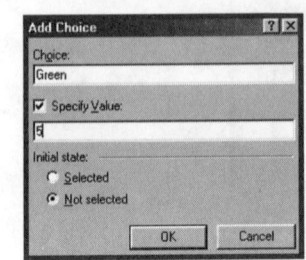

Figure 3.52

The Add Choice dialog box

> ### CHOICES AND VALUES IN DROP-DOWN MENUS
>
> If you look at Figure 3.51, you can see that each color option has been assigned a numeric value. This means that when this form element is processed, the choice that the user makes is given a number value (Red=1, Blue=2, and so on). Then, rather than passing the actual color to the form-processing page, the assigned value is passed.
>
> Why would you want to do this? In many cases (especially where information entered on a form is processed and inserted into a database), companies use codes for their products. While these codes might be very useful and logical to the company, they typically make little sense to the consumer, who would rather see the actual product name than its secret code. Therefore, the choice is assigned as the product name, but the value is given the company-specific code. Since the customer doesn't see the value, this works for both parties.
>
> How you insert data into your database (including how you assign values to form options) is another important element of Web design. You'll learn more about this in tonight's session.

Double-click the push button element to view the Push Button Properties dialog box (see Figure 3.53).

Use the Submit button type to serve as a trigger to send form results to a processing page. You can use the Reset button type to clear the data that was entered into all form elements on a given page.

You'll learn more about submitting form data in both tonight's and tomorrow's sessions. For now, do some more experimenting on your FormTest.htm page, adding and deleting various form elements, and experimenting with the each element's unique Properties dialog box.

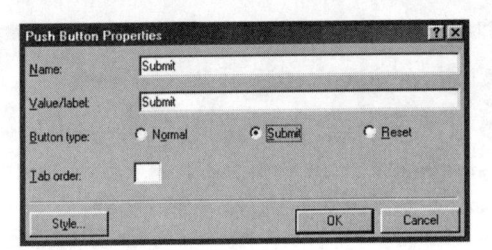

Figure 3.53

The Push Button Properties dialog box. In this example, Submit was selected as the button type.

Adding Hyperlinks

The final topic of discussion before the dinner break is how to add hyperlinks to your Web pages. As you know from surfing the Web, hyperlinks enable you to quickly jump from one Web page to the next. They can also be used to move you quickly from one location in a page to another location in the same page. Hyperlinks are the defining navigation tool of the Web; they allow you to jump—literally—across the world with just a few clicks of the mouse.

For your small business Web site, hyperlinks are an essential element for allowing your customers quick and easy access to all your services and products. For example, you might have hyperlinks to your product catalog, an order form, a feedback form, or to additional Web pages within your site.

Thanks to FrontPage, adding hyperlinks to your Web pages is very easy. You are not limited to using text as your links; you can use graphics as hyperlinks, too. An example of this might be a graphic of one of your products that, when clicked, takes the customer to an order form or production information for that particular product.

Adding Text Hyperlinks to Your Pages

Let's begin the discussion of hyperlinks by creating textual hyperlinks. Just follow these steps:

1. So that you can really see the functionality of hyperlinks, you should work in a frames page. From within your SmallBiz Web, open the FrameTest.htm file.

SATURDAY AFTERNOON Advanced FrontPage Functionality   107

> **NOTE**
> Depending on how much you experimented when this page was created, your frames page may look different from the figures in this section. If so, that's OK! The hyperlink discussion will work just the same, no matter what your frames page looks like.

2. If you made the left frame (frameleft.htm) very small, increase its size. You'll need some space to add textual hyperlinks in this frame (see Figure 3.54).

3. If you turned the borders off, turn them back on for this exercise.

4. Now add some text to the left frame. To do so, click inside the frame and then type some text so that your frames page looks like the one shown in Figure 3.55.

5. First, you'll create a hyperlink to the New Products information. Therefore, you need to create a New Products page. When customers

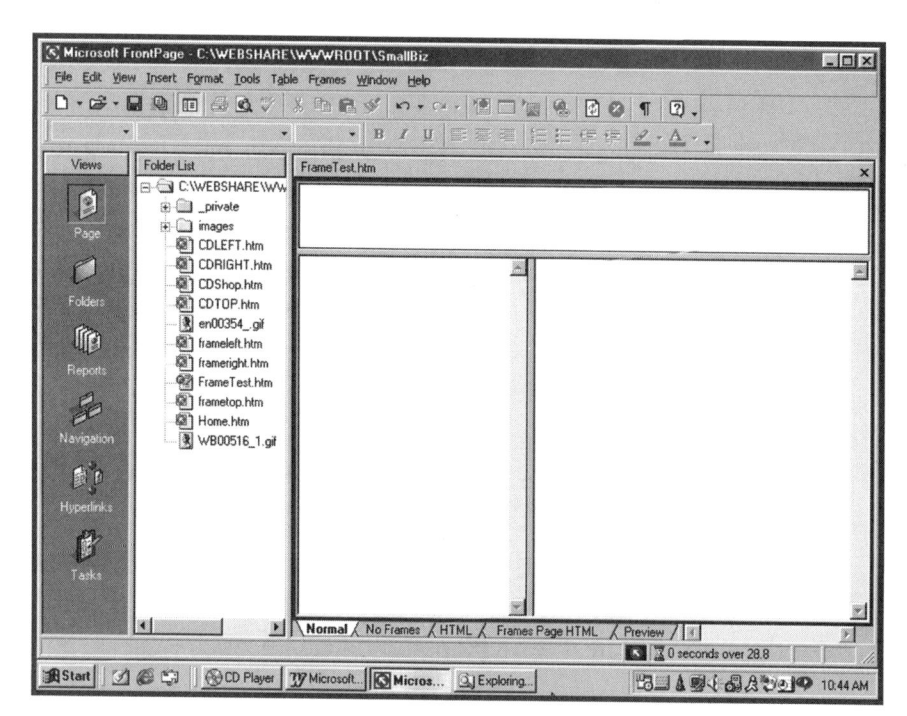

Figure 3.54

Your left frame should be at least wide enough to add some text.

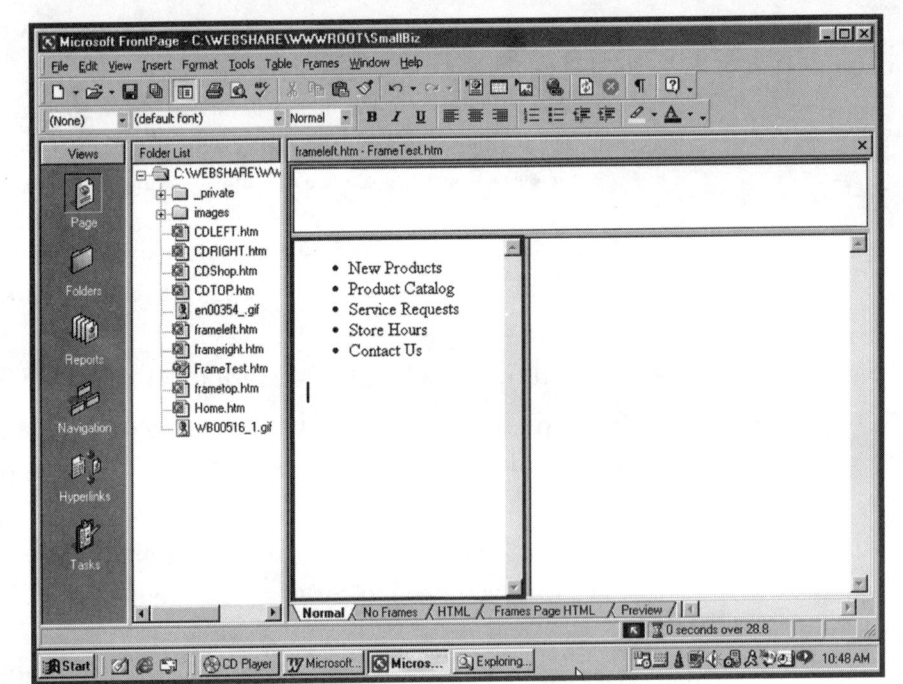

Figure 3.55

In this frame layout, the left frame is often used as a table of contents window, where you provide links to information that will appear in the right frame.

click this link, the New Products page loads into the frame; in this case, it will load in the right frame. From within the SmallBiz Web, create the New Products page and then save it as NewProducts.htm. Add some text to the page (anything you like—just type something!). After the page is created, experiment with all the formatting you've learned up to this point, perhaps adding a table or two, a form element, and so on. Make the page look the way you like!

6. Now, turn the text you created in Step 4 into individual hyperlinks. Bring the FrameTest.htm page back into focus by selecting the name of the page from the Window menu.

7. Start with the New Products line. Drag your mouse pointer over this line of text so that it is selected, then choose Insert, Hyperlink. The Create Hyperlink dialog box appears, as shown in Figure 3.56.

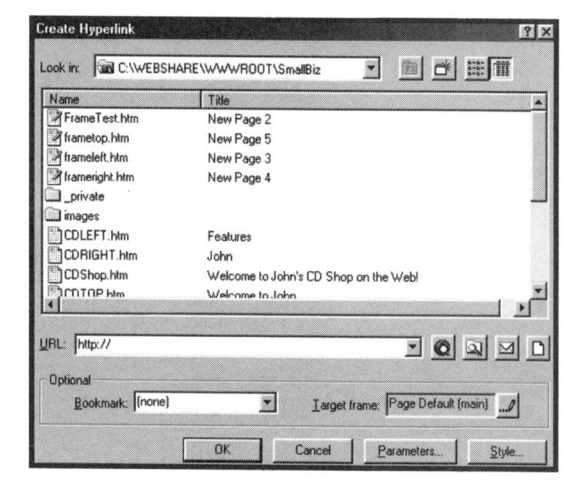

Figure 3.56

The Create Hyperlink dialog box

8. The URL field stores the page to which you want this hyperlink to point. For this example, since you are working in a frames page, the links in the left frame will open information in the right frame. Also, since you are creating the New Products hyperlink, this hyperlink will point to the NewProducts.htm page. From the list of files presented in the Create Hyperlink dialog box, select NewProducts.htm. This will cause NewProducts.htm to appear in the URL field, as shown in Figure 3.57. Don't click OK just yet!

9. There is one other thing to note before the hyperlink is put in action. Since hyperlinks are created within a frames page, you must be sure that the page loads into the correct frame when the user clicks on the link. In this case, the NewProducts.htm page should load into the right frame. The frame to which the hyperlink points is specified by selecting a target frame in the Target Frame dialog box, accessed from the Create Hyperlink dialog box. Click the button that appears to the right of the Target Frame field in the Create Hyperlink dialog box. The Target Frame dialog box appears, as shown in Figure 3.58.

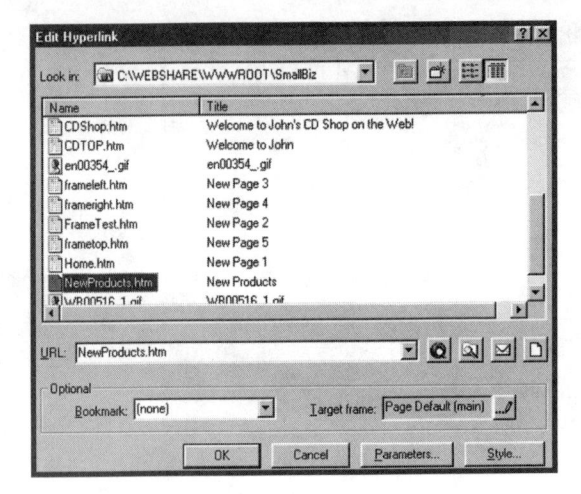

Figure 3.57

The URL field contains the name of the file (Web page) to which the hyperlink points.

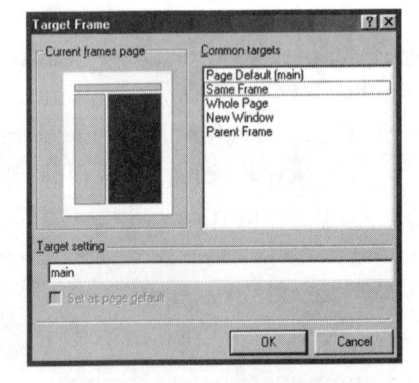

Figure 3.58

The Target Frame dialog box

10. In the Current Frames Page section of this dialog box, click inside each of the three frames. As you do, notice how the Target setting changes. Set the Target setting to main, then click OK.

11. Finally, click OK in the Create Hyperlink dialog box, then choose File, Save. You are now ready to test your hyperlink in a Web browser.

Testing Hyperlinks in a Browser

You can now see the New Products hyperlink in action. Open your Web browser and type the address of your FrameTest page. Your address should be something like: http://127.0.0.1/SmallBiz/FrameTest.htm.

SATURDAY AFTERNOON Advanced FrontPage Functionality   111

When you click on the New Products link, the NewProducts.htm page is loaded into the right frame, just as you specified when you created the hyperlink (see Figure 3.59).

Adding Graphical Hyperlinks to Your Pages

Turning an image into a hyperlink is as easy as creating a textual hyperlink. Just follow these steps:

1. Go back into FrontPage, and open the FrameTest.htm page. Click in the left frame (frameleft.htm). Click at the bottom of the list of items and then choose Insert, Picture, Clip Art.

2. Browse through the clip art collection until you find a graphic that appeals to you. Select it and insert it into your page.

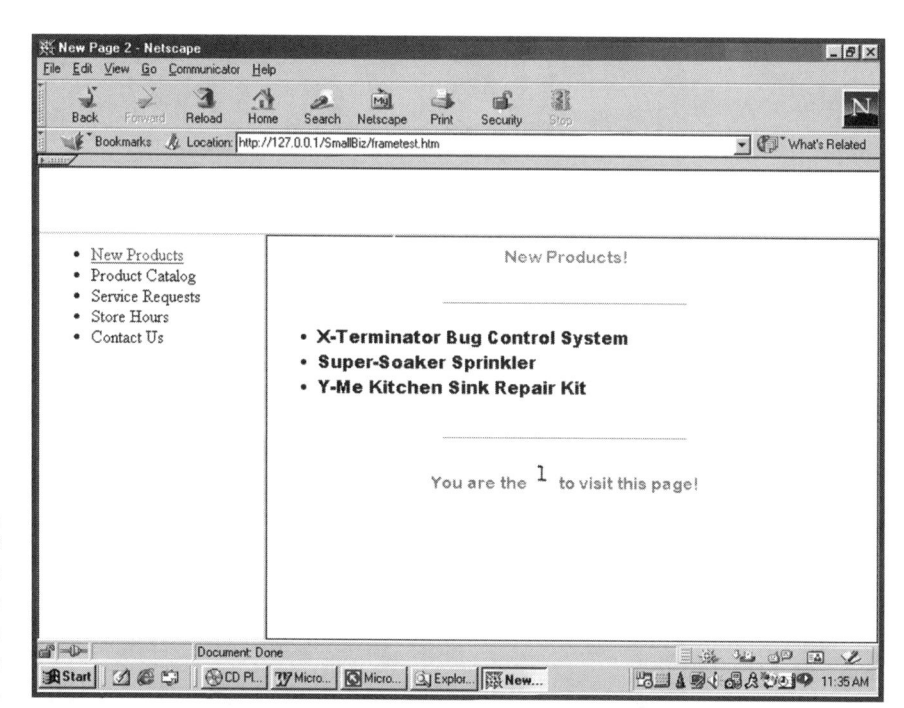

Figure 3.59

The New Products hyperlink loads the NewProducts.htm page into the right frame.

3. Now, click the graphic and select Insert, Hyperlink. Repeat the steps you performed when you created a textual hyperlink. For now, link this graphic to the same NewProducts.htm page. Don't forget to set the target frame to main, just as you did when you created a textual hyperlink. Also, don't forget to save your work!

4. Reload the FrameTest.htm page in your browser. Then, click the graphic. Your New Products page should again load into the right frame, as shown in Figure 3.60.

There is much more you can do with graphical and textual hyperlinks, but this preliminary discussion should give you the basic design concepts. In tomorrow's sessions, you'll be focusing more on the special design considerations of using hyperlinks (both textual and graphical). Stay tuned!

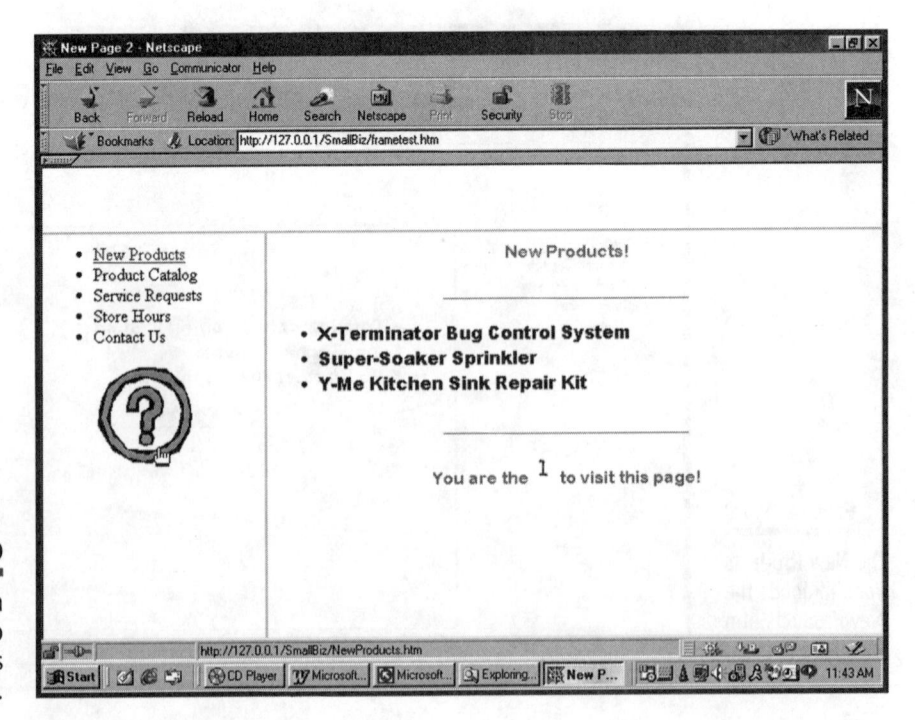

Figure 3.60

You can easily turn graphics into hyperlinks, just as you did with text.

Session in Review

That about does it for this afternoon's session. A tremendous amount of FrontPage ground has been covered. Take a look back at what you've accomplished:

- First, you learned how to navigate through your FrontPage Webs.
- Then, you spiced up your Web using FrontPage Wizards and Themes.
- Later, you began to organize your information using tables.
- You learned how to utilize the power of frames and forms.
- Finally, you added both textual and graphical hyperlinks to your Web page.

If you're feeling overwhelmed by all this talk of tables, frames, forms, and hyperlinks, stay calm! Everything will become clearer as you create more Web pages, finish the remainder of this book, and study the full-fledged, Web-enabled small business example tomorrow afternoon.

After dinner, you'll be ready to jump into the real meat and potatoes of Web-enabling your small business—exploiting the power of having your Web pages interact with a database. It's gonna be fun; I guarantee it!

SATURDAY EVENING

Dynamic Webs: Processing Forms and Integrating Databases

- What's So Dynamic about Dynamic Webs?
- Active Server Pages 101
- Processing Forms
- The Background of Dynamic Webs
- Using a Database
- Preparing Your Access Database for the Web
- Inserting Information: Advanced Database Integration

As I've mentioned several times in other sections of this book, a major component of a successful small business Web site (or any Web site, for that matter) is ensuring that its content is current and accurate. Think of the times you've visited sites only to discover a tag line, perhaps at the bottom of the page, reading "Last Update: January 1, 1996." Certainly, this doesn't fill you with confidence in the accuracy of the site.

Worse still, this untimely updating of information is often indicative of another major problem: *The Web site of the company in question is not fully integrated into the internal processes of the company.* Remember that a Web site is ultimately another tool in your company's overall business process strategy. While it can play a large or small role, it absolutely, positively, must be an integrated component—regardless of its size—of your entire functional process. (The role you choose for your Web site, of course, depends on the size of your company, the level of importance you place on e-commerce, and so on.) Otherwise, the Web site is simply gimmicky window dressing for your company.

Fortunately, this scenario can be avoided by planning how your site can be partnered with your other processes, such as ordering, billing, product information distribution, and customer service. A central component of this integration is allowing your site to be dynamic, which means always providing current information and having a site that is easy to update.

CAUTION It probably goes without saying that having outdated information on your Web site, aside from providing inaccurate information, also seriously reduces the credibility of your company. It is easy to see how customers who visit your site for product news and find old information could easily be turned off by your lack of devotion to providing the most current material.

Not to repeat myself, but if you take the time to build a site and establish a Web presence, you should also take the time to ensure that the information you are presenting is accurate and timely! Anything else is a sure sign that your Web site is not an integral part of your business, and your ability to move into and benefit from the exciting world of e-commerce will be seriously handicapped.

What's So Dynamic about Dynamic Webs?

So how do you make your small business Web site dynamic? Well, you've come to the right place! In tonight's session, you'll learn about two central and easy to implement features that will really make your Web site come alive: processing form information and allowing your site to read from, and write to, a database (in this case, Microsoft Access).

Once you gain an understanding of these two concepts, you will be well on your way to developing not only a functional site, but also one that can be integrated into your company's overall processes. Let's get going!

Active Server Pages 101

Not that long ago, processing a form was a complicated matter. While it has always been relatively easy to create a form like you did in this afternoon's session, actually manipulating, storing, and using the information entered into the various form elements was another story entirely. There simply wasn't an easy way to work with form information unless you were an experienced programmer.

SATURDAY EVENING Dynamic Webs: Processing Forms and Integrating Databases

> ### A LITTLE HTML CAN GO A LONG WAY
>
> You've probably heard the term HTML many times. HTML is the special code from which Web pages are built. When a Web browser such as Internet Explorer loads these pages, HTML is decoded and the pages are displayed on your screen.
>
> What's interesting about working with an application such as FrontPage is that you don't have to know any HTML to construct Web pages. Rather, FrontPage, by using the traditional what-you-see-is-what-you-get (WYSIWYG) interface, constructs the HTML code automatically.
>
> Although this is a powerful feature of FrontPage (and puts Web page creation into the hands of everyone—programmers and non-programmers alike), you still might need to get in and "mess around" with the actual HTML code sometimes. That's why in the FrontPage editor, you see the HTML tab at the bottom of your screen. You looked at this tab briefly in this afternoon's discussion of how frames are constructed.
>
> In this session, the HTML tab will be used more extensively. You'll need to add just a few things to the HTML code to make your Web pages dynamic. Don't be apprehensive about playing with the actual code generated by FrontPage—even though it looks complicated, HTML is extremely easy to use. By knowing just a few simple lines of HTML code, you can do some amazing things. Those amazing things—processing form results and allowing your Web pages to communicate with databases—are the subjects of this chapter.
>
> Finally, if you are interested in learning more about HTML, be sure to check out Prima's *Learn HTML In a Weekend*!

Fortunately, those days are behind us. When Microsoft introduced its Active Server Pages (ASP) technology, non-programmers (as well as traditional programmers) took a big step forward. Not only could they create forms, but the data could be easily inserted in a database, passed to another Web page, and so on.

> **BUZZ WORD**
>
> ◄◄◄◄◄◄◄◄◄◄◄◄◄◄◄◄◄◄◄◄◄◄◄◄◄
>
> *Active Server Pages* is a special component that runs on a Web server, such as the Personal Web Server that you've installed and worked with this weekend. Rather than having to know and use large chunks of programming code, ASP wraps the code into easily accessible objects, which can then be called from your Web pages. Sound complicated? It's actually quite easy, and it brings a tremendous amount of functionality and power to your Web pages.
>
> ◄◄◄◄◄◄◄◄◄◄◄◄◄◄◄◄◄◄◄◄◄◄◄◄◄

Throughout tonight's chapter, you'll call on various Active Server Page objects to both work with form data and insert information into a database. What's even more exciting is that you'll be able to implement the vast majority of this powerful functionality without ever leaving the FrontPage environment. You'll be using wizards, as you've done before, to program your Web pages to work with Access databases.

> **NOTE**
>
> As I promised early in the weekend, you don't have to be a programmer to Web enable your small business. That's my story, and I'm sticking to it. However, after reading this evening's session and discovering how easy it really is to use ASP technology, you just might be inclined to delve a little deeper into Web programming. You may want to learn in more detail about everything that ASP can bring to your Web. If this is the case, then I suggest you check out *ASP 3 Fast & Easy Web Development* (Prima, 2000).

Getting Your Web Ready for ASP

Before beginning a discussion of how to use ASP in conjunction with forms and databases, you need to be sure that your Web is properly configured to work with ASP. This is not a difficult task, but you should take the time now to go through the following steps so that you can unleash the full power (not to mention fun) of working with ASP.

SATURDAY·EVENING Dynamic Webs: Processing Forms and Integrating Databases — **121**

1. Click the Personal Web Server icon in the taskbar. When the Personal Web Manager opens, click the Advanced button. Scroll down the list until you see your SmallBiz folder (indicated by /SmallBiz). Your screen should look similar to Figure 4.1.

2. The Default Document(s) field should read, Default.htm,Default.asp. If it doesn't, type it in now. You are now ready to use Active Server Pages with your SmallBiz Web!

> **TIP**
> You may be wondering how all the special modifications that you're making on your own machine will translate to your ISP when it comes time to actually publish your pages to the Web. Don't worry—your ISP will take care of these modifications on their own servers for you. You will need to provide them with some general information, but they'll take care of the overly technical stuff involved in activating your ASP-enabled Web site.

Processing Forms

Okay, you have your SmallBiz Web configured for ASP and you're now ready to make your pages truly dynamic. Here is a simple example to

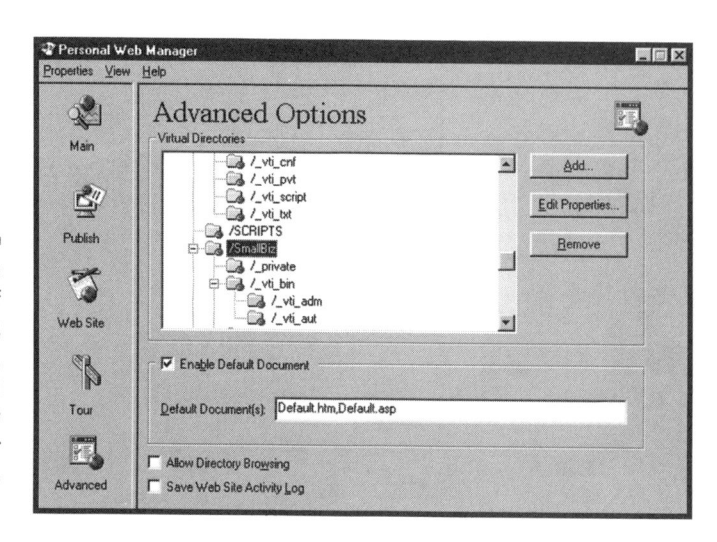

Figure 4.1

Depending on the number of FrontPage Webs you've created, your Virtual Directories list may be longer or shorter than the one displayed here.

make sure that you understand the basics of working with form processing in ASP. You'll then move on to more functional examples that will really highlight the power of ASP.

1. From within your SmallBiz Web, create a new page and name it FormA.htm.

2. Now add a few form elements to the page. At the top of the page, type **Enter your full name here:** and press Enter a few times.

3. Next, from the Insert menu, choose Form, One-Line Text Box. Your page should look similar to Figure 4.2.

4. Now make the text box bigger and adjust some of its other properties. To do so, double-click inside the text box to access the Text Box Properties dialog box, shown in Figure 4.3.

5. Change the Name to FullName and the Width in Characters value to 30, and then click OK.

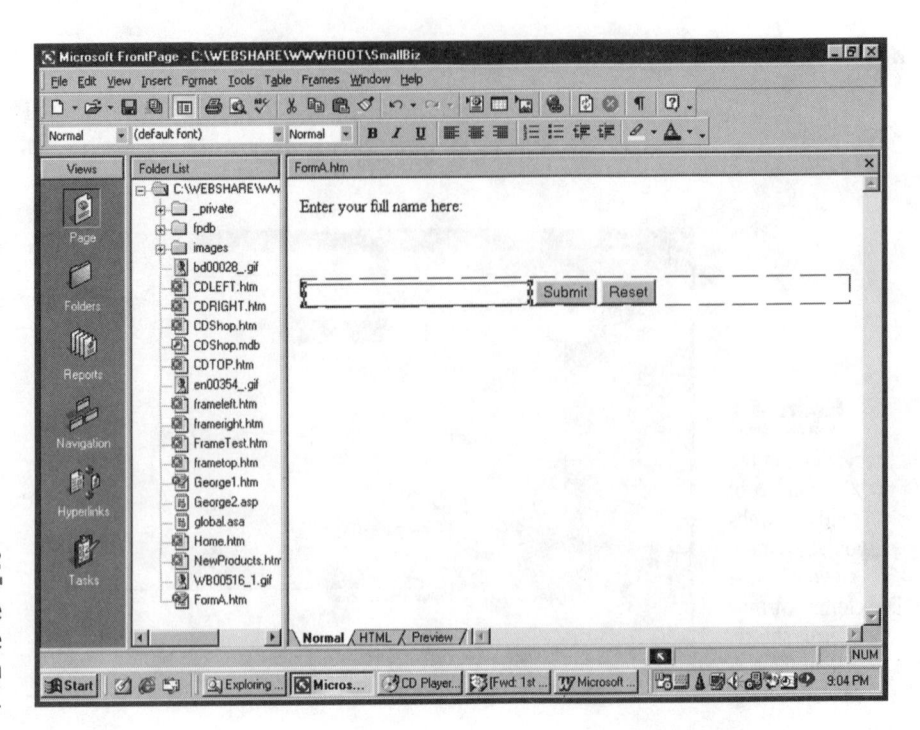

Figure 4.2

Your simple page now has a one-line text box form element.

Figure 4.3

Configuring the text box form element

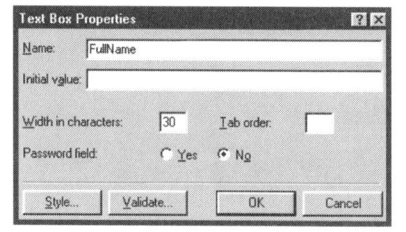

6. You must now set the actual properties of the form, not just the individual form field properties. Right-click within the form (inside the dotted line), but not on an actual form element. From the shortcut menu that appears, choose Form Properties. The Form Properties dialog box appears, as shown in Figure 4.4.

7. Select Send to Other and, from the drop-down menu, select Custom ISAPI, NSAPI, CGI, or ASP Script.

NOTE Don't be concerned about terms like ISAPI, NSAPI, and CGI. The only component you'll use in this session is ASP.

8. Next, in the Form Properties dialog box, click Options. The Options for Custom Form Handler dialog box appears, as shown in Figure 4.5.

Figure 4.4

Configuring properties for the entire form itself, not just the individual form elements

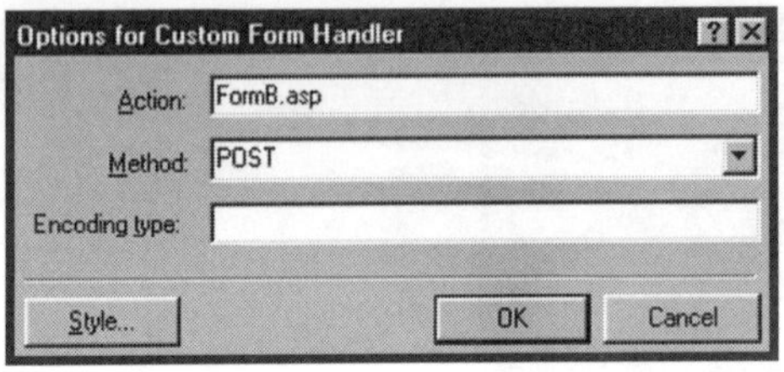

Figure 4.5

Determining form processing characteristics

9. Leave the Method set to POST, but change the Action to FormB.asp.
10. Click OK, then OK again (in the Form Properties dialog box) to return to your form.

Creating a Form-Processing Web Page

Now that you have a usable form (in this case, a simple form that asks for your full name), you need a page to process the data (your name) that will be entered on the FormA.htm page. This is where ASP comes in very handy. Use these steps to create a form-processing page, and then you can see the two pages together in action.

1. From within your SmallBiz Web, create another page. When you save the page, name it FormB.asp, then select Active Server Pages from the Save as Type drop-down menu, as shown in Figure 4.6.
2. Now you're ready to work with the form collection component of ASP to process the information entered on FormA.htm. Make sure you have FormB.asp open, then click the HTML tab at the bottom of the window (see Figure 4.7).
3. In order to process the form information, you'll need to type some special information directly into the HTML code of FormB.asp. Take a close look at Figure 4.7. Between the <BODY> and </BODY> tags, you should see the following line:

```
Hello, <%=request.form("FullName")%>! Welcome to the
     world of ASP!
```

SATURDAY·EVENING Dynamic Webs: Processing Forms and Integrating Databases   125

Figure 4.6

Creating an ASP page

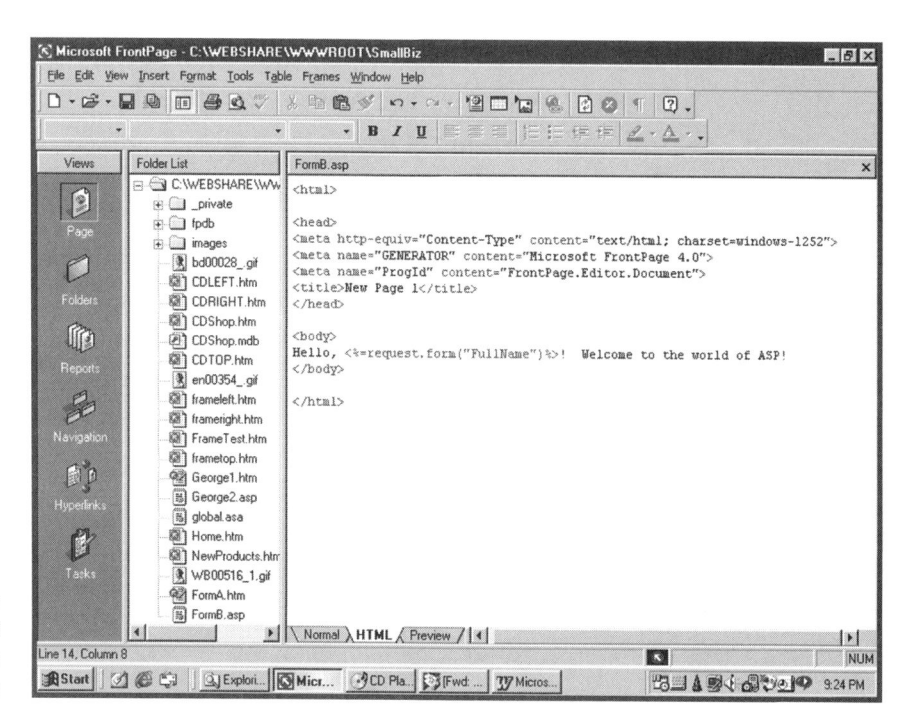

Figure 4.7

The HTML code for FormB.asp

What's happening in this line? Take a closer look:

- The key statement of this line reads `<%=request.form("Full-Name")%>`, where `request.form` refers to the form collection of ASP. By adding this line directly into the HTML code of FormB.asp, you are requesting that ASP help process the information entered on FormA.htm.

- `"FullName"` refers to the name of the actual form element to be processed. Remember that the one-line text box element in FormA.htm was named FullName. What you are doing now is asking the ASP-enabled page to retrieve the data that was entered into the FullName form element.

- The `%=` and `%` symbols indicate where your ASP code begins and ends. It is important that you use these indicators. Otherwise, you will receive errors when your page is processed.

4. It's now time to see these pages in action. Save both FormA.htm and FormB.asp, then open your browser. Type the URL for FormA.htm (it's probably similar to http://127.0.0.1/smallbiz/FormA.htm). When the page loads, type your full name in the text box, then click Submit (see Figure 4.8). You should see the results similar to those shown in Figure 4.9.

Pretty neat stuff, eh? I told you that using ASP would be easy!

The next set of steps illustrates one more example of processing form results, this time using a slightly more complicated form.

1. Open your FormA.htm page again. Insert a few check boxes and a group of radio buttons so that the page looks like Figure 4.10.

2. Now, customize the form elements just a bit. Make no changes to the one-line text box. Remember that the size was set to 30, and it was named FullName.

3. Change the name of each of the check boxes, respectively, to CheckBox1, CheckBox2, and CheckBox3. In addition, change the value attribute for each check box to Yes, as shown in Figure 4.11.

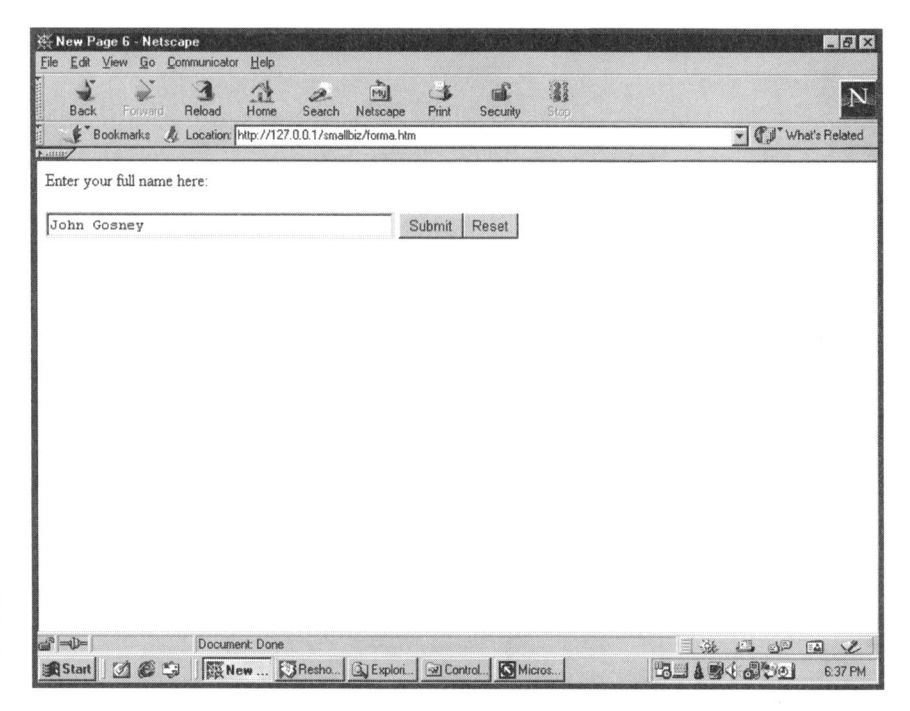

SATURDAY·EVENING Dynamic Webs: Processing Forms and Integrating Databases 127

Figure 4.8

The FormA.htm form

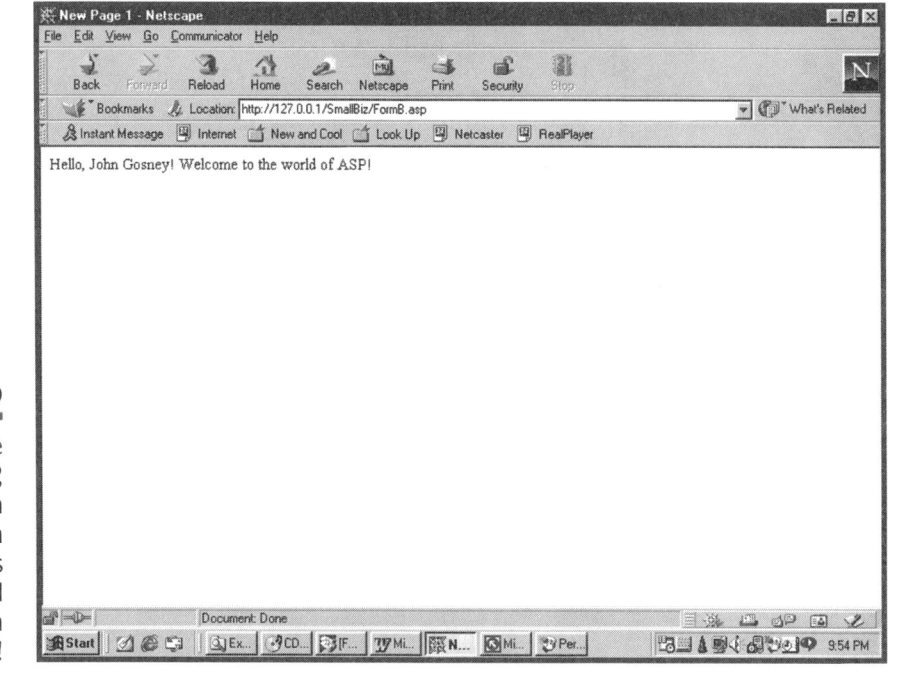

Figure 4.9

Through the magic of ASP, the information you entered in FormA.htm is passed to and processed on FormB.asp!

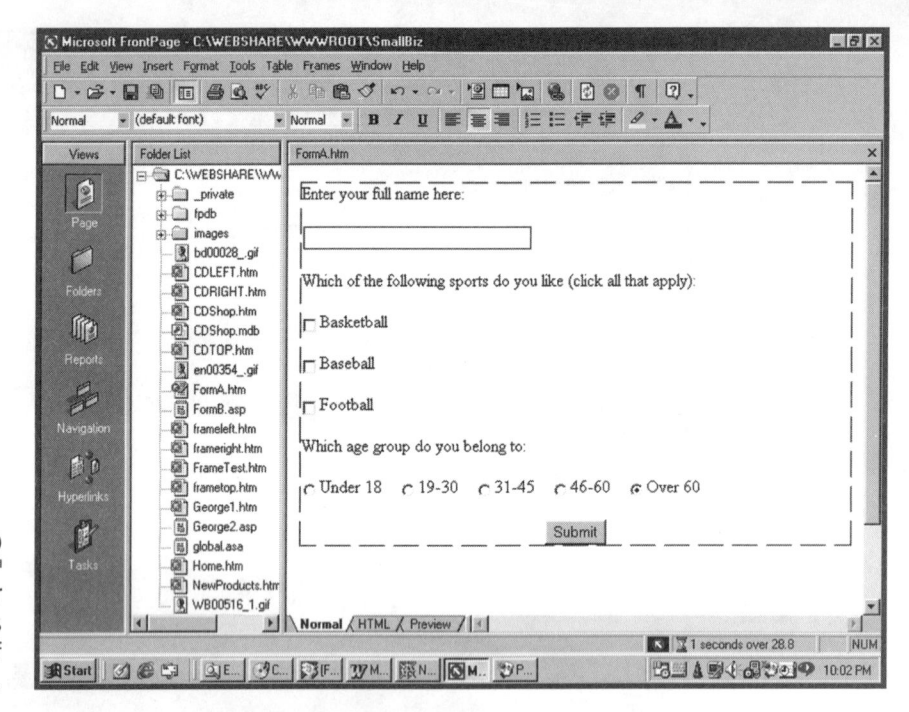

Figure 4.10

FormA.htm after adding check boxes and a group of radio buttons.

Figure 4.11

Naming the form elements in this uniform manner makes it easier to work with them.

4. For each of the radio buttons, leave the Group Name as R1, but change the value to the name of each respective radio button, as shown in Figure 4.12.

5. Now open FormB.asp (see Figure 4.13). Click the HTML tab so that you can add ASP-specific code.

SATURDAY-EVENING Dynamic Webs: Processing Forms and Integrating Databases   **129**

Figure 4.12

Changing the value of each radio button

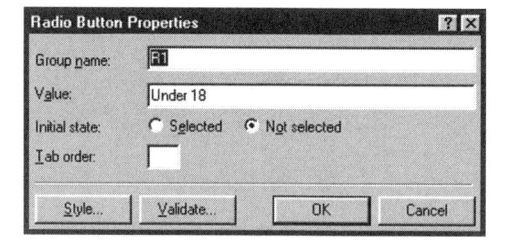

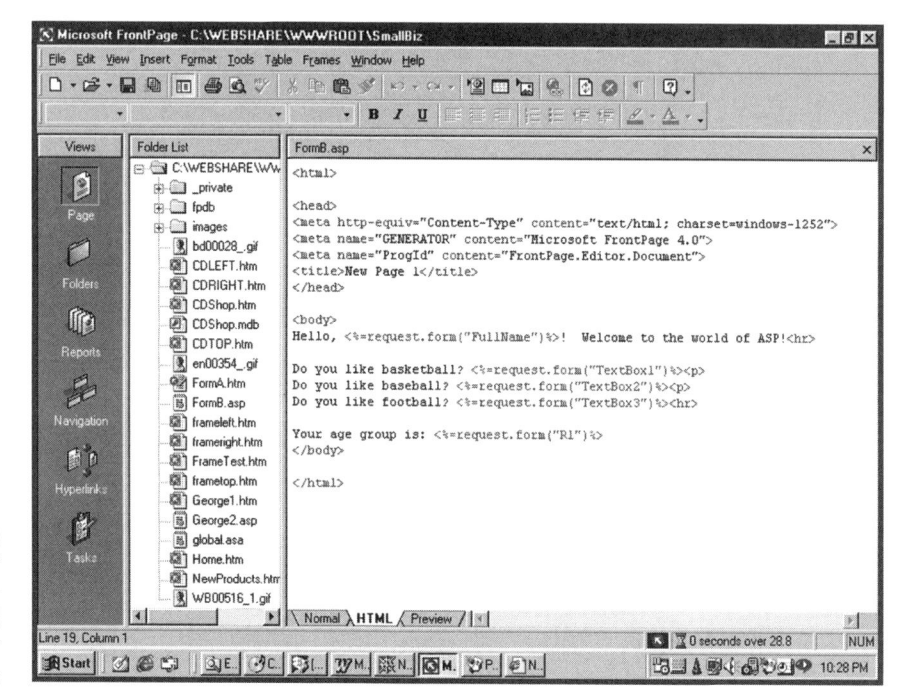

Figure 4.13

The new-and-improved HTML code for FormB.asp

6. Take a closer look at what has been added to the HTML code:

   ```
   <html>

   <head>
   <meta http-equiv="Content-Type" content="text/html;
       charset=windows-1252">
   <meta name="GENERATOR" content="Microsoft FrontPage 4.0">
   <meta name="ProgId" content="FrontPage.Editor.Document">
   ```

```
<title>New Page 1</title>
</head>

<body>
Hello, <%=request.form("FullName")%>! Welcome to the
    world of ASP!<hr>

Do you like basketball? <%=request.form("TextBox1")%><p>
Do you like baseball? <%=request.form("TextBox2")%><p>
Do you like football? <%=request.form("TextBox3")%><hr>

Your age group is: <%=request.form("R1")%>
</body>

</html>
```

The added HTML code enters a request.form for each of the new elements. Notice, however, that only one request.form was added for the radio buttons. Why? Since radio buttons are grouped, only one value is passed. Grouping the buttons ensures that only one option can be selected, no matter how many are presented.

7. Now do a little experimenting. Save the page and reload it in your browser. It should appear similar to Figure 4.14.

8. Type your name, select the first two check boxes and your age group, then click Submit. You are presented with a screen similar to the one shown in Figure 4.15.

   Notice how the values for the two check boxes you selected (baseball and basketball) are passed (the *Yes* value is presented), but for football, there is nothing. Why isn't the text "Do you like football?" followed by a "No," since it wasn't selected? Unfortunately, check box elements are not passed unless they are selected. Therefore since you didn't select football as a sport you liked on FormA.htm, no value was passed for this check box.

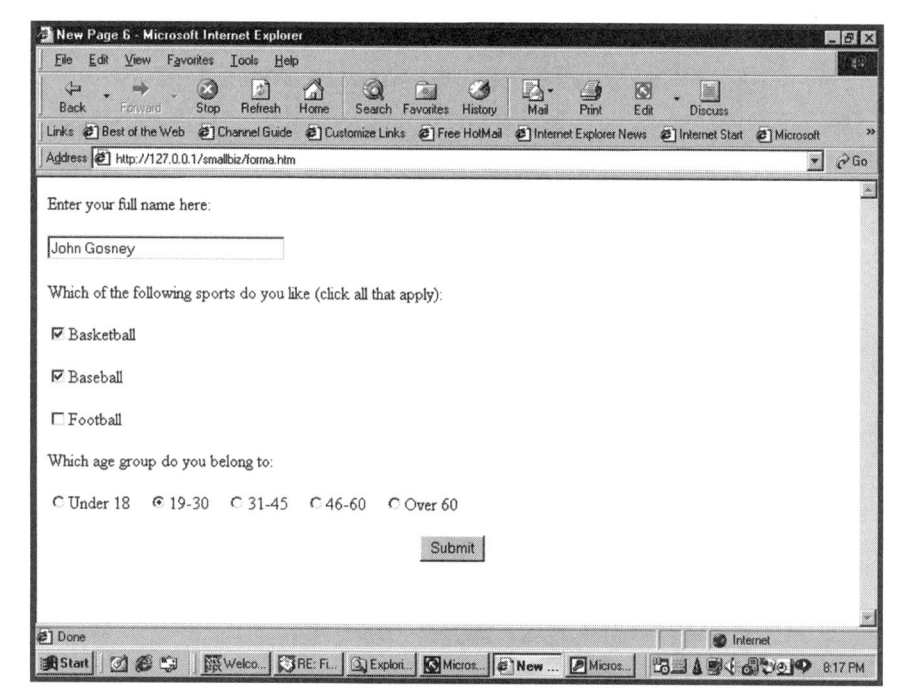

SATURDAY·EVENING Dynamic Webs: Processing Forms and Integrating Databases   **131**

Figure 4.14

Your form is ready for input.

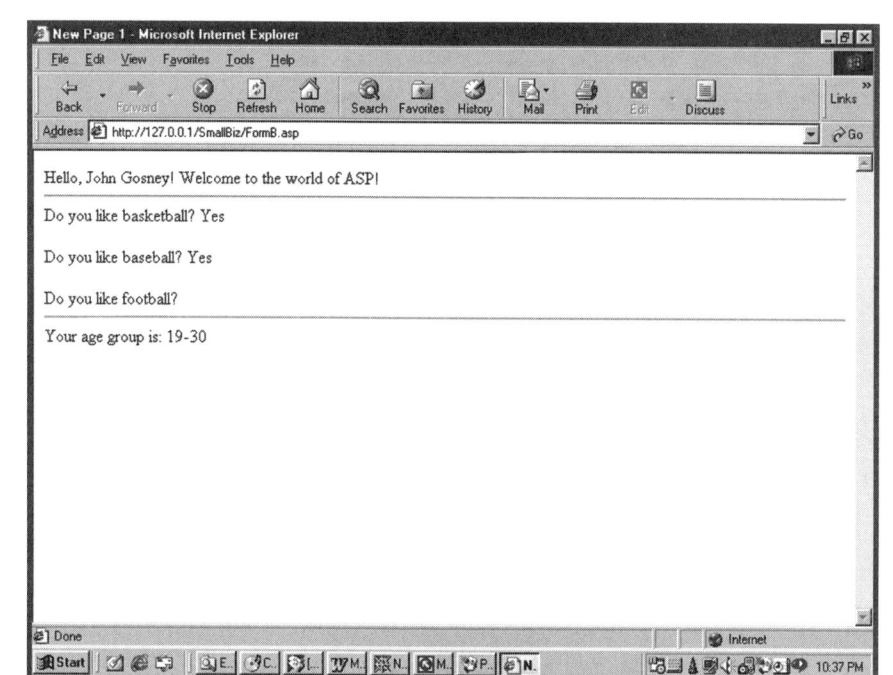

Figure 4.15

Depending on the information you provided on the form, your results may vary somewhat from those illustrated here.

FOR THE PROGRAMMER INSIDE YOU!

You don't have to know a lick of programming to get your small business Web site up and running. As I've demonstrated in this chapter, by using simple ASP code you can build dynamic forms that actually pass information entered into specific form elements to a different page. You can present the information in a variety of ways.

This is all fine and great, and the functionality of ASP will get even better as you learn how to insert data into—and read data from—an Access database. However, for those of you reading this book who are now asking, "Wow, this ASP stuff is pretty cool. What is the real limit to what I can do with it?" I'd like to take just a minute and whet your Web appetite.

As I said earlier, programming for the Web used to be a very difficult task and was not for the faint of heart. With the evolution of advanced Web development software, such as FrontPage 2000, as well as Web scripting languages, such as Active Server Pages (and to a lesser degree, JavaScript), the power of building really awesome, functional Web pages is in the hands of people like you and me.

Still, ASP is an advanced topic. Go ahead and pat yourself on the back for venturing, perhaps unknowingly, into a *power user* level of working with the Web! There have been many books written on the subject (thick books, I might add), and its ultimate functionality is limited only by the imagination of the developer.

That said, there is really nothing you can't do with a Web page, if you use ASP. And, believe it or not, some *really* advanced functionality isn't that terribly difficult, once you master the basics.

Unfortunately, a full discussion of ASP (even the full basics) is beyond the scope of this book. Besides, I want to live up to my promise that you don't have to program to get your small biz on the Web. If you feel at all comfortable and interested in what ASP can offer, however, I strongly suggest you pursue the topic. You can use the outstanding *ASP 3 Fast & Easy Web Development* (Prima, 2000), Microsoft documentation, and an infinite number of ASP tutorial-based Web sites.

Happy programming, if indeed you discover a programming affinity lurking inside you!

SATURDAY EVENING Dynamic Webs: Processing Forms and Integrating Databases

Now that you know how to process form elements, it's time to move ahead with a discussion about adding the power of database functionality to your Web pages. In tomorrow afternoon's session, I'll give you a complete, integrated example of all this dynamic functionality.

Take a Break!

You've spent a good deal of time learning the elements of form processing. Before diving into working with databases, take a break! Set the VCR to tape *Saturday Night Live* (just in case you decide to stay up late and do some Web experimentation), grab some refreshments, and I'll see you back here when you're ready.

The Background of Dynamic Webs

Welcome back. It's now time to learn how to get data from (and into) a Microsoft database so that you can make your Web site truly functional and dynamic.

Remember from our previous discussion that there is a difference between static and dynamic Webs. With static Webs, your information is hard coded into the page. In other words, static information is a permanent part of the page and can only be changed by manually loading a Web page editor, such as FrontPage, and physically changing the information.

Dynamic Web pages, on the other hand, allow information to be changed and updated on the fly. Therefore, rather than having information hard coded into their actual design, these types of Web pages only include a placeholder for information. The information is then loaded into the location of the placeholder from some kind of data source (for example, Microsoft Access or SQL Server).

The great thing about dynamic Web pages is that you can present custom information to your customers depending on criteria such as:

- Their personal profile information (age, gender, geographic location, specific interests, and so on)

- Their previous order information (for example, the types of items they've purchased or the quantity of items)
- Specific appointments they might have made with your company and now wish to check (when a representative will arrive for service, the location for service, and so on)
- Specific order tracking information (for example, when their order was processed and when it was shipped)
- Updates to your general product catalog (for example, new items or services you offer, or the removal of outdated items and special offers)

From this list, it should be easy to see that a dynamic Web page is more current and accurate. You present customers with up-to-the minute information related to their own specific orders, as well as general information about your company. If you were to try to manually enter this information by physically changing the Web page through FrontPage, you would constantly be updating your page—probably not a task you relish!

This is where a data source like Access really comes in handy. By having all of your information stored and updated in a central location, you can then have your Web pages simply read data from there. For the rest of tonight's session, you'll learn about the following components of producing a dynamic Web through the integration of an Access database:

- **Designing your database.** You'll learn how to store information in your database so that it is structured and organized in a way that dovetails neatly into your actual business processes and makes it easy to get that information into a Web page.
- **Establishing a connection between your database and Web page.** So that you can get information out of your database and into your Web page, you'll learn how to establish a connection between the two.
- **Making your Web pages dynamic.** You'll also learn about the actual process (automated through FrontPage) of getting data from

the database into your Web page. You'll see simple, powerful examples of how to use the database language, SQL, to make your dynamic Webs even more functional.

Using a Database

Microsoft Access, the database application of Microsoft Office, is an exceptionally easy-to-use application. However, you shouldn't take this as an indication that the product is simple or basic. Underneath the well-designed user interface, Access is a robust, powerful application, capable of storing and manipulating data in a myriad of ways.

NOTE For this discussion of dynamic Webs, you can use either Access 97 or the 2000 version. Although the interface appears slightly different between the two versions, the functionality (at least in terms of what is discussed here) is the same.

But guess what? You don't have to come anywhere close to these powerful (but admittedly complex) features of Access in order to get the application to work with your Web pages. Rather, you can use the power of FrontPage wizards and just a little bit of ASP code to make your pages sing and dance with information.

Access is a relational database in that relationships between different data sets (such as a customer profile and the types of products ordered by that customer) can be established and exploited. For example, consider a database with the following three tables:

- **Customers.** This table includes basic customer information, such as name, address, telephone number, and e-mail address.
- **Products.** This table contains information about your current products, such as description and price.
- **Orders.** This table stores information about specific orders, such as which customer ordered what product, when the order was placed, the total cost of the order, and so on.

Since each table includes specific information rather than a complete record of every transaction, you can determine relationships between data in a number of ways. For example, you could query the database to determine how many Widgets that John Smith bought in a specific time frame. Or, perhaps you are interested in comparing the number of Widget sales across specific geographic regions—which is possible because you have a unique record of every order and you store your customers' locations in the Customers table.

Relational databases are very powerful. Using tools presented to you in FrontPage, you can easily and quickly take this relational information and put it to work in your Web pages.

NOTE Unfortunately, space is limited in this discussion of Access, so you won't learn all the details of this very powerful application. If you're interested in learning more about Access, check out Appendix B, "Access Essentials," or read *Access 2000 Fast & Easy* (Prima, 1999).

Organizing Your Business Process Flow

Large companies spend millions of dollars every year in the design, maintenance, and use of their data sources. You've probably heard the phrase, "information is power." This is becoming even more true in the "e-world" of today, as companies seek to exploit the power of information to find new relationships between their products and their customers, and thus gain an edge over their competitors. Terms such as *business intelligence* and *customer relationship management* are new methodologies for applying the power of the machine to organize and crunch data. These methods are used to uncover new buying patterns, sales opportunities, and other cutting-edge business applications.

While this is a very exciting field, it is truly a field! Thousands of articles and books are being written on how to best manipulate business information. This, combined with new technology emerging on a daily basis, makes it very difficult to keep up with all the changes.

However, you can still jump aboard this information revolution without being a database design expert (or even a financial guru, for that matter). The simple fact of the matter is that tools like FrontPage and Access (not to mention the Web itself) are putting more power into the hands of people like you and me than anyone could have ever imagined. What you can do with FrontPage and Access in a few hours would have boggled the mind of even the most skilled computer scientist ten years ago. We are truly in the information revolution—don't let it pass you by!

OK, enough of the pep talk. I'm assuming that if you've come this far, you are interested in what you can do with these tools to give your small business an "e-presence." You'll begin with the most important issue of all—making sure your database is an accurate reflection of how your company actually works!

Unfortunately, databases are only as useful as their design. If your database is poorly organized, then the information you place into the database won't be of much use. For this discussion, the most important thing to consider is that *the process in which you update, read, and store information must fit with your actual company process.*

Process Flow and Web Design: A Bad Example

The Doe Company has decided to allow their customers to make appointments via the Web. The Doe Company is a garage door install and repair outfit, so they want customers to be able to set their own appointments using a Web interface. The company has paid an outside Web design firm a significant amount of money to design a slick-looking Web page and allow the Web page to talk to a data source (Access, for this example). The day has come to go live with the new system, so they have spent additional funds to advertise their new Web site.

Just a few days into the implementation, things start to go wrong. An irate customer calls in saying that they received an electronic confirmation of their appointment but that no one has yet to show up. This customer has taken off valuable work time to be at home for the installation, and is demanding a reason why a telephone call wasn't received to explain that (perhaps?) the technician was running late.

> **NOTE** A quick note on this example: Funds paid to an outside Web design firm can quickly amount to tens of thousands of dollars. Believe this figure; it is not an exaggeration. Consultants will charge you—big time—to do the same thing you're learning how to do in this book, perhaps even using the same tools. Don't get me wrong; professional Web design is often worth the money and there is something to be said for skilled individuals. But get ready to "show them the money" if you go outside for an e-commerce Web solution.

A few minutes later, another customer telephones saying that the technician arrived with the wrong kind of garage door opener, although he requested (via the Web site) a specific model. The model the technician arrived with is very expensive, the customer doesn't want to pay the extra money, and (like the other customer) he has stayed home from work.

Fortunately, the Doe Company has an on-site computer tech that checks the system. Everything is working okay, so how did these customer orders get so confused? The answer doesn't lay with the technical implementation; the consulting company did their job well. The Web site is attractive and is reading information from and writing information to the database.

Rather, the problem is with how the Web site fits (or rather, doesn't fit) into the overall process flow of the Doe Company. When the consulting firm and the company management sat down to map out how appointments are scheduled for a garage door opener installation, they didn't consider all the components involved, such as:

- **Notification of service.** Once a customer makes an appointment via the Web, an e-mail message is automatically generated and sent to the customer, verifying the information they provided (such as name, address, desired service date, and special instructions). Although this order is then saved in a database and an e-mail message is generated, the Web system does not take into account how to internally notify the appropriate individuals that a service call has been made. Put simply, the Web service request does not communicate with the traditional phone-in request, so the scheduling department does not get service requests on a consistent basis. Therefore, conflicts between requested service dates and times are not resolved.

- **Inventory is not updated quickly enough for Web time.** Remember the discussion of Web time from Friday evening's session? This is the most common error companies make when trying to Web enable their processes—they simply do not account for the speed at which transactions can take place over the Web. Customers expect and demand that the information presented to them on a Web page is both timely and accurate. In the example of the second customer, the Web page that lists the in-stock items was only being internally updated every week. Due to increased demand for a particular product, the availability of that product was quickly depleted, but this information was not reported to the Web. The result? Customers were ordering products that had gone out of stock.

- **The site doesn't provide effective customer relationship management.** As mentioned above, rather than providing a method to check the status of their orders and appointments, customers are required to telephone with their problems. One key to a successful Web implementation is to ensure that the customer service features you provide elsewhere (perhaps by fax or telephone) integrate with those you provide via the Web.

Process Flow and Web Design: Steps to Success

By reviewing the example of the Doe Company, you can see some of the things that can go wrong if you don't take the time to ensure that your Web site is an accurate reflection of your internal processes.

Aligning your e-business component with the rest of your company doesn't have to be a disaster the first time out. By using project management skills (through the use of trained project managers along with software such as

Microsoft Project), you can phase the implementation of your Web services so that your company can grow with your Web site. This minimizes the potential burden of achieving the new business ideology of doing business on Web time.

This doesn't mean, however, that your small business Web site has to be a long-term development project. You should ask yourself the following questions:

- **Who is your target audience?** By determining who are your primary customers (internal employees versus external customers), you can go a long way in making sure you are not overwhelmed in your initial implementation. In the example presented in the next section, you'll see that by first tackling a specific target audience set, you can take time to develop your internal business process infrastructure so that it blends with your Web component.

- **What do you want to accomplish with your Web site?** There is nothing wrong at first with simply having a Web presence that provides basic information about your company—perhaps its history, hours of location, services and products you provide, and so on. While this kind of Web presence would likely be a static presence—your customers probably wouldn't be able to interact with your site in terms of submitting information about themselves or ordering products—it would give you time to map out your internal process flow.

- **Can you maintain the Web site with limited external assistance?** Whether you design and implement your own site or have an outside consulting firm do the work for you, the final product should be easy to maintain and, of course, functional. Think of the ways you'll want to interact with the site once it is up and running:
  - **You'll want a way to easily update general information.** Rather than having to manually open a page (as with a static Web site) in FrontPage to move, update, or change information, this

process should be somewhat automated. In other words, you should have a method—a dedicated management side to your Web site—that allows you to easily make changes.

- **You'll want a way to access all data stored in the database.** I've often seen Web sites that store large amounts of information, but which only provide limited access to that data. You should always have full access to all information, whether by accessing the database directly or through some kind of management system that allows you full access to the information.

- **You'll want to be able to generate reports of different types and query data using various methods.** Remember that information is power. You'll want an easy way of generating reports on the customer data that you've collected and stored. This can be done either through direct access to the database or through a management system.

The information presented here is, at best, a cursory overview of the things you need to consider when mapping your business process to the Web. But don't be intimidated by all the rules. The key, quite simply, is to take the time to ensure that your Web site is a logical extension of your internal business processes and procedures. As you build your site, you may need to adjust some aspects of various processes. This is a natural outgrowth of a medium (the Web) that moves at a much faster pace than traditional business models.

Furthermore, depending on the size of your business, your processes may actually be quite limited, so don't make a mountain out of a molehill (so to speak). Since you are reading this book, your business is likely of sufficient size, where integrating your Web site with your business processes will not be a Herculean undertaking.

That said, you can now move forward to an example of Web enabling an Access database. You'll see how a business process can be both reflected and extended using the Web.

Preparing Your Access Database for the Web

Guess what? Getting your Access database connected to your Web pages is easy, and you still won't have to do any programming to accomplish this task. Once connected, you can take full advantage of the incredible power and fun of having a database-enabled Web page by both presenting customers with dynamic information and gathering information from your customers. The data possibilities are endless.

Establishing a Data Source Name (DSN)

The first thing you need to do is establish a data source name (DSN), which will identify your database as being available for use by your Web pages. This is not difficult, but it does require a few steps.

NOTE For the rest of this session, the sample database CDShop.mdb file on the enclosed CD-ROM will be used.

1. Copy the CDShop.mdb file from the CD-ROM into your SmallBiz Web folder. The CDShop.mdb is the sample database that will be used in tomorrow's case study session. By establishing all the connections now, you'll not only learn how to do so, but you'll also be ready to jump right into the case study tomorrow!

NOTE The CDShop.mdb file is located in the Book Example Files on the CD-ROM. When you unzip the sample files, they will be placed on your hard drive in a folder called WebEnableSmallBusiness. To copy the files into your SmallBiz Web folder instead, simply click Install, then click the Browse button and select the SmallBiz Web folder.

2. Now that you have the database on your machine, you need to establish a connection (the DSN) to that database. Open the

SATURDAY·EVENING Dynamic Webs: Processing Forms and Integrating Databases **143**

Control Panel by choosing Start, Settings, Control Panel and then double-click the ODBC Data Sources (32-bit) icon (see Figure 4.16). The ODBC Data Source Administrator dialog box appears.

3. Click the System DSN tab (see Figure 4.17).
4. Click Add, which displays the Create New Data Source dialog box, shown in Figure 4.18.
5. Select Microsoft Access Driver from the list of available drivers and click Finish.
6. Complete the ODBC Microsoft Access Setup dialog box to specify the data source to which you want to connect (see Figure 4.19).
7. In the Data Source Name field, type **CDShop** and then click Select. You will be asked to select a data source (or database) to which you want to establish a connection.

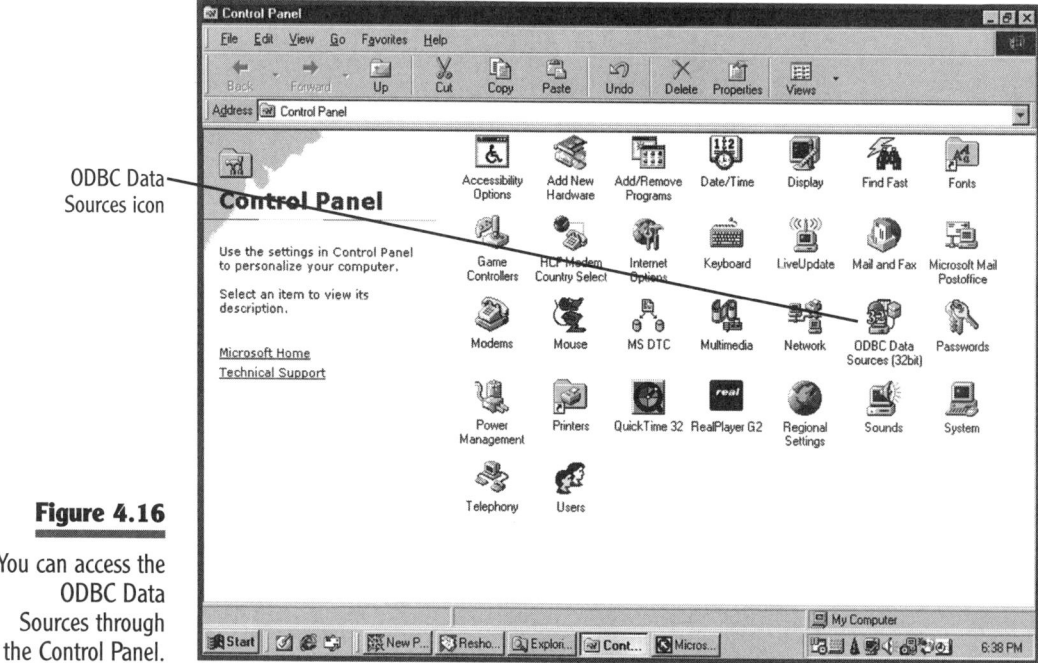

Figure 4.16

You can access the ODBC Data Sources through the Control Panel.

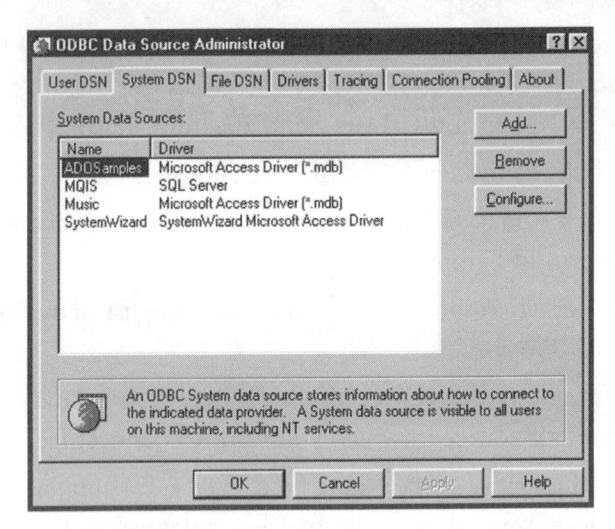

Figure 4.17

An ODBC System data source stores information about how to connect to the indicated data provider.

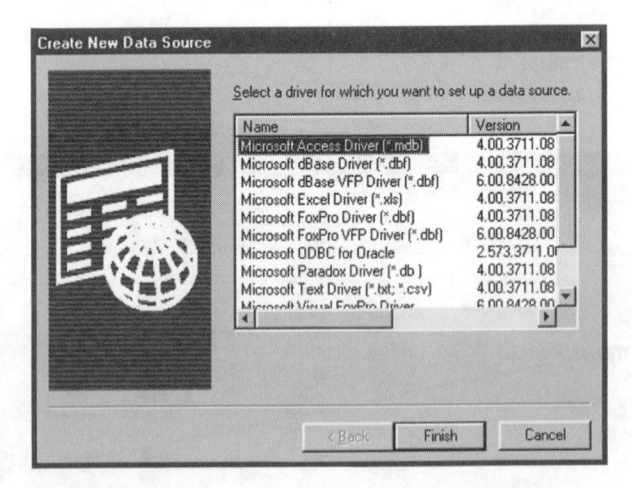

Figure 4.18

Note the various types of data sources you can use.

8. Navigate to the CDShop.mdb file, as shown in Figure 4.20. (If you copied this file to your Web folder, the CDShop.mdb database file should be in your SmallBiz folder.) Select the file, then click OK to close this dialog box. Then, click OK again to close the ODBC Microsoft Access Setup dialog box. The CDShop database appears in the list of available System Data Sources in the ODBC Data Source Administrator dialog box, as shown in Figure 4.21.

9. Click OK to close this dialog box.

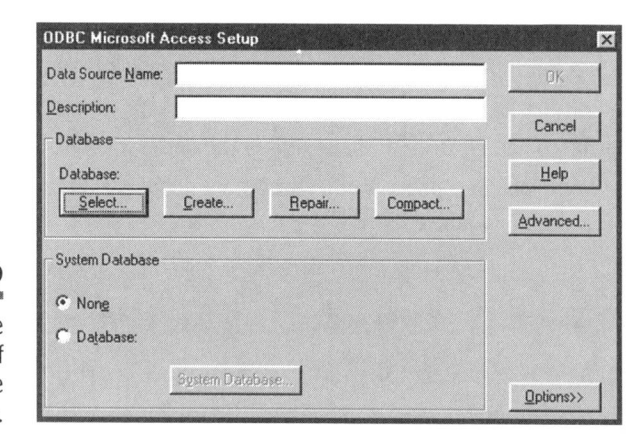

SATURDAY EVENING Dynamic Webs: Processing Forms and Integrating Databases

Figure 4.19

You can change the attributes of the data source at any time.

Figure 4.20

You can now select the CDShop as a data source to use within your Web pages!

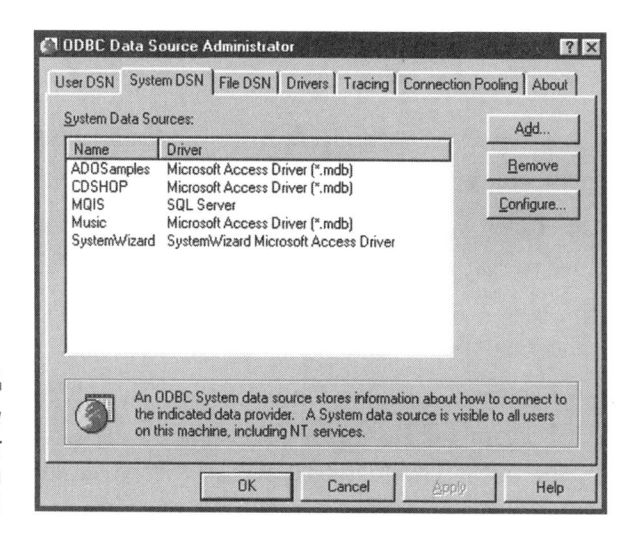

Figure 4.21

You can now access your database through your Web pages!

> **NOTE**
>
> When you upload your Web pages and database to your Internet Service Provider, they will establish this ODBC connection on the server where your Web will reside. They will ask you what to name the data source; this is the name you will use when accessing the database from your Web pages. You'll learn more about this in the next section.

Creating Your First Database-Driven Web Page

Now that you have established a connection to the CDShop database, you can use it in your Web pages. FrontPage 2000 provides a handy wizard that you can use to connect your Web pages with a database. Here's an example of how to use that wizard:

> **CAUTION**
>
> Microsoft has made some major enhancements to the Database Results Wizard in FrontPage 2000. Therefore, this is one area where FrontPage 2000 and FrontPage 98 will differ significantly.
>
> That said, in order to take full advantage of the information provided in this section, you really need to be using FrontPage 2000. While it is possible to make a connection between a database and a Web page with FrontPage 98, the process is not nearly as intuitive as it is with the 2000 version of the program.

1. For this example, information from the Catalog table of the CDShop database will be displayed. This table is shown in Figure 4.22.
2. Create a new page in your SmallBiz Web, and name it database. Be sure to save the database with the Active Server Page extension (.asp). This is critical to ensure that your connections with the CDShop database will work as they should!
3. Now it is time to call on the FrontPage 2000 Database Results Wizard. From the Insert menu, choose Database, Results, as shown in Figure 4.23. The Database Results Wizard dialog box appears.

SATURDAY·EVENING Dynamic Webs: Processing Forms and Integrating Databases **147**

Figure 4.22

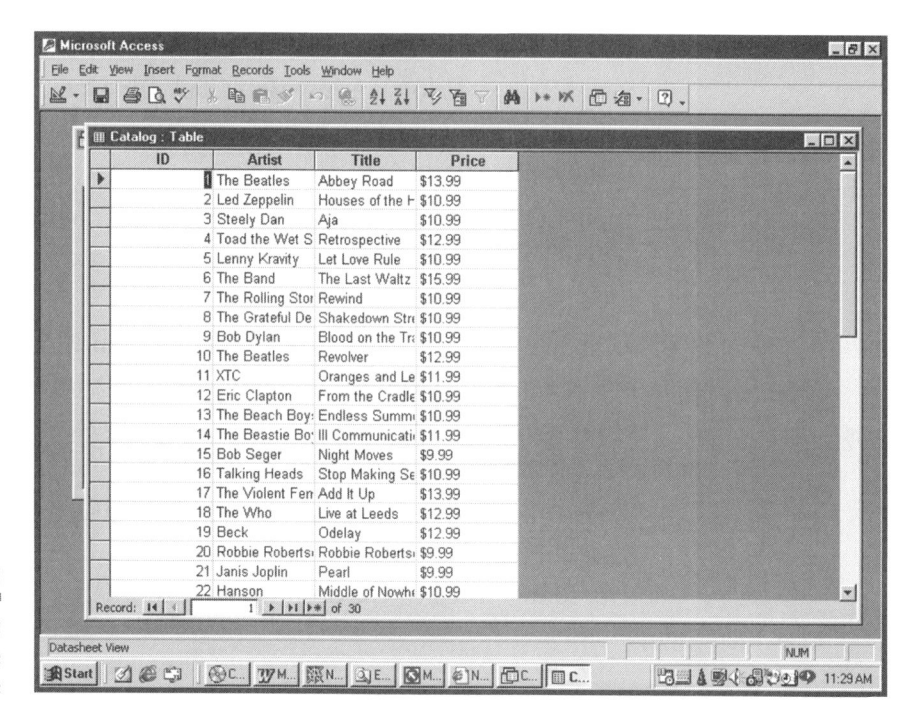

The Catalog table from the CDShop database

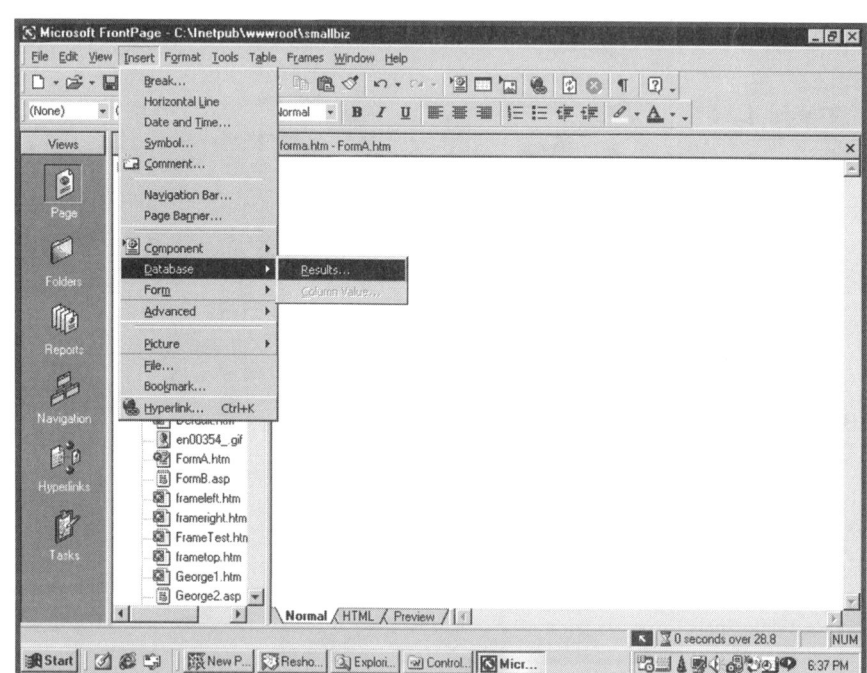

Figure 4.23

Calling the Database Results Wizard

4. Select Use a New Database Connection, then click Create. The Web Settings dialog box appears. Click the Database tab, and then click Add. The New Database Connection dialog box will appear, as shown in Figure 4.24.

5. Type **CDShop** in the Name field, then select System Data Source on Web Server. You'll need to identify this specific data source, so click Browse.

6. As shown in Figure 4.25, select CDShop and then click OK. Click OK again so that you are left with the Web Settings dialog box. From there, click the Apply button. FrontPage will create the necessary connections for this data source.

7. When the cursor is returned to you, click OK. You should now be back at Step 1 of the Database Results Wizard, with the CDShop data source listed in the drop-down menu. Click Next.

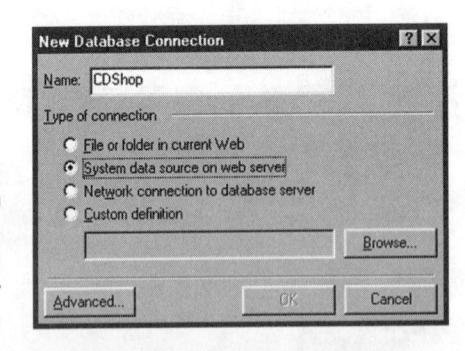

Figure 4.24

Defining a new database connection for your Web page

Figure 4.25

Be sure to select CDShop as your data source. Remember that you can change this selection later if you want to access a different data source.

SATURDAY·EVENING Dynamic Webs: Processing Forms and Integrating Databases   149

8. Step 2 of the Database Results Wizard asks you to select a Record Source from which to retrieve data. In this case, Record Source refers to the various tables within the CDShop database. For this example, select Catalog from the drop-down menu and then click Next, as shown in Figure 4.26.

9. Step 3 of the Database Results Wizard presents you with a list of all the fields contained in the Catalog table (ID, Artist, Title, and Price). You can choose to remove specific fields so they don't display in your Web page. For now, though, leave them all in. Click Next to continue to Step 4.

10. Step 4 of the Wizard presents you with options of how the returned data should be displayed (see Figure 4.27). For the formatting in this example, select Table-One Record Per Row from the drop-down menu and click Next.

11. The final step in the Wizard presents you with options as to how the data should be grouped. A neat feature of this Wizard is that it allows you to split records into groups rather than presenting the entire contents of a table all at once. Select the Split Records into Groups option and leave the default number of records returned set to 5.

12. Click Finish. After a few seconds, you return to the FrontPage Normal View. Your page should look like Figure 4.28.

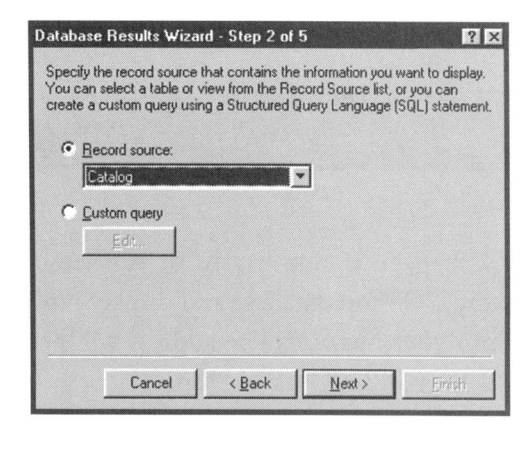

Figure 4.26

FrontPage 2000 makes it easy for you to pull specific information from a database.

Figure 4.27

Note that no matter which formatting method you select, you can customize it later from within the FrontPage Editor.

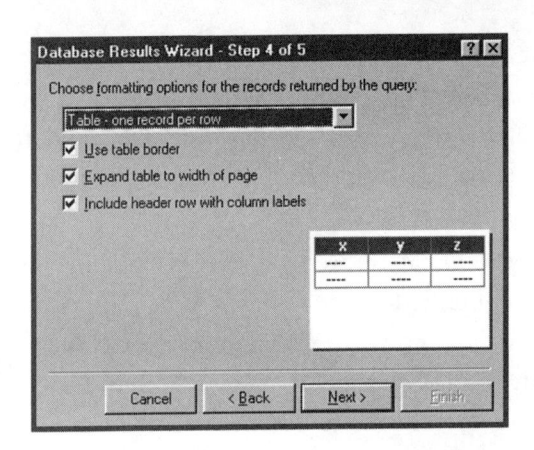

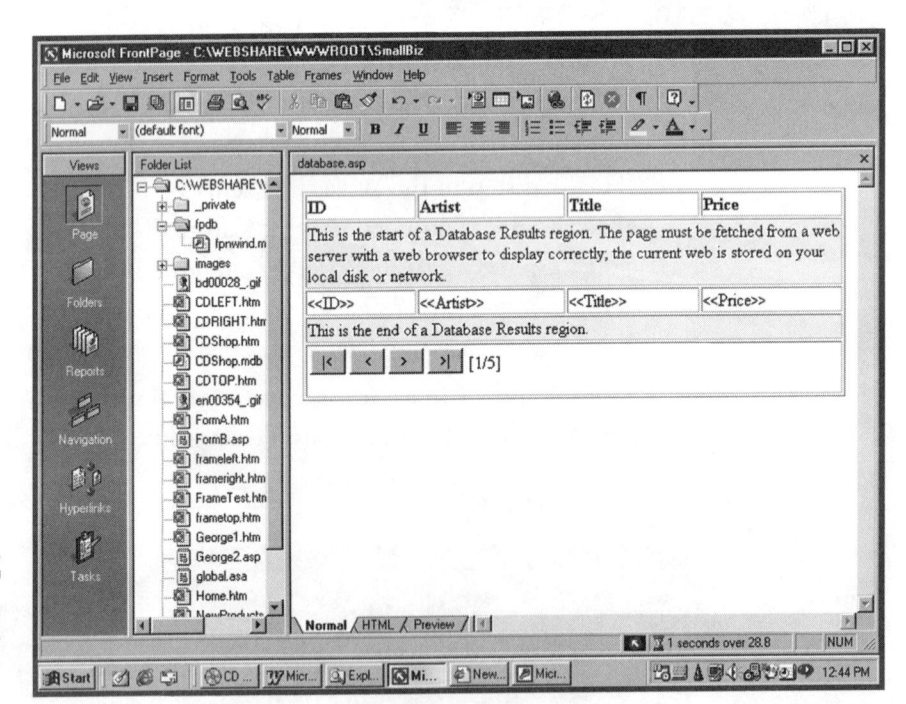

Figure 4.28

The database results region has been inserted into your Web page.

Your dynamic Web page is now ready to read information from the Catalog table of the CDShop database and display those results on screen. Load the page into your browser. The address will be something similar to http://127.0.0.1/SmallBiz/Database.asp.

SATURDAY·EVENING Dynamic Webs: Processing Forms and Integrating Databases   151

Notice how the Database Results Wizard also inserted navigation buttons underneath the returned record set (see Figure 4.29). Experiment with these buttons to see how you can easily move through the records.

> **NOTE** Unlike previous versions of FrontPage, the Web pages generated with the Database Results Wizard in FrontPage 2000 will work equally well in Internet Explorer and Netscape Navigator.

Adding a Search Form

The previous example is pretty nifty and shows how easy it is to get information stored in a database into your Web pages. But this is just the tip of the iceberg in terms of functionality. For example, what if you want to present your customers with a way of searching your database? This would be particularly useful if, for example, you allowed customers to enter a search word so they could see if there was a match in your product catalog.

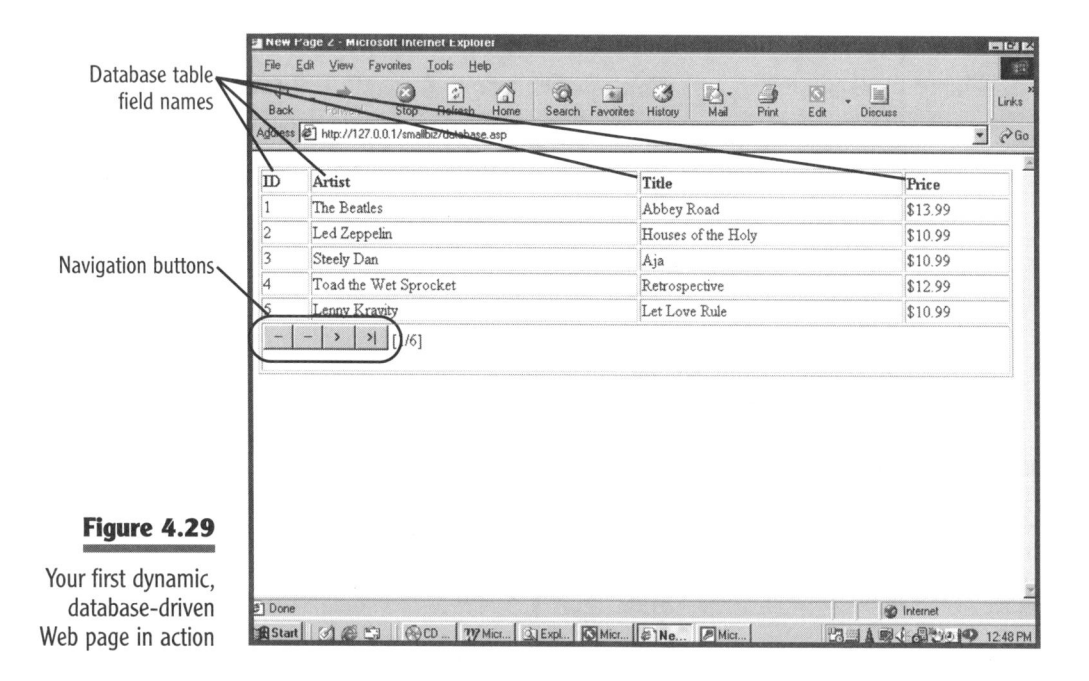

Figure 4.29

Your first dynamic, database-driven Web page in action

The Database Results Wizard allows for this kind of search function. Here's how it is done.

1. The first step in adding a search feature to your Web site is to build a search form. Start by creating a new page within your SmallBiz Web, and name it SearchA. You can save it with a regular .htm extension.
2. Add two elements to the page, so that it looks similar to Figure 4.30.
3. Assign these attributes to your elements:
   - Make the one-line text box, named Search, 30 characters in width (see Figure 4.31). You can make this width attribute any value you wish—I have just chosen 30 to allow a text box big enough to allow longer search terms the user might enter.
   - Name the submit button Search the database! (You can label it anything you want, just be sure that the button type is submit.)

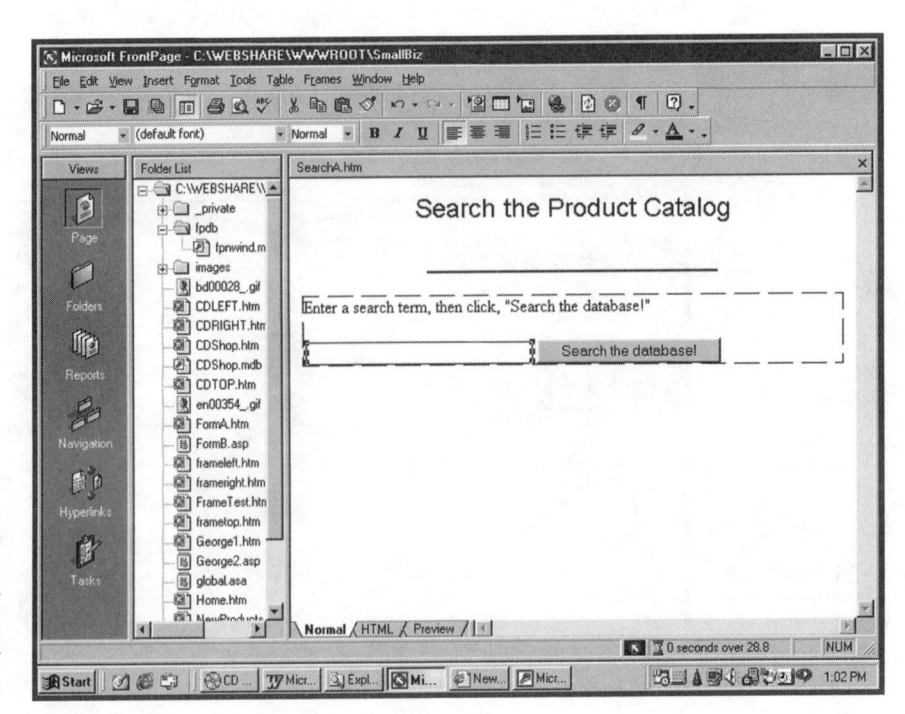

Figure 4.30

Adding form elements to your page, and specifying their attributes

SATURDAY·EVENING Dynamic Webs: Processing Forms and Integrating Databases   **153**

Figure 4.31

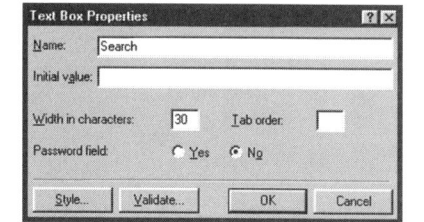

Attributes of the one-line text box

> **TIP**
>
> Remember that you can review all of these form elements and how they function by taking another look at the information presented in this afternoon's session, "Advanced FrontPage Functionality."

4. Now you need to direct this page to the Web page, which will display the search results. To do so, you must first adjust the form attributes. The steps are similar to those used to process forms. Right-click within the form boundary (noted by the dotted line), and choose Form Properties from the shortcut menu that appears.

5. From the Form Properties dialog box, select the Send to Other option, as shown in Figure 4.32.

6. Click Options in the Form Properties dialog box. The Options for Custom Form Handler dialog box appears, as shown in Figure 4.33.

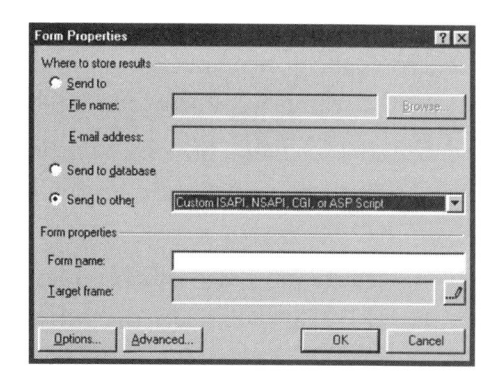

Figure 4.32

Adjusting form properties

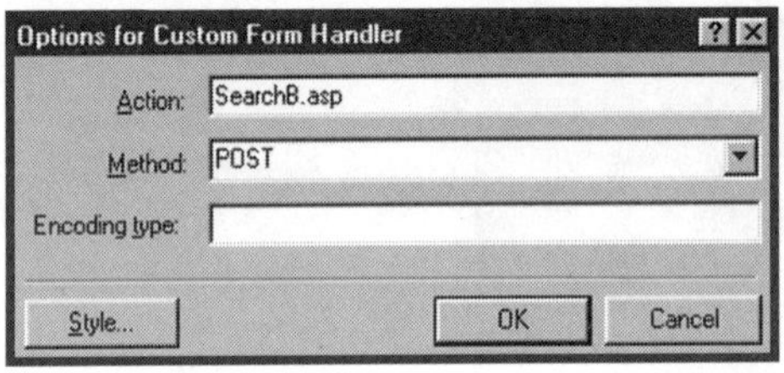

Figure 4.33

Directing form results to a processing page

7. In the Action text box, type **SearchB.asp**. Remember that in the Action field, the form is told where to send its results. SearchB.asp will be the search results page, which will be created next. Be sure to save SearchA.htm to ensure that all your work has been captured.

8. Now, create the actual page that will display the search results. To do so, create another new page within your SmallBiz Web and save it as SearchB.asp. Be sure to save this page with the .asp extension, otherwise your database connection will not function.

9. Choose Database, Results from the Insert menu. The wizard starts.

10. Select the Use an Existing Database Connection option, and from the drop-down menu, choose CDShop. Click Next.

11. In Step 2 of the Wizard, click the Record Source option and select Catalog from the drop-down list. Click Next.

12. In Step 3 of the Wizard, click Options. The Options dialog box appears. Click Criteria to display the Criteria dialog box, then click Add. The Add Criteria dialog box appears, as shown in Figure 4.34. From here, you can specify how you want your database to be searched, based on the search term provided by the customer.

13. Complete the Add Criteria dialog box. Be sure to select Use this Search Form Field. Here's an explanation of the fields in this dialog box:

    - **Field Name.** This selects the specific field to be searched in the Catalog table. For this example, select the Artist field.

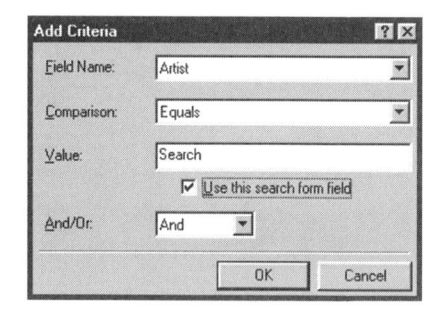

Figure 4.34

The Add Criteria dialog box

- **Comparison**. This field presents a variety of operators used to compare the term entered by the customer with what is available within the database. In this example, choose Equals from the drop-down menu. This ensures that only exact matches will be returned.

> **TIP**
> Use the Contains operator to return all records that include the search term somewhere in the record. For example, the search term *beat* would return both *Beatles* and *Beat Generation*, since this term is contained in both entries.

- **Value**. The Value field is the search criteria. In this case, the term entered by the customer on SearchA.htm will be used, so type Search in this field. This corresponds to the name of the one-line text box on the search form. Be sure to select the Use this Search Form Field check box to identify your value as coming from a form field.
- **And/Or**. Since searching will only occur on one term, leave the And/Or field set to And.

14. When you've filled in the Add Criteria dialog box, click OK. The Criteria dialog box reappears, with the options you specified in the Add Criteria dialog box (see Figure 4.35).

Figure 4.35

Your search criteria are defined.

15. Click OK until you return to Step 3 of the Database Results Wizard. Then, click Next until you reach Step 5. Once there, click Finish.//
16. Save both SearchA.htm and SearchB.asp to ensure that all your work is recorded.

Now, try out your new search form. Open your SearchA.htm page in your browser, and type **The Beatles** in the search box, as shown in Figure 4.36.

When you click Search the database!, two records are returned, as shown in Figure 4.37.

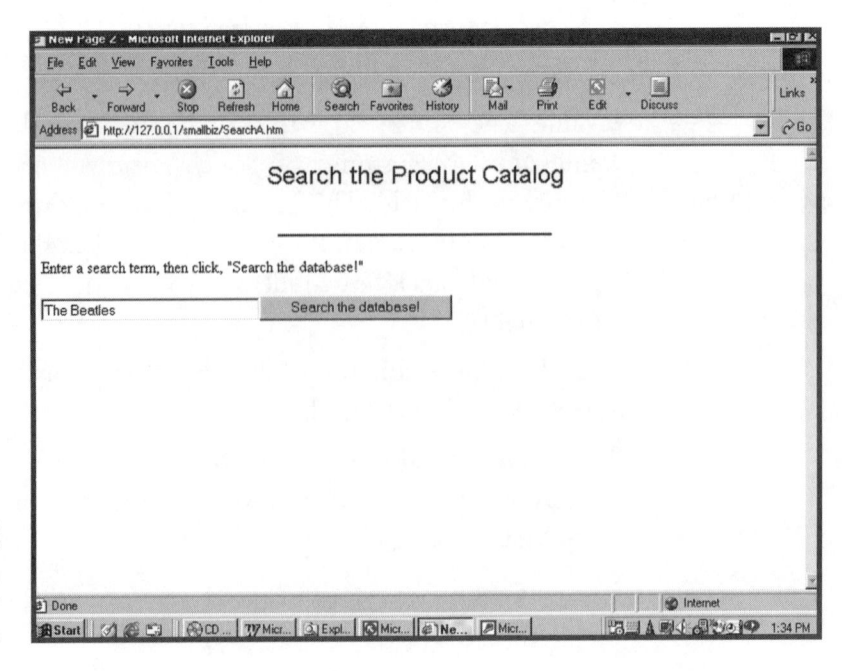

Figure 4.36

Preparing to search the database for The Beatles

SATURDAY·EVENING Dynamic Webs: Processing Forms and Integrating Databases 157

Figure 4.37

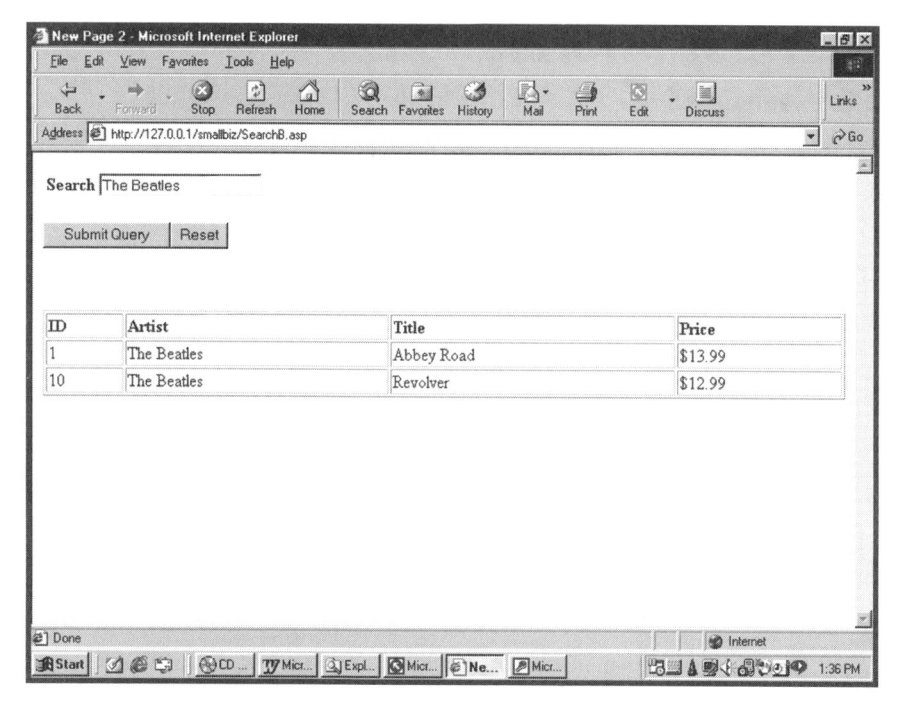

Results of searching for The Beatles

Notice that you are also presented with a search field on the actual search results page, compliments of the Database Results Wizard. All in all, great functionality, and very easy to implement.

Take a Break!

Well, you've gone through quite a bit of material already this evening, learning how to connect to and search a database and how to return search results in a Web page.

It only gets better. After your break, I'll show you how to capture information from customers and store it in your database, as well as a few other neat tricks that really put the *d* in dynamic Web page!

Inserting Information: Advanced Database Integration

If you want your small business Web site to be truly dynamic, you'll eventually want to capture information from customers.

In what ways would you do this? Consider the following:

- You've provided a "Send Us Your Comments" feedback form and are interested in storing those comments in a comment table in your database.
- You want your customers to schedule appointments online, so you need a method of capturing their chosen times.
- You want to allow your customers to place orders online.

This is a short list, but it gives you an idea of the very powerful functionality you can present to your customers. You can allow them to send you information directly and have that information stored in a database from which you can retrieve it later.

In this section, I'll show you how to provide your customers with a method of sending you information. While the example will be somewhat basic, tomorrow's case study in the afternoon session, "Examining a Web-Enabled Small Business Example: BestPop CD Shop," will present a more robust e-commerce solution, using everything you've learned up to this point.

Inserting Information into a Database

FrontPage 2000 provides an easy method of writing information to a database. This example will take you through the process.

1. First, create yet another new page within your SmallBiz Web. Save this page as Insert.asp, making sure to give it the .asp extension.
2. Add three individual one-line text boxes, as shown in Figure 4.38. Also, be sure to include a submit button.

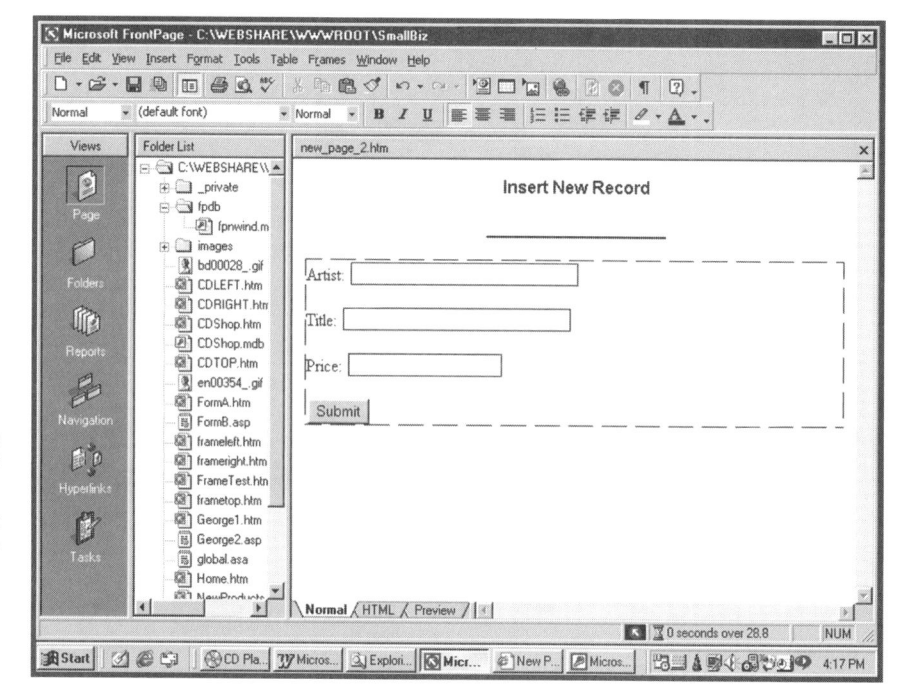

Figure 4.38

Preparing a data insert form, so that you—or your customers—can enter information directly into your database

3. Right-click within the form and choose Form Properties from the shortcut menu that appears. Select Send to Database and click OK. The Options for Saving Results to Database dialog box appears, as shown in Figure 4.39.
4. Select CDShop as the Database Connection to Use. Then select Catalog as the Table to Hold Form Results.
5. Click the Saved Fields tab (see Figure 4.40). From here, you will map your form field elements, the three one-line text boxes with corresponding fields in the Catalog table.
6. Three form elements (artist, title, and price) must be created to match the three corresponding fields in the Catalog table. Click Add to access the Add Field dialog box, shown in Figure 4.41.

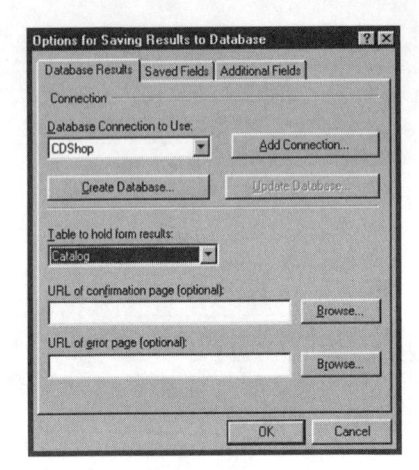

Figure 4.39

Configuring the options for inserting information into your database

Figure 4.40

The Saved Fields tab before you've selected the fields into which you want to save data that will be entered into form elements

Figure 4.41

Matching form fields with database fields

7. From the Database Column to Save to drop-down menu, you'll need to match each form field with its corresponding database column name. For each field, click Add, select a field from the Form Field to Add list, then select its corresponding database column name and click OK.

8. When you've finished matching each form field with its corresponding database column name, your Form Fields to Save box should resemble the one shown in Figure 4.42. Click OK and you will return to the Form Properties dialog box.

9. Click OK to close the Form Properties dialog box and save the Insert.asp page. You are now ready to test the page in your Web browser.

To test your page, load the Insert.asp page into your Web browser. It should resemble Figure 4.43.

Complete the form, adding an artist and title of one of your favorite CDs. Enter a price, too. When you click Submit, you will be presented with a confirmation that your entry was accepted, as shown in Figure 4.44.

Just to illustrate the point and power of this feature, open the actual CDShop.mdb file in Access. Then, open the Catalog table and scroll through the list until you see your entry (see Figure 4.45).

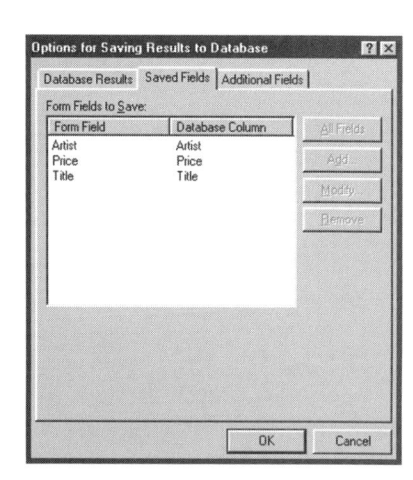

Figure 4.42

All form elements have been mapped to corresponding database column names in the Catalog table.

Figure 4.43

Your Insert.asp page, ready to accept a new catalog entry

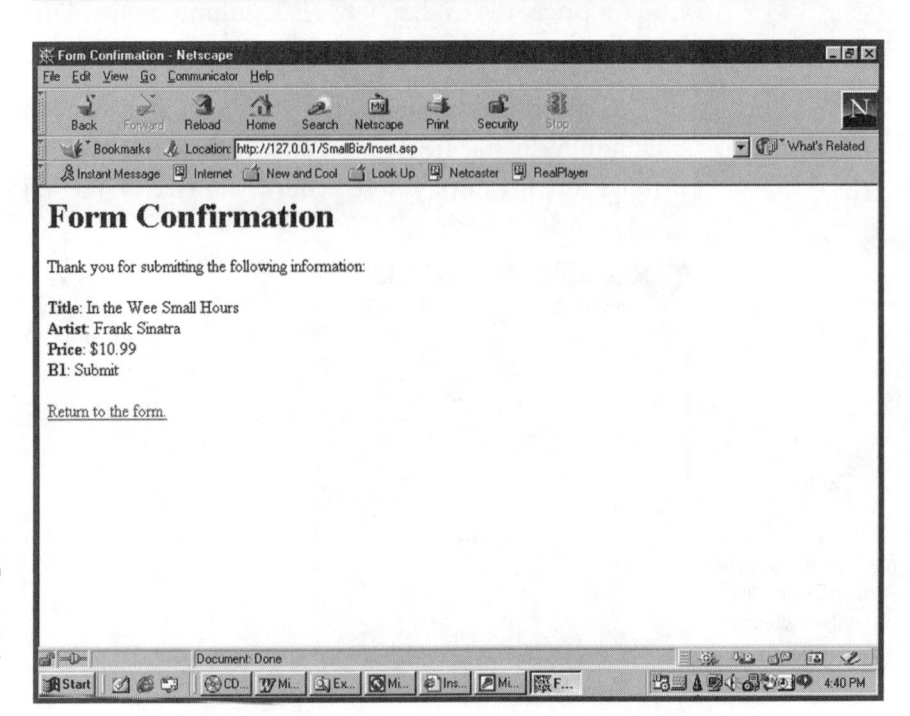

Figure 4.44

Receiving confirmation that your entry was accepted

SATURDAY·EVENING   Dynamic Webs: Processing Forms and Integrating Databases

Figure 4.45

Your entry is inserted into the Catalog table of the CDShop database, just as you entered the information on the Insert.asp page!

There are many great uses for this ability to store information directly in a database. By using this feature, you provide customers with a way to send you information, such as comments on your site, product orders, and so on. This information can then be presented to the customer at a later time, such as on a return visit to verify a previous order. The possibilities are endless.

In tomorrow afternoon's session, you'll see how these database features can be used in a real-world example. For now, though, start thinking about different types of information that you would like to capture from your customers. Then, in tomorrow's session, you can see how this process actually takes shape.

> **NOTE** FrontPage 2000 also makes other features available with the Insert Data feature. For example, instead of the default confirmation page shown in Figure 4.44, you can specify a Web page to display for this confirmation. I'll discuss some more of these advanced features in tomorrow afternoon's session.

Session in Review

Time to hit the hay again. You've come a long way in your Web adventure:

- You've learned the fundamentals of database organization, and how it should fit into your overall business process strategy.

- You've learned how to process form information, so your customers have a way to provide you with data.

- Finally, you've learned how to make a connection between an Access database and a Web page, so your small business Web can really come alive by capturing information entered by customers.

Good things are still to come! Tomorrow morning, I'll cover some neat features that will make your Web site more personal, not to mention more interesting and functional. You'll learn about graphics, sound, and e-mail features. Then, in the afternoon, you'll see a full example of a Web-enabled small business. Finally, during tomorrow evening's session, you'll be presented with the final issues about how to bring your developed Web to life through an ISP.

Sweet, small-business Web dreams!

SATURDAY EVENING Dynamic Webs: Processing Forms and Integrating Databases

TIP OF THE DYNAMIC WEB ICEBERG

I know I might be starting to sound like a broken record, but I want to keep my promise: You don't have to be a programmer to Web enable your small business.

However, after working through tonight's session, you might be thinking, "How do I delete information from a database?" or "How do I update a record that has already been entered?"

These are legitimate questions. These tasks are quite possible and not that complicated. However, FrontPage doesn't offer a friendly wizard to walk you through update and delete processes, as it does with the general reading data from, and writing data to, features.

In order to update and delete information, you need to dig a little deeper in Active Server Page scripting. While it isn't difficult, it does involve some explanation that would probably make your eyes glaze over at this late hour! It also comes awfully close to—dare I say it—programming.

Active Server Pages technology is a great leap forward in bringing the true power of the Web to all of us. If you are interested in exploring all the power of e-commerce, you might benefit by checking out a book on ASP. The basics of ASP aren't really difficult to learn. Check out *ASP 3 Fast & Easy Web Development* (Prima, 2000) for more information.

Sunday Morning

Adding FrontPage Spice: Form Validation, DHTML, and E-Mail

- Validating Forms
- Integrating E-Mail with FrontPage Webs
- Working with DHTML Effects
- Adding a Search Feature to Your Web Site

In the old days of the Web (those ancient times circa 1995-1996), there were many a simple HTML page. You remember these pages, right? They might have had annoying blinking text. Maybe some of the fancy ones even had animated GIF graphics—you remember…the animated e-mail links or the various spinning/spiraling "Under Construction" graphics. The interesting thing about these sites was that they were the progenitors of the great stuff to come: widespread use of JavaScript and true, bandwidth-friendly, graphic applications like Macromedia Flash.

Adding various special effects to your Web pages is both a blessing and a curse. On the positive side, well-designed, temperately-placed graphics can really bring your site to life by adding a distinctive flair to the its mood and feel while reflecting your company's own distinct personality. However, the down side is that many people go overboard. To make an analogy to the glorious '70s and the "Days of Disco," there is a reason we aren't still all decked out in polyester and standing in the freezing cold to get a spot in Studio 54—excess. Too much of a good thing can be bad, resulting in Web pages with excessive loading time and a lack of focus. With the '70s…well…you remember "Saturday Night Fever," right?!

This morning's session will introduce you to some of the more useful extras of Web design, as well as how to easily implement them into your Web pages. And, by the way, I'll try to keep the disco analogies in check.

> **NOTE** The spicy enhancements discussed in this session will focus primarily on functional enhancements, such as adding e-mail and validating forms, rather than how to add a animated picture of John Travolta to your Web page. For a more complete description of the graphical aspect of Web design, check out Prima's *Electrify Your Web Site In a Weekend* (1999).

Validating Forms

You may have noticed during one of your visits to your favorite e-commerce site that if you don't provide all required information in a form (for example, mailing address or telephone number), you receive a message such as "Please complete all required fields" when you try to submit the form.

How does a Web site know when you have left certain required fields blank? And how do you determine which fields are required? These are all aspects of form validation. As with many aspects of Web design, form validation used to be a difficult programming task. But like many Web-related tasks now, FrontPage makes things a whole lot easier. In this section, you'll look at how to incorporate form validation into your own Web pages, to be sure you are capturing all the required information from your customers.

Determining Required Form Fields

To begin the discussion of form validation, work with a form created in last night's session, "Dynamic Webs: Processing Forms and Integrating Databases."

> **NOTE** If you don't have this form saved, no sweat! Just create a new form with at least one text box field, one group of radio buttons, and one check box. Then follow along with the instructions presented.

SUNDAY MORNING Adding FrontPage Spice: Form Validation, DHTML, and E-Mail

1. First, open your SmallBiz Web and the page FormA.htm. This form should look similar to Figure 5.1.

2. For this initial example, pretend that you've determined the text box field (Enter Your Full Name Here) to be required. Double-click the actual form element to display the Text Box Properties dialog box, shown in Figure 5.2.

3. Click Validate to display the form element's validation properties. The Text Box Validation dialog box appears (see Figure 5.3).

NOTE Different form elements will display different validation dialog boxes. For example, the Radio Button Validation dialog box appears when a radio button is selected for validation.

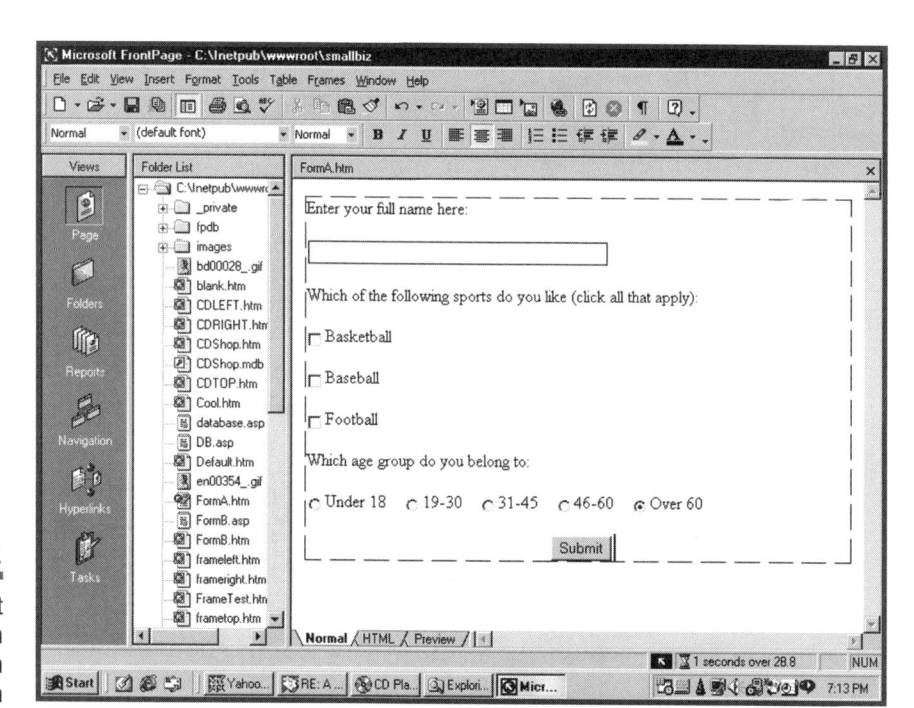

Figure 5.1

Preparing to set validation properties on a form

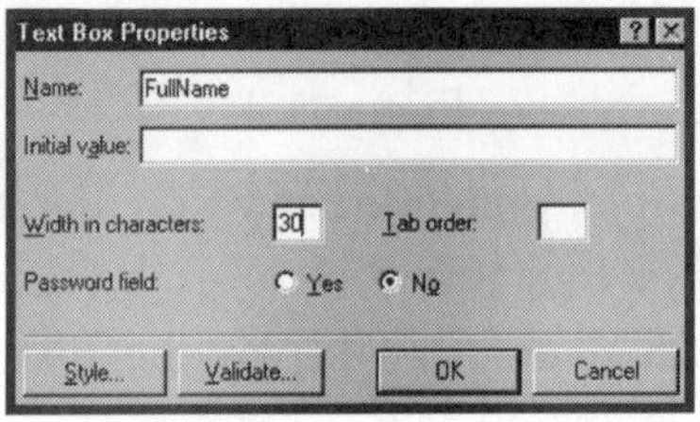

Figure 5.2

The now-familiar Text Box Properties dialog box

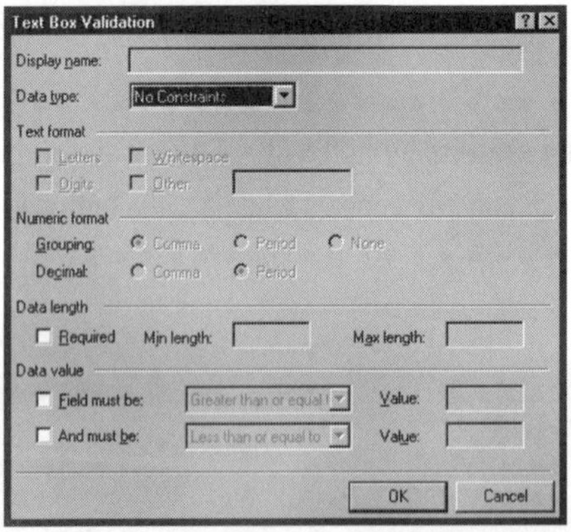

Figure 5.3

The Validation dialog box for a Text Box form element

This box appears complicated, but is actually quite simple. Take a closer look at some of the different kinds of validation properties you can set:

- **Data Type.** This drop-down menu allows you to set the specific type of data that can be entered into the form element. There are four types: No Constraints, Text, Integer, and Number. Depending on the data type you select, the Text Format options of the dialog box might be activated. For example, if you select the Text option, both the Text Format options and the Display Name will become active, as shown in Figure 5.4. This enables selection of the text formats that will be allowed in the text box form element, such as letters, digits, and white space. You can also include the message that will be displayed if the user does not enter information in the form field, or enters characters that are not acceptable.

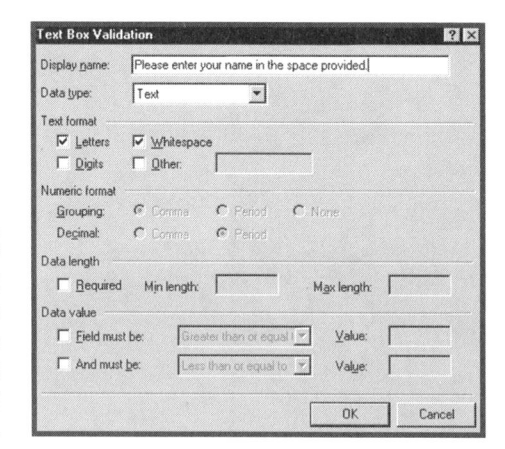

SUNDAY MORNING Adding FrontPage Spice: Form Validation, DHTML, and E-Mail

Figure 5.4

By selecting different data types, you can access specific form validation properties.

> **CAUTION**
>
> ◆◆◆◆◆◆◆◆◆◆◆◆◆◆◆◆◆◆◆◆◆◆◆◆◆◆◆◆◆◆◆◆◆◆◆◆
>
> Use caution when setting the Text Format properties of a form element. In Figure 5.4, the Text Format properties were set to allow for letters and white space. However, if users were to enter any numbers or any special characters, such as a comma, in this field, the error message would display upon submission.
>
> When setting form validation, take time to think about the type of information your users will enter in the form fields. For example, if you have a form field requiring a phone number, then you'd want to set the Text Format property to allow for numbers and special characters, such as a hyphen or parentheses.
>
> ◆◆◆◆◆◆◆◆◆◆◆◆◆◆◆◆◆◆◆◆◆◆◆◆◆◆◆◆◆◆◆◆◆◆◆◆

- **Data Length.** This section allows you to determine the number of characters that can be entered in the field. Note that there are both maximum and minimum value properties.
- **Data Value.** This section allows you to set specific parameters regarding the range in which the data must fall (such as greater than or less than), which is especially useful for capturing numeric data.

4. Set the validation properties for this form element to match those shown in Figure 5.5.

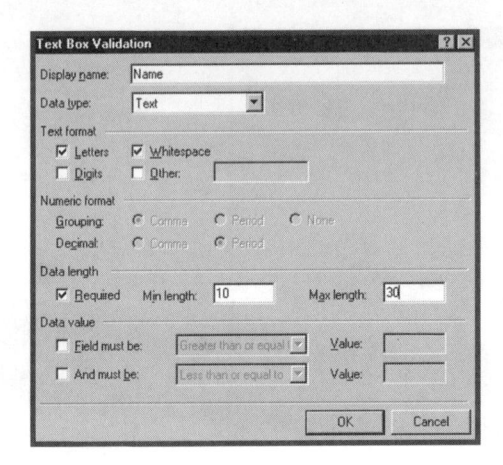

Figure 5.5

Setting validation properties for the text box

5. Save and close this page. You can now test the form validation properties in a browser.

Testing Form Validation in a Browser

By loading the page in a Web browser and using Personal Web Server, you can test the form validation properties that have just been set.

1. Load the FormA.htm page into your browser of choice (see Figure 5.6). The URL for this page is probably something like http://127.0.0.1/smallbiz/forma.htm.

2. To see the effect of the validation settings on the text box field, click the Submit button before entering any information in the field.

3. When Submit is clicked without any information in the Name field, a validation error appears, just as specified in the form validation dialog box for this specific form element (see Figure 5.7).

NOTE Note that the form validation message box indicates it is using JavaScript. Through the magic (did someone say convenience?) of FrontPage, the underlying JavaScript code is inserted into your pages automatically—no programming involved!

SUNDAY MORNING Adding FrontPage Spice: Form Validation, DHTML, and E-Mail   **175**

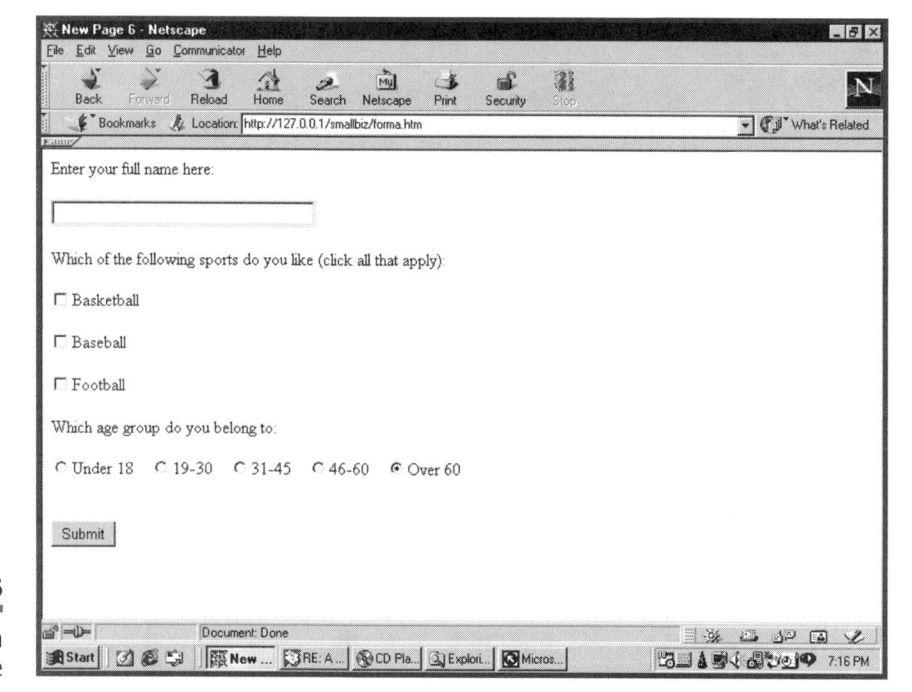

Figure 5.6

The FormA.htm page

Figure 5.7

Form validation in action

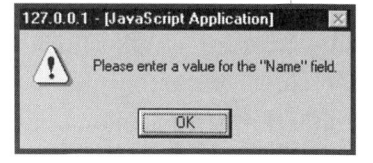

4. Remember from Figure 5.5 that the Text Format properties were set to allow only for text and white space. Try entering some numbers in the Name field, but enter less than 10 numbers. Then, try entering more than 10 numbers and compare the differences in the error messages you receive (see Figures 5.8 and 5.9).

   Due to the specified validation properties when less than 10 characters are entered, the error message in Figure 5.8 was displayed when you entered just a few numbers. However, when you entered more than 10 numbers, that particular validation requirement was met. But since numbers were entered rather than text, the error message in Figure 5.9 was displayed.

Figure 5.8

By using specific properties of form validation, you can determine parameters of data entered into fields.

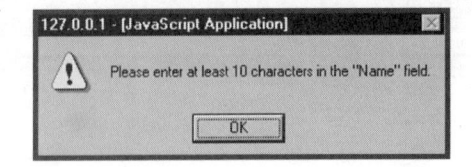

Figure 5.9

Form validation allows you to specify numeric versus text information allowed for entry into form fields.

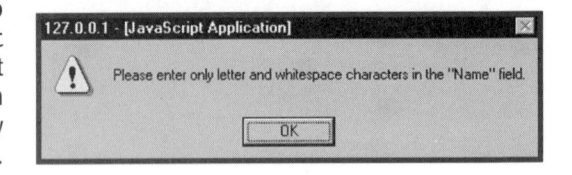

As you can see from this example, form validation provides a powerful, easy-to-implement method of ensuring that data is captured in just the way you want it. Combined with some planning on your part, you can use form validation as both an error check and a powerful customer support tool. For example, if customers are given direction on what types of data to enter, you can respond to their requests much more efficiently.

Validating Other Form Elements

You can use form validation with other form elements, too. In essence, they all follow the same principle as text boxes in that you set specific requirements for the type of data that can be entered, selected, or checked. You can refer to your FormA.htm page to see to what other types of form elements you can apply form validation.

When you validate a group of radio buttons, you set the requirement that the user must select one of them. Double-click one of the radio buttons and then click the Validate button in the Radio Button Properties dialog box. This will display the Radio Button Validation dialog box (see Figure 5.10).

SUNDAY MORNING Adding FrontPage Spice: Form Validation, DHTML, and E-Mail

Figure 5.10

Simple radio button validation

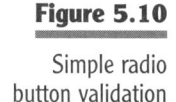

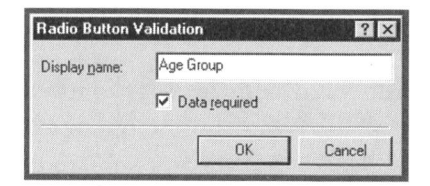

If the user does not select one of the radio buttons when validation is active, the error message presented in Figure 5.11 appears.

The other useful form validation feature is for drop-down menus. Although a drop-down menu does not exist on FormA.htm, Figure 5.12 illustrates the validation dialog box for this form element.

One neat thing about the validation features for drop-down menus is the Disallow First Item option. By selecting this, you prevent the user from selecting the first item in the list. That way, you can use the first item on the list as an instructional option, such as "Select from the following list," without worrying about the user actually selecting this option.

As with other cool FrontPage functionality, form validation requires that the FrontPage Components be installed on the server.

Figure 5.11

The error message displayed when the user does not select one of the radio buttons

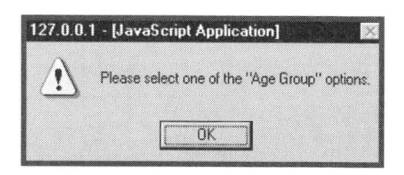

Figure 5.12

Setting validation for a drop-down menu form element

Take a Break!

Now that you've experimented with form validation, take five—maybe dig out that "Saturday Night Fever" CD. Come on, I know you have a copy somewhere in your collection! When you get back, you'll learn how you can integrate e-mail functionality into your FrontPage Webs.

Integrating E-Mail with FrontPage Webs

By utilizing the FrontPage e-mail features, you can turn your Web site into your own personal secretary. But rather than having hundreds of those old "While You Were Out" message forms lying all over your desk, you can configure your small business Web site to automatically send you an e-mail when an order is placed.

How is this done? Quite simply—take a look:

1. Since you've already added some nifty form validation to your FormA.htm page, continue to work it.

2. From within FrontPage, right-click anywhere within the form boundaries (not on a specific form element, but just somewhere inside the dotted lines), and select Form Properties from the shortcut menu. The Form Properties dialog box appears (see Figure 5.13).

3. First, take a look at the Where to Store Results section of this dialog box. In last night's session, you used the Send to Other option to specify a page to which form results would be submitted, so the information could be inserted into an Access database. For this example, click the Send To option and enter your e-mail address. Then, click OK.

   You will likely receive the FrontPage error message shown in Figure 5.14 when you select Send to E-mail Address. What is this rather detailed error message and why are you receiving it? In order for FrontPage to automatically generate e-mail, the e-mail server needs to be properly configured. For this section, therefore, you'll have to

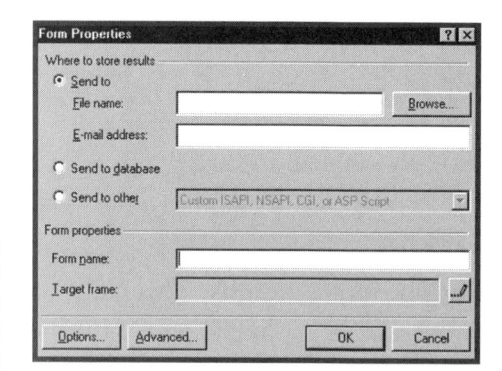

SUNDAY MORNING Adding FrontPage Spice: Form Validation, DHTML, and E-Mail   179

Figure 5.13

The Form Properties dialog box

Figure 5.14

Remember, you need the Server Extensions installed to really take advantage of the full power of FrontPage!

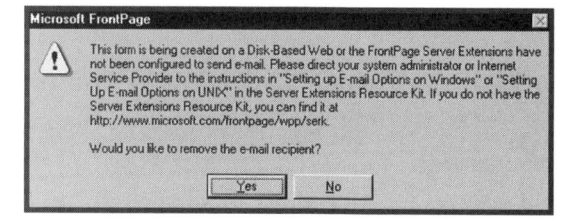

take my word that this feature really does work, even though you might not be able to see a live demonstration on your own machine running Personal Web Server. If you do see this message when you develop your Web on PWS, just go ahead and click No. Then, when your site is activated by your Web Presence Provider, you'll be ready to go.

NOTE Since you are using Personal Web Server, you really don't have access to a server with this capability. However, your Web Presence Provider will have configured their e-mail servers for you. All you need to do is select the Send to E-mail Address option, and you'll be all set. When users submit the form, you will receive notice via the e-mail address you specified in the Send To field.

4. With the Send To option selected, click Options. This will display the Options for Saving Results of Form dialog box, shown in Figure 5.15.

5. Click the E-mail Results tab to specify related e-mail features of FrontPage. The E-mail Results tab has a few specific properties you can set:

   - **E-mail address to receive results.** This is the address to which the message will be sent (most likely, your e-mail address).

   - **E-mail format.** Depending on the type of e-mail client used (for example, Microsoft Outlook or Netscape Messenger), the format of the e-mail text can have different styles, such as HTML formatting, formatted text, and so on. The default format is formatted text.

   - **E-mail message header.** This allows you to specify the subject and reply-to line of the e-mail. Ideally, the subject line will be indicative of the message contents. The reply-to line can be an e-mail address (again, your e-mail address or your company's general e-mail address) to which your customers can respond, if necessary.

6. After you specify the properties, click OK to return to the Form Properties dialog box. Click OK again to close this dialog box and return to the FrontPage editor.

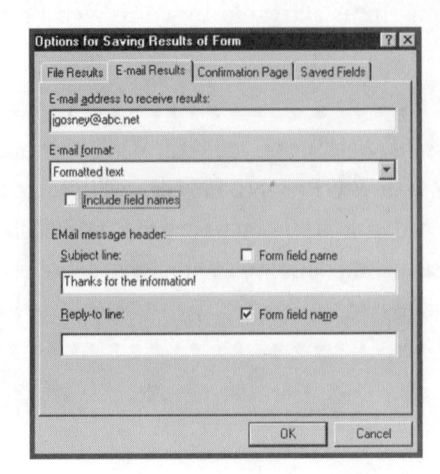

Figure 5.15

Specifying e-mail options, including the message header

TIP Check with your Web Presence Provider for more details on how they support FrontPage's e-mail features.

> ### WHY E-MAIL YOUR CUSTOMERS?
>
> You may be wondering why you should even bother sending e-mail to your customers. The answer is simple: An informed customer is a happy customer. Using the speed and convenience of e-mail, you ensure that your customers know not only the status of their orders, but also how to contact you if something is wrong.
>
> For example, imagine that customer Joe Smith places an order for ZXY Widget on a small business Web site. He has provided sensitive information (personal information, such as his phone number and address, not to mention credit card information), trusting the electronic process of the site to place his order so his goods arrive on time. By sending a simple confirmation of his order as well as another message that his product has been shipped, Joe is kept informed and is thus confident that his order is being handled well, and that he is being treated like a VIP.
>
> Be sure to note that using e-mail to keep the customer informed is a key to successful e-commerce—don't forget about this powerful, easy-to-use FrontPage feature!

Working with DHTML Effects

The Web is not a static medium. Given the ever-increasing bandwidth offered by devices such as cable modems, not to mention increased processor speeds and the generally out-of-this-world cool applications being developed, we are truly in the digital revolution, with the Web as our collective technological flagship.

That said, one of recent advances has been in HTML itself. HTML was originally designed to be a static method of displaying text (hence the *markup* in Hypertext Markup Language), not unlike preparing a book for a printer. HTML has received some much-needed shots in the arm using advances such as DHTML, which is the focus of this section.

So, what is DHTML? This acronym stands for *Dynamic Hypertext Markup Language*. In essence, it allows traditional HTML to come alive using exact text positioning on a screen, along with all kinds of interesting special effects. Using a combination of cascading style sheets and JavaScript, skilled DHTML programmers can do some amazing things to bring a boring, static Web page to life.

However, you don't have to program to use the DHTML effects that are available through FrontPage. Here's an example of how you can add DHTML to your Web pages using FrontPage.

CAUTION

Despite the cool applications that Microsoft develops, they are not the only fish in the Web pond—they might be the biggest, but they are not the only one. That said, the technology used by Microsoft to implement DHTML in their browser (Internet Explorer) is not the same as the method used by Netscape to implement this technology in their browser.

So guess what? The DHTML effects you add to your Web pages with FrontPage may look fantastic in IE, but may not work at all in Navigator, or they may work differently. Bottom line: Don't bet the farm on the use of DHTML effects in your Web pages, as they can very often be implemented quite differently in different browsers.

1. Keeping the caution on DHTML use in mind, do a little experimenting. Create a new page in your SmallBiz Web and name it Cool.htm.
2. Type **Dropping in to say hello, this is an example of DHTML** and format the text in some fashion. I've bolded, changed the font, and increased the text size in the example.

SUNDAY MORNING Adding FrontPage Spice: Form Validation, DHTML, and E-Mail

3. With your cursor on the same line as the text, choose Format, Dynamic HTML effects.

4. The DHTML toolbar appears, as shown in Figure 5.16. From the On drop-down menu, choose Page Load, and from the Apply drop-down menu, choose Drop in by Word. Notice that your text is now outlined in blue.

5. Save your page.

6. Load this page into Internet Explorer (see Figure 5.17). The address should be similar to http://127.0.0.1/SmallBiz/Cool.htm.

Figure 5.16

Determining the type of DHTML effect you wish to apply

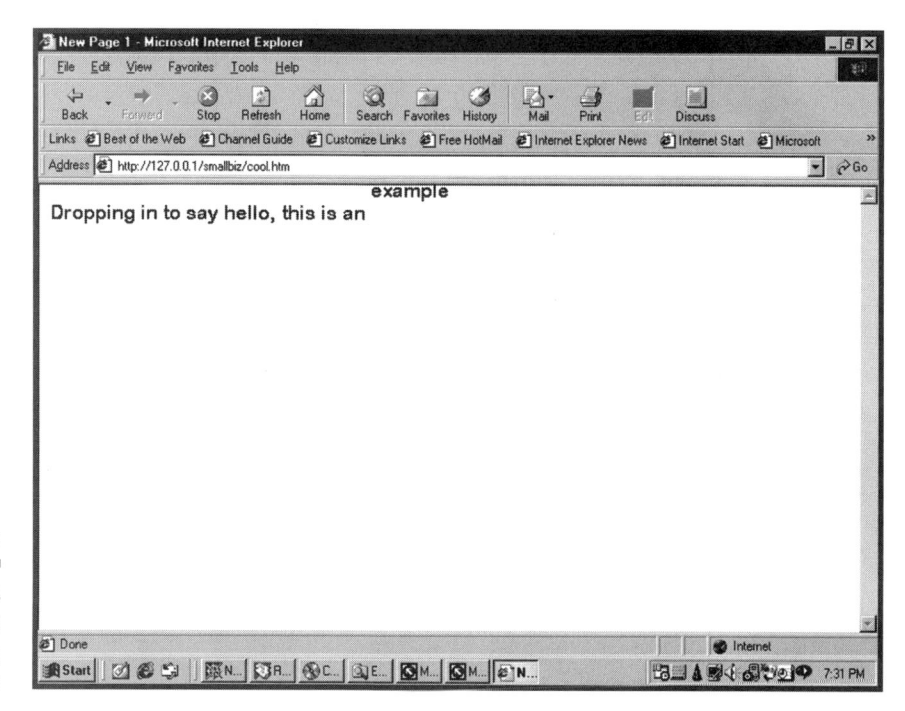

Figure 5.17

Your text "drops in," just as you specified in FrontPage

7. If you have Netscape Navigator, try loading the same page so that you can see the differences in effect. Instead of dropping in word by word, the entire sentence drops in at once. Still a cool effect, although admittedly not quite as snazzy as in Internet Explorer.

Adding a Search Feature to Your Web Site

Every great e-commerce Web site allows you to search the site for specific information. For example, look at the Amazon.com home page, shown in Figure 5.18.

> **TIP**
>
> DHTML is fun, and with the use of FrontPage it's easy to implement. However, as you've just seen, differences in how various browsers interpret DHTML can produce mixed results, to say the least.
>
> A much better alternative is to use a browser plug-in that can produce the same effect regardless of which browser your customers use. Probably the best such application available today is Macromedia Flash. Although it is somewhat difficult to master, Flash can produce absolutely stunning audio and visual effects within your Web page. (For a great example, check out the Chrysler Web site for their new PT Cruiser at http://www.chryslercars.com.)
>
> Also, check out *Flash 5 Fast & Easy Web Development* (Prima, 2000) to help you learn more about the power of Flash.

Amazon.com is probably just a *little* bit bigger than your small business Web site, but a search feature can come in handy no matter how big your site. Customers like to be able to quickly navigate to areas of interest, and a search feature can provide this functionality.

How do you add a search feature to your Web site using FrontPage? Simply follow these steps.

1. Create a new page in your SmallBiz Web and save it as SearchCheck.htm.

SUNDAY MORNING Adding FrontPage Spice: Form Validation, DHTML, and E-Mail — **185**

Figure 5.18

The search tool on Amazon.com is immediately accessible when the home page loads, so customers can quickly find specific information.

2. From the Insert menu, choose Component, Search Form. The Search Form Properties dialog box appears, as shown in Figure 5.19.

3. Leave all of the default selections and click OK. You will now see the Search Form element in the FrontPage editor (see Figure 5.20).

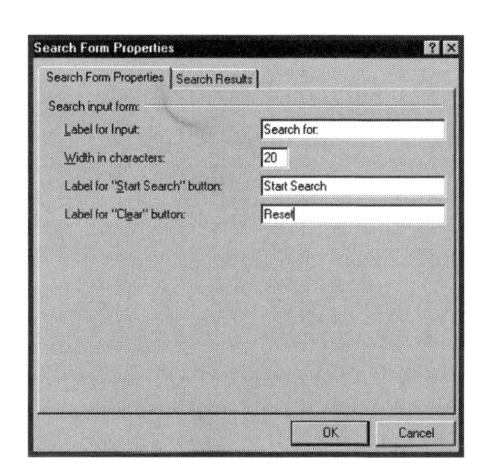

Figure 5.19

Determining search form properties

Figure 5.20

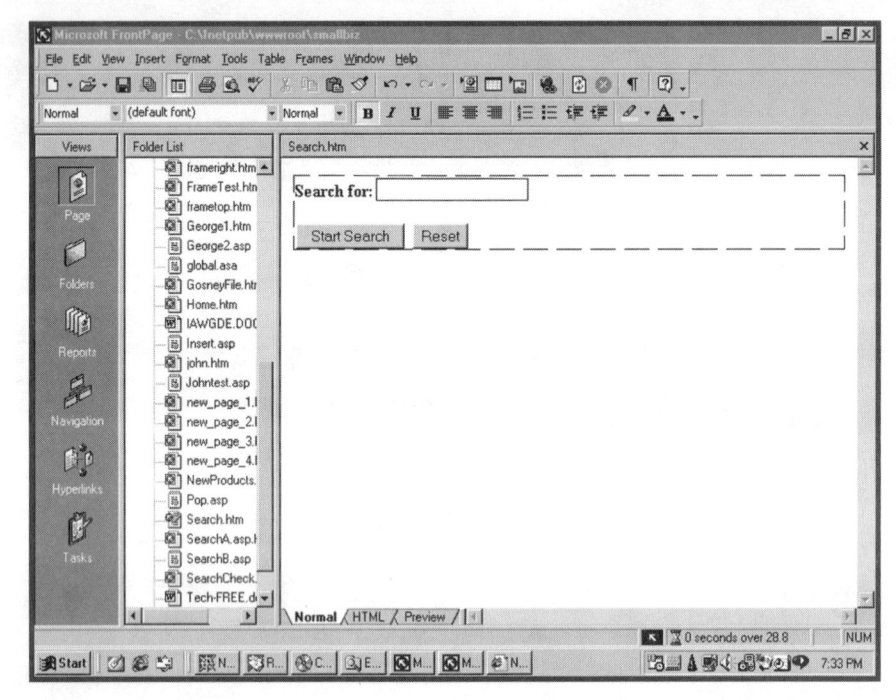

The Search element added to your Web page

4. Save this page and open any other page in your SmallBiz Web. Once you open another page, type your name somewhere on the page. To test the search component, you'll look for your name.

5. Now save the page onto which you just typed your name.

6. Load the SearchCheck.htm page into your browser, as shown in Figure 5.21. Again, the address should be something like http://127.0.0.1/smallbiz/searchcheck.htm.

7. Type your name and click Start Search. The search results should display a link to the page that contains your name, as shown in Figure 5.22. By clicking the hyperlink, you will be taken to the page where your search term appears.

NOTE The number of returned hits may vary, depending on your search term and the number of pages within your SmallBiz Web where the term appears.

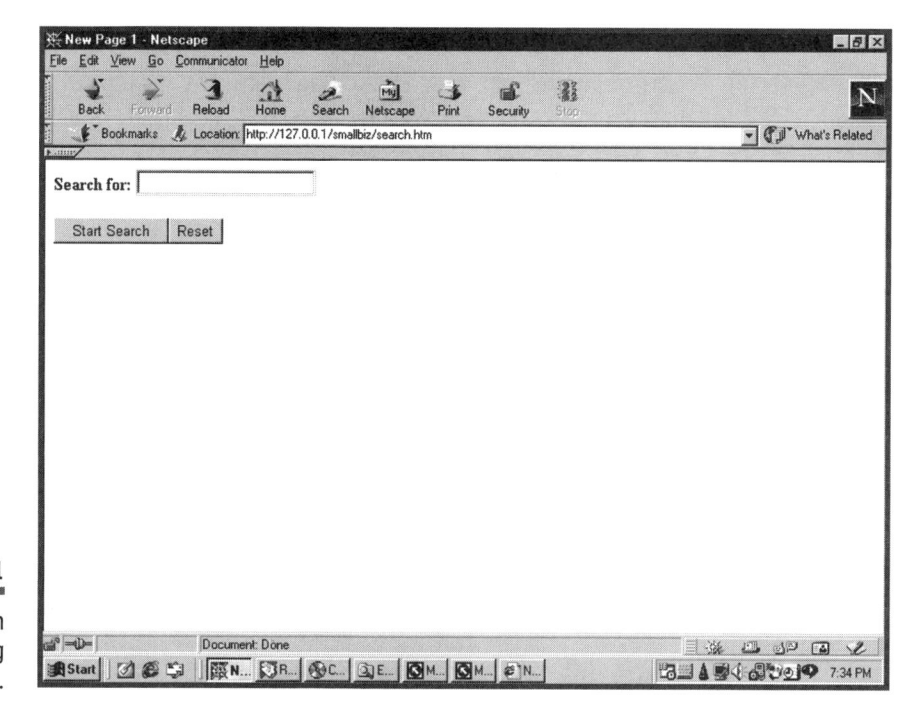

SUNDAY MORNING Adding FrontPage Spice: Form Validation, DHTML, and E-Mail   **187**

Figure 5.21

Begin the search process by entering a search term.

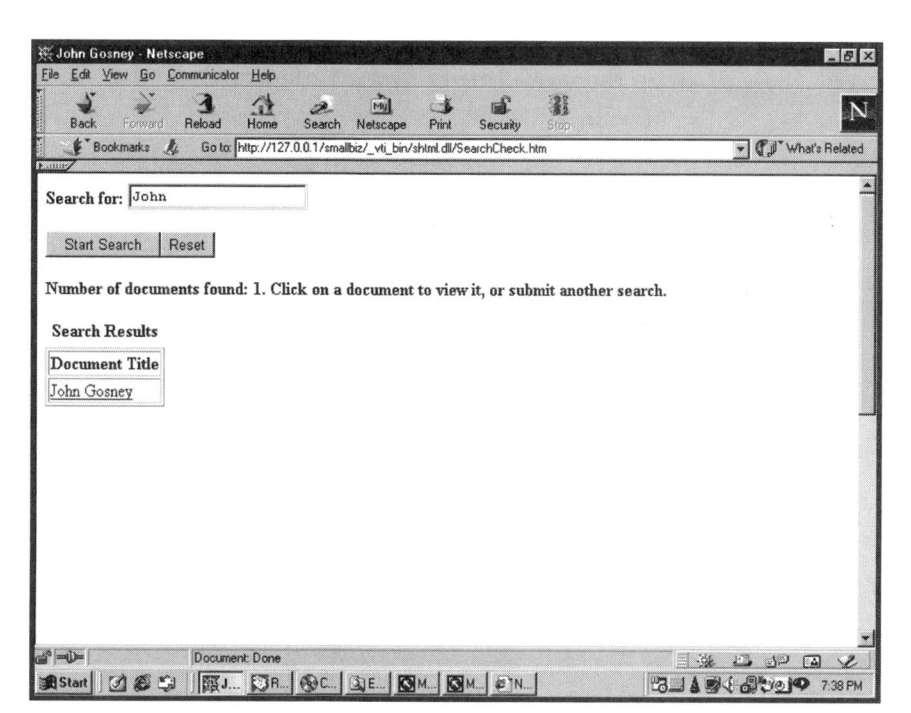

Figure 5.22

Your search results are displayed.

Take advantage of this powerful FrontPage component to provide your customers with a quick way to navigate through your Web site. They can then quickly search for the information in which they are most interested.

Session in Review

In this morning's short session, you've reviewed some easy ways to add powerful spice to your Web cooking.

- First, you learned how to validate forms on your Web site.
- Next, you integrated e-mail functionality into your FrontPage Web.
- Then, you learned to work with some DHTML effects to make your Web more dynamic.
- Finally, you added a Search feature to your page, so your customers can quickly locate the information for which they are searching.

Form validation, search forms, and e-mail are all essential components of a well-planned, customer-friendly Web site. Each of these features will ensure that you gather the information you require from your customers, keep them informed of their order status, and allow them to easily navigate your Web site.

This afternoon's session will provide a complete example of a Web-enabled small business Web site. So, take a break for now. Watch your favorite Sunday morning news program and when you come back it'll be time to pay a visit to the BestPop CD Shop.

SUNDAY AFTERNOON

Examining a Web-Enabled Small Business Example: BestPop CD Shop

- History of BestPop CD Shop
- Overview of the BestPop Web Site
- Examining the BestPop Database
- Analyzing the Pages
- Wrapping up with the BestPop Web Site

Throughout the weekend you have learned a variety of concepts (both organizational and technical) in regard to Web enabling your small business. You've looked at everything from how to build a simple Web page utilizing FrontPage to using more advanced dynamic Web techniques in which you allow your Web pages to interact with an Access database.

Along the way, you might have found yourself asking, "You know, this is all fine and good. But what I'd really like to see is a complete example of how I can use all this fancy technical stuff you're teaching me to get some real results!"

If you indeed were asking yourself that question, then I'm happy to report that I have an answer for you: a tangible, hands-on example is what this afternoon's session is all about. To give you a better idea of how this session is organized, take a quick look at how the discussion will move along:

- To begin the example, I'll give you some important background information on BestPop, in terms of the company history and what the owners wish to accomplish with their Web site.

- Next, you'll take a peek inside some organizational meetings that were held prior to implementing the BestPop Web site. Here, you'll discover the thought process behind the features of the site and, most importantly, how those features were integrated with the actual business processes of BestPop.

- Then, you'll dive into the actual, technical, functioning of the Web site. You'll take a look at the pages that comprise the BestPop Web site, as well as the underlying (Access) database that is used to make the site dynamic.
- Finally, you'll see a wrap-up of how the BestPop Web site has been designed to grow with the company. You'll also look at how the site is managed by its owners, in cooperation with their Web Presence Provider.

NOTE In case you haven't guessed, BestPop is a fictional company, despite my best intentions of someday opening a small music shop that specializes in providing only the finest rock 'n roll available. That said, take the example with a grain of salt, but be assured that the processes described in building the site are indicative of what you would go through to Web enable your own small business.

History of BestPop CD Shop

Back in 1996, Jim Lamoureux and Dugan Ballard, two friends, decided to fulfill a life-long dream of opening a small CD shop, specializing in rock 'n roll music. Jim and Dugan were both musicians and were also co-workers at a local music store. Having gotten frustrated with their jobs at the store, the two decided they could offer their town something it was desperately missing: a healthy dose of rock music (at the most affordable prices, of course).

Both had some business knowledge from their work experience and a few courses at the local college. That, in addition to having a lawyer friend, gave them all the tools they needed to open the shop. After the usual growing pains, the shop began to flourish. Not surprisingly, the local community college provided a well-informed, interested clientele for the BestPop merchandise. Moreover, since the shop was the only real CD store within several miles, it provided a convenient location for music lovers to grab the latest releases (as well as the classics) without driving into the larger city.

Flash-forward to 2000: BestPop has expanded into two locations (the second store opened in another college town within the state, about 75 miles away), and continues to experience solid business. However, Jim and Dugan realize that to provide the best service to their customers (not to mention an easy way of organizing inventory and general communication between their two stores), a Web presence is the next logical step in their business evolution.

Investigating the Web Construction Options

Since Jim was the more computer-savvy of the two partners (having used Quicken and Microsoft Excel to computerize much of the paperwork of the business), he was asked to take the lead in investigating the steps involved in building a Web site.

To begin, Jim arranged some meetings with a few local Web design firms to get a general idea of the time and cost involved in constructing a Web site. Going into the meetings, Jim was excited about bringing BestPop to the Web and was confident this could be accomplished quickly and cheaply. Unfortunately, upon returning from the meetings and reporting the results to Dugan, both partners were discouraged due to the following results:

- Although all the firms said they could build the site in a relatively quick time frame (about six weeks was the average), the cost was far beyond what BestPop expected to pay. Initial design of the site, including the underlying database structure, ranged from $20,000 at the low end to $28,000 at the high end.

- Even though the firms were courteous, all of them seemed to be *telling* Jim how to build his company's site, rather than listening to his ideas and specific needs. Although Jim was cognizant of his limited Web knowledge, he felt that he was quite competent with computers in general and had a strong business sense. Instead of giving him the impression they were interested in his ideas, their tone was, in general, patronizing and demeaning: "You don't worry about any of the technical stuff—it's above your head, anyway."

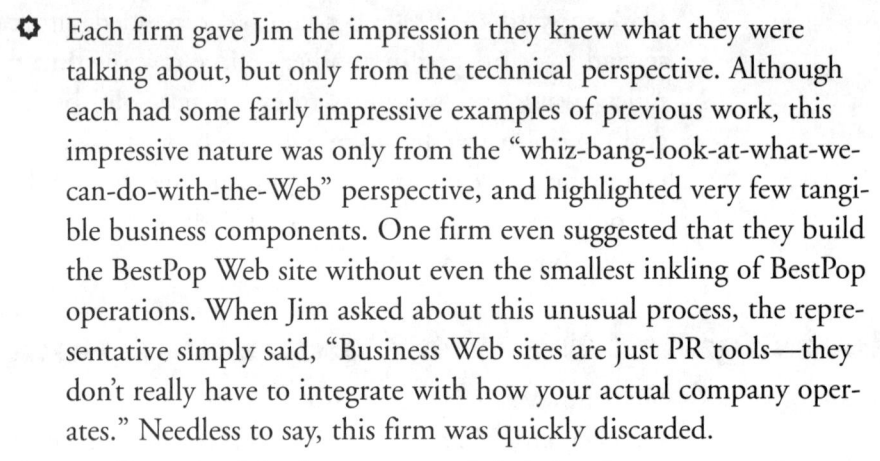

- Each firm gave Jim the impression they knew what they were talking about, but only from the technical perspective. Although each had some fairly impressive examples of previous work, this impressive nature was only from the "whiz-bang-look-at-what-we-can-do-with-the-Web" perspective, and highlighted very few tangible business components. One firm even suggested that they build the BestPop Web site without even the smallest inkling of BestPop operations. When Jim asked about this unusual process, the representative simply said, "Business Web sites are just PR tools—they don't really have to integrate with how your actual company operates." Needless to say, this firm was quickly discarded.

- Finally, each of the firms suggested that they have a continuing hand in how the BestPop Web site (and thus, by default, the company itself) would be maintained in the future. Again, although Jim didn't know much about how Web sites functioned, he was confident he wouldn't need some third-party company controlling part of his business just because BestPop now had a Web site.

Considering the Web Design Firm Suggestions

After meeting with a few consulting firms, Jim gathered his notes for review with Dugan. Although Jim was impressed with what the firms were able to perform from a technical perspective, he left each meeting with a wary feeling of being told how to run his company, and a lingering doubt about how he felt about investing so much time and money in a long-term commitment to a third-party.

After consulting with Dugan, the two partners decided against using a consulting firm to build their Web site, for a variety of reasons:

- The initial design costs were simply too much to swallow. When BestPop budgeted funds for their Web site, they were thinking, at most, of a $10,000 limit for design and implementation. However, the lowest bid of $20,000 fell far above the budgeted allotment. Even though the partners were impressed with what they saw, they just couldn't afford that kind of monetary commitment.

SUNDAY AFTERNOON Examining a Web-Enabled Small Business Example

> ### THE REAL STORY ON COMPUTER CONSULTING COMPANIES
>
> If, after reading about Jim and Dugan's findings, you were starting to think, "Geez! Are all Web design companies in cahoots with the devil himself?!," let me slow down your conspiracy-minded train of thought.
>
> While it's true that some consulting companies are only out to make a (very expensive) quick buck, the vast majority of such companies offer trained professionals with a ton of experience, who are ready, willing, and able to help your company with all its computing needs, Web site design or otherwise. Having been a consultant for a major consulting firm, I know the high degree of professionalism and experience these companies demand of their employees; consulting firms are a dime a dozen these days, and only the best survive. That said, the best have to be very, very good, and they usually are.
>
> However, this level of professionalism doesn't come inexpensively (and for good reason). As described here, many consultants have a lot of computer knowledge, but very little business knowledge. The bottom line is that e-commerce has exploded into today's business world and thus requires "computer guys" to be jacks of all trades (technically skilled, business savvy, masters of organization, and so on). No one is perfect, of course, so to demand that someone know all components of e-commerce might still be a bit too much to ask.
>
> That said, be wary of investing too much time and money on consulting firms when you can do much of the work yourself by using your own business savvy and the help of *Web Enable Your Small Business in a Weekend*!

- Being musicians themselves and having started (and maintained) their own business, both Jim and Dugan were very wary of being told how to incorporate their business processes into the functioning of their Web site. While they were willing to concede that they knew very little about Web design, Jim had constructed a simple Web page using FrontPage and knew that the basic mechanics were not above his technical ability. Moreover, although they respected the consultants' experience and skill in terms of Web design, the partners were fairly confident that they possessed greater business savvy. Maybe they didn't know the intricacies of e-commerce, but they most certainly knew the intricacies of their own business, which they considered the most important thing.

- Finally, when the idea for a BestPop Web site originated, the idea was to use a third party to build the site. That third party would then step aside when the site was up and running. But after speaking with the design firms, Jim noticed they were all hinting at continued involvement, including continuing to manage the technical functioning of the site (and thus, being involved in the day-to-day operations of BestPop). Jim and Dugan had started the company themselves and had made it into a successful operation, too. Again, although they weren't above considering outside involvement, they wanted control to remain firmly in their hands.

Building a Web Site on Their Own

Although the partners decided against using an outside consulting firm, they still wanted a Web site. Again, Jim was fairly computer savvy and had doodled around a bit with FrontPage, not to mention organizing much of BestPop's inventory with Access. So, he was confident he could build a functional site by himself.

Flash-forward again one month: BestPop has a functioning, dynamic, attractive Web site that dovetails with existing business processes. Furthermore, it is dynamic in that it interacts with an Access database. Best of all, Jim constructed the site on his own at very little cost, other than the initial minimal cost of establishing the site with a Web Presence Provider.

How did he do it? As he was browsing through the computer section in the local bookstore, he noticed a book entitled, *Web Enable Your Small Business In a Weekend*. By combining his intermediate knowledge of computers (especially Microsoft Office) with an interest in getting a site up and running, Jim was able to construct the BestPop Web site quickly and easily.

> **TIP** The rest of this afternoon's session will provide an analysis of the BestPop Web site, from design to function. Be sure to consult the enclosed CD-ROM for the actual files (including the database) used in this description.

Overview of the BestPop Web Site

Start by looking at Figure 6.1, which illustrates the BestPop home page, to get an idea of the kind of information and features that the site has to offer.

- **General information.** General information about the store (location and hours), as well as a history of BestPop CD Shop can be found within these links.

- **Online catalog search.** This option allows customers to browse through the BestPop inventory, searching by title or artist.

> **NOTE** The BestPop Web site is driven by a Microsoft Access database, which allows dynamic interaction with the site. A detailed look at this database, including its general structure and the type of information it stores, appears a bit later this afternoon, in the section, "Examining the BestPop Database."

- **Customer feedback.** These features include an electronic guest book where customers can leave their comments, as well as a form they can complete to join the BestPop mailing list.

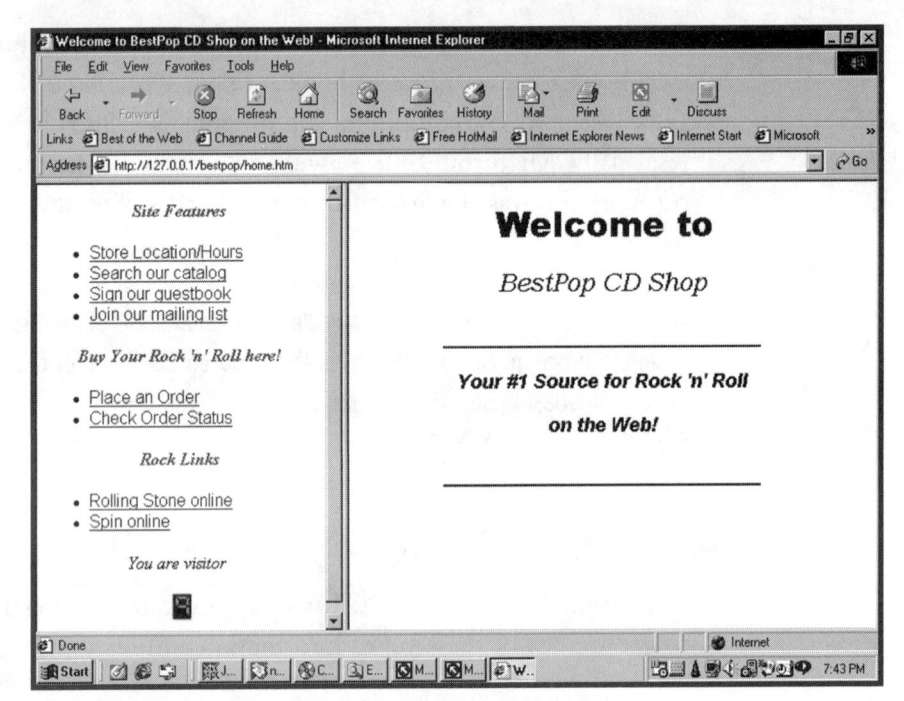

Figure 6.1

The BestPop home page

- **E-commerce features.** A great small business Web site will allow some amount of online commerce, and BestPop is no exception. Customers can place an order online, and also check the status of their orders.
- **Related links.** As another customer support feature, BestPop offers a few links to online rock magazines (*Rolling Stone* and *Spin*).

> **TIP**
> You should consider providing related subject links on your Web site, too. This increases the frequency at which customers will visit, since they know they will be presented with a list of related links in one convenient location—your site—rather than having to search through the Web to find them. It also allows you to serve as a kind of portal or kiosk for the particular industry you serve, which in turn increases traffic to your site.

SUNDAY AFTERNOON Examining a Web-Enabled Small Business Example

In order to demonstrate each of the features of the BestPop Web site, this afternoon's session will discuss each of these points in more detail. That way, you will see how the feature was constructed and how it integrates with other features on the BestPop site.

Looking at the BestPop Home Page Design

You should note from yesterday's discussion of frames that the BestPop home page uses frames. When viewed within the FrontPage editor, you can see that the home page consists of three distinct pages: homeleft.htm, homeright.asp, and home.htm (see Figure 6.2).

Take a closer look at these three pages:

○ **Home.htm.** This is the frame *container*, or the page that pulls the other two pages (homeleft.htm and homeright.asp) together to form the BestPop home page. You can see this clearly by looking at the HTML code that is used to build the BestPop home page.

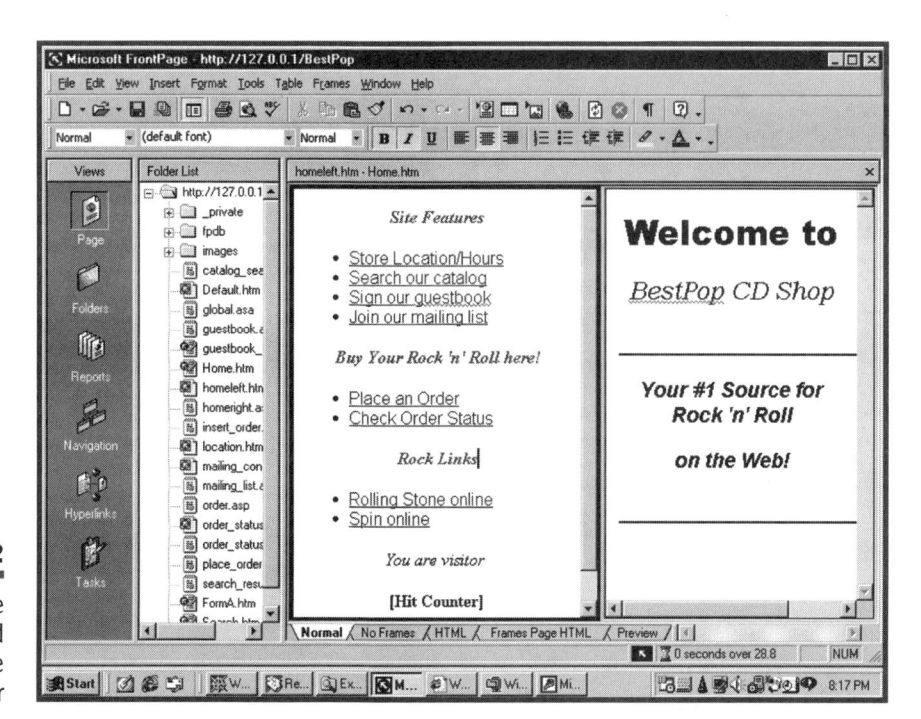

Figure 6.2

The BestPop home page, viewed within the FrontPage editor

1. If it's not already running, start FrontPage and open the Home.htm file from the CD-ROM. When the page opens in FrontPage, it should look similar to Figure 6.2.
2. Click the Frames Page HTML tab at the bottom of the window. You will see the HTML code behind the home.htm page, as shown in Figure 6.3.
3. By looking at the HTML code, you can see the two pages that are used to build the home.htm frames page (homeleft.htm and homeright.asp). Review yesterday's discussion of frames for more information about the mechanics of building frames pages.

- **Homeleft.htm.** This is the table of contents frame. If you look back at Figure 6.1, the left side of the window (where all the hyperlinks are) is the homeleft.htm page. When a link is clicked there, its contents are displayed in the right, or main, frame. Aside from the hyperlinks, homeleft.htm also uses a hit counter component so you and your customers can see how many people have visited the BestPop home page.

- **Homeright.asp.** This is the title page for the BestPop Web site. When different links are clicked in the left frame, their results are displayed in this frame.

> **TIP**
> Why the difference in file extensions (.htm versus .asp) between homeleft.htm and homeright.asp? You may remember that the .asp extension stands for Active Server Pages; you need to use Active Server Pages when retrieving information from or inserting information into your Access database. The BestPop designers have given the homeright page an .asp extension so that, in the future, they can pull information from a database directly into this page.

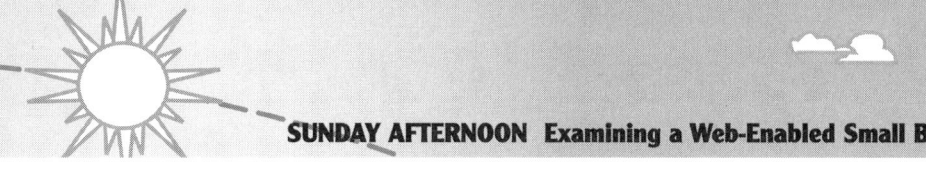

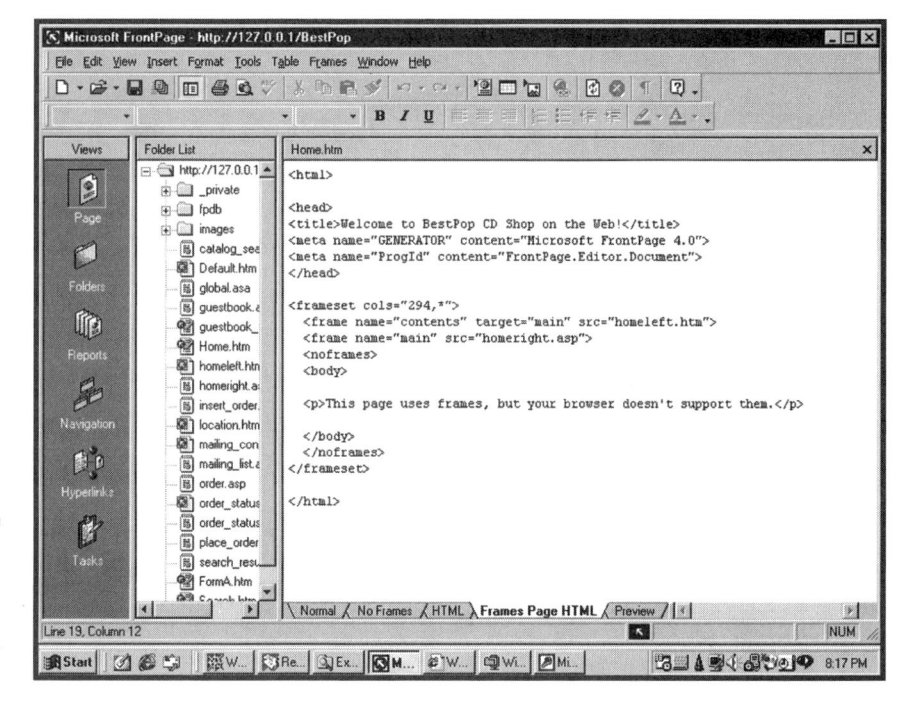

SUNDAY AFTERNOON Examining a Web-Enabled Small Business Example   201

Figure 6.3

Notice the two frame names (main and contents) and their associated src (source) pages.

As you move through your exploration of the BestPop Web site, experimenting with the functionality, feel free to tweak the pages to your liking. For example, you might want to change the appearance of the hit counter on homeleft.htm, or you might want to see if you can pull information from the underlying Access database into homeright.asp. Experiment all you want—the master copy of the site remains on your CD-ROM in case you get lost or want to restore the site to its original condition.

Examining the BestPop Database

Before you begin analyzing how the BestPop Web pages are designed, take a look at the Access database that makes the BestPop Web site dynamic, user-friendly, and ultimately quite powerful (see Figure 6.4).

Figure 6.4

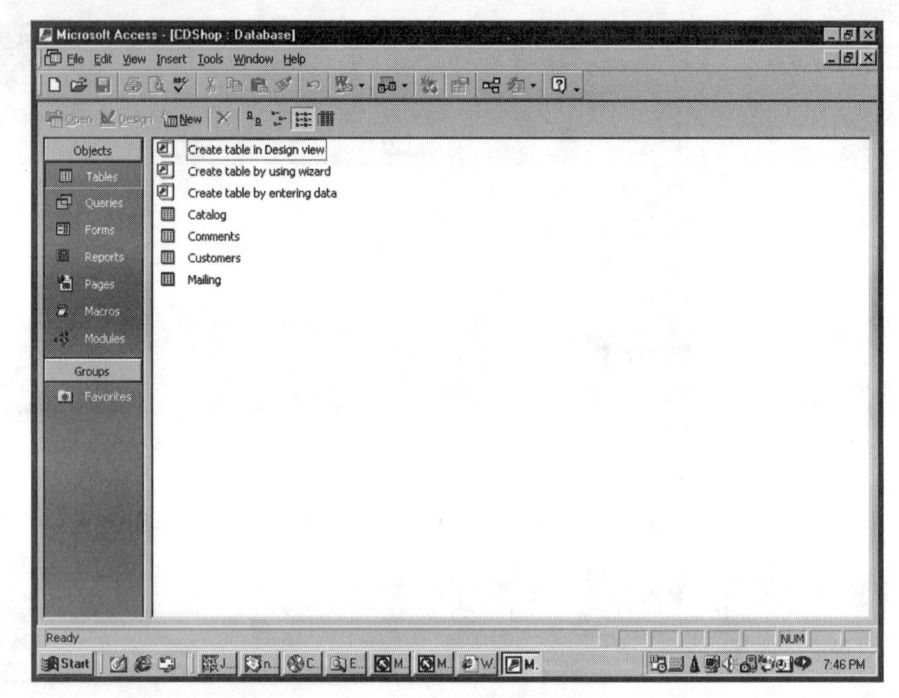

The BestPop database, as constructed with Microsoft Access 2000

> **TIP**
>
> Depending on the size of your Web site, you may want to consider asking your Web Presence Provider about using SQL Server as your database engine. SQL Server, a robust, full-featured production application, allows far more power and reliability (for high-volume Web sites, that is) than Access, which really wasn't designed for this type of usage.
>
> However, to get your feet wet and get your site up and running, Access is just fine. It is also a great way to introduce yourself to the world of databases and dynamic Web pages.

The BestPop database consists of the following tables:

- **Catalog.** The Catalog table is a current inventory of all CDs that BestPop carries. The table consists of four fields: ID, Artist, Title, and Price, as shown in Figure 6.5.

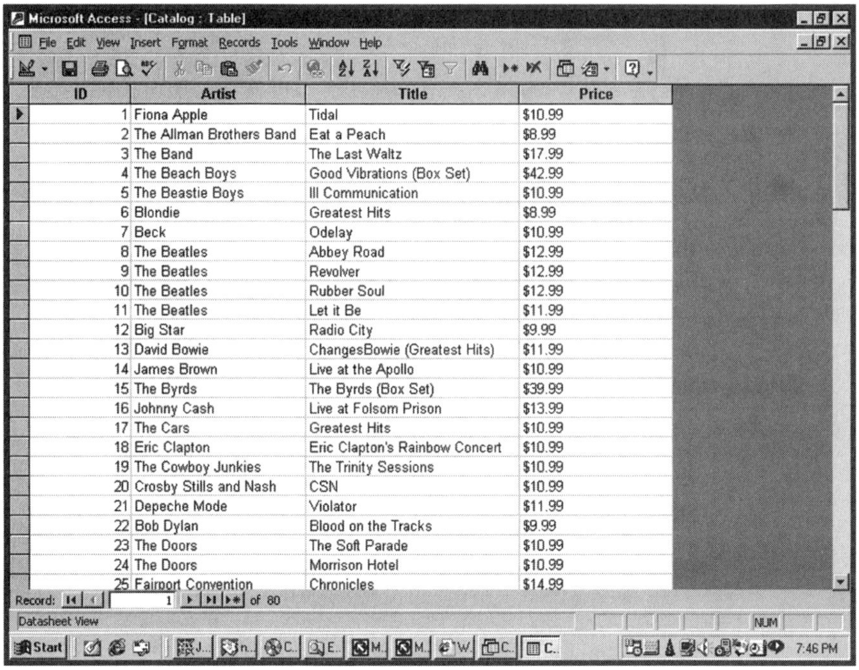

ID	Artist	Title	Price
1	Fiona Apple	Tidal	$10.99
2	The Allman Brothers Band	Eat a Peach	$8.99
3	The Band	The Last Waltz	$17.99
4	The Beach Boys	Good Vibrations (Box Set)	$42.99
5	The Beastie Boys	Ill Communication	$10.99
6	Blondie	Greatest Hits	$8.99
7	Beck	Odelay	$10.99
8	The Beatles	Abbey Road	$12.99
9	The Beatles	Revolver	$12.99
10	The Beatles	Rubber Soul	$12.99
11	The Beatles	Let it Be	$11.99
12	Big Star	Radio City	$9.99
13	David Bowie	ChangesBowie (Greatest Hits)	$11.99
14	James Brown	Live at the Apollo	$10.99
15	The Byrds	The Byrds (Box Set)	$39.99
16	Johnny Cash	Live at Folsom Prison	$13.99
17	The Cars	Greatest Hits	$10.99
18	Eric Clapton	Eric Clapton's Rainbow Concert	$10.99
19	The Cowboy Junkies	The Trinity Sessions	$10.99
20	Crosby Stills and Nash	CSN	$10.99
21	Depeche Mode	Violator	$11.99
22	Bob Dylan	Blood on the Tracks	$9.99
23	The Doors	The Soft Parade	$10.99
24	The Doors	Morrison Hotel	$10.99
25	Fairport Convention	Chronicles	$14.99

Figure 6.5

The Catalog table

- **Comments.** The Comments table allows customers to provide feedback on the site. The table consists of eight fields: RecNum, FirstName, LastName, Address, City, State, Zip, and Comments (see Figure 6.6).
- **Customers.** When a customer wishes to place an order request online, they are asked to make an entry into the Customers table (see Figure 6.7). This table consists of seven fields: ID, LastName, FirstName, Product_ID, Email, Title, and Date.
- **Mailing.** The Mailing table is where information is stored once the customer completes the form to join the BestPop mailing list (see Figure 6.8). This table consists of eight fields: RecNum, FirstName, LastName, Address, City, State, Zip, and Email.

This is a relatively simple database, but when integrated with the BestPop Web site (through the power of FrontPage, of course!), it can produce some really powerful results.

Figure 6.6

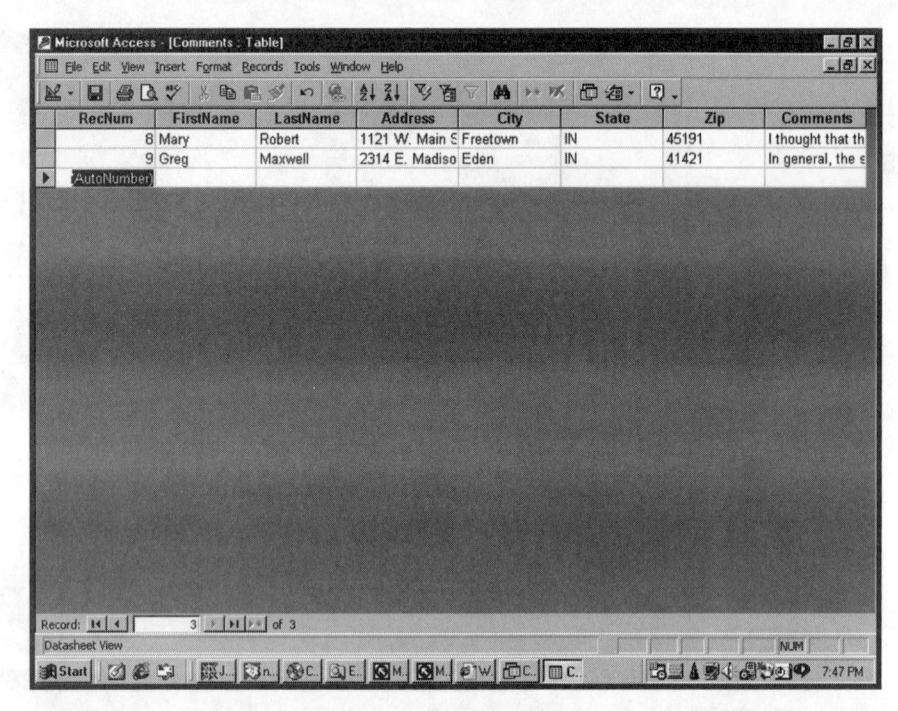

The Comments table

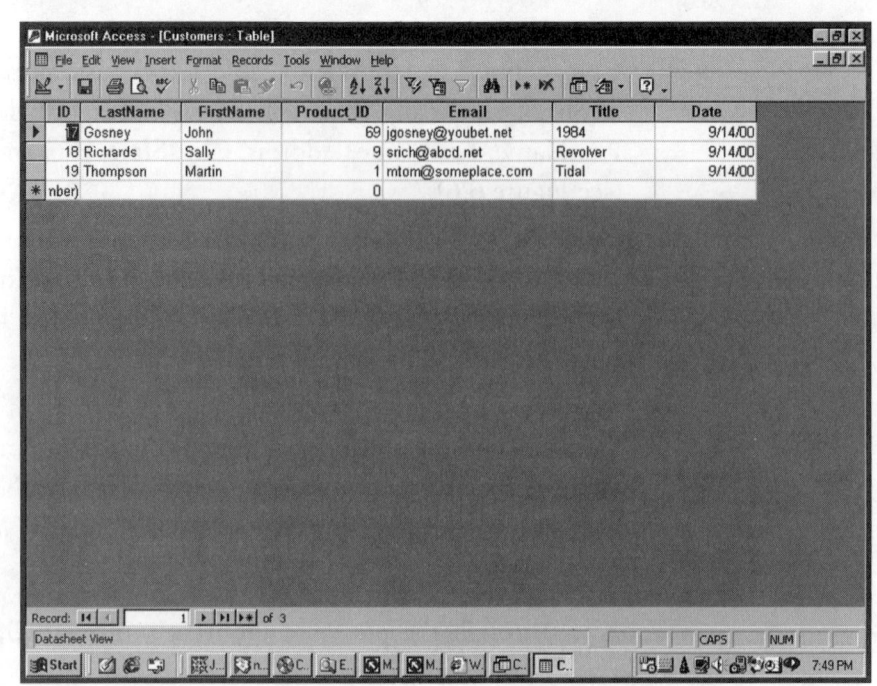

Figure 6.7

The Customers table

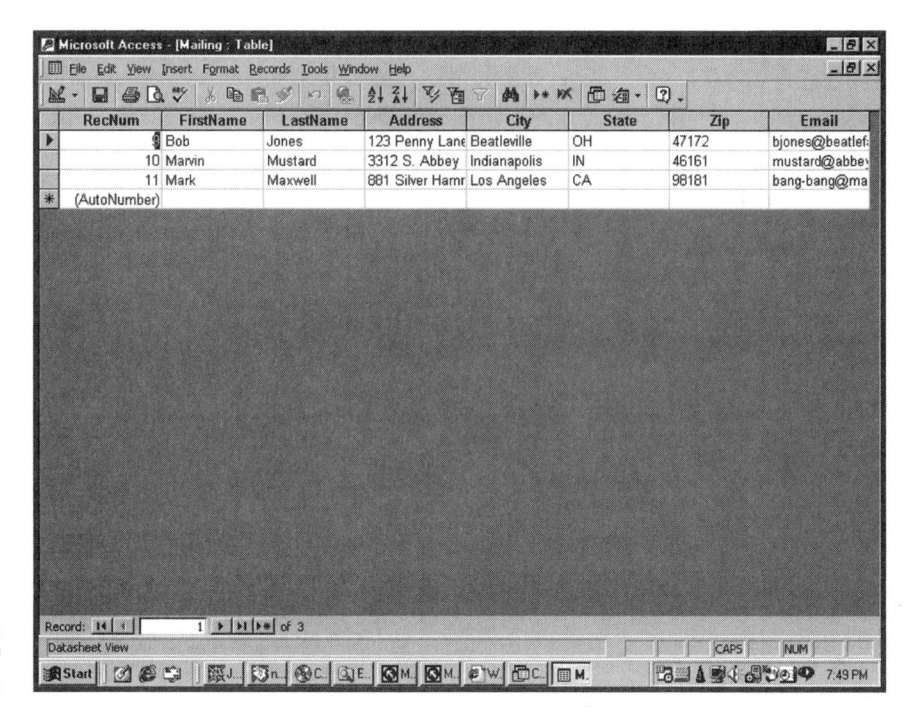

SUNDAY AFTERNOON Examining a Web-Enabled Small Business Example **205**

Figure 6.8

The Mailing table

As you move through the discussion of each page and feature of the BestPop Web site (especially those that interact with the database), I'll offer a detailed explanation of how each field in the respective tables stores information. I'll also let you know, in general, how the relational nature of the individual tables work together to produce the functionality you see in the BestPop Web.

> **NOTE** Obviously, with a production Web site (one that is in use), there will be far more records stored within the tables than are illustrated in this example. After all, a typical record store of the BestPop type would have thousands of items and not just the 80 individual titles listed in the Catalog table. These small numbers are designed for demonstration purposes only. Don't think that your database has to be this small to be functional—there's plenty of room to grow within a typical Access database.

Web Enable Your Small Business In a Weekend

> **TIP**
>
> In order to get the BestPop site to function on your computer, you'll not only need to load the site into a FrontPage Web named BestPop, but you'll also need to establish an ODBC connection to the database. Refer back to last night's session if you need a refresher on how to establish this connection.

Analyzing the location.htm Page

The location.htm page provides basic store information about BestPop, including store hours, contact information, and directions for how get to the two stores (see Figure 6.9).

This page is a straightforward HTML page with a bit of formatting, but it contains primarily unformatted text. Notice how the link for this page is constructed on the homeleft.htm page.

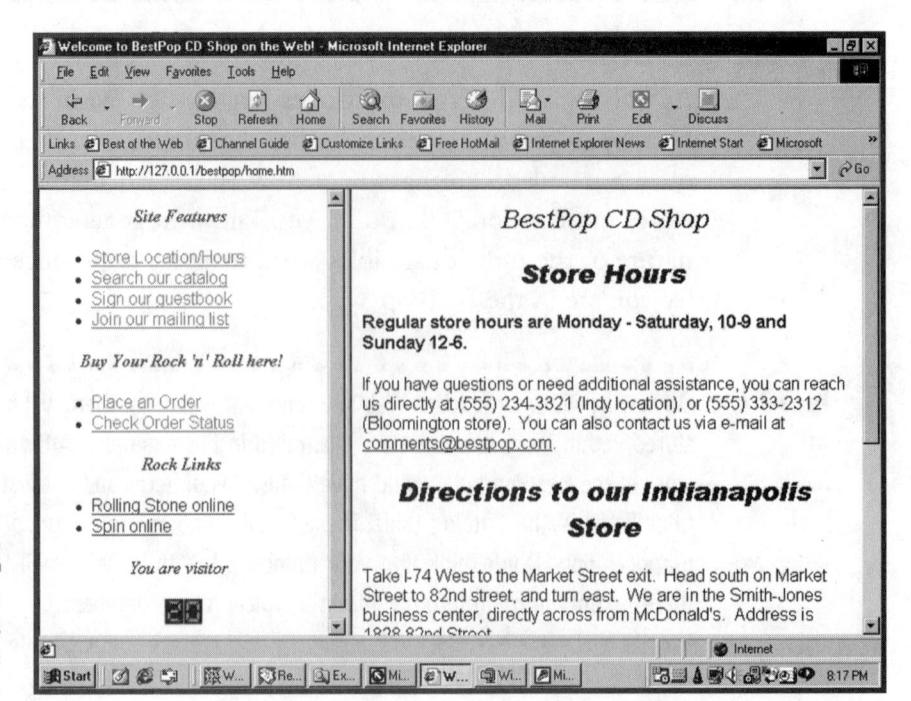

Figure 6.9

The location.htm page provides general store information.

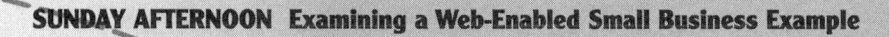

SUNDAY AFTERNOON Examining a Web-Enabled Small Business Example   **207**

1. Load home.htm into FrontPage. Place your cursor on the Store Location/Hours hyperlink. Right-click, and from the shortcut menu, choose Hyperlink Properties. The Edit Hyperlink dialog box appears, as shown in Figure 6.10.
2. Notice the full URL for location.htm (http://127.0.0.1/bestpop/location.htm). Also, notice that the Target Frame location is set to main. Click the icon that appears to the right of the Target Frame box. This displays the Target Frame dialog box, as shown in Figure 6.11.

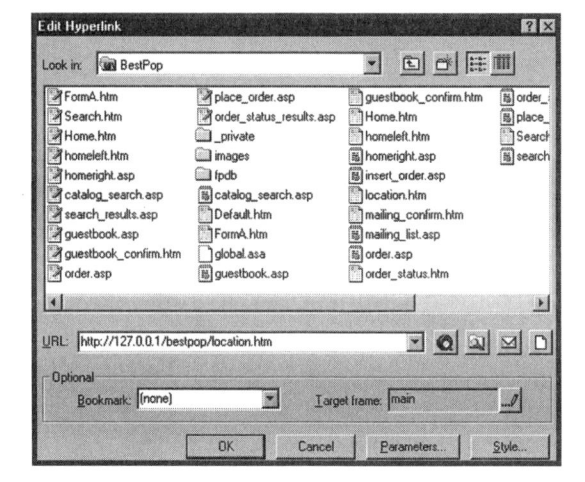

Figure 6.10

The Edit Hyperlink dialog box

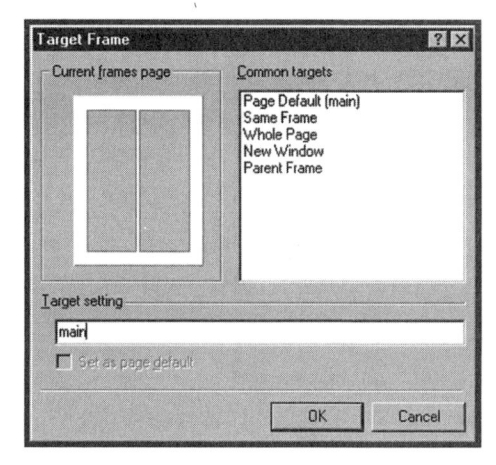

Figure 6.11

The Target Frame dialog box

3. You can see that the Target setting is set to main. This means that when you click on the location.htm hyperlink in the left frame, the results of this action will display in the right, or main, frame.

4. To see what happens when you change this target setting, set the target setting to contents by clicking in the left frame of the Current Frames Page graphic, as shown in Figure 6.12.

5. Click OK to close the Target Frame dialog box, then click OK again to close the Edit Hyperlink dialog box. Save main.htm to capture your changes and reload main.htm in your Web browser.

6. Now, click on the Store Location/Hours hyperlink. Rather than displaying in the right, or main, frame, it is displayed in the left, or contents, frame, as shown in Figure 6.13.

7. For now, go back into FrontPage and home.htm, and change the Target setting of this link back to main. You should notice, though, how easy it is to change the Target setting of a hyperlink with a frames page. Save and reload the page, then click again on the Location/Hours hyperlink. Now, the information loads in the main, or right, frame, as shown in Figure 6.14.

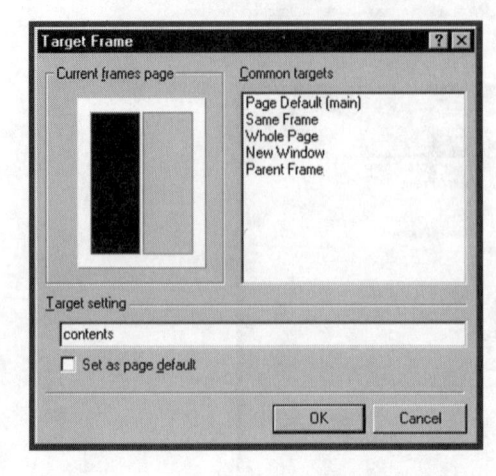

Figure 6.12

Changing the target setting of a frames hyperlink.

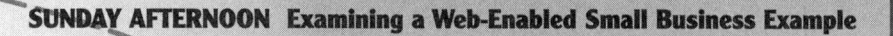

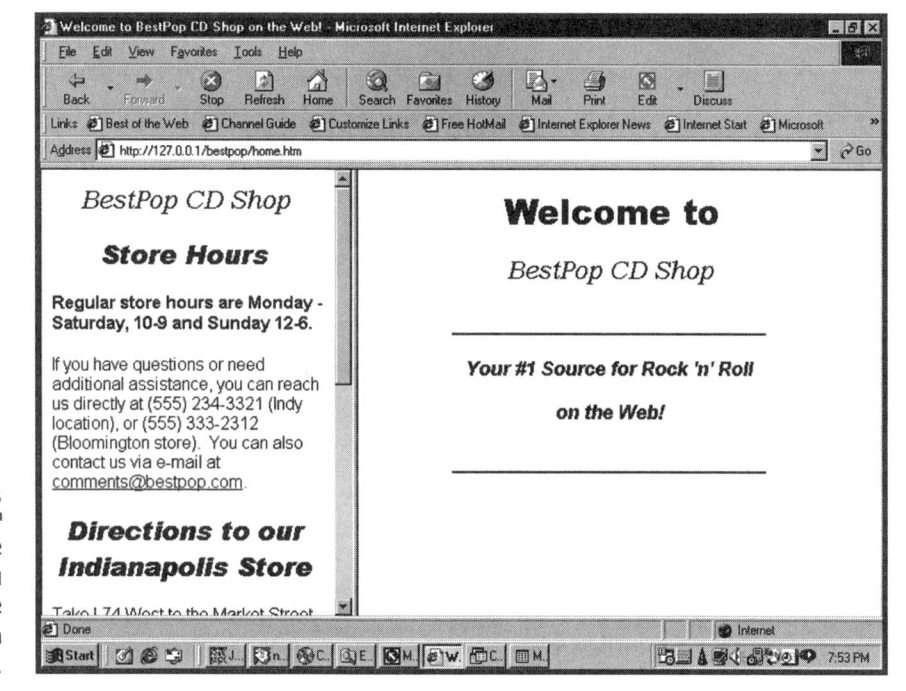

SUNDAY AFTERNOON Examining a Web-Enabled Small Business Example   209

Figure 6.13

By editing the target setting, you can change the location to which a hyperlink points.

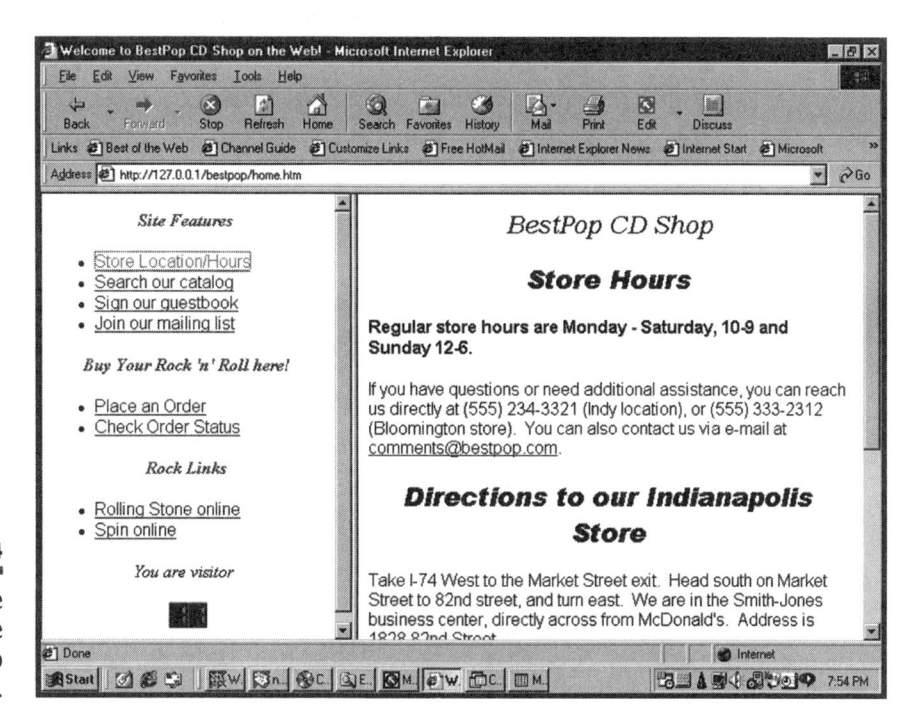

Figure 6.14

The hyperlinks are pointing from the contents frame to the main frame.

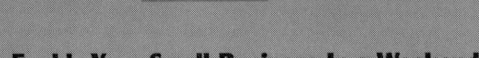

Notice that all the hyperlinks in the left frame point to the main frame. This is done to give the left frame a table of contents feel, with all subsequent information being presented in the right, or main, frame.

Analyzing the catalog_search.asp and search_results.asp Pages

The next hyperlink in the contents frame is entitled, "Search our catalog." This page utilizes the FrontPage database component to allow customers to search through the Access database (see Figures 6.15 and 6.16).

How does this page work? Here's how it was constructed:

1. Open catalog_search.asp in FrontPage, as shown in Figure 6.17.
2. Double-click in the text box. You'll see that the name of this field is Artist. Now click on the Validate button. You should see that the

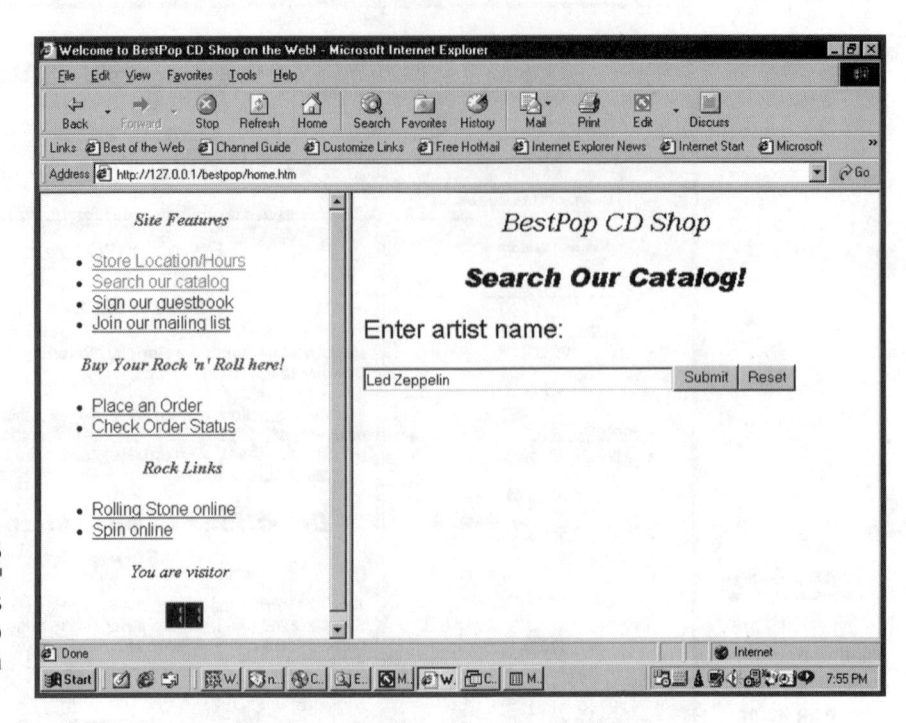

Figure 6.15

BestPop allows their customers to search through a current catalog...

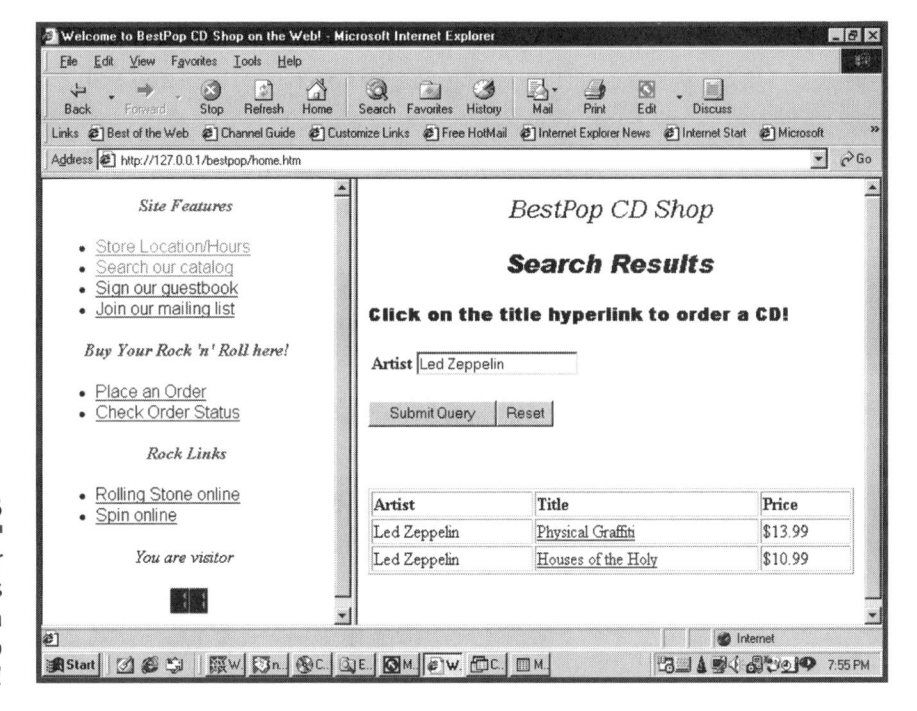

SUNDAY AFTERNOON Examining a Web-Enabled Small Business Example   **211**

Figure 6.16

...and have their search results displayed with a direct hyperlink to the order page!

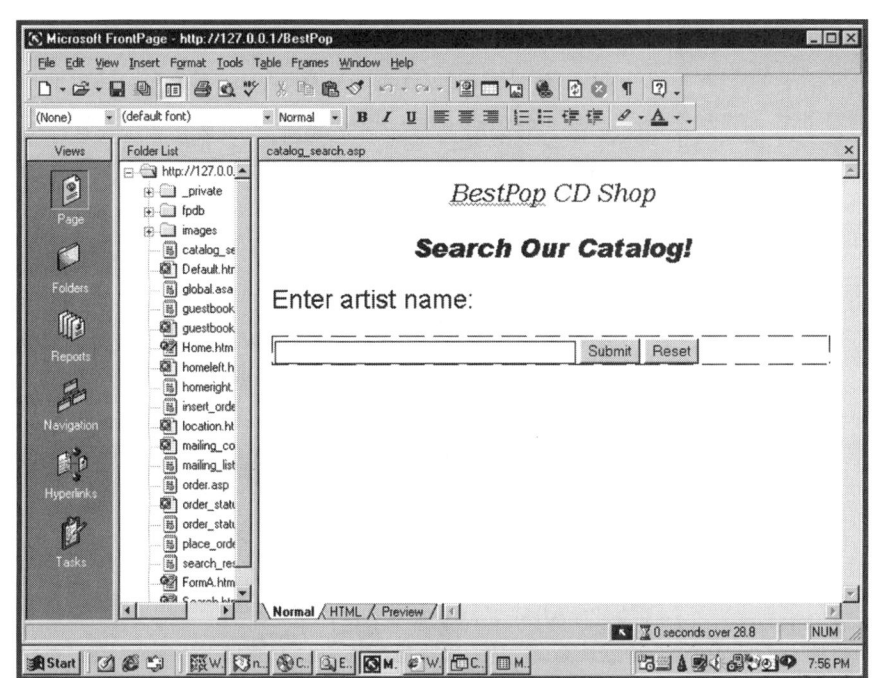

Figure 6.17

Catalog_search.asp uses a simple one-line text box.

Data length property has been set to Required. As you learned this morning, setting this property to Required will force the user to enter a search string.

3. Now, right-click inside the form (but not within the form field itself) and choose Form properties from the shortcut menu. Click the Options button to access the Options for Custom Form Handler dialog box (see Figure 6.18). It is within this dialog box that the target is set for the form, in this case, the search results page, search_results.asp.

4. That's it for search_catalog.asp. The real action takes place on the search results page, so look at that now. Open search_results.asp within FrontPage (see Figure 6.19).

5. Examine more closely what is happening on this page. Right-click within the table (the database results component) and choose Database Results Properties from the shortcut menu. The Database Results Wizard appears, as shown in Figure 6.20.

6. Notice that the database connection is named Database1. Click Next. The Catalog table was chosen as the record source, as this is the table to be queried (because the Catalog table is where the BestPop inventory is stored).

7. Click Next again. You should be looking at Step 3 of the Wizard. Now, click the More Options button, and you will see the More Options dialog box, shown in Figure 6.21.

8. Notice the text that is displayed if a match does not exist for the search criteria—"No records match your search term." Now, click the Criteria button to display the Criteria dialog box, shown in Figure 6.22.

Figure 6.18

Specifying where the search_catalog.asp page should point

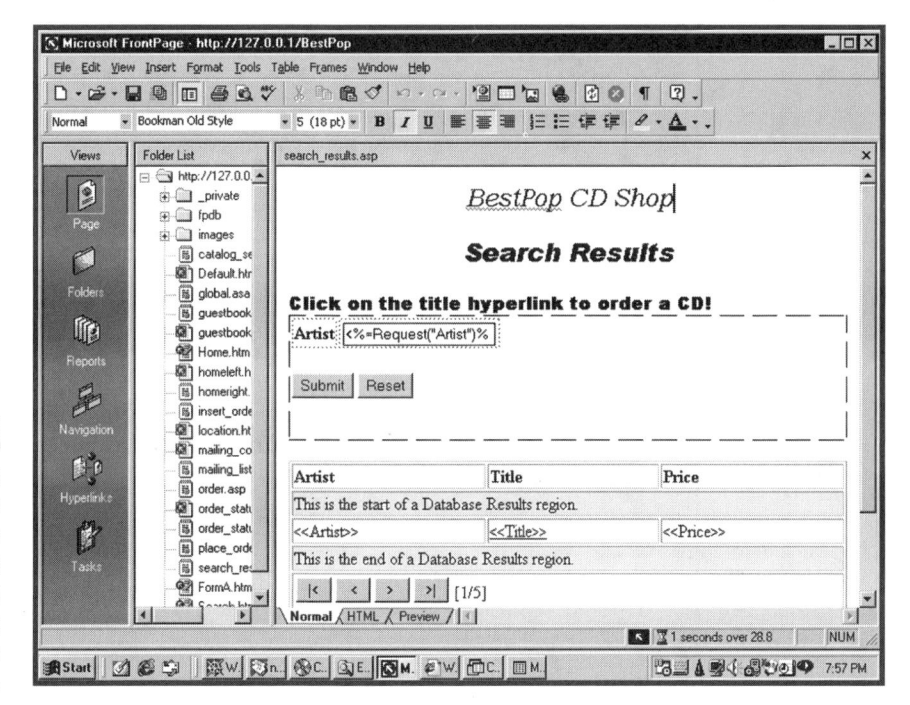

SUNDAY AFTERNOON Examining a Web-Enabled Small Business Example   213

Figure 6.19

The search_results.asp page uses the database results component to display information directly from the database.

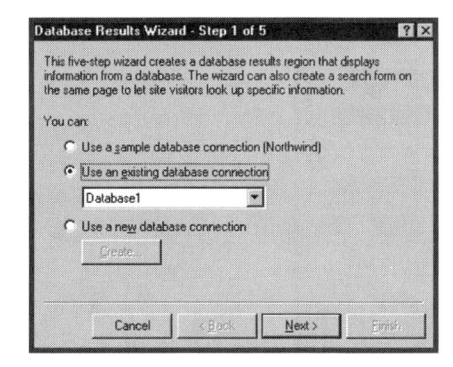

Figure 6.20

The Database Results Wizard makes it easy to pull information from a database into your Web pages.

9. Click the word Artist to select this criterion, then click Modify to view how this search criterion was established (see Figure 6.23).

10. By looking at Figure 6.23, you can see that the Artist field in the Catalog table is the field being queried. The Contains comparison is used so that any match between what the customer entered in

Figure 6.21

Search criteria and other properties related to the search are specified here.

Figure 6.22

The Criteria dialog box specifies how the search term entered by the customer should be used when searching through the Catalog table of the database.

Figure 6.23

By using this simple dialog box, you can build your query of the database, using the customer's entered search term.

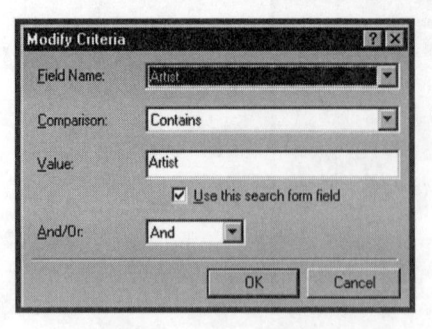

the Artist search field (back on catalog_search.asp) and values contained within the Artist field of the Catalog table will be returned as matches.

11. Click OK until you return to Step 3 of the Wizard, then click Next. The final two steps of the Wizard are used to determine how the search results are displayed.

SUNDAY AFTERNOON Examining a Web-Enabled Small Business Example   215

You should look at one other thing to see the real power of this search page. If you examine Figure 6.24, you'll notice that the titles of the matching records are hyperlinks. Within your Web browser, rest your mouse pointer over one of these titles and look at the status bar. You'll notice that, along with the usual page pointed to by the hyperlink, there is an addition to the end of the hyperlink.

If you open the Catalog table in the CDShop database and scroll down to record number 36, you'll see that the ID field is indeed 36, and it corresponds to the selected title ("Houses of the Holy"), as shown in Figure 6.25.

Why is this important? By including the ID and Title fields within the hyperlink, you can quickly reference the returned record on another page—in the case of the BestPop site, the Order page. This means you don't have to ask your customers to do another search to find the item of interest, because you can simply carry over the returned record of interest to another page.

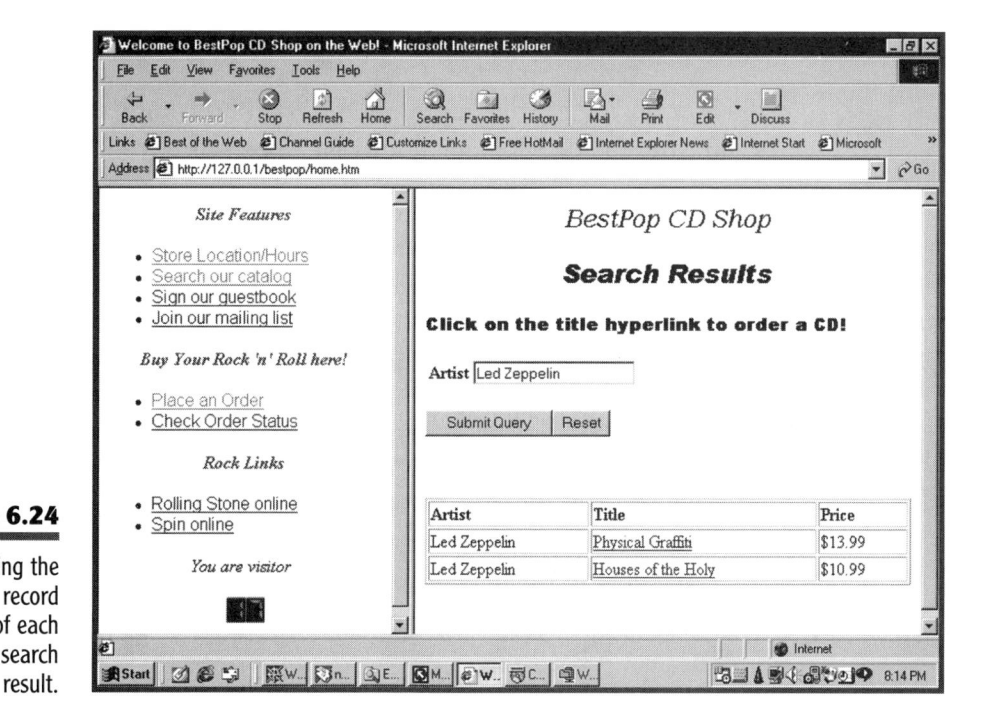

Figure 6.24

Specifying the unique record number of each returned search result.

Figure 6.25

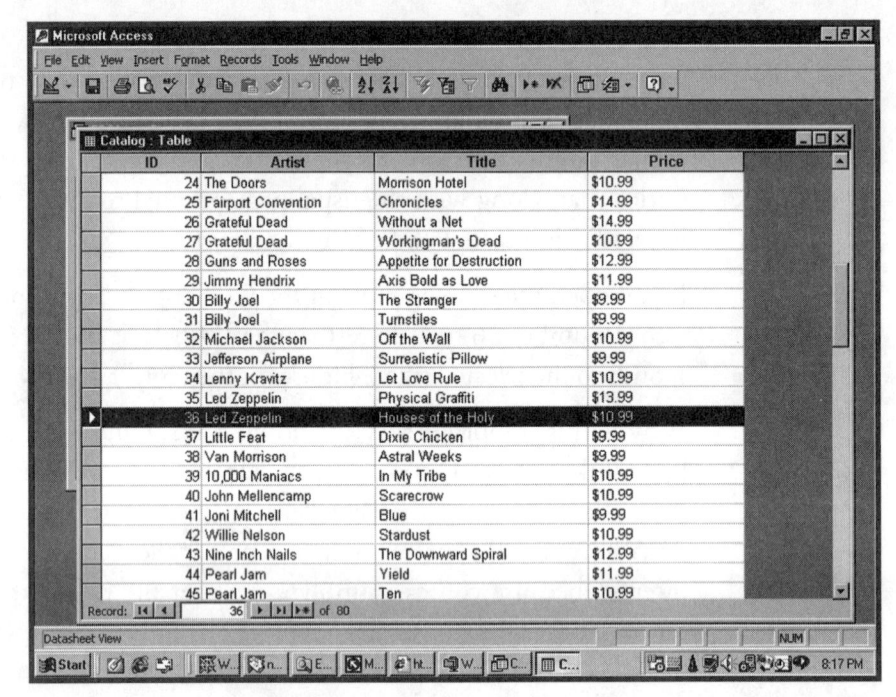

The ID number displayed in the hyperlink matches the returned record's title.

So how do you get that unique identifier (in this case, the value of the ID field from the Catalog table) into the hyperlink?

1. Go back into FrontPage and bring search_results.asp to the forefront. Right-click on the blue, underlined Title text, and choose Hyperlink Properties from the shortcut menu. The Edit Hyperlink dialog box appears.

2. Click the Parameters button to display the Hyperlink Parameters dialog box, shown in Figure 6.26.

3. In the Path field, the page to which the Title hyperlink will point is entered (in this case, the order form for BestPop). The value in the Query String field indicates that the ID and Title fields should be included in the hyperlink and that its value should be assigned the corresponding match from the Catalog table.

Figure 6.26

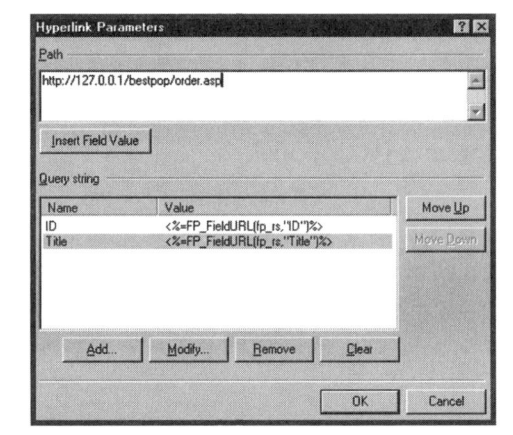

The Hyperlink Parameters dialog box

4. Click the ID text within the Query String field to select it, then click the Modify button. The Modify Parameter dialog box appears, as shown in Figure 6.27.

5. The items listed in the Name drop-down menu are all the field names from the Catalog table, while the items in the Value drop-down menu correspond with their returned values. In this case, the value for the ID field is 36, as that matches the value of the ID field for our selected search result (the "Houses of the Holy" title).

6. Repeat this process for the Title field; in other words, go back to the Hyperlinks Parameters dialog box (shown in Figure 6.26), and click the Title text within the Query String field to select it. Then, click the Modify button to view the parameters that have been set for the Title field.

Figure 6.27

The Modify Parameter dialog box allows you to specify your query string values (in this case, the ID value).

You'll see further how this query string ID and Title value comes into play during the discussion of the Order page. For now, take note of this important feature and realize its usefulness as it enables you to reference a returned search item on additional pages.

> **TIP**
> Feeling a bit overwhelmed by all this talk of Database Results Wizards and query strings? If so, take a breather and review last night's session for a refresher on this topic.

Take a Break!

This analysis of the BestPop Web site is getting pretty deep. Take a quick break and when you get back, be ready to finish up the initial exploration of how each of the pages function.

Analyzing the guestbook.asp and guestbook_confirm.htm Pages

Welcome back. As you know, the ever-present guest book is a popular method of gathering feedback in a variety of environments (business seminars, weddings, funerals...you name it). Wherever a desire exists to capture the names of individuals who were in attendance for an event, you can be sure to find a guest book nearby.

The Web is no exception. BestPop has decided to provide a guest book feature so customers can leave comments (anonymously, if they wish) about their experiences with the site. This is accomplished through guestbook.asp.

Working with the guestbook.asp Page

Building a guest book page like the one displayed in Figures 6.28 and 6.29 is incredibly easy. Here's how it's done!

SUNDAY AFTERNOON Examining a Web-Enabled Small Business Example 219

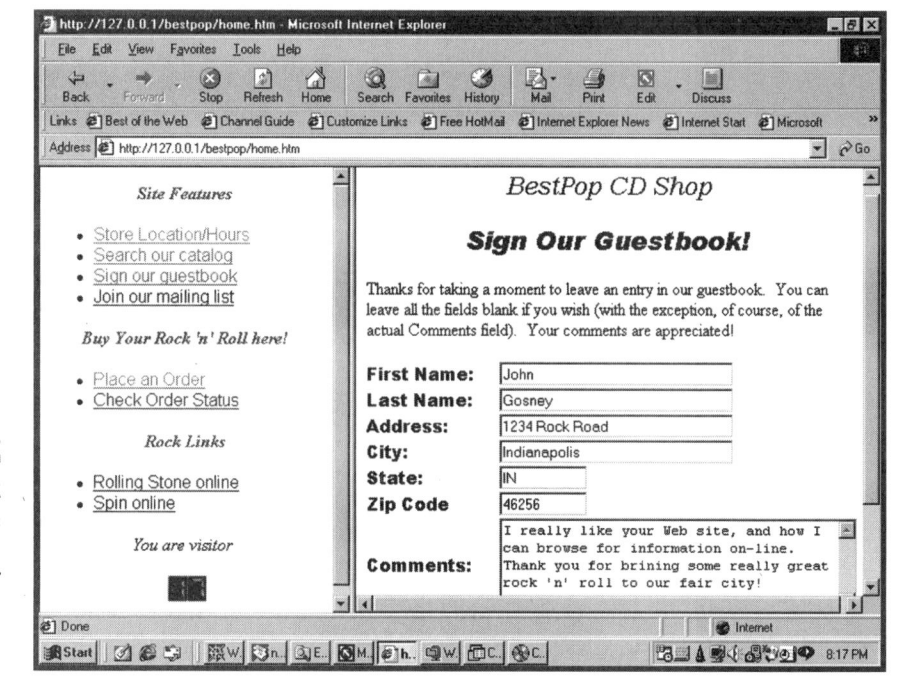

Figure 6.28

The guest book page of the BestPop Web site. Customers enter their comments, click Submit, and then...

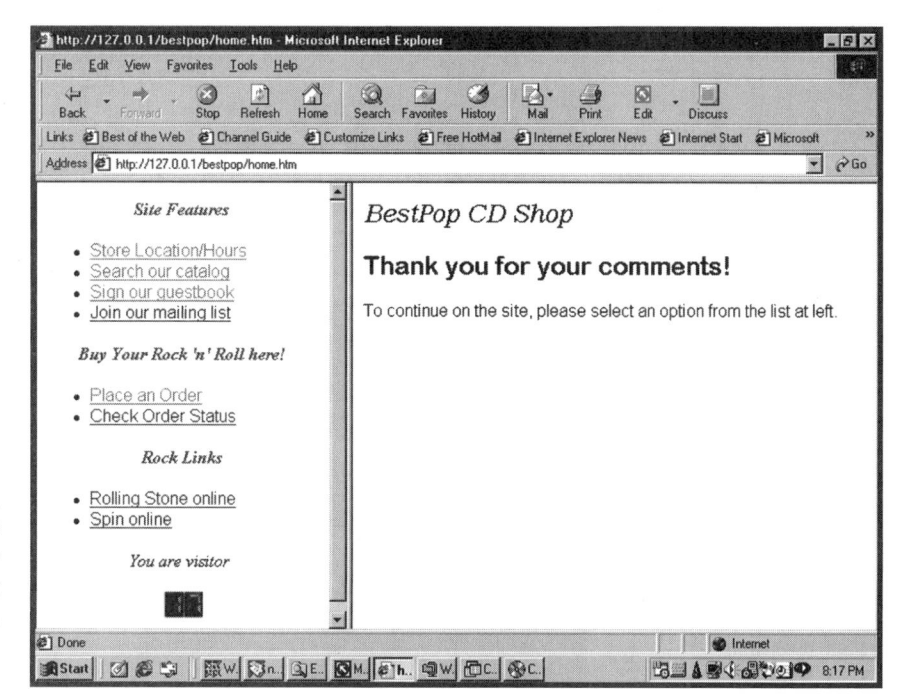

Figure 6.29

...receive a friendly confirmation that their comments have been recorded.

1. Within FrontPage, open the guestbook.asp page. The page consists of some explanatory text at the top and then several form fields (such as first name, last name, and so on), which are used to capture information from the customer (see Figure 6.30).

2. Open the CDShop database and view the Comments table in Design View. You will see that the guestbook.asp page has a form element to match each field (with the exception of RecNum, which is an AutoNumber field) of the Comments table (see Figure 6.31).

    If you examine the properties for each form field, you will notice that the BestPop designers have given them the same names as their corresponding fields in the Comments table. This identical naming comes in handy when you go to insert data, as you'll see in just a moment.

3. To see how the information entered by the customer is inserted in the Comments table, right-click within the form and choose Form Properties from the shortcut menu that appears. When the dialog box appears, notice that the Send to Database option is selected.

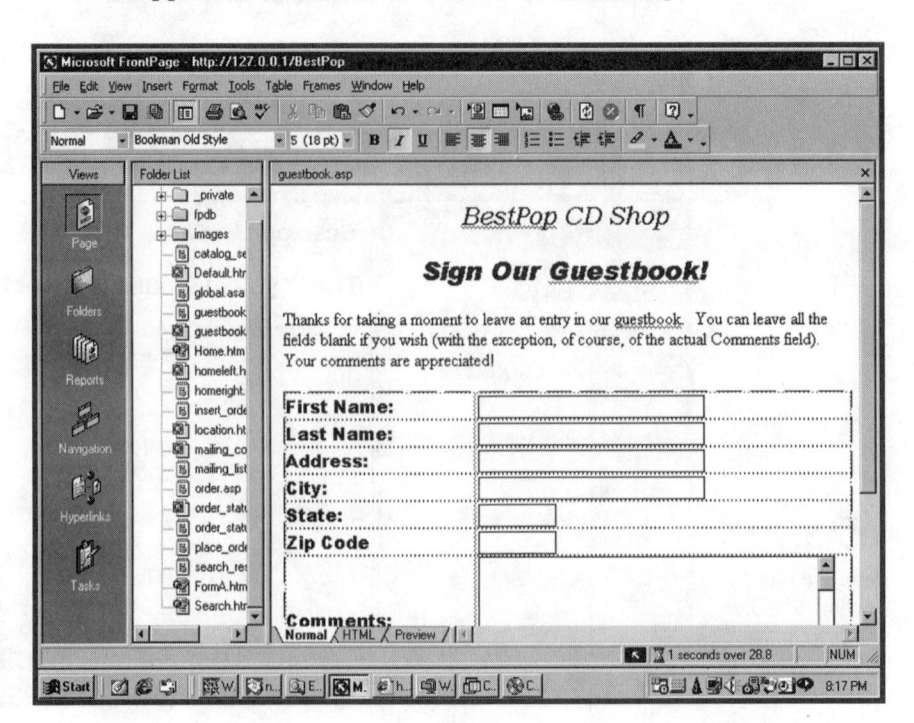

Figure 6.30

The guestbook.asp page opened in FrontPage

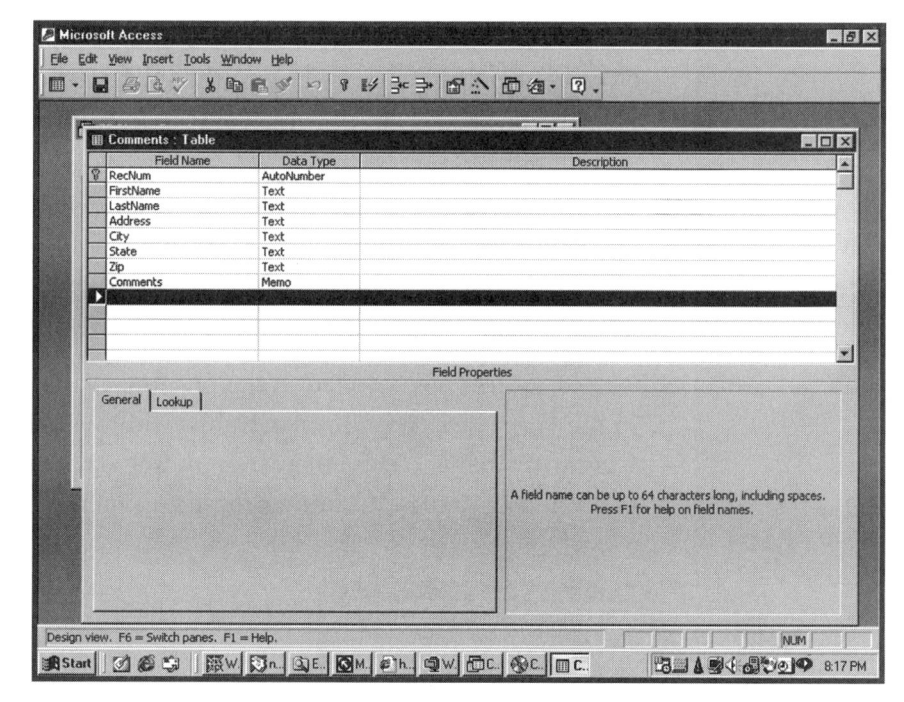

SUNDAY AFTERNOON Examining a Web-Enabled Small Business Example   **221**

Figure 6.31

The Comments table, opened in Design View in Microsoft Access 2000

4. Click the Options button to display the Options for Saving Results to Database dialog box, shown in Figure 6.32.

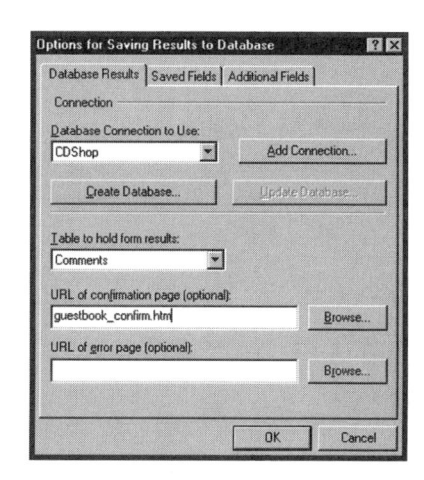

Figure 6.32

Set specific options regarding inserting customers' comments into the database in this dialog box.

5. Notice that the Table to Hold Form Results option is set to the Comments table. Also notice that the URL of the confirmation page has been set to guestbook_confirm.htm (more on this page in a minute).

6. Click the Saved Fields tab to display the form fields whose values will be inserted into the Comments table (see Figure 6.33).

7. Select the Address Form Field, then click Modify. This displays the Modify Field dialog box, shown in Figure 6.34.

8. The form field you selected in the previous dialog box appears here in the Form Field box. To match this field to a field within the Comments table, choose its corresponding database table field from the Save to Database Column drop-down menu.

Figure 6.33

By mapping form fields to specific database table fields, you can be sure that the information entered by the customer is correctly recorded within the database.

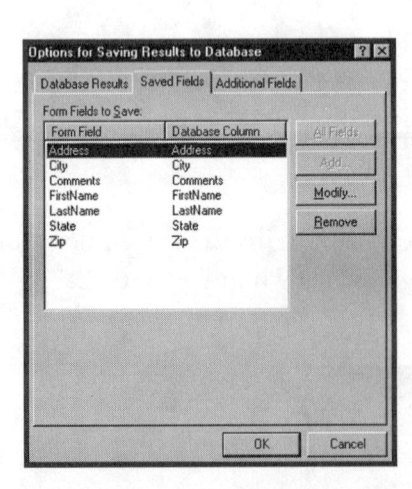

Figure 6.34

Use the Modify Field dialog box to match form fields in the guestbook.asp page with corresponding fields in the Comments table of the database.

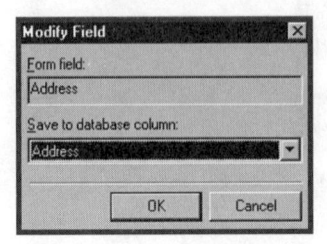

9. To capture all information entered by the customer, you'll need to match each form field with a corresponding database field. If you look again at Figure 6.33, you can see that each field on the guestbook.asp page has been matched with a corresponding field in the Comments table of the database.

10. To see this in action, load the guestbook.asp page into your Web browser. Fill out the form, making sure you enter at least some text in the Comments field (if you don't, you'll get an error message, asking you to enter something). Click Submit and you should then be presented with the guestbook_confirm.htm confirmation page, as illustrated in Figure 6.29.

Understanding the guestbook_confirm.htm Page

This page is a simple confirmation page, used to show customers that their comments have been recorded (see Figure 6.35). Be sure to use these confirmation pages whenever you ask customers to provide information. A friendly confirmation page is not only good net-etiquette, but it also provides customers with peace of mind, knowing that their (sometimes confidential) information has been submitted in good faith.

Analyzing the mailing_list.asp and mailing_confirm.htm Pages

The mailing list page is nearly identical to the guest book page, with the exception that all fields are required on the mailing_list.asp page. In addition, a field for the customer's e-mail address is also included (see Figure 6.36).

The functionality of this page is nearly identical to that of guestbook.asp, so an extended discussion of how this page was constructed is not included here.

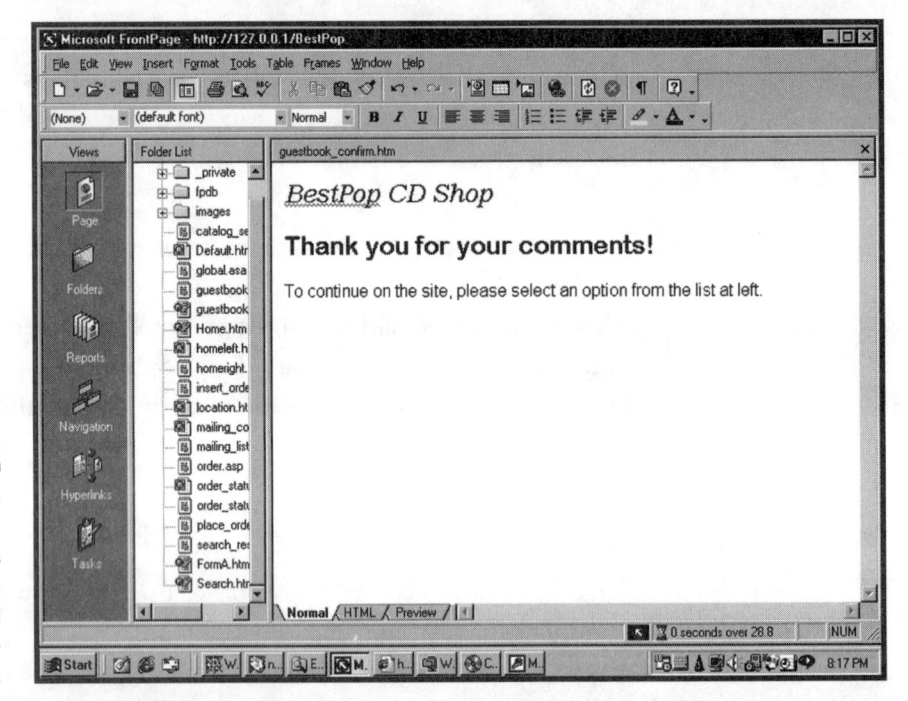

Figure 6.35

The guestbook_confirm.htm page, as viewed within FrontPage, is coded with straightforward HTML.

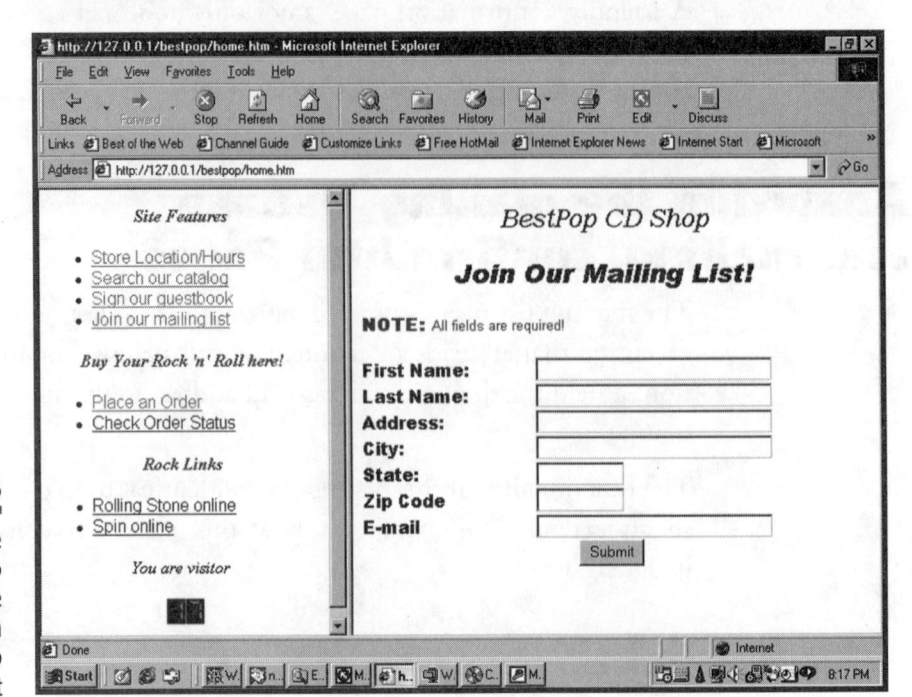

Figure 6.36

The mailing_list.asp page, where customers can join the BestPop mailing list

After they complete the mailing_list.asp form, the mailing_confirm.htm page provides verification to customers that they have been added to the BestPop mailing list (see Figure 6.37). It functions much like the guestbook_confirm.htm page.

Just a reminder of the simple rule with confirmation pages: Use them! Customers will appreciate knowing your system is working properly, and that the information they have taken the time to enter has been recorded.

Analyzing the order.asp Page

You've now arrived at the e-commerce enabled pages of the BestPop Web site. When Jim and Dugan sat down to think of all the functionality they wanted to add to the BestPop site, they knew they wanted some method for customers to request orders online. When they started out, they weren't sure that they were comfortable with processing actual transactions over the Web, such as having customers enter credit card numbers,

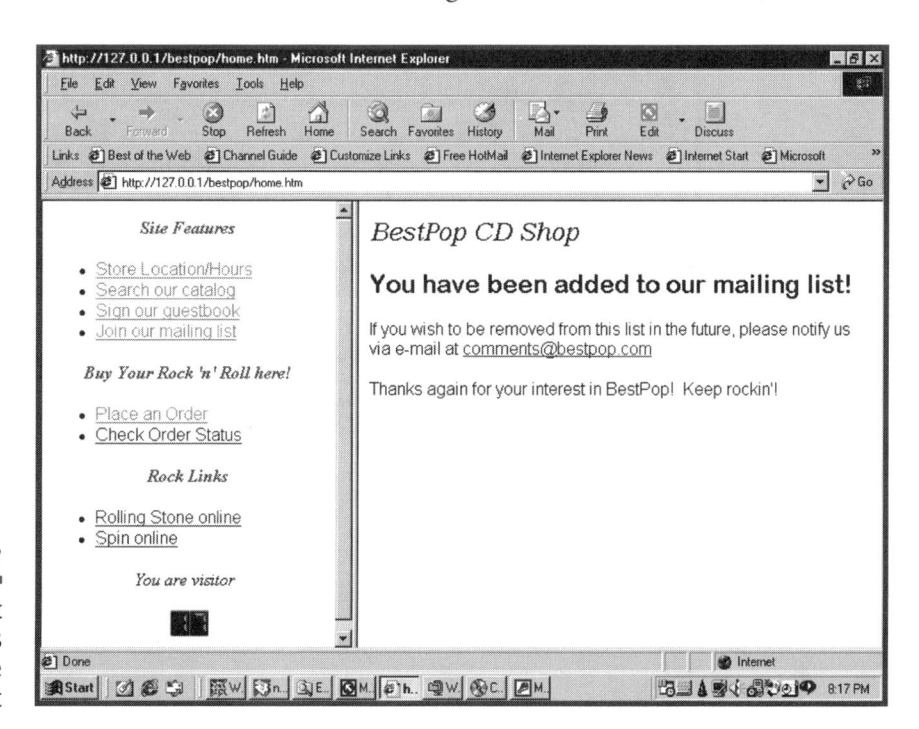

Figure 6.37

Confirming that a customer has been added to the BestPop mailing list and so on. However, they still wanted a way for customers to shop from home and then have the order ready when they walked into the store.

By utilizing the FrontPage Database Results Wizard and just a tiny bit of ASP coding, they were able to provide just this kind of *shop at home* feature. You can see how they did it by looking at the order.asp page, shown in Figure 6.38.

As you can see, the order form is smart, in that it knows which title the customer selected from the search_results.asp page. Take a look at the following sequence of actions, which will demonstrate the entire search and order process:

1. First, the customer searches the database for the artist of choice (see Figure 6.39).
2. Next, results of the search are returned, as shown in Figure 6.40.

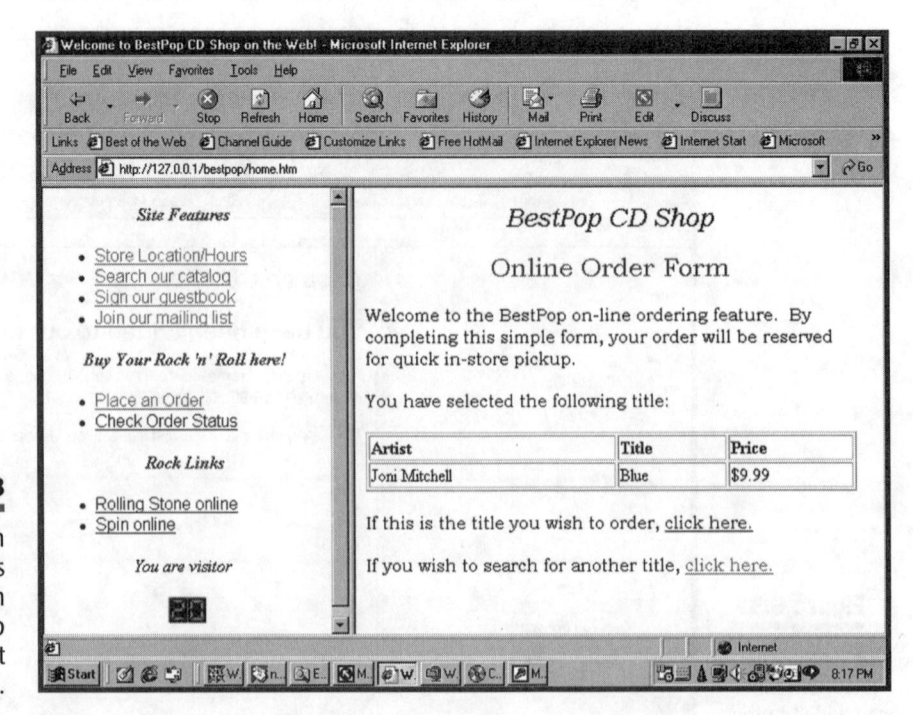

Figure 6.38

Customers can place orders directly on the BestPop Web for pick-up at the store.

> ### GETTING YOUR FEET WET WITH E-COMMERCE
>
> This type of browse at home feature is a great way to introduce yourself to the world of e-commerce. By starting out this way, you can be sure to get your internal business processes organized (especially the processes that revolve around your current inventory), so that, eventually, you can provide your customers will a complete e-commerce Web site.
>
> You may be asking yourself, "What good is placing the catalog online, if the customers still need to come into the store to pick up their order?" The answer is that the "search at home" (but not necessarily "buy from home") feature allows you a safety net, which is especially important when you are just beginning with e-commerce. This allows you more time to get your inventory in order before you allow customers to purchase online.
>
> Processing credit card information will be discussed in tonight's session, so you can get an idea of how you might move from this more basic search feature to a full-fledged e-commerce site that allows customers to actually order directly from the site.

3. By clicking on the hyperlinked title of choice (in this case, "Blue"), the customer is brought to the order.asp page (see Figure 6.41).

NOTE When the customer clicks on the Place an Order hyperlink, the search_catalog.asp page loads. This way, the customer is always forced to start from square one when placing an order; in other words, they have to first select a product before they can order it. BestPop uses the search_catalog.asp page as a convenient way of allowing customers to select the item in which they are interested.

Web Enable Your Small Business In a Weekend

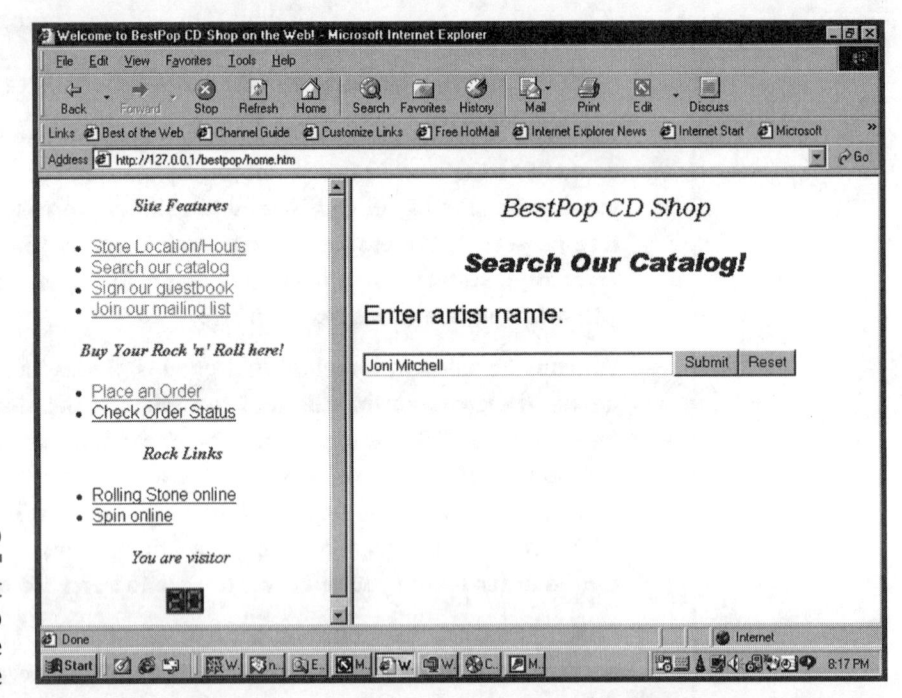

Figure 6.39

Providing an artist name for which to search within the CDShop database

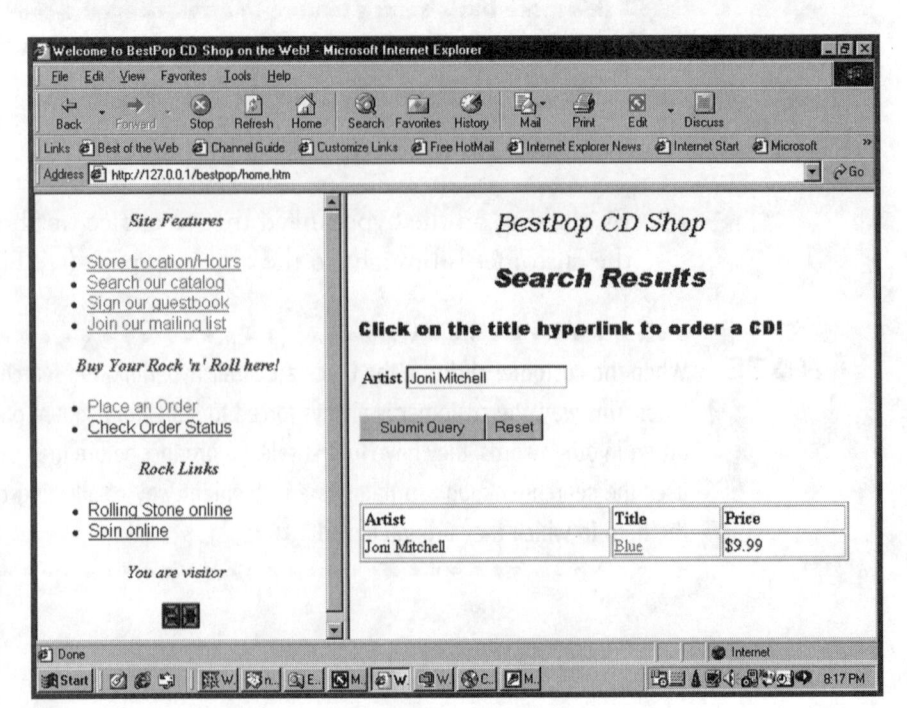

Figure 6.40

In this case, the CDShop database contains one entry for Joni Mitchell.

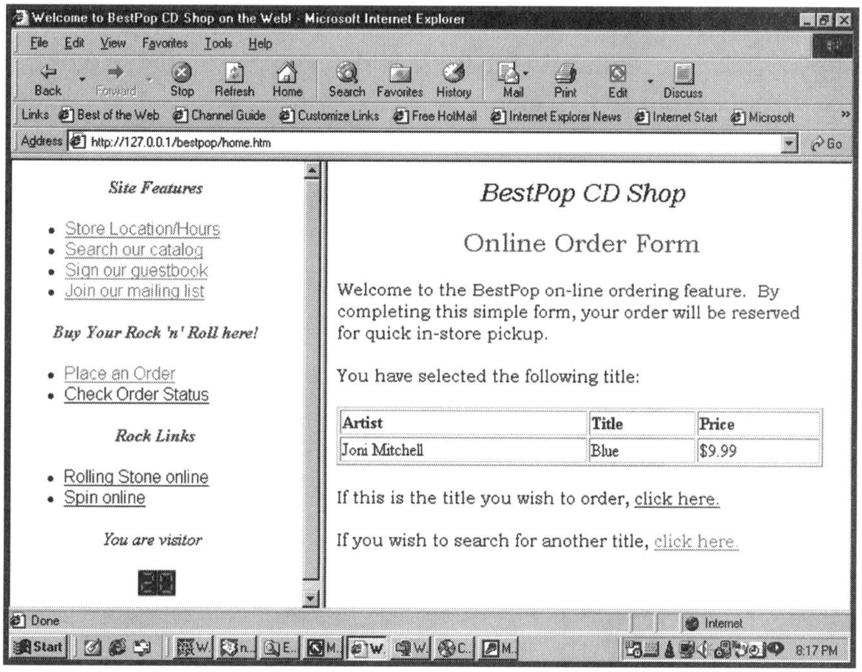

Figure 6.41

The customer is ready to select the returned search item for their order.

Now, examine how the order.asp page is constructed and how the selected title is passed to the order page from the search_results.asp page.

1. Open order.asp in FrontPage. As with search_catalog.asp, the order page uses the database results component (see Figure 6.42).

    Remember that when a user selects a title on the search_results.asp page, information on that title is passed directly to the order form. Therefore, the customer doesn't have to enter additional information on order.asp to select their desired CD. This is done through the power of ASP and the database results component.

2. How exactly is this done? Right-click the Database Results Region and choose Database Results Properties from the shortcut menu.

3. Click Next on the Database Results Wizard dialog box until you get to Step 3. Then, click the More Options button.

4. Within the More Options dialog box, click the Criteria button to display the Criteria dialog box (see Figure 6.43).

Figure 6.42

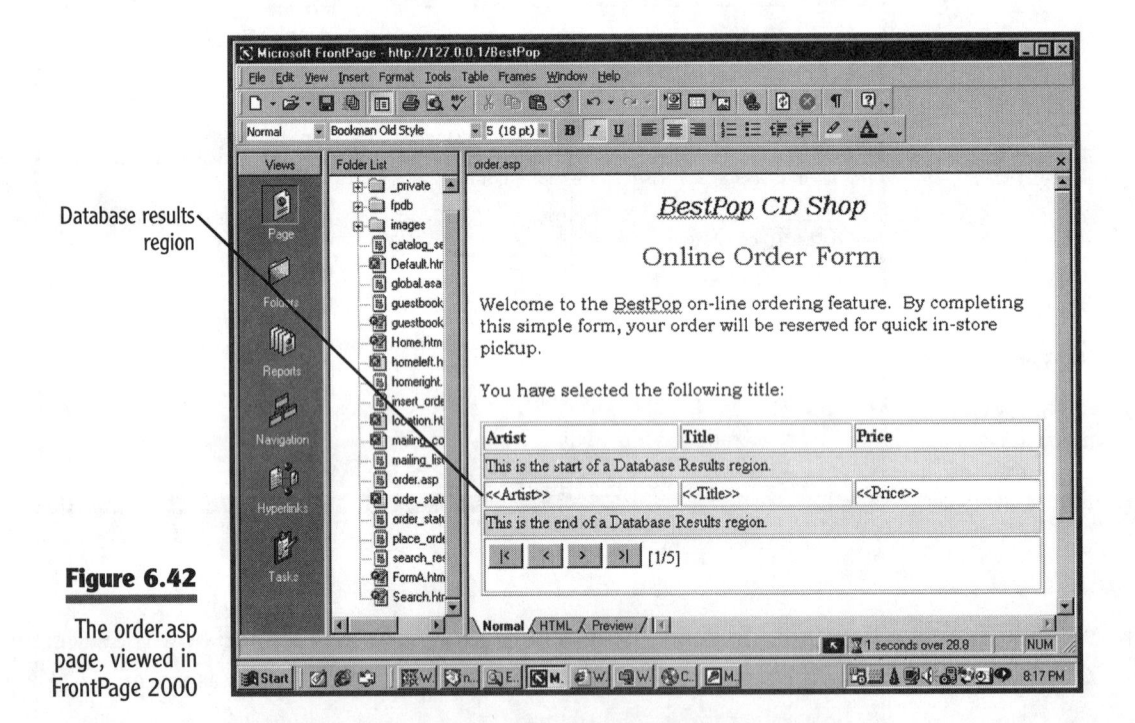

The order.asp page, viewed in FrontPage 2000

Figure 6.43

The Criteria dialog box is where you determine how your Access database will be queried for information.

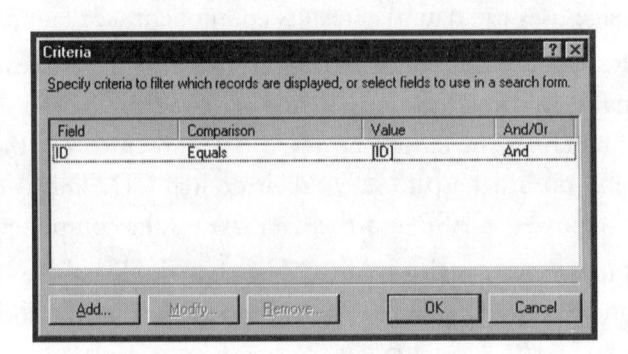

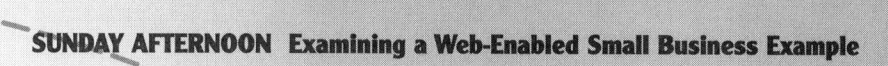

SUNDAY AFTERNOON Examining a Web-Enabled Small Business Example   **231**

5. Select the record, then click Modify. The Modify Criteria dialog box appears, as shown in Figure 6.44. In this dialog box, you can determine how you will query the database. In this case, a match between the ID of the selected title and the ID field within the Catalog table of the database is needed.

6. It's necessary to match the ID field because that is the link to the selected title. If you recall from the discussion of search_results.asp, the unique ID of the selected title (again, as found in the Catalog table of the database) is assigned to the customer's selected hyperlink, which in turn takes them to the order.asp page. By assigning the Field and Value properties in the Modify Criteria dialog box to the same value, in essence the two fields are matched.

> **TIP**
> Matching two fields refers to:
> - the value assigned to ID in the hyperlink query string, and
> - the unique value of the ID field in the Catalog table, which corresponds to the title selected by the customer.

Analyzing the place_order.asp Page

When a customer decides to purchase an item, they click on the link, "If this is the title you wish to order, click here," as illustrated in Figure 6.41. By clicking this link, they are taken to the actual ordering page, place_order.asp, shown in Figure 6.45. Customers are asked to enter their first and last names, as well as their e-mail address. Notice that all form fields on this page are required.

In reality, this page functions very much like the pages described previously. The Database Results Wizard is used to query the database (again, using the query string ID value). Moreover, customers are asked to enter their first name, last name, and e-mail address. All of this information is then inserted into the Customers table of the database when the Submit button is clicked.

Web Enable Your Small Business In a Weekend

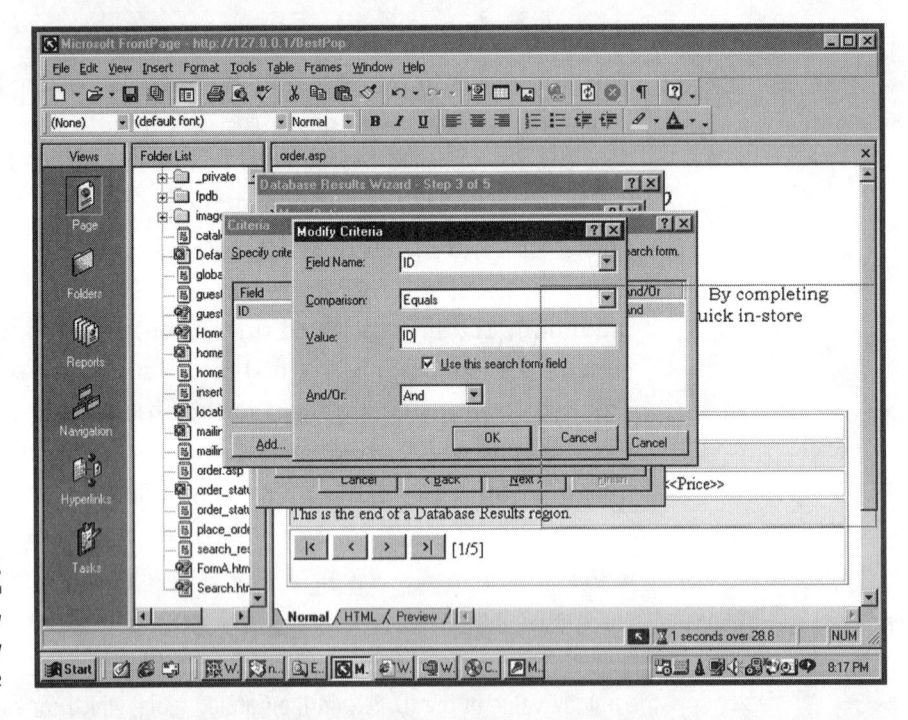

Figure 6.44

Determining how you will query the database

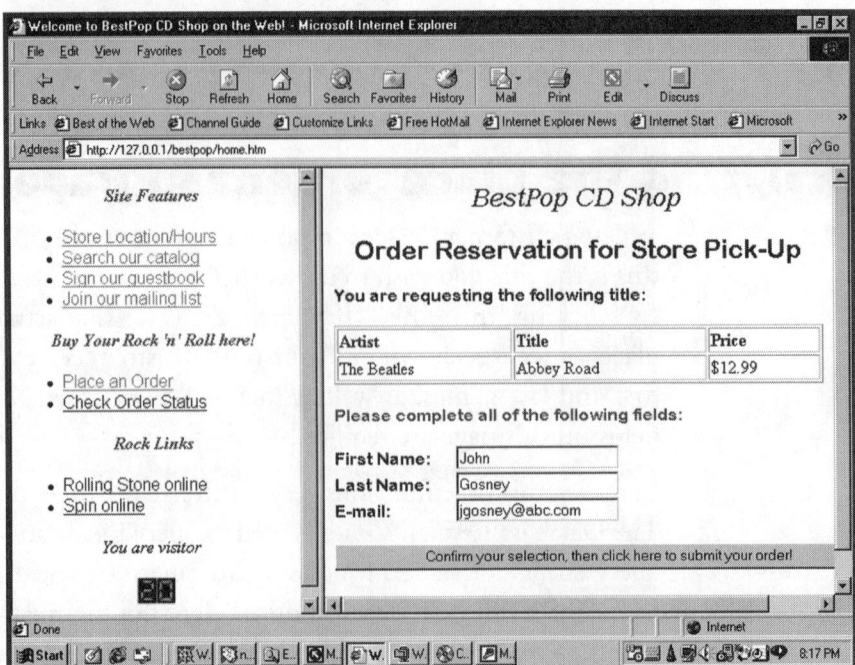

Figure 6.45

The BestPop order page

One additional task this page does perform, however, is to use the hidden field capability of FrontPage to also insert the ID of the selected title into the database along with the customer's information.

Take a look at an entry within the Customers table of the database. The Product_ID field is a cross-reference to the Catalog table. In the case of Figure 6.46, look at the corresponding record in the Catalog table (see Figure 6.47).

The value that is inserted into the Product_ID field is captured via a hidden form field on the place_order.asp page, as is the value that is inserted into the Title field. Here's how this is accomplished.

1. Open the place_order.asp page in FrontPage. Right-click in the form and choose Form Properties from the shortcut menu that appears. The Form Properties dialog box appears.

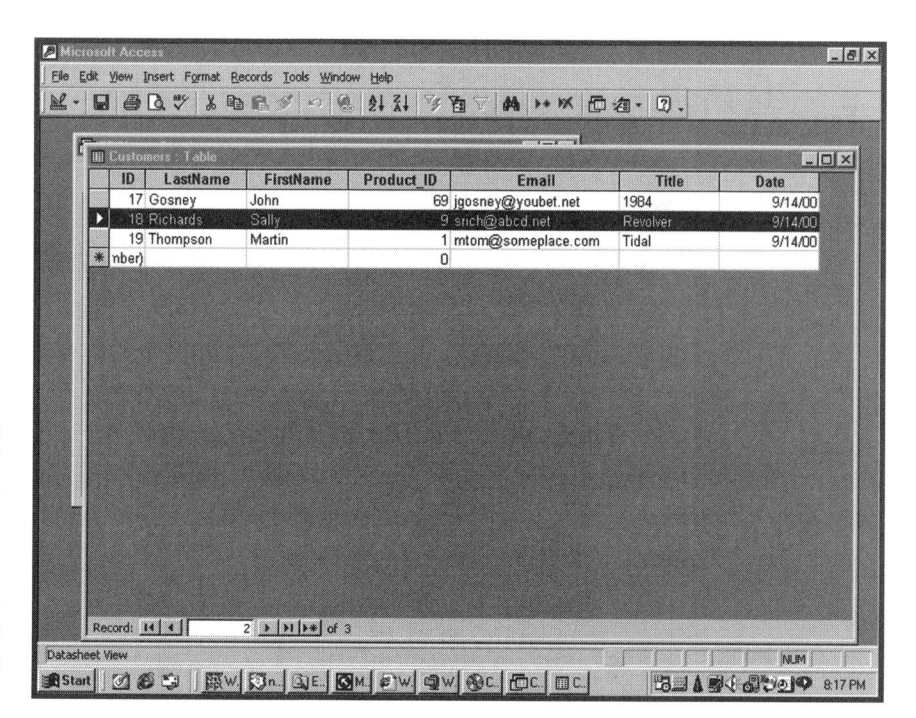

Figure 6.46

The Customers table captures all information entered on the order form, including the unique ID and title of the selection (the Product_ID field).

2. Click the Advanced button to display the Advanced Form Properties dialog box, shown in Figure 6.48.

3. Select the ID record and click Modify. This will display the Name/Value Pair dialog box, shown in Figure 6.49.

Figure 6.47

The Product_ID in the Customers table corresponds to a unique record in the Catalog table.

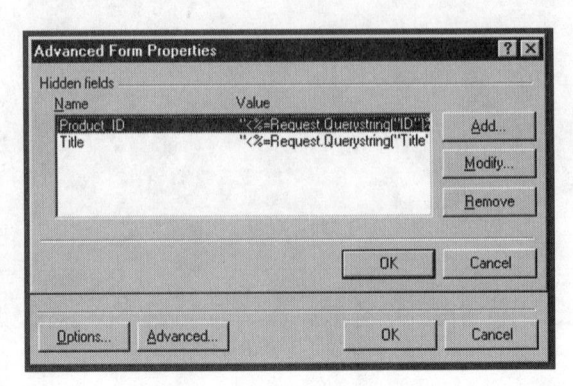

Figure 6.48

The Advanced Form Properties dialog box, where you can manipulate hidden form fields

4. As you can see in Figure 6.49, the hidden form field has the name Product_ID to match the corresponding field name in the Customers table of the database.

5. Then, you must provide a value for this hidden form field. Since you want to use the specific ID for the selected title and since the value will be passed using a querystring, a bit of simple ASP script (also known as VBScript) will pull the querystring ID value into this hidden form field.

   ```
   <%=Request.Querystring("ID")%>
   ```

6. That's all there is to it! Now, when the rest of the form is submitted (in other words, first name, last name, and e-mail address), this hidden form field will also be submitted, along with its value.

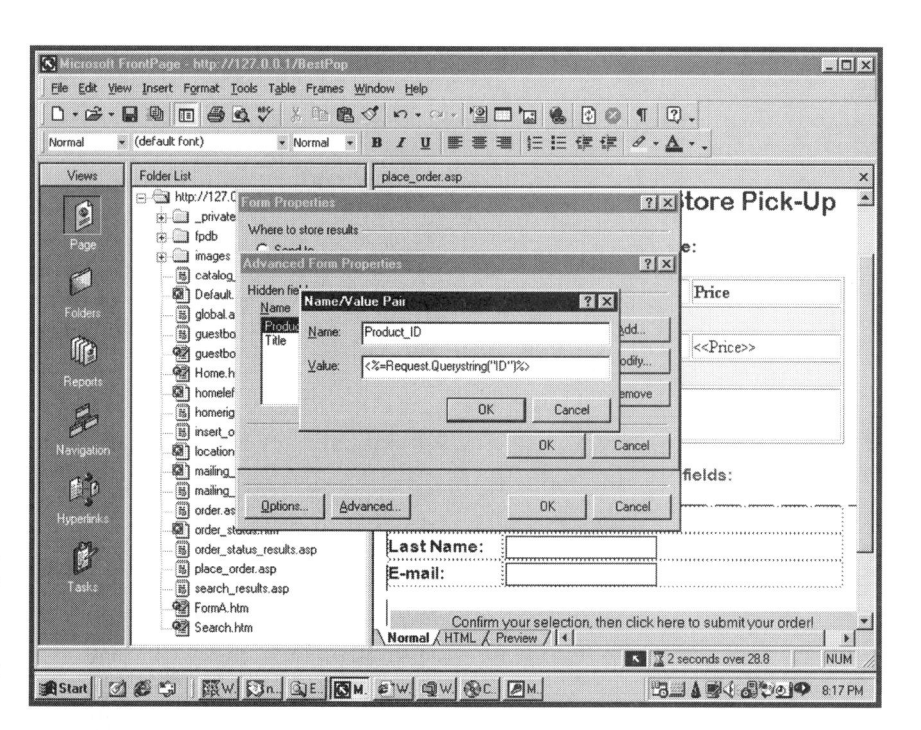

Figure 6.49

Establishing a hidden form field and the value it will contain

> **NOTE**
>
> The form field is hidden because it doesn't appear to the customer on screen. However, it is assigned a name (in this case, Product_ID) and a value (the unique ID of the selected title, as passed in the querystring via the ID value). The value inserted into the Title field is done in exactly the same way. To examine its attributes, select the Title record, as illustrated in Figure 6.48, and repeat steps 3–6.

Analyzing the insert_order.asp Page

Similar to the other confirmation pages on the BestPop site, insert_order.asp verifies that the customer's order was placed (see Figure 6.50).

Analyzing the order_status.htm and order_status_results.asp Pages

These pages allow a returning customer to view what orders they have placed through the BestPop Web site.

I won't give a detailed analysis of these pages, as they are nearly identical in function to how the catalog_search.asp page functions, but here is a brief description of how they work:

1. First, the user enters their e-mail address, as illustrated in Figure 6.51, and clicks the Submit button.
2. This page (order_status.htm) points to order_status_results.asp, which uses the same database wizard as search_results.asp. The only difference is that, with order_status_results.asp, the form field in question is the e-mail address provided by the user.
3. The value entered into this field is searched for within the Email field of the Customers table of the database. Depending on how many hits are made (or, how many orders the customer has placed), the full record of the order is returned for the customer to view (as shown in Figure 6.52).

SUNDAY AFTERNOON Examining a Web-Enabled Small Business Example   237

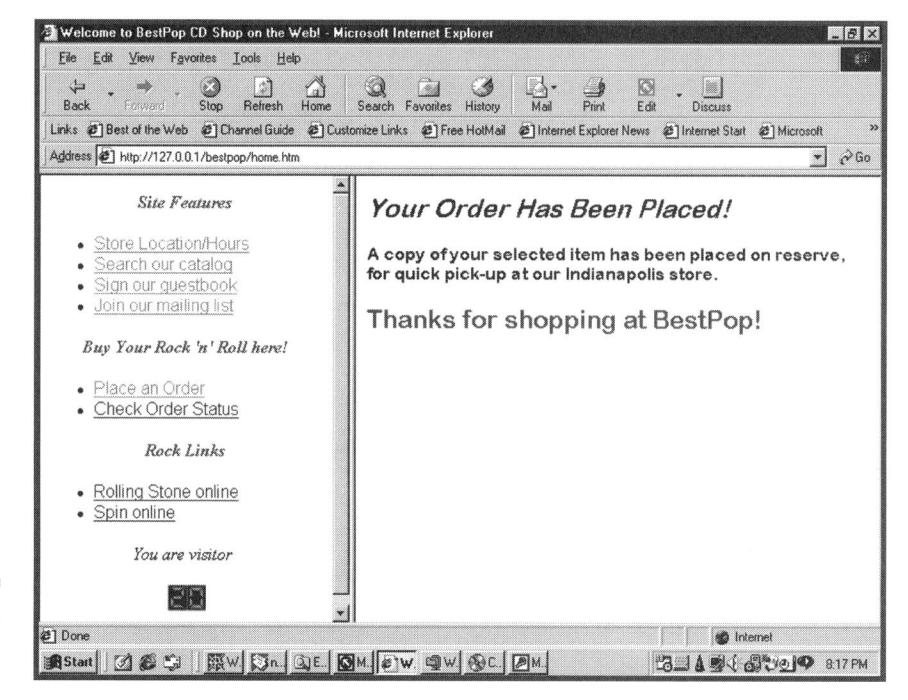

Figure 6.50

Confirming that an order has been placed

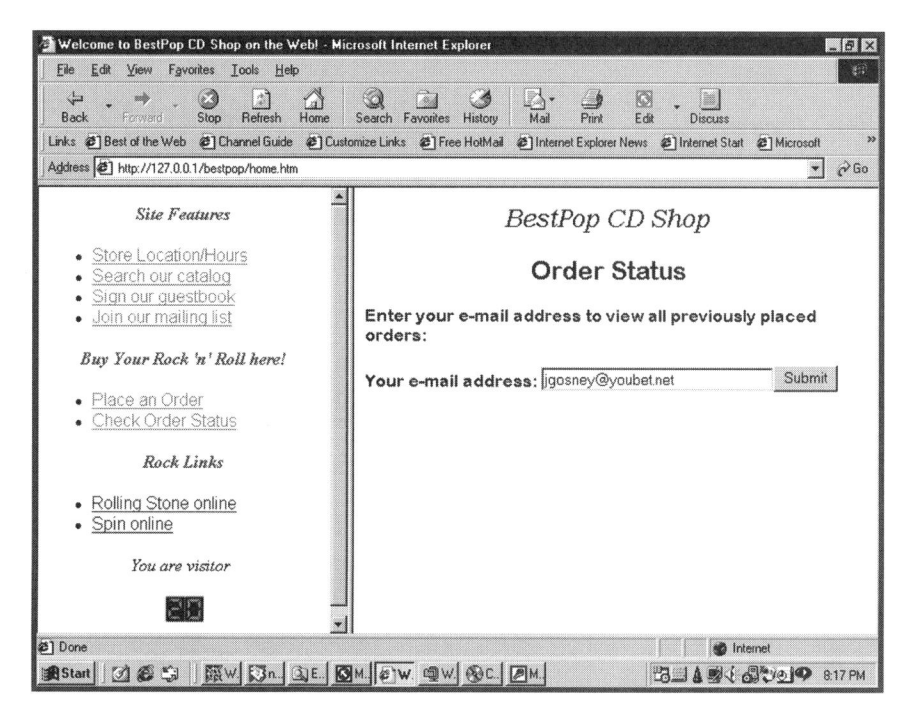

Figure 6.51

When customers enter their e-mail addresses...

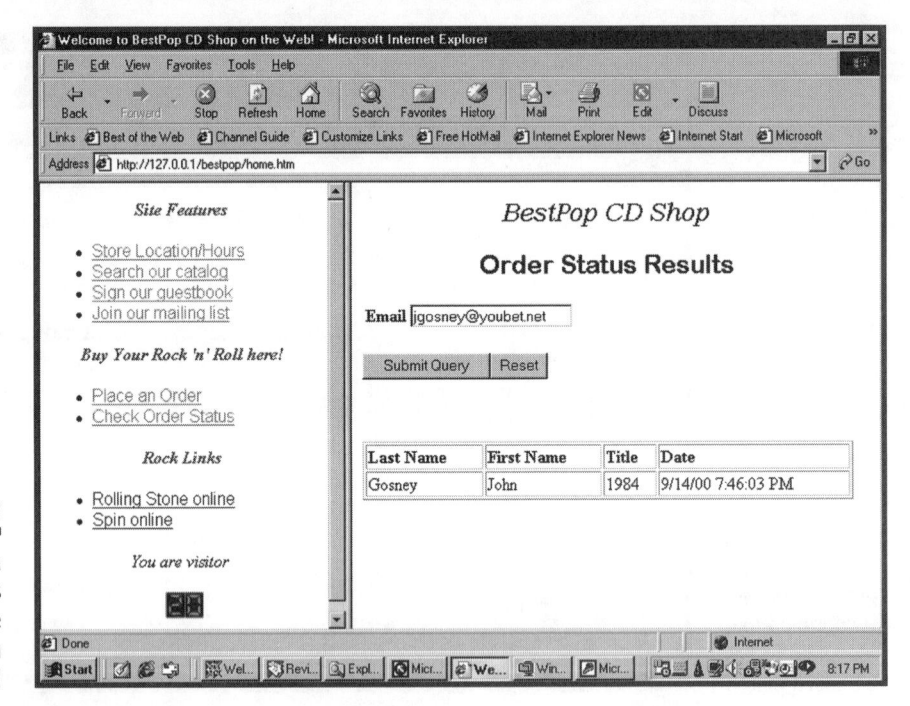

Figure 6.52

...they can view a listing of previous orders they have placed with BestPop!

> **TIP**
>
> Always provide customers with a method of reviewing what they have ordered, as it builds confidence that your site is functioning. Put simply, when customers can verify that their order has been placed, they are comfortable in knowing that the information they provided to you has been recorded (and presumably, acted upon) by the company.

Wrapping up with the BestPop Web Site

Although the BestPop site is in its early version, it is still quite functional. Consider how much the site allows, in terms of functionality:

- It allows customers to search a current product listing.
- It allows customers to reserve orders online.

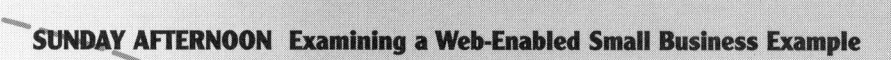

- It offers an automated mailing list.
- It allows customers to sign a guest book and thus leave comments on the site.
- It provides general store information about BestPop (store hours and directions).

All in all, not a bad little site. Jim and Dugan realize that there is more work to be done, but they were able to get the site up and running in a weekend. All they really had to do was establish a connection to their pre-existing Access database and build a few Web pages using FrontPage. By utilizing the extremely powerful and easy-to-use Database Results Wizard, they were able to capture information provided by customers and allow customers to search the BestPop product catalog.

Session in Review

You've come a long way this weekend. You've learned some advanced features of FrontPage, as well as how to bring an Access database online.

In tonight's final session, you'll wrap up the weekend and learn some additional tips (and general information) on the finishing touches of Web enabling your small business.

SUNDAY EVENING

Publishing Your Web

- Registering a Name for Your Web Site
- Publishing Your Web with the FrontPage Server Extensions
- Publishing Your Web without the FrontPage Server Extensions
- Promoting Your Small Business Web Site
- Performing Monetary Transactions on the Web

First of all, congratulations on making it through the weekend! Hopefully, you are feeling really good about all the new Web knowledge you've gained this weekend, especially how it relates to bringing the exciting world of e-commerce (and the Web in general) to your small business. From the basics of FrontPage to integrating databases with your Web site, you've covered a tremendous amount of ground.

Now, there is only one thing left to do: Take that fantastic, small business Web site and actually make it active! As with almost everything else, FrontPage provides a nice set of tools that can make it easy to publish your Web site. Tonight's wrap-up session will move you quickly through these features, as well as talk a bit about publicizing your Web site. You'll have some time to reflect on everything you've learned this weekend and get ready to move forward with your Web-enabled small business come Monday morning.

> **TIP** There are some useful tools on the enclosed CD-ROM to help you publish your Web. Be sure to check out Appendix C, "What's on the CD-ROM?," for more information!

Registering a Name for Your Web Site

You may be wondering how customers will find your small business on the Web. Put simply, when they connect to the Web, what URL will they type in so that your site begins to load in their browser?

Although we'll talk about how to advertise your site in the "Promoting Your Small Business Web Site" section later tonight, you should take some time to think about your site's domain name.

So how do you go about registering a domain name for your site? Your best bet is to pay a visit to register.com.

Using Register.com to Find a Domain Name

Register.com is a service that allows you to perform several important tasks.

- You can enter a desired domain name (for example, bestpop or johngosneyweb) and see if it is available.
- If your initial choice of domain name is available, you can register it on the spot. If it is not available, register.com will provide you with a list of closely related, alternative names, or allow you to search for a different name.
- You can also study register.com's simple instructions for maintaining your domain name.

NOTE Remember, there are a lot of sites out there in cyberspace, so your first choice of domain name may not be available. Indeed, your second, third, and maybe even fourth choice might have already been taken! Be patient, and be creative, too. Utilize the alternative names that register.com suggests to come up with perhaps even a better name than your initial idea!

To use register.com:

1. Enter the URL for register.com into your Web browser (http://www.register.com). The home page for register.com loads (see Figure 7.1).

2. In the space provided, enter a term you would like to register as your domain name, then click the Check It button.

Figure 7.1

The home page for register.com

3. After a few seconds, register.com will let you know if the term you want to use is already taken. As you can see in Figure 7.2, bestpopcd is available.

4. If the term you entered is already taken, you will be presented with a list of alternative names from which to choose, as shown in Figure 7.3.

Register.com walks you through the entire domain name registration process and provides you with pricing and update information. Take advantage of this friendly, easy-to-use service to ensure the domain name for your Web-enabled small business is exactly what you want!

Remember, too, that a good domain name can be an important tool to ensure that your small business Web site is quickly found. Try to keep the name as short (yet descriptive) as possible, so your customers can quickly type it into their browsers.

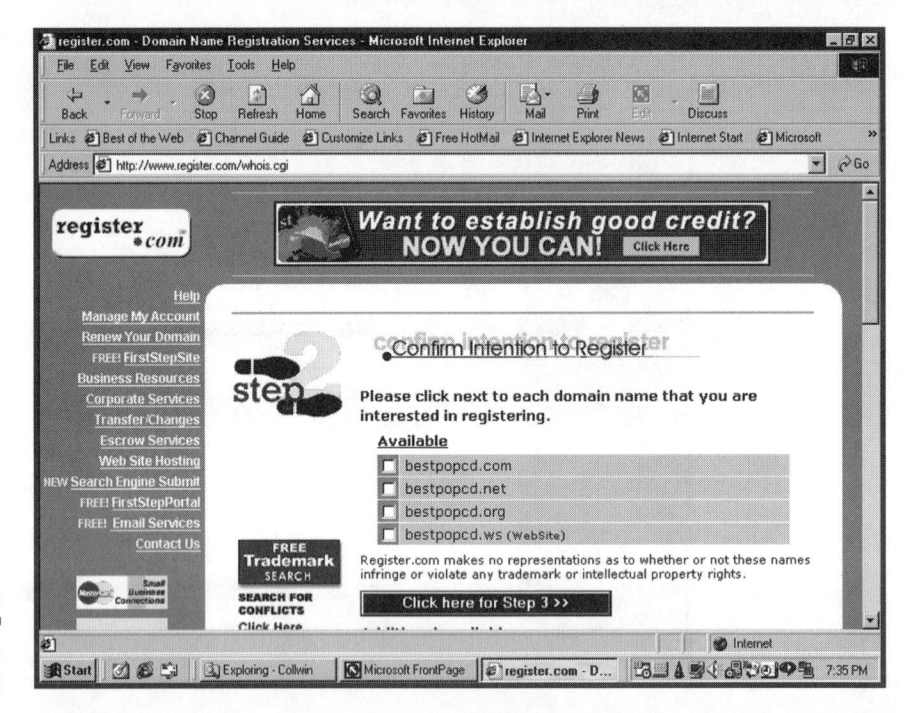

Figure 7.2

The desired term is available!

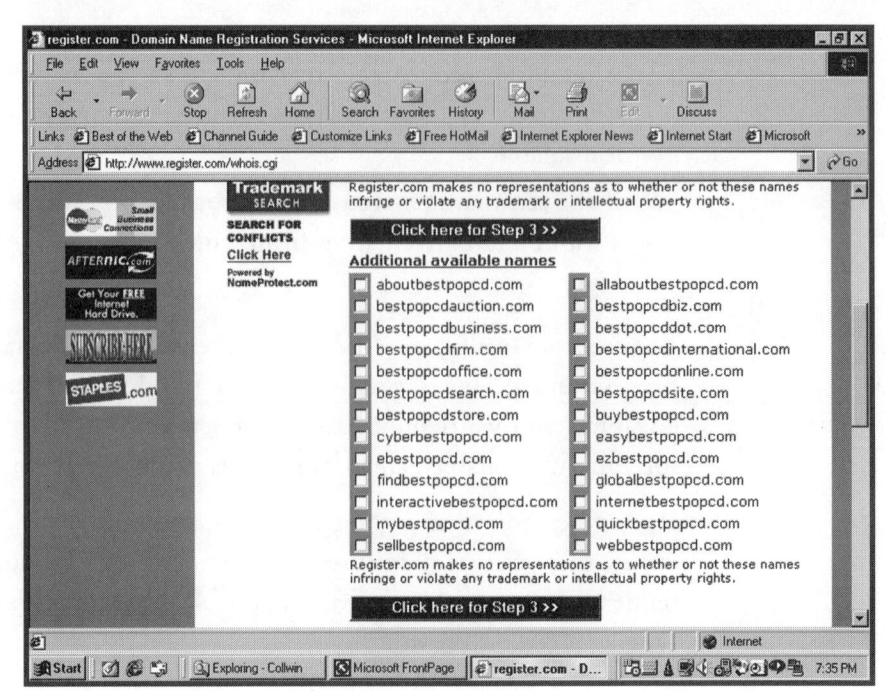

Figure 7.3

Choose an alternative domain name if your first choice is already taken.

Publishing Your Web with the FrontPage Server Extensions

FrontPage Server Extensions: Making life easier for novice Web developers for quite some time!

If this sounds like a slogan, it should be! Through the magic of the Extensions, you can avoid a lot of headaches and tedious programming. That said, you need to be sure your ISP uses the FrontPage Extensions. While it is possible to publish to a server without using the Extensions, you will lose some of the more powerful functionality that working within FrontPage provides, with features such as:

- Search Components
- Save Results Components
- Confirmation Field Components
- Discussion Components
- Registration Components
- Hotspot Image Maps
- Forms

Although Appendix A, "Finding a Web Hosting Service," offers a listing of ISPs, you should also check out the FrontPage section of Microsoft's Web site, at http://www.microsoft.com/frontpage. From this page, check out the Solutions and Resources link for information on an ISP that provides support for the Extensions.

> **TIP**
> Remember that your ISP doesn't have to be in the same town where you live when you are talking about publishing your Web. These Web Presence Providers (WPPs) can be anywhere, since your Web site can be accessed from anywhere in the world. Just be sure to work with a WPP that provides the best service. See Appendix A to learn more about the types of questions you should ask when deciding on a WPP.

Take a look at the Web publishing features of FrontPage in action, so you can get a feel for how this important task works. For this example, the SmallBiz Web will be published to Personal Web Server. Although you've been creating your Webs using PWS, by republishing to PWS you can see the Publish Web feature of FrontPage in action.

1. Open your SmallBiz Web and select File, Publish Web. The Publish Web dialog box appears, as shown in Figure 7.4.
2. Click Options to take a look at the extra features available when publishing a Web (see Figure 7.5).
3. You can publish only the pages that have changed since the last time you published, or you can publish all pages, thus overwriting any pages already on the server. Select the Publish Changed Pages Only option. Then, in the location field, type the location of your PWS (probably http://127.0.0.1).
4. Click the Publish button. You will see the progress of the publication process, as shown in Figure 7.6.

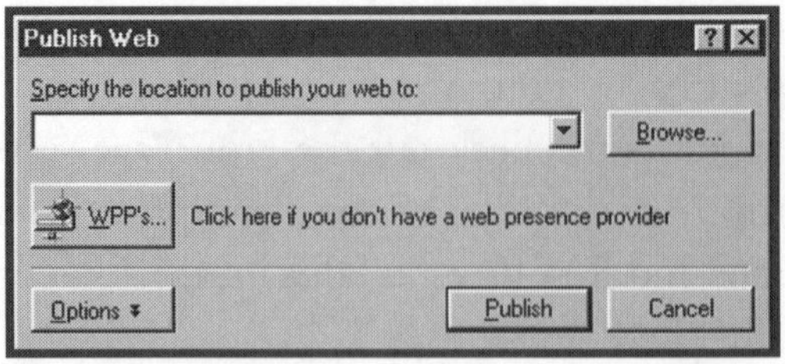

Figure 7.4

FrontPage 2000's Publish Web feature includes an information link to help you locate a WPP.

SUNDAY EVENING Publishing Your Web **249**

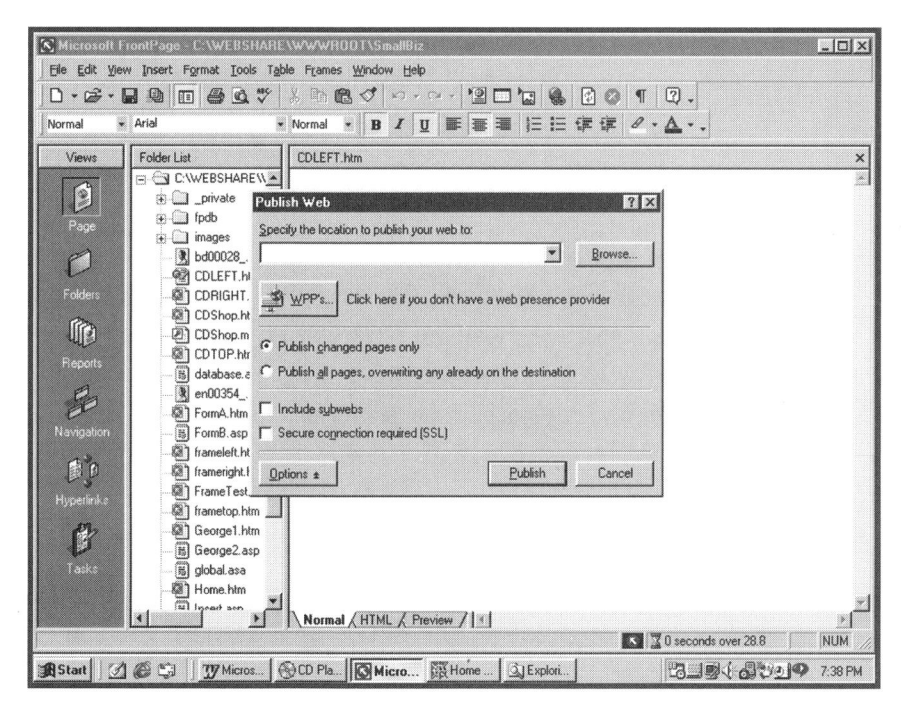

Figure 7.5

Extra features you can use when publishing your Web

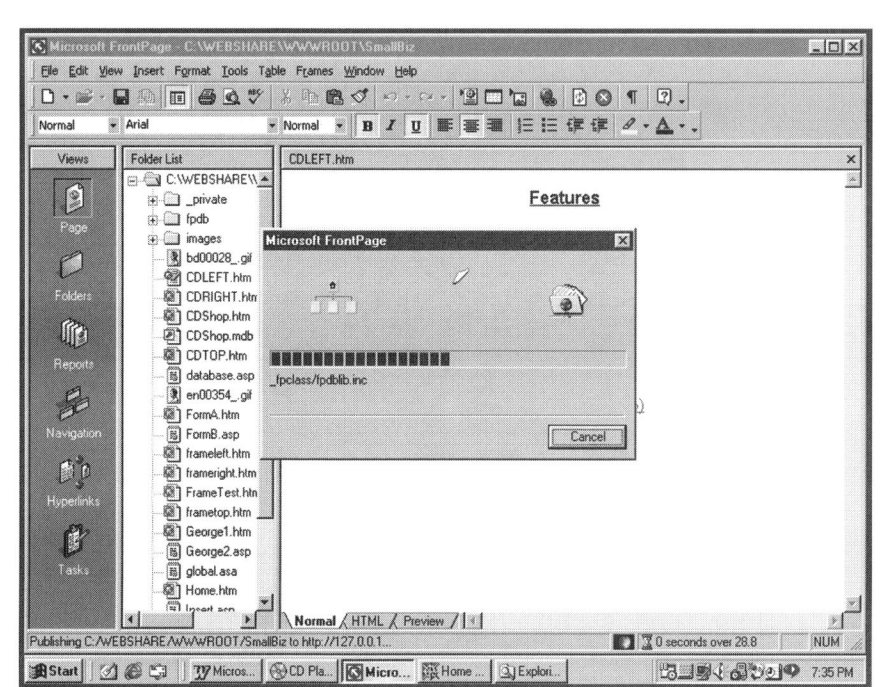

Figure 7.6

Publishing your Web to the server

5. After a few moments, you are presented with confirmation that your Web has successfully published, as shown in Figure 7.7.

6. That's all there is to it! Click the link to begin viewing your published Web site.

> **TIP**
> Is publishing a Web really that simple? The answer is yes, especially if you use a WPP that supports the FrontPage Server Extensions. Should you encounter any problems, any WPP worth their cyberspace weight will provide plenty of friendly, free technical support to help you get your site up and running.

Editing Pages on the Web Server

What makes the FrontPage Server Extensions even more useful is that once you publish your Web with your WPP, you can edit your Web pages

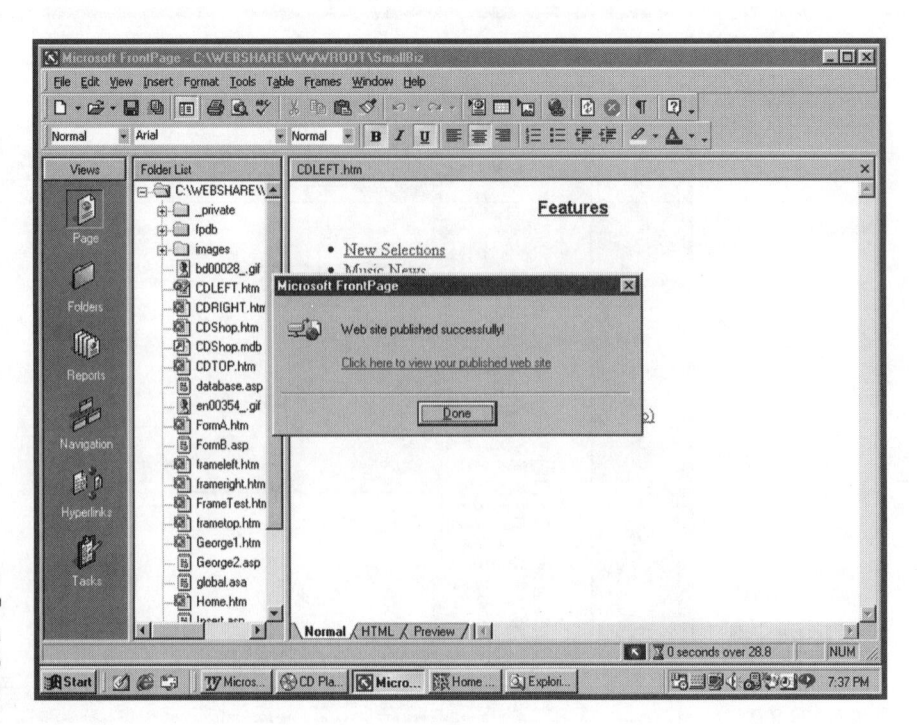

Figure 7.7

Confirmation of a successful Web publishing!

directly on the server. This allows for quick changes because you don't have to first make the change on your local machine and then publish the page to your WPP again.

To edit on the server, follow these steps:

1. From the File menu, select Open Web. When the Open File dialog box appears, click the Web Folders icon. All of the Webs that you have published will be displayed, in the format (Web name) on (Server). For example, in Figure 7.8, the SmallBiz on 127.0.0.1 listing indicates that the SmallBiz Web has been published on the server 127.0.0.1

2. Open the Web folder and select the page you want to edit. Make the necessary changes, then save the page again. Your changes should be automatically posted to your WPP server.

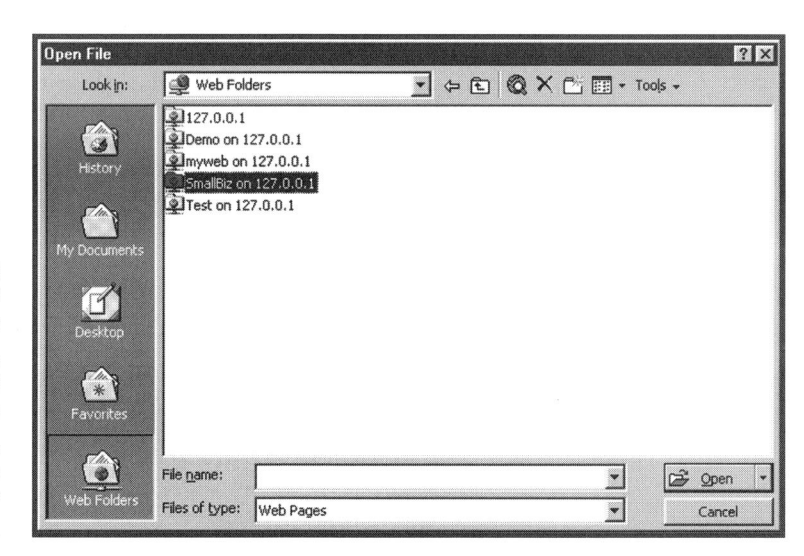

Figure 7.8

By editing directly on the Web server, you can make changes quickly and efficiently, without having to republish your affected pages.

CAUTION Although this is uncommon, some WPPs use cached versions of their Webs. This means that the Webs are stored in the virtual memory of the server machines. When requests are made for these pages, they can be sent out without actually involving any processing on the part of the server. While this can speed delivery time, the cached pages are obviously not the most current pages. For example, if your WPP only updates its cache twice a day, the changes you make to your Webs won't be reflected until these updates occur. Be sure to check with your WPP to see their policy on using cached Webs.

Selectively Publishing Web Pages

FrontPage doesn't limit you to publishing an entire Web. Rather, you can decide which specific pages to publish.

1. Making sure you have your local copy (the copy that is not on the WPP server) of the Web open, select Reports, Publish Status from the View menu. The Publish Status report appears.

2. Right-click in the right corner of the Publish field to view the drop-down menu shown in Figure 7.9. Select Don't Publish to prevent publishing that particular page. Use the Publish or Don't Publish setting to determine which pages to include when you publish your Web.

CAUTION Don't confuse this Publish/Don't Publish feature with the options presented in the Publish Web dialog box shown in Figure 7.5. The options presented in the Publish Web dialog box only refer to pages that have been marked for publication. In other words, if you select a page to not be published (as shown in Figure 7.9), it will not be included, regardless of which option you have selected in the Publish Web dialog box.

SUNDAY EVENING Publishing Your Web   253

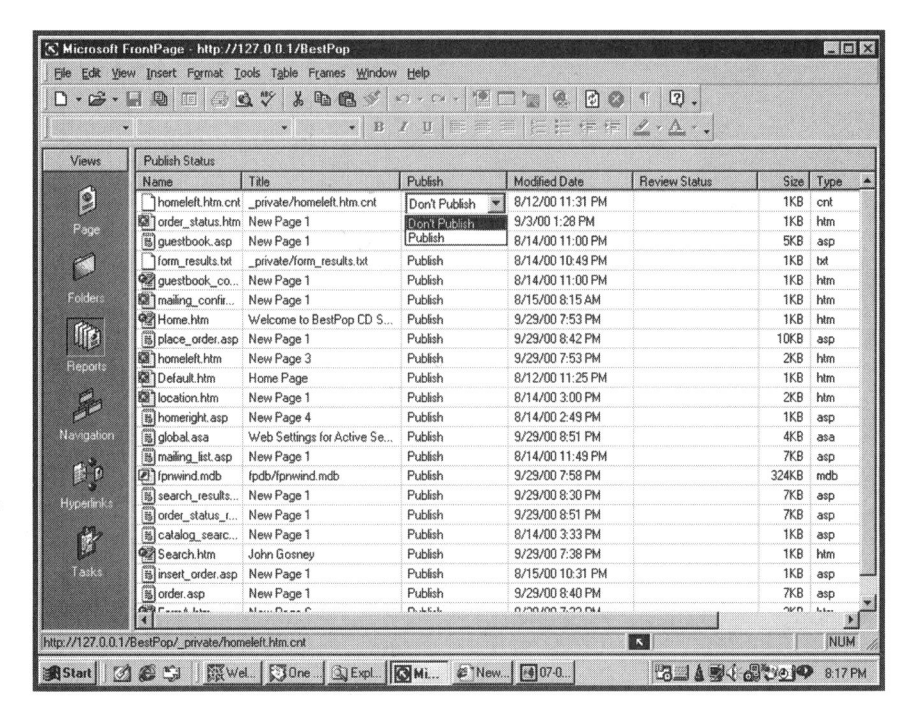

Figure 7.9

The Publish Status report, where you can specify which pages to include when you publish your Web

Publishing Your Web without the FrontPage Server Extensions

If your WPP of choice not does support the FrontPage Server Extensions, your Web can still be published, although any functionality that uses the FPSEs will not work.

There are a couple ways in which you can publish your Web without the FPSEs. You can do so by using FrontPage, or by using the Windows 98 Web Publishing Wizard.

> **TIP**
> You can also publish your Webs using a separate FTP program. Be sure to check out this book's CD-ROM for an example of such an application (CuteFTP).

Publishing Your Web Using FrontPage

You can still use FrontPage to help you publish your Web to a WPP that doesn't support the FPSEs. To do so, follow these steps:

1. Within FrontPage, open the local copy of the Web you want to publish.
2. From the File menu, choose Publish Web.
3. Click Browse. The Open Web dialog box appears, as shown in Figure 7.10.
4. From the Look In drop-down menu, select Add/Modify FTP locations. The Add/Modify FTP Locations dialog box appears, as shown in Figure 7.11.
5. Type the name of the FTP site, then select User.
6. Type your user name and password. Click Add, and then click OK.
7. In the Open Web dialog box, select the name of the FTP server you just entered. The Publish Web dialog box appears. Click Publish, and the process will begin.

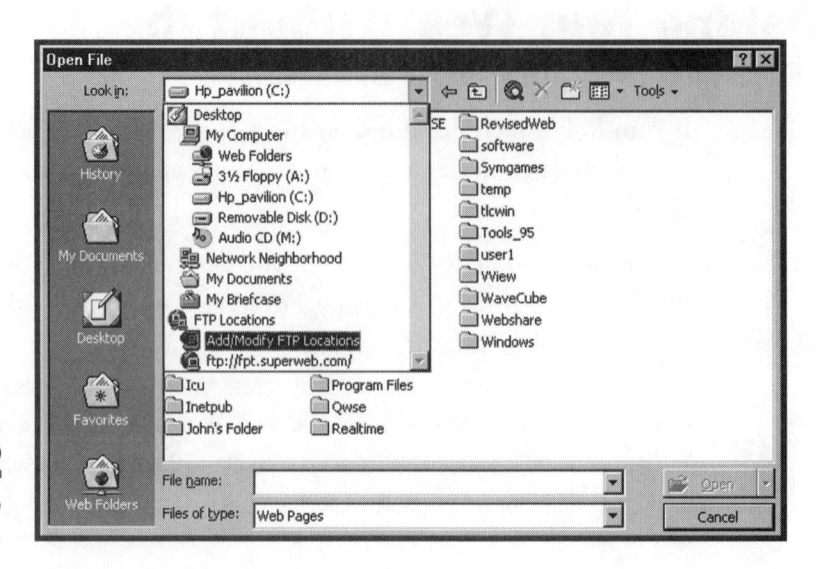

Figure 7.10

The Open Web dialog box.

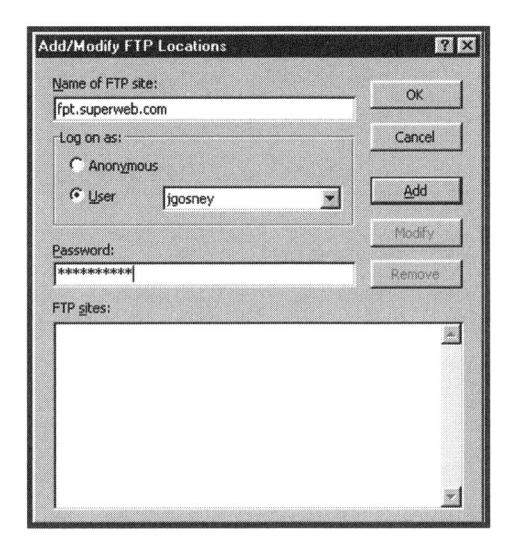

Figure 7.11

Providing the necessary information to FTP your Web

> **NOTE** During the publication process, you might be presented with a dialog box indicating that pages within your Web containing FrontPage components will not work with a server that doesn't support FPSEs. This is normal, although the functionality you have inserted in these pages probably won't work!

Publishing Your Web Using the Windows 98 Web Publishing Wizard

You can use the Windows 98 Web Publishing Wizard as another method of publishing to a WPP that does not support the FPSEs. Simply follow these steps:

1. From the Start menu, select Programs, Internet Explorer, Web Publishing Wizard. When the Web Publishing Wizard opens, click Next.

2. Click Browse Folders to navigate to the location of your local Web (the location on your machine where your Web is stored, probably c:\inetpub\wwwroot\your Web name).

3. Click OK, then click Next. Then, type a description for your Web server and click Next.

4. Type the URL for the Web site to which you are attempting to publish, and type the path to the Web to be published (this has probably been completed for you). Click Next.

5. Depending upon whether you use a dial-up connection or have a constant connection, you will be connected to the Internet.

6. Type your password, then click Next again.

7. Type the FTP server name and subfolder path (you should have received these from your WPP), then click Next.

8. Click Finish. The publication progress will be tracked. When everything is complete, you will be presented with a confirmation message indicating the successful publication of your Web.

9. Open your Web browser of choice, and test your newly published Web!

Take a Break!

Before completing the discussion for the weekend, take a quick break. Catch the Simpsons—even if it happens to be a rerun—or just grab a snack. When you get back, we'll wrap things up with a discussion of how to promote your new small business Web site.

Promoting Your Small Business Web Site

Web promotion is a tricky thing. Despite the tremendous power of having your Web site accessible from (literally) anywhere in the known universe, getting the word out about its exact location (in other words, the URL of your Web) can be a different matter entirely.

That said, you'll want your site to appear in as many search engines as possible. For example, if your small business specializes in oriental rugs and you happen to live in Columbus, Ohio, it would be nice if when users go to their favorite search engine and type, "Oriental Rugs Ohio," your business name shows up in the list.

So, how do you promote your Web site? Consider the following methods:

- Go with Yahoo!, the big boy of search engines. In competition with other search engines, Yahoo! is still probably the most popular gateway for everyday users seeking information on the Web. You can suggest your site to Yahoo! by going to http://www.yahoo.com/info. Note my use of the word *suggest*. As you might expect, Yahoo! receives a huge number of requests to have individual Web sites listed, and not all are posted (for a variety of reasons). So, be aware that even though you suggest your site to Yahoo!, it might not show up in any of the lists returned by the search engine.

- There are also other ways to get noticed on the Web. Be sure to check out the Exploit Submission Wizard on the enclosed CD-ROM, which allows you to quickly enter general information about your Web site. The program then sends this information to a variety of search engines, without asking you for additional input.

- Try http://www.submit-it.com. This service is free for submissions to up to 20 search engines; you must pay a fee for a submission to up to 400 search engines. It can also get you noticed quickly. Not all search engines that receive your request will actually file your site, so the bigger the number of search engines you submit to, the better your chances of actually getting noticed.

- In a more traditional vein, be sure to include the URL of your small business Web site on your business cards, on your company letterhead, in advertisements (whether radio, television, or printed), and so on. This is a great way to spread your site's URL quickly.

- Have some promotional material printed up that includes your URL. For example, the ever-popular refrigerator magnet (with your company name, telephone number, and URL), coffee mugs, pens.... The possibilities are endless. This is another good way to get your site noticed.

- Finally, just be cognizant of the fact that you have entered the 21st century and have taken the brave, exciting step of establishing yourself as a Web presence. In meetings, general conversation, and e-mail messages to friends and customers alike, be sure to mention something like, "Hey, have you checked out my company's Web site?" Word of mouth is always a good way to spread a message.

Performing Monetary Transactions on the Web

Although our BestPop case study from this afternoon's session didn't touch on online sales, it is a very real possibility that you'll want to allow for this type of information transaction in the near future. Certainly, the ability to perform e-commerce transactions can be a powerful, convenient sales tool for your business.

Fortunately, there are services available that make this process easy to use and administer, as well as providing your customers with a tangible sense of security when they provide sensitive information (for example, credit card numbers) over the Web.

One of the best services available to help you with e-commerce transactions is Cybercash (http://www.cybercash.com), shown in Figure 7.12. If you choose to use Cybercash as a facilitator for your online transactions, you'll want to use their CashRegister service, shown in Figure 7.13

Just like register.com, Cybercash offers a tremendous amount of easy-to-understand information on their Web site, and will walk you through the necessary steps to help you add this powerful e-commerce component to your small business Web site. Again, take advantage of services like these to really catapult your small business into the exciting world of e-commerce!

SUNDAY EVENING Publishing Your Web 259

Figure 7.12

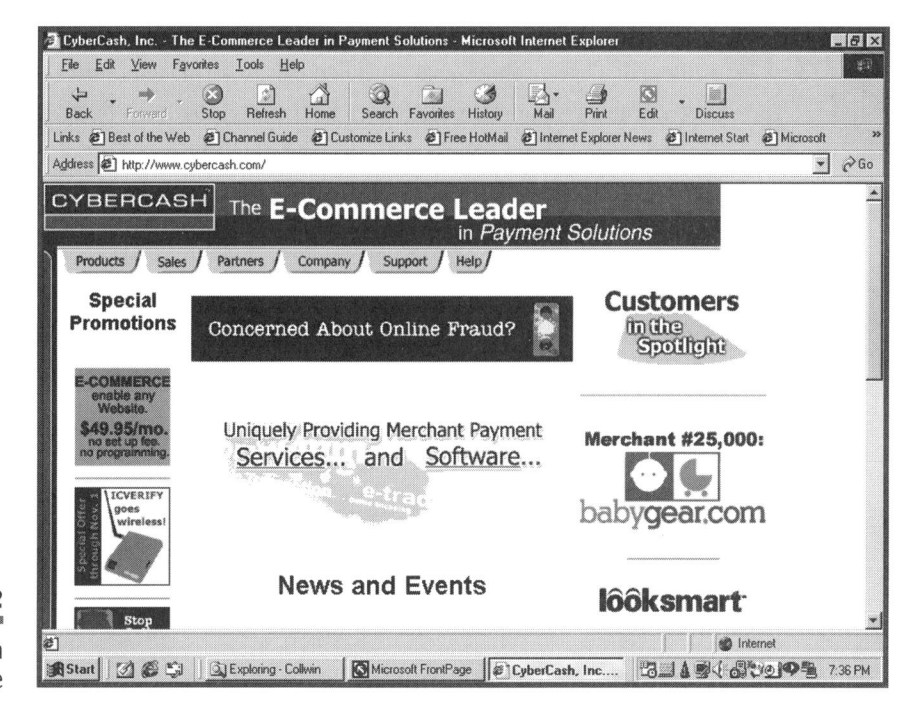

The Cybercash.com home page

Figure 7.13

The CashRegister service, available from Cybercash.com

> **NOTE**
> If you don't feel comfortable providing electronic monetary transactions at this point in your Web development experience, don't worry! The focus of this weekend has been on establishing an online presence for your small business. Primarily, this has included some moderate Web design with FrontPage, and allowing you to capture information provided by your customers by integrating your Web site with a database.
>
> So, take some time to get comfortable with your new Web site and how it integrates with the rest of your business. Then, when you're ready, you can utilize services like Cybercash to take your e-commerce to the next level.

Weekend Wrap-Up

You've come to the end of the weekend. How do you feel? Ready to set the world on fire with your fantastic small business Web site? I hope so!

Remember that it's okay to start out small with your Web presence. Hopefully, aside from showing you the technical aspects of publishing your Web, this book has also illustrated the need for your Web site to be a logical extension of your actual business processes. Remember that a Web site that functions as a separate entity from the rest of your business is nothing more than an expensive toy. It can cost you dearly in lost credibility (if customers get outdated or incorrect information from a poorly kept site, for example) and general bad advertising. Take the time to be sure your Web site is updated properly and treat it as the effective, powerful business tool it can really be!

Finally, as a closing thought: the Web is a constantly evolving place. While you should consider the development of your first small business Web site a major accomplishment, there will be newer versions of FrontPage, Access, Internet Explorer, and so on just around the corner. While you shouldn't feel pressured to upgrade to the latest and greatest technology the minute it hits the shelves, you should keep your eyes open for new technology that will make your business run smoother—and thus, make your life easier.

Thanks for your time this weekend. I hope you enjoyed working through this book as much as I enjoyed writing it. Good luck with all your e-commerce undertakings! See you in cyberspace!

APPENDIX A
Finding a Web Hosting Service

○ A Sample Listing of Web Hosting Providers

This appendix contains a sample overview of some different Web hosting services available that support FrontPage Extensions and/or NT Server. As you investigate each listing (or any company, for that matter, who you might want to have host your site), be sure to ask the following questions:

- **What technical support hours does the service provide?** Is it 24-7 (including weekends), or is support only available during regular business hours? From our discussion in the Friday Evening session, remember that e-commerce doesn't recognize traditional business hours. Your customers can (and will) visit your site at all hours of the day and night. Therefore, if your site goes down, you want to be sure to have quick, responsive, technical support to get things up and running again. The old adage, "time is money," is especially true on the Web.

- **Does the service provide database support?** Some hosting services might support FrontPage extensions, but offer no database support. Remember that the heart of your small business Web site is the database that both accepts information from and delivers information to your customers. If the hosting service doesn't provide database support either in the form of Microsoft Access or SQL Server, you should look elsewhere.

- **When new versions of software are introduced (for example, new versions of Windows, FrontPage, and so on), what testing methodology does the provider use to evaluate the new software?** Put simply, you want your hosting service to stay on the cutting edge of technology, but not necessarily the bleeding edge. New technology can be cool, but often requires a fair amount of testing to ensure that it is compatible, secure, and functional with existing technology and procedures.

- **How much storage space are you allowed on the server?** Is going over this amount permitted, and if so, how much additional money will it cost you? Depending on the size of your Web site, storage space on the server may be less of an issue in the beginning. You can be assured, however, that as your site grows (as you add Web pages, and as your database increases in size), you'll need more space.

- **What administrative rights do you have to your own Webs?** Some hosting services only allow limited outside access to personal Webs. While this can be okay in some situations, if you need to make an emergency adjustment to your Web site, you should have the ability to do so yourself. You won't want to rely completely on technical support that may not be as fast as your customers' demand. The great thing about using FrontPage as your development environment is that it is easy to make changes and then upload those changes to a host machine. Take advantage of this ability, and if the hosting service is too restrictive in what they allow, look elsewhere.

- **Does the hosting service use server caching to deliver pages?** Some hosting services cache (store) older versions of Web pages on their server in order to decrease the processing load on the server. This is okay in some instances, but if you need to make immediate changes to your material, you might have to wait several hours to see those changes implemented. A hosting server using server caching only refreshes the pages it delivers to browser requests during certain times of the day.

APPENDIX A   Finding a Web Hosting Service

As a last word of advice on choosing a hosting service, be sure to look through your local Yellow Pages to see what services are available in (or near) your hometown. While it is perfectly fine to do business with a hosting service in a different city, state, or even country, when something goes wrong, it is nice to have your hosting service nearby. At least you won't get stuck with a huge long distance bill while you're on the phone with technical support.

A Sample Listing of Web Hosting Providers

There are many Web hosting services out there, and the following list is merely a sample of them. You can start with these, but also look around on your own. Take your time and select the Web hosting service that best fits your small business needs.

- 1st Choice International Internet Services (http://www.1stchoice-nt.net)
- Active Server Pages Network (http://www.asppages.net)
- AKOS (http://fp.akos.net)
- American Business Web (http://usbusinessweb.net)
- BitShop.com (http://www.bitshop.com)
- CCC Webbs (http://cccwebbs.com)
- Comtrack (http://www.comtrack.com)
- Concentric (http://www.concentric.com/index.shtml)
- Cybertronic.Net (http://www.cybertronic.net)
- EZ Web Host (http://www.ezwebhost.net)
- FreeWebspace.net (http://freewebspace.net)
- Get On The Web Internet Services (http://www.ntwebhosting.com)
- HalfPrice Hosting (http://www.halfpricehosting.com)
- HosTek.com (http://www.hostek.com)
- IndoLinks (http://www.indolinks.com)

- Infinities (http://www.infinities.com)
- iNNERHOST (http://www.innerhost.com)
- Luxline (http://www.luxline.net)
- MidWeb.net (http://www.midweb.net/index.html)
- NetCulture (http://www.netculture.net)
- NetData4 (http://www.netdata4.net)
- ORCS Web, Inc. (http://www.orcsweb.com)
- Ozelink (http://www.ozelink.com)
- PacificNet Productions (http://www.pnpro.com)
- PAC-Web (http://www.pac-web.net)
- RGM Webb Net (http://www.rgmwebb.net)
- Server 101 (http://www.server101.com)
- SpaceNet (http://www.spacey.net)
- The Hosting Company (http://www.hostco.net)
- The Web Power (http://www.thewebpower.net)
- Web Site Hosting (http://www.websitehosting.net)
- Wired Hosting (http://www.wiredhosting.com)

APPENDIX B

Access Essentials

- Creating a Database
- Creating Tables in Design View
- Entering Data into a Table Using the Datasheet View
- Modifying a Table that Contains Data
- Using the Access Simple Query Wizard

Throughout this book, especially during the Saturday Evening and Sunday Afternoon sessions, I've focused on taking your Microsoft Access databases and integrating them with your small business Web site.

FrontPage 2000 makes this process very easy by utilizing some powerful database connection wizards and allowing users to generate the special search commands (also known as SQL queries) that search through specific database tables for requested information.

> **TIP**
>
> Access 2000 is a deceptively simple program. However, don't let that perceived simplicity convince you that it is not a robust, powerful member of the Office 2000 suite. Although you will learn the basics of working with Access in this appendix, be sure to check out *Access 2000 Fast and Easy* (Prima, 1999) for a more complete overview of the basic Access essentials.

So, in reality, you don't need to know much about Access in order to integrate your databases with your Web pages. But what if you need a bit of a refresher in the fundamentals, such as how to create a database from scratch or how to insert tables and modify fields? Well, you've come to the right place! This short appendix will introduce you to the Access essentials. Along the way, you'll take a peek at some of the query-generating tools that are also available within the application.

> **NOTE**
>
> What's all this talk about queries? As you might remember from our discussion in the Saturday Evening session, Access uses a special language called SQL (*Structured Query Language*), which is standard across most database applications. SQL was developed to provide a uniform method of accessing information from databases using a standard syntax. Although a full discussion of SQL is well beyond the scope of this book, I'll briefly discuss the Access Query Wizard a bit later in the "Using the Access Simple Query Wizard" section of this appendix.
>
> Remember, though, that the FrontPage database wizards generate most (if not all) of the SQL you'll need to use. So if you aren't interested in this topic, don't worry—you can live without it!

Creating a Database

Take some time now to create a database from scratch. Even though you can work with the sample Access database found on the enclosed CD-ROM (the database used in the Sunday Afternoon case study), you should still become familiar with the essential steps of database creation in Access.

1. Open Access. A dialog box immediate appears, asking you to create a new database or open an existing file, as shown in Figure B.1.

Figure B.1

Determining how to create your new Access database

2. Select the Blank Access Database option, then click OK. The File New Database dialog box appears, as shown in Figure B.2.

3. Give your database a name and select a location in which to save it.

> **TIP** If you plan to integrate your database with a FrontPage Web, you might want to place the database within the actual Web folder, so you keep all your related files together.

4. Click the Create button. After a few seconds, your database will be created (see Figure B.3).

You are now ready to begin working with your new database. Next, you'll move through some more of the essential features of Access, including how to create and modify tables, as well as specific fields within those tables.

Creating Tables in Design View

You need a place to store the information that you'll work with in your database. That's where tables come into play.

Access tables are powerful repositories of data that allow you to view information in a variety of ways, through the use of simple sorting features and SQL queries. Creating them is very easy; take a look at how it's done.

Figure B.2

Saving the database to the C drive, with a name of TestDatabase

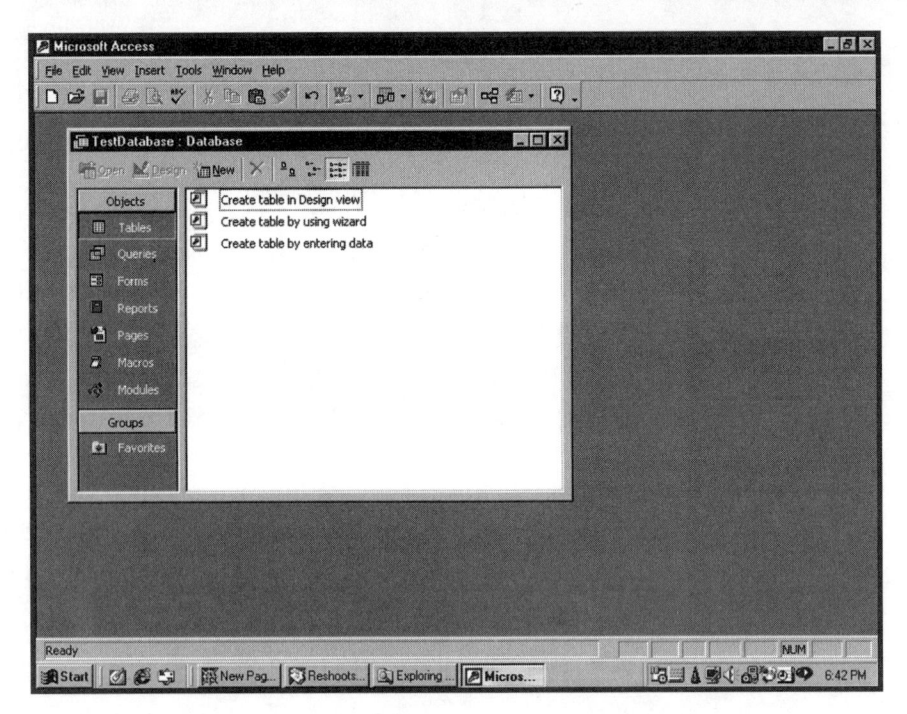

Figure B.3

Your newly created Access database

There are three ways to create a table in Access 2000: in Design View, through the use of a wizard, or by entering data. The traditional process is to create a table in Design View.

1. Double-click on Create Table in Design View. Design View for a new table appears, as shown in Figure B.4.

2. Notice the three column names in Design View: Field Name, Data Type, and Description. As you create specific fields within a table, each of these columns will contain a value. (Stay with me here! All of this will be illustrated as you move through the process of table creation.) Click in the first Field Name position, if your cursor isn't already there.

3. For this example, you'll create a table to store information similar to that found in a personal address book. Type **ID** to make ID the name of your first field. Then press Tab, so that your cursor appears

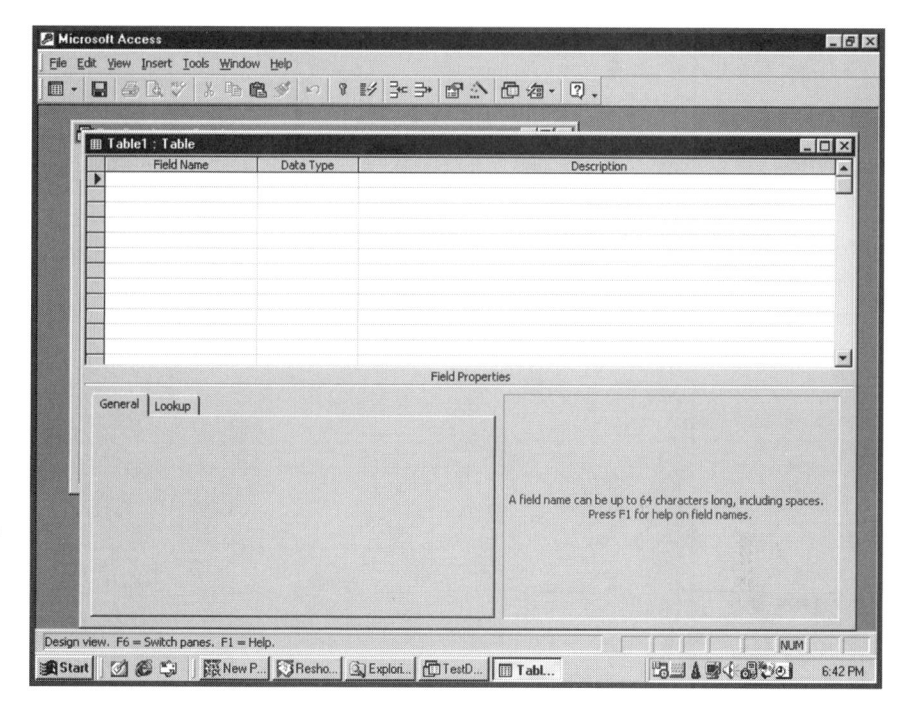

Figure B.4

Your new table, in Design View. Notice the default naming convention applied: Table1.

in the Data Type field, as shown in Figure B.5. You'll notice that when you tab across to the Data Type column, information in the Field Properties section appears.

4. The Data Type column is where you specify (surprise!) the type of data you are going to be storing within the specific field. Click the Data Type down arrow to display the different data types available, as shown in Figure B.6.

5. Select AutoNumber. This will make the ID value automatically increase in increments of one, so that as new records are entered into the database, they are assigned a unique identifier (in other words, they are given a specific ID).

6. You want to make the ID field the primary key field for your database. To do so, right-click within the ID field and select Primary Key from the menu that appears, as shown in Figure B.7.

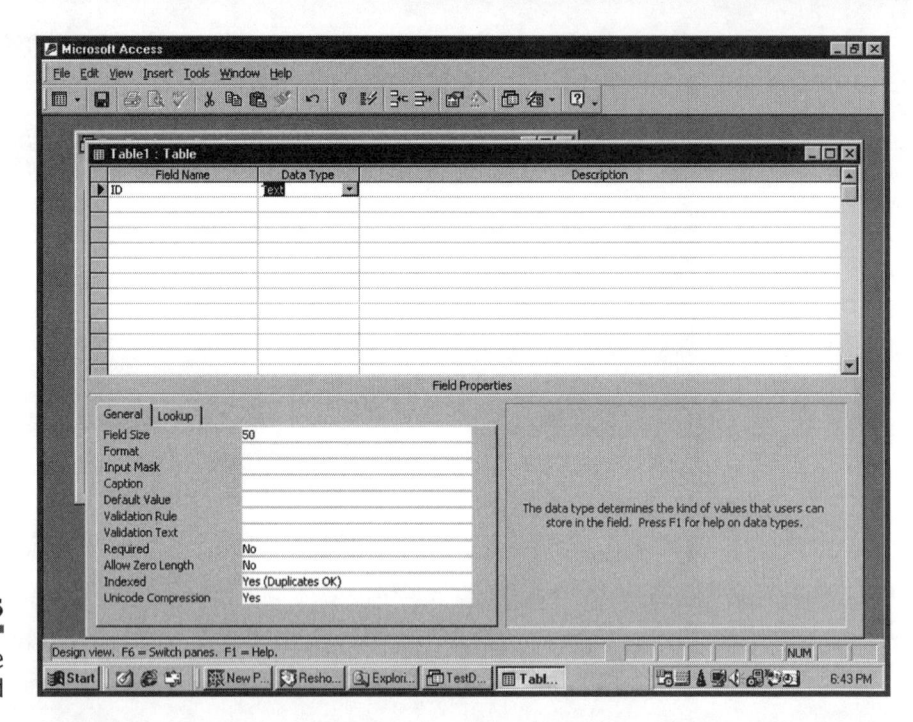

Figure B.5

Creating a name for the first field

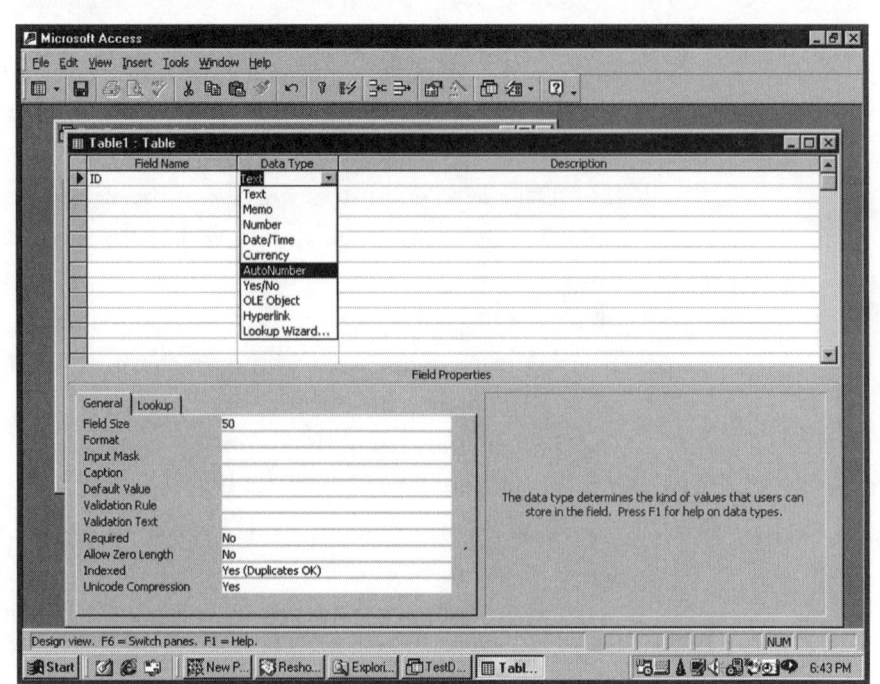

Figure B.6

Exploring the different data types available in Access 2000

APPENDIX B Access Essentials 277

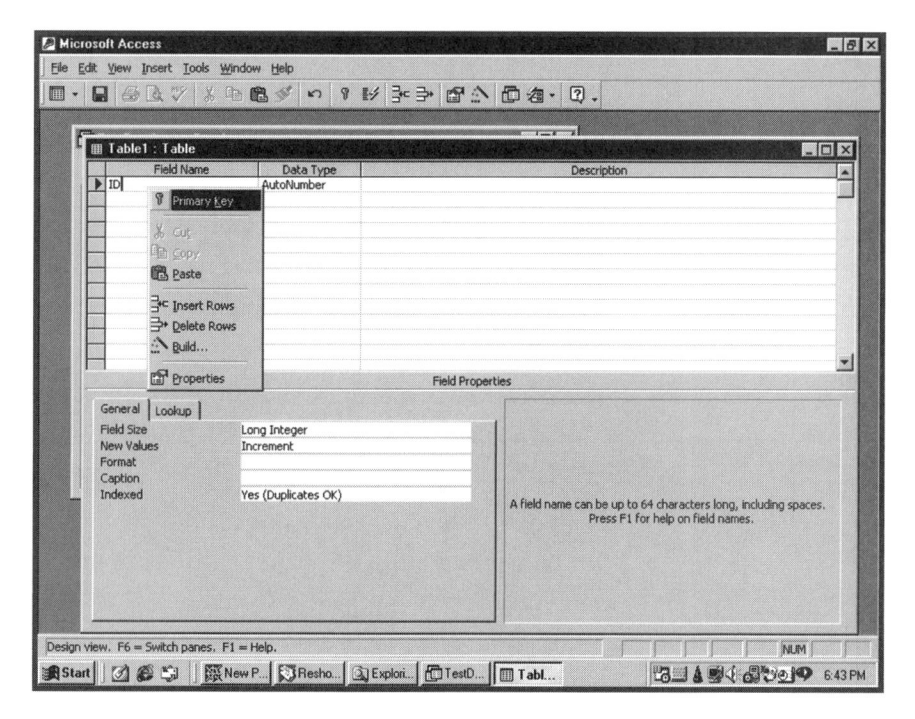

Figure B.7

Assigning the ID field as the primary key for this table

BUZZ WORD

◄◄◄◄◄◄◄◄◄◄◄◄◄◄◄◄◄◄◄◄◄◄◄◄◄

A *primary key* field uniquely identifies each record stored within a table. Doing so allows the full relational powers of Access to function, as data can be quickly located, sorted, and manipulated using this primary key. Every table should have a primary key.

◄◄◄◄◄◄◄◄◄◄◄◄◄◄◄◄◄◄◄◄◄◄◄◄◄

7. Now, create a few other fields for your address book table. For this example, say you want to store the following information about each person in your address book:

    - First name
    - Last name
    - Street address
    - City
    - State

- Zip code
- Phone number

There are seven fields of information you want to store about each person in your address book, so you'll need to create seven specific fields within your Access table. Place your cursor in the field directly beneath the ID field and type **FirstName**. Then, press Tab and select Text from the Data Type drop-down menu, as shown in Figure B.8.

8. Notice the Field Properties section of the screen. The fields in this section, including Field Size and Format, allow you to assign specific characteristics to each field. For now, take note of these fields:

    - **Field Size**. This determines how many characters of information can be stored within a specific field. This can vary, depending on the type of field you have selected.

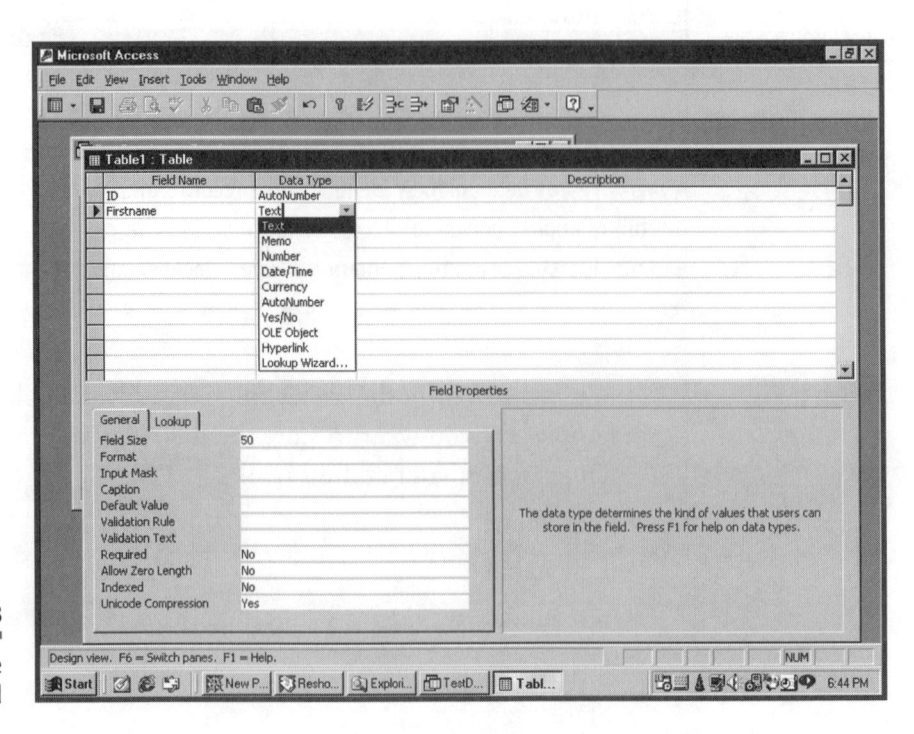

Figure B.8

Creating the FirstName field

- **Required**. This determines whether information must be present in a field, for the specific record. In the discussion about validating Web forms, remember how a user was presented with an error message if he or she didn't enter a value for a specific form field? Think of the Required property in the same way; information must be included if the Required property is set to Yes.

- **Allow Zero Length**. This determines whether a "zero length" input is allowed—in other words, whether it is OK to have a blank space in this specific field.

For the FirstName field, leave the Field Size property at its default setting of 50. Then, set the Required property to Yes and the Allow Zero Length property to No (see Figure B.9).

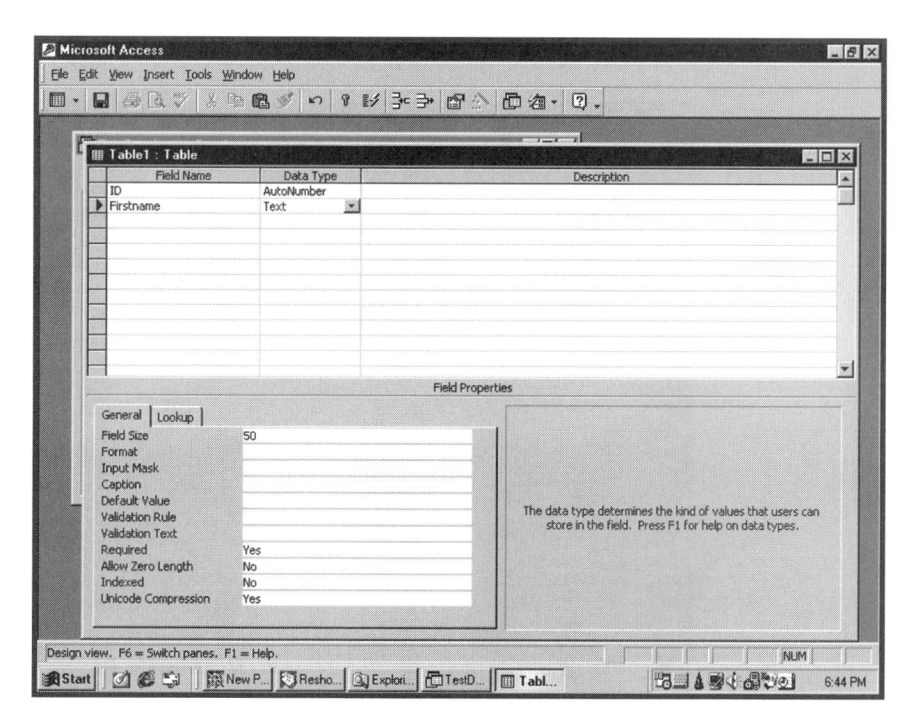

Figure B.9

Setting field attribute properties for the FirstName field

> **NOTE**
>
> Generally speaking, if you have the Required field property set to Yes, you should set the Allow Zero Length property to No. This will ensure that some type of information will be entered into the specific field within your table.

9. You are now ready to create the fields for the remaining pieces of information (Last Name, Street Address, and so on) in your address book. Repeat Steps 7 and 8 for each of the fields you wish to create in your address book, and make sure you set the following attributes for each field:

    - **Data Type.** Set this to Text for each field (see Figure B.10).

    - **Field Size.** This property can be left at the default of 50 for each field except StreetAddress, for which it must be set to 255.

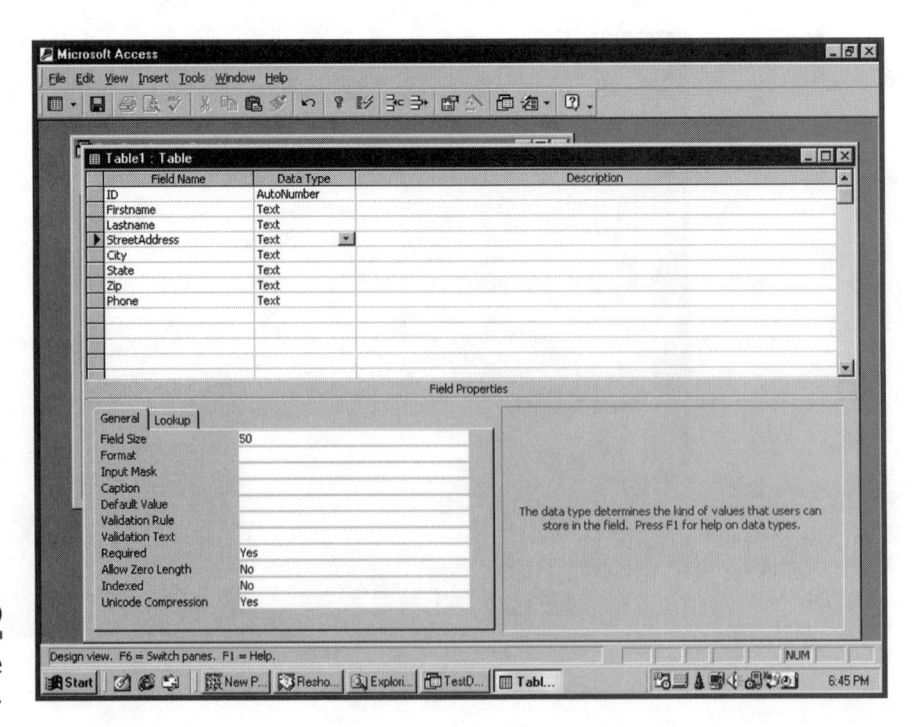

Figure B.10

All fields have been entered.

APPENDIX B Access Essentials

- **Required**. Set this property to Yes.
- **Allow Zero Length**. This property should be set to No.

10. Now that you have created all the specific fields, it is time to save the table. Click the Save icon on the toolbar. The Save As dialog box appears, as shown in Figure B.11.

11. Click OK to save your table. Then, close the Design View for this table by selecting File, Close. Your table is now included as part of the TestDatabase, as shown in Figure B.12.

That's about it for table creation. Of course, this has been a very quick introduction (to put it mildly!) to creating tables in Access. While the actual process is quite easy, planning which tables to create and which fields to store within them can be quite complex, depending on the amount of information you are storing and the relationships you wish to

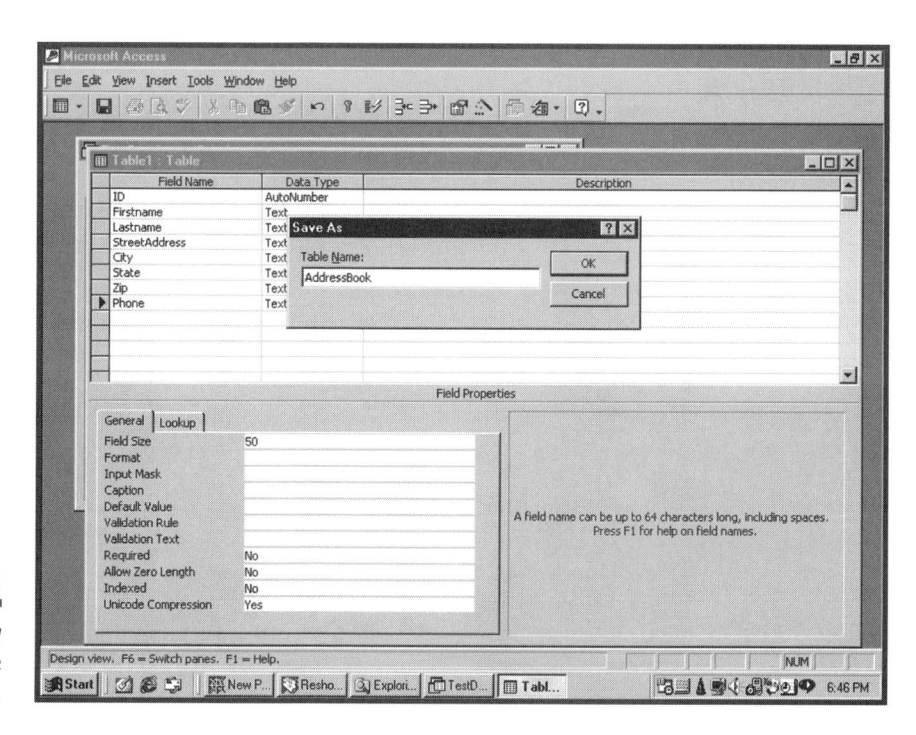

Figure B.11

Give your new table a name to save it.

establish between specific tables. Again, a complete discussion of database creation is far beyond the scope of this book. For now, though, remember the following tips for table creation:

- Set a primary key in each table you create.
- Assign specific data types (for example, Text or AutoNumber) and specific field properties for each field you create.
- Plan ahead! Think about the kind of information you want to store in specific tables, and how that information can be broken down into specific fields. For example, in the AddressBook table you just created, you wanted to store the usual pieces of information for each person listed in your address book, such as first name, last name, address, and so on. By thinking about which types of information you want to store, you can make the table creation process that much easier and save yourself time later, because you won't have to go back and add fields you forgot to create in the beginning.

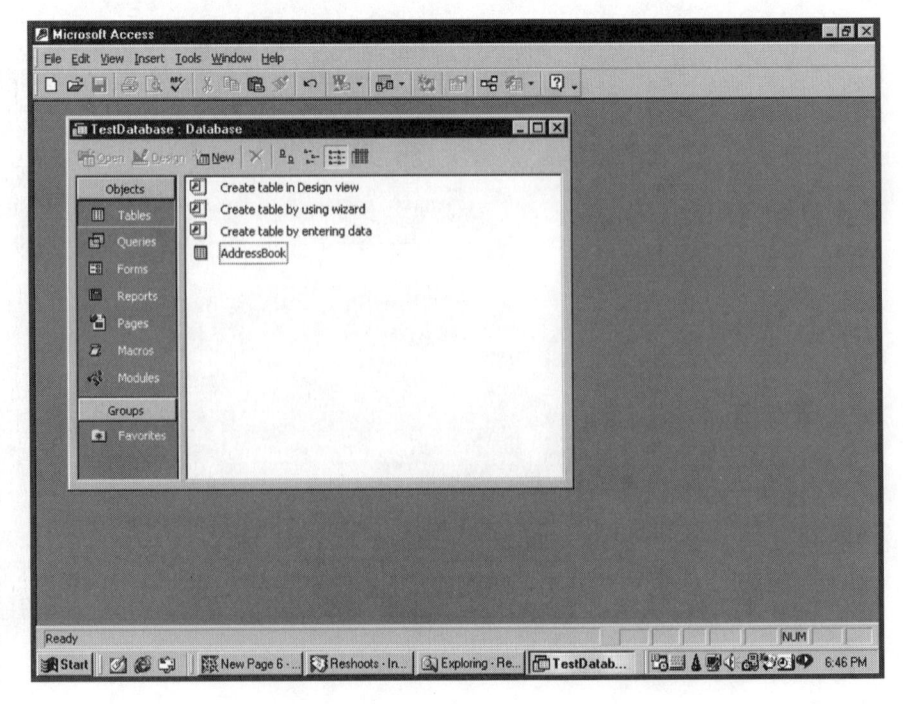

Figure B.12

Your AddressBook table is now part of the TestDatabase!

APPENDIX B Access Essentials   283

Entering Data into a Table Using the Datasheet View

Now that you've created a table, it's easy to enter data into the table from within Access.

1. In your newly created TestDatabase, double-click on the Address-Book table you just created. The table opens in Datasheet View, as shown in Figure B.13.

NOTE What's the difference between Design View and Datasheet View? Use Design View to create your table (as you did in the previous section), so that you can easily designate your specific names, data types, and field properties. Use Datasheet View to enter data into your already created table.

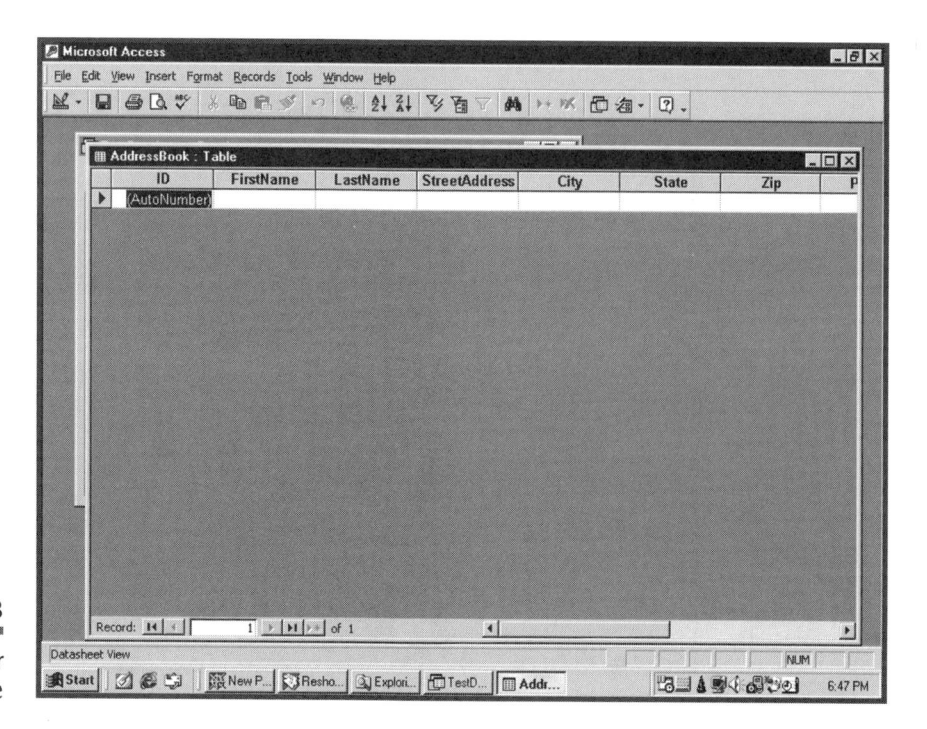

Figure B.13

Preparing to enter data into the table

2. Enter some data into your AddressBook table. In this case, you are transcribing information from your old-fashioned(!) pen and paper address book into the high-tech world of an Access database. Notice that as you enter records, the ID field automatically increases by one, as shown in Figure B.14.

Modifying a Table that Contains Data

Imagine that you want to add a field to a table, after you've already begun entering data. Do you have to start from the beginning again, and lose all the data you've already entered? Of course not! Access 2000 makes it easy to insert a new field (or delete an existing field, for that matter), even if you've already started entering information into a table.

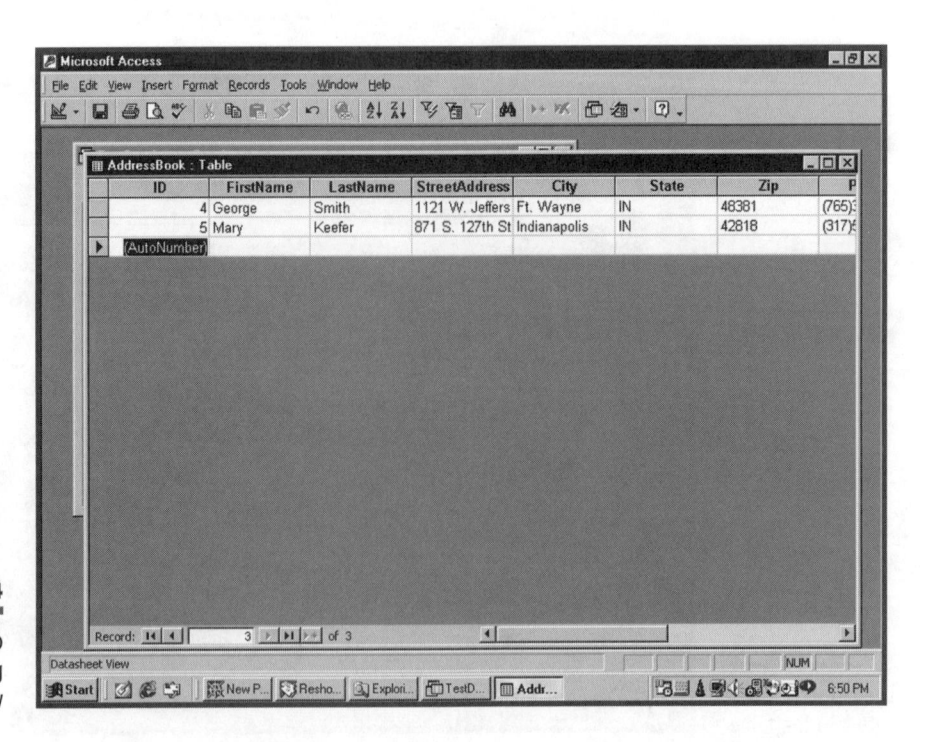

Figure B.14

Entering data into your table using Datasheet View

Inserting a New Field into an Existing Table

Follow these steps to quickly insert a field into an existing table:

1. Imagine that you want to add a Fax field to your existing AddressBook table. This is easily done in Design View, so go ahead and open the table in Design View now (see Figure B.15).

2. You could simply tack the new field onto the end of the field listing by placing it after the Phone field. But for this example, place it right after the StreetAddress field. To do so, click on the City field to highlight it, right-click to display the menu, and select Insert Rows, as shown in Figure B.16.

3. There should now be a blank space between the StreetAddress and City fields. Type **Fax** into this blank space, press the Tab key, and select Text as the Data Type, as shown in Figure B.17.

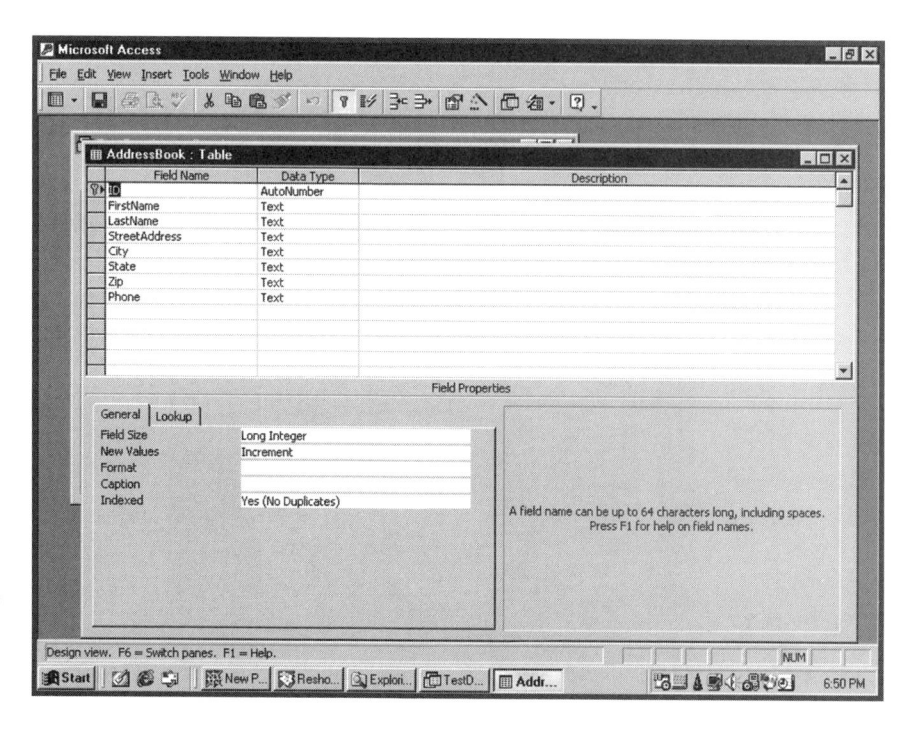

Figure B.15

Another look at the AddressBook table, in Design View

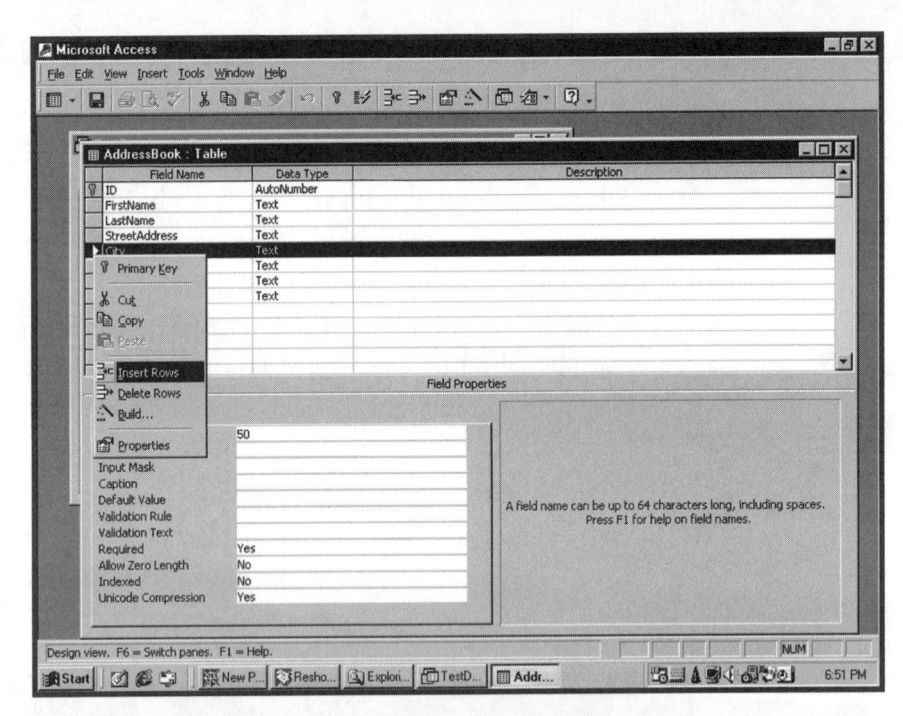

Figure B.16

Preparing to insert a new field into an existing table

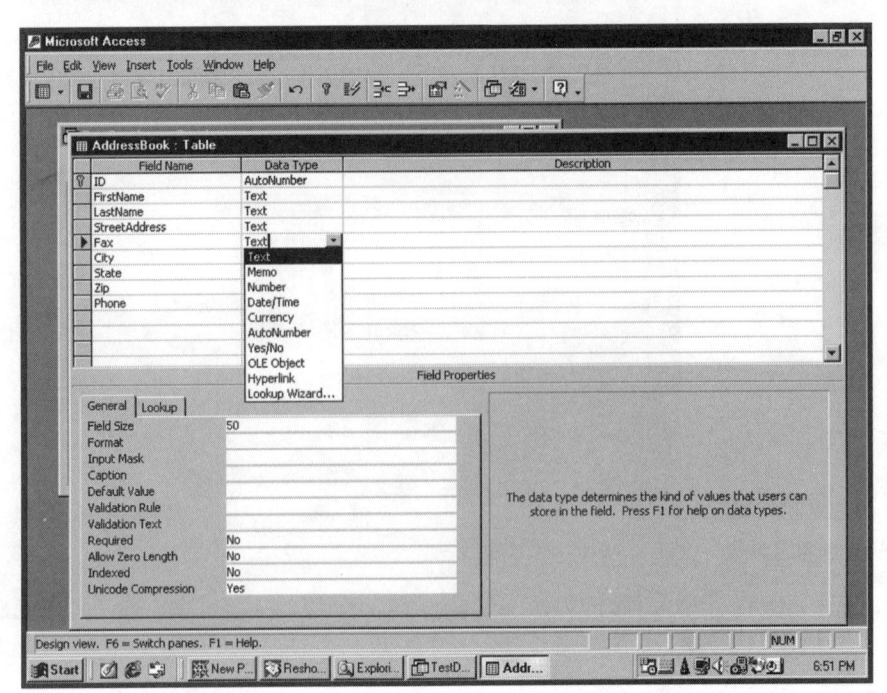

Figure B.17

Don't forget to set the Data Type and specific field properties!

Now, when you view the table in Datasheet View, you will see the new field in place (see Figure B.18). You can go back and enter the specified information (in this case, a fax number) for each record that exists in the table.

Deleting a Field from an Existing Table

You can also easily delete fields from an existing table. To do so, follow these steps:

1. Open the AddressBook table in Design View.
2. For this example, delete the newly created Fax field. Click within the field to select it, right-click to display the menu, and select Delete Rows, as shown in Figure B.19.
3. Before the deletion process goes any further, Access will caution you about the action that you are about to take, as shown in Figure B.20.
4. Go ahead and click Yes. The field is deleted.

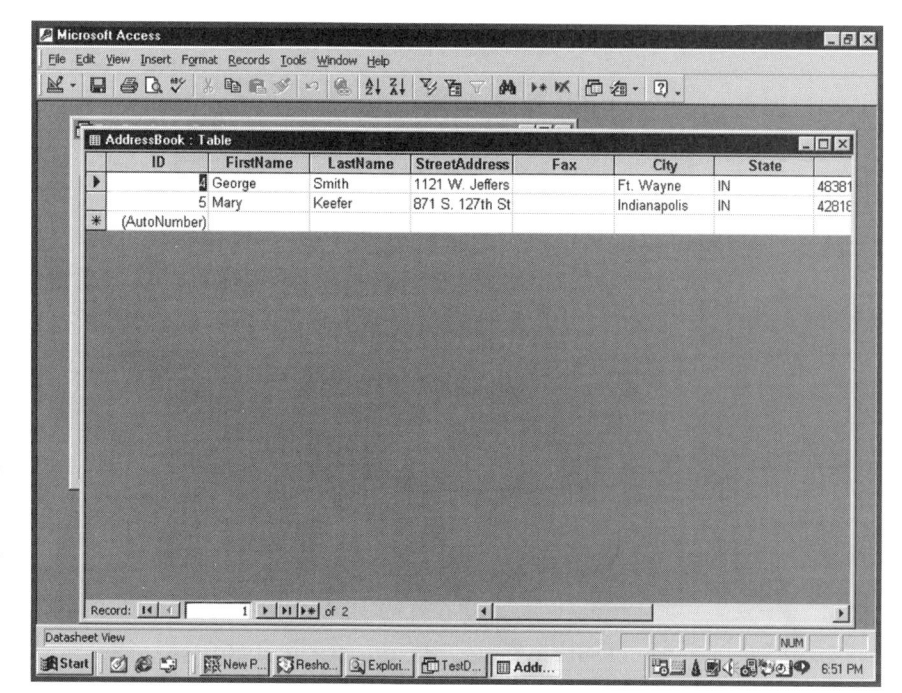

Figure B.18

You'll need to add the fax number for each record that currently exists in the AddressBook table.

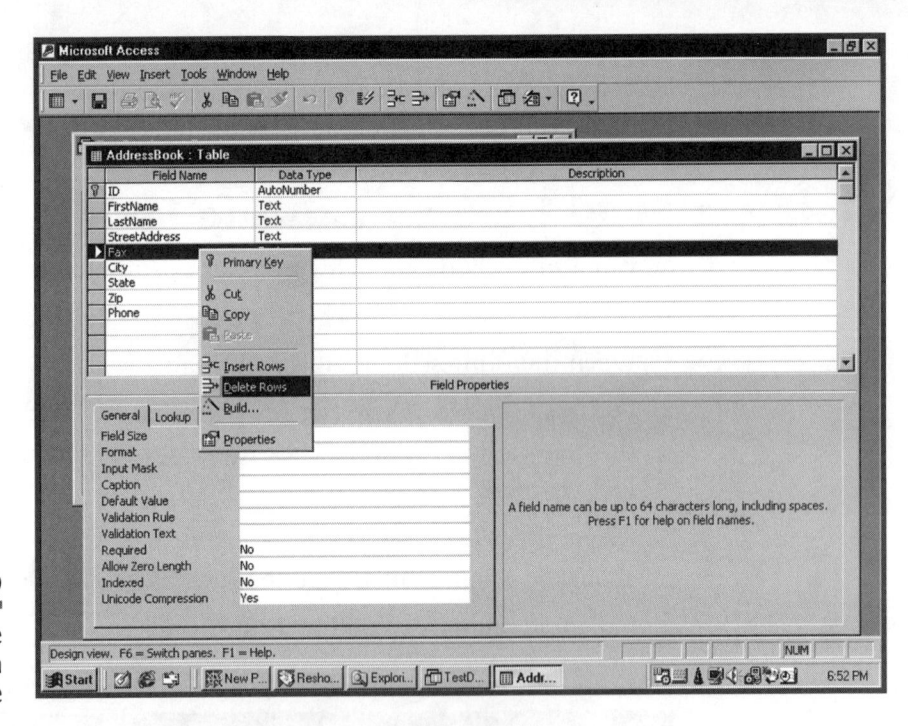

Figure B.19

Preparing to delete a field in an existing table

Figure B.20

Use the Delete action with caution.

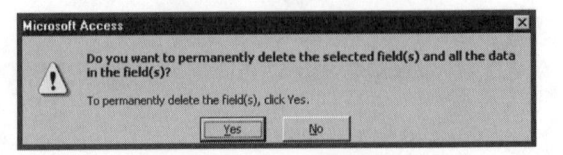

Modifying a Field Data Type

Another modification you might want to make is to change a field's data type in an existing table.

1. Again, open the AddressBook table in Design View.
2. Place your cursor in the Data Type column for the Phone Field.
3. Click on the down arrow, and change the Data Type from Text to Number, as shown in Figure B.21.
4. Save this table, but notice the dialog box that appears when you try to save (see Figure B.22).

APPENDIX B Access Essentials   289

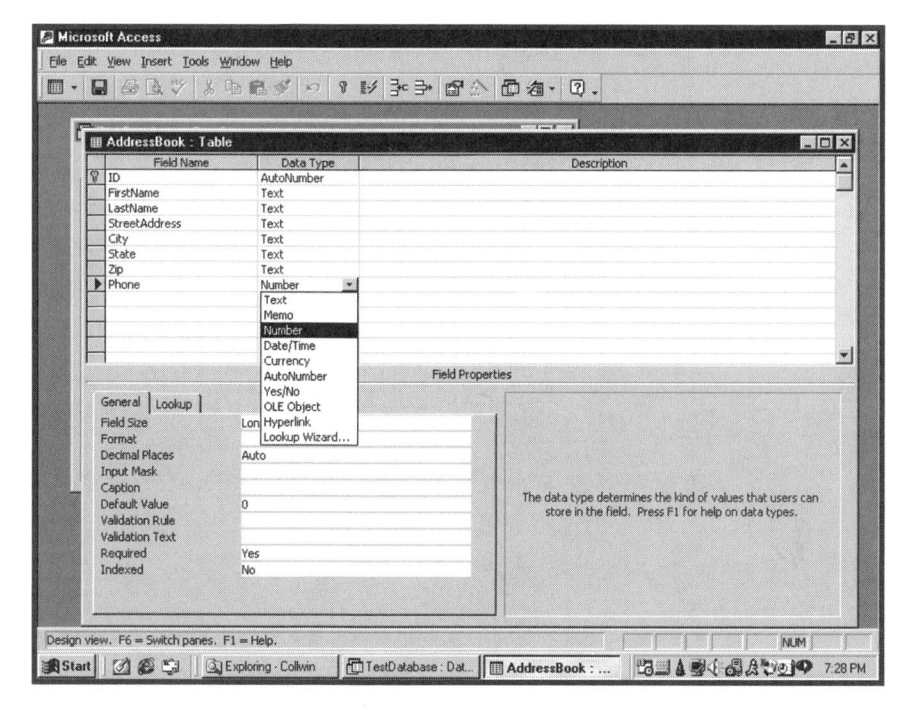

Figure B.21

Changing a field Data Type attribute

Figure B.22

Again, Access warns you about potential data loss, this time due to a change of Data Type properties.

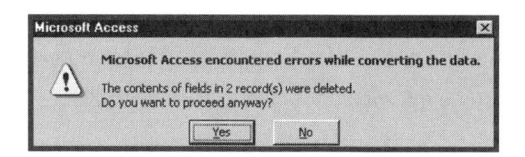

What does this mean? When you entered data into the AddressBook table, you probably used the following format in the Phone field:

(Area Code)XXX-XXXX

So, for example, a typical phone number was listed as:

(317)555-1212

Since this field was a text field, the parentheses around the area code and the hyphen between the prefix and the remaining four digits of the number were acceptable. But now that you've changed the Data Type from Text to Number, the parentheses and hyphen can no longer be part of the number, because they are text elements rather than numbers. In this case, Access is telling you that in order for the Data Type change to occur, you must delete the information previously entered into the Phone field.

5. For this example, go ahead and click Yes. If this were a real application, you'd need to go back and enter the information into the Phone field again, without any text elements like parentheses or hyphens.

Again, this example shows that you need to do some planning before you start constructing your database tables (or, at the very least, before you get too far in your data entry). So, plan ahead as much as possible!

> **CAUTION**
> If this were a Web-enabled Access database and you tried to enter text information into a number field using a Web form, you would be presented with an error message in your Web browser. As with any error on your small business Web site, this detracts from the displayed professionalism of your site and could potentially cost you money in lost customer orders. Therefore, take the time to troubleshoot your Web forms and ensure that you do not allow customers to enter data into specific form fields in a way that would cause an error when the information is sent to your database.
>
> For more information on the topic of form validation, see the Sunday Morning session, "Adding FrontPage Spice: Form Validation, DHTML, and E-Mail."

Using the Access Simple Query Wizard

You'll remember from previous discussions that a query is a method of sorting and otherwise looking at your data in a specific way. SQL, the universal database language, is a powerful method for querying your data.

APPENDIX B Access Essentials

But, as usual, Access has a helpful wizard to guide you through the process of querying your data, so you don't have to worry about learning SQL to powerfully manipulate your data to see new informational relationships.

In this section, we'll take a quick look at the Access Simple Query Wizard, which helps you sort your data by doing most of the legwork for you.

> **NOTE** For this section, you'll be using the CDShop.mdb sample database, which is included on the enclosed CD-ROM. This is the same database you used in the Sunday Afternoon session, "Examining a Web-Enabled Small Business Example: BestPop CD Shop."

1. Open the CDShop.mdb file, and click on the Queries button. Two different methods of creating queries will appear, as shown in Figure B.23.
2. Double-click on the Create Query by Using Wizard option. The first step of the Simple Query Wizard appears, as shown in Figure B.24.
3. In the Tables/Queries field, select the Catalog table.
4. For this query, you'll want to include the Artist and Price fields. So, select each of these fields one at a time and click the inclusion button to add them to the Selected Fields list (see Figure B.25).
5. Click Next. The final dialog box for the Simple Query Wizard appears, as shown in Figure B.26.

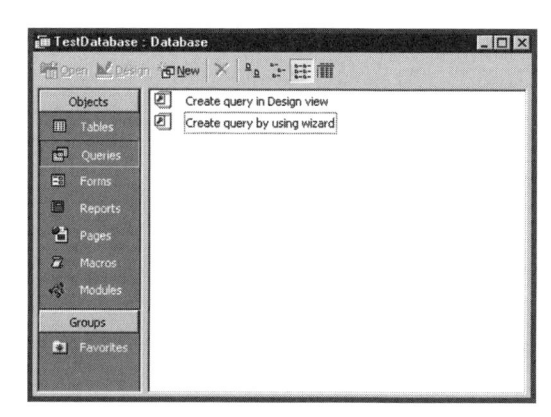

Figure B.23

You can create a query in Design View or by using a wizard.

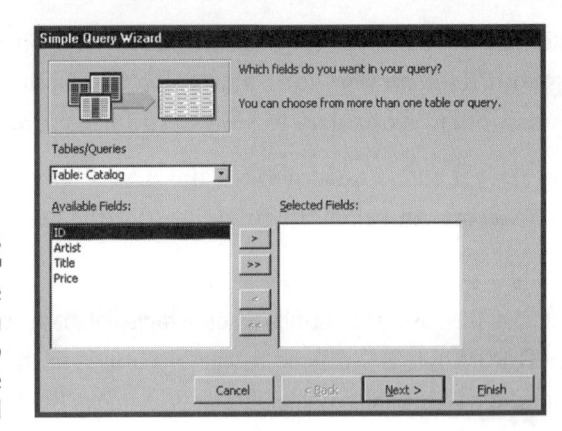

Figure B.24

Beginning the query creation process, with help from the Simple Query Wizard

Figure B.25

Determining which fields to include in the query

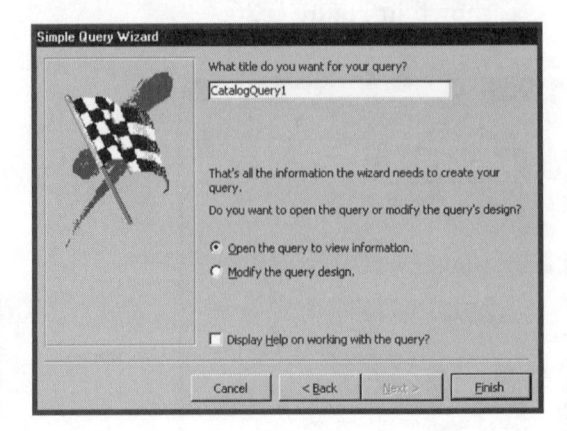

Figure B.26

The final steps in the Simple Query Wizard

APPENDIX B Access Essentials

6. Leave the title of the query as the default Catalog Query. Also, make sure the Open the Query to View Information radio button is selected.

7. Click Finish. The Catalog table, sorted by artist and price, appears, just as you specified in your query (see Figure B.27).

NOTE Again, the Simple Query Wizard is just the beginning of the data sorting and data manipulation abilities of Access 2000. As your interest guides you, take the time to investigate the advanced querying abilities of Access and learn more about SQL. As your small business Web site grows, you might want to learn more about how to present, store, and retrieve information on your site. Advanced querying and SQL (in conjunction with Active Server Pages) can make this possible.

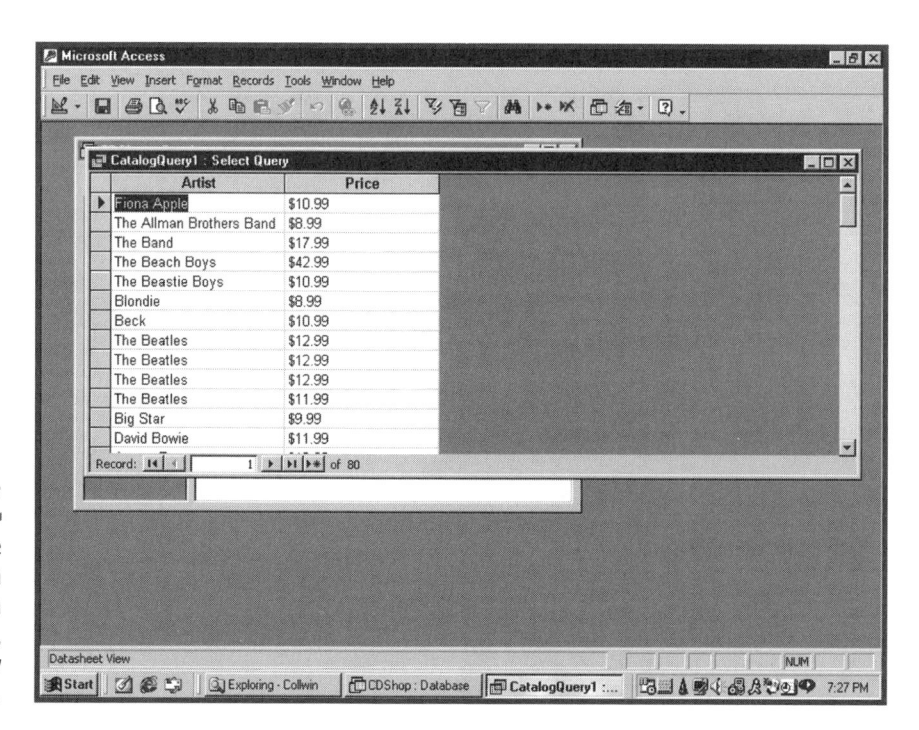

Figure B.27

The Simple Query Wizard can quickly return your information, sorted in the way you specified.

APPENDIX C

What's On the CD-ROM?

- Running the CD
- The Prima License
- The Prima User Interface
- The Software

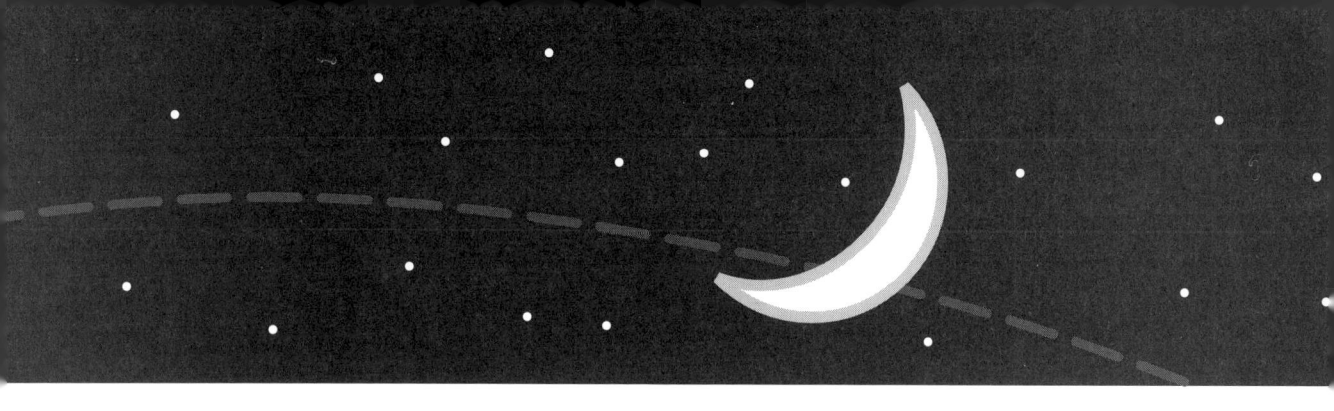

The CD-ROM that accompanies this book contains shareware and freeware that will help you use what you learned in this book more effectively.

Running the CD

To make the CD-ROM more user-friendly, and to take up less of your disk space, no installation is required. This means that the only files transferred to your hard disk are the ones you choose to copy or install.

CAUTION This CD has been designed to run under Windows 95/98/2000/Me and Windows NT 4. Neither the CD itself nor the programs on the CD will run under earlier versions of Windows.

Windows 95/98/NT4/2000/Me

Since there is no install routine, running the CD-ROM in Windows 95/98/NT4/2000/Me is a breeze, especially if you have autorun enabled. Simply insert the CD in the CD-ROM drive, close the tray, and wait for the CD to load.

If you have disabled autorun, place the CD in the CD-ROM drive and follow these steps:

1. From the Start menu, choose Run.
2. Type **D:\CDInstaller.exe** (where D:\ is the CD-ROM drive).
3. Click OK.

The Prima License

The first window you will see is the Prima License Agreement. Take a moment to read the agreement, then click the I Agree button to accept the license and proceed to the user interface. If you do not agree with the license, click the I Decline button to close the user interface and end the session.

The Prima User Interface

Prima's user interface is designed to make viewing and using the CD contents quick and easy. The opening screen contains a two-panel window with three buttons across the bottom. The left panel contains the structure of the programs on the CD. The right panel displays a description page for the selected entry in the left panel. The three buttons across the bottom of the user interface make it possible to install programs, view the contents of the CD using Windows Explorer, and view the contents of a help file for the selected entry. If any of the buttons are grayed out, it means that button is unavailable. For example, if the Help button is disabled, it means that no Help file is available.

Resizing and Closing the User Interface

As with any window, you can resize the user interface. To do so, position the mouse over any edge or corner, hold down the left mouse button and drag the edge or corner to a new position.

APPENDIX C What's On the CD-ROM? 299

To close and exit the user interface, either double-click on the small button in upper-left corner of the window, or click the Close button in the upper-right corner of the window.

Using the Left Panel

The left panel of the Prima user interface works very much like Windows Explorer. To view the description of an entry in the left panel, simply click the entry. For example, to view the general information about Prima Tech, click the Prima-Tech entry.

Some items have subitems that are nested below them. Such parent items have a small plus (+) symbol next to them. To view the nested subitems, simply click the plus sign. When you do, the list expands and the subitems are listed below the parent item. In addition, the plus symbol becomes a minus (-) symbol. To hide the subitems, click the minus symbol to collapse the listing.

> **TIP**
> You can control the positon of the line between the left and right panels. To change the position of the dividing line, move the mouse over the line, hold down the left mouse button (the mouse becomes a two-headed arrow), and drag the line to a new position.

Using the Right Panel

The right panel displays a page that describes the entry you select in the left panel. Use the information provided to read details about your selection, such as what functionality an installable program provides. In addition to a general description, the page may provide the following information:

- **World Wide Web site**. Many program providers have a Web site. If one is available, the description page provides the Web address. To navigate to the Web site using your browser, simply click the

Web address (you must be connected to the Internet). Alternately, you can copy the Web address to the clipboard, and paste it into the URL, or *address*, line at the top of your browser window.

- **E-Mail address.** Many program providers are available via e-mail. If available, the description page provides the e-mail address. To use the e-mail address, click it to open your e-mail program (to send e-mail, you must be connected to your Intranet or the Internet). Alternately, copy the address to the clipboard, and paste it into the address line of your e-mail program.

- **Readme, License, and other text files.** Many programs have additional information available in files with such names as Readme, License, Order, and so on. If such files exist, you can view the contents of the file in the right panel by clicking the indicated hyperlink. When you are done viewing the text file, you can return to the description page by re-clicking the entry in the left panel.

Command Buttons

You should find this CD quite easy to use. The following list gives a short explanation of the command buttons.

- **Install.** Use this button to install the program corresponding to your selection onto your hard drive.

- **Explore.** Use this button to view the contents of the CD-ROM using Windows Explorer.

- **Help.** Use this button to display the contents of the Help file provided with the program.

Pop-Up Menu Options

You can use the pop-up menu options to do the following:

- **Install.** If the selected title contains an install routine, choosing this option begins the installation process.

- **Explore.** Choosing this option allows you to view the folder containing the program files using Windows Explorer.
- **View Help.** Using this menu item displays the contents of the Help file provided with the program.

The Software

This section gives you a brief description of the shareware and evaluation software you'll find on the CD-ROM.

> **NOTE** The software included with this publication is provided for your evaluation. If you try this software and find it useful, you must register the software as discussed in its documentation. Prima Publishing has not paid the registration fee for any shareware included on the CD.

- **1st Theme Factory for FrontPage (Entertainment).** The Entertainment version of 1st Theme Factory for FrontPage provides professionally designed themes with an entertainment subject. Each theme contains a ready-made package of background images, bullets, buttons, color schemes, images, and navigation bars. All themes are modeled for FrontPage, so they are easily swapped, added, or removed via the FrontPage command buttons.
- **1st Theme Factory for FrontPage (Series 1).** Choose from an exciting new range of ten professionally designed themes (with at least three variations of each) for use in your FrontPage-created Web sites. Theme titles are Africa, Highway, Ice, Klingon, Maritime, Money, Music, Soccer, Starship, and Wine. Each theme contains a ready-made package of background images, bullets, buttons, color schemes, images, and navigation bars. All themes are modeled for FrontPage, so they are easily swapped, added, or removed via the FrontPage command buttons.

- **1st Theme Factory for FrontPage (Sports).** 1st Theme Factory assists you with creating a sports-related Web site easily and quickly using FrontPage. It includes ten sports-related themes titled Baseball, Formula 1, Golf, NBA, NFL, NHL, Riding, Scuba, Soccer 2, and Tennis.
- **4004 Background Images and Sounds.** Over 4,000 professional images and sound files are available for your use in this extensive and ever-enlarging gallery.
- **Blounkser.** Running Blounkser from your Web server allows you to automatically change background or other GIF and JPEG image files on your site. And, you can predefine the sequence in which you wish them to rotate.
- **Cool Edit 2000.** Cool Edit is a digital sound editor for Windows. You might think of it as a paint program for audio. Just as a paint program enables you to create images with colors, brush strokes, and a variety of special effects, Cool Edit enables you to *paint* with sound: tones, pieces of songs and voices, miscellaneous noises, sine waves and sawtooth waves, noise, or just pure silence.
- **CuteFTP.** CuteFTP is a Windows-based File Transfer Protocol (FTP) client that allows you to utilize the capabilities of FTP without needing to know all the details of the protocol itself. This excellent FTP program includes a lot more than just a pretty interface.
- **Exploit Submission Wizard.** Submission Wizard offers Web users the ability to submit their sites automatically—without hassle or complication—to the ever-increasing number of search engines on the Internet. Once the required data has been gathered, the program uses a standard Internet connection to submit a site to a host of major search engines and high-traffic sites without requiring any further input. This trial version allows submission to 20 engines and is compatible with Windows 98.

- **FastStats: Log File Analysis.** FastStats gives you vital information about your Web site: how many hits per day you get, which search engines and keywords are used to access your Web site, what documents are missing (404 errors), and how well your Web server is performing (incomplete or server busy requests). FastStats is written in C++, with the speed-critical portions written in C and assembly language. FastStats uses fast data collection and sorting algorithms, allowing it to process your log files at high speed. You can sort data in both ascending and descending order and view graphs as tables, which allows you to see the raw data behind the graphs.

- **GifArt Clip Art Collection.** GifArt provides a wide range of clip art and other graphics. You can explore the site, viewing the graphics available there, as well as taking advantage of a multitude of links to other graphics Web sites. The latest collection of free graphics available at press time is included on this CD; simply use the Explore button to view the collection of graphics and either use them directly from the CD or copy them to your hard drive. The collection includes a wide range of bars, buttons, controls, backgrounds, icons, and animations.

- **Internet Audio Mix.** Internet Audio Mix is an intuitive multi-track recording and WAVE/MP3 sound mixing software package with integrated support for RealAudio.

- **My Creations Clip Art Collection.** My Creations provides a wide range of clip art graphics. You can explore the site, viewing a wide range of categories of clip art, and use much of it free. The latest collection available at press time is included on this CD. Simply use the Explore button to view the collection of graphics, and either use them directly from the CD or copy them to your hard drive.

- **NetStudio.** NetStudio allows you to design graphics for your Web site without requiring you to draw the pictures by hand. The program offers one-click creation of text, buttons, navigation bars, banners, and other essential Web graphics components. You can also manipulate your image objects in a variety of ways. For example, you can adjust brightness and contrast, apply drop shadows, emboss items, incorporate washout and transparency effects, and so on. You can also insert more than one object onto a canvas to create a composite image, while retaining the ability to edit each individual object. This is a 30-day trial version. The full version includes more styles, templates, and pictures, featuring new Easy Hover buttons.

- **Paint Shop Pro.** Paint Shop Pro is an award-winning, image-editing tool that supports more than 30 image formats and several painting and drawing tools. The program is one of the easiest and most powerful you may ever use for image viewing, editing, and converting. Included are dockable toolbars, enhanced selection options, built-in special effects filters, RGB color separation, support for new image formats (Progressive JPEG, Mac PICT, and PNG with transparency), resampling, and masking options. Relatively new are features such as multilevel undo functionality, complete layer support, "picture tube" brushes, CMYK separation, and pressure-sensitive tablet support. The program also includes enhancements to Paint Shop Pro's flexible painting and retouching brushes, adjustable cropping and selection tools, and images.

- **Password.** The password applet is used to provide a password protection scheme for Web pages that do not rely on server intervention.

- **Purp's World Graphics Clipart Collection.** Purp's World provides a wide range of clip art and other graphics. You can explore the site, viewing such subjects as Graphics Tips, HTML Tips, and even download a collection of free graphics. The latest collection available at press time is included on this CD. Simply use the Explore button to view the collection of graphics and either use them directly from the CD or copy them to your hard drive. The collection includes a wide range of banners, buttons, arrows, and other separators.

- **Signpost.** If you decide to move your Web site to a new server, you'll want to notify all those people who bookmarked your old address. Signpost can change all your old Web pages into re-directors or pointers (signposts) to your new address. For examples of signpost pages, open the examples.htm file included with this program in any Web browser.

- **Viewer.** This is a shareware slide show applet. It will show the pictures you specify with a delay between each picture. The applet supports GIF and JPEG pictures and it will automatically resize the viewing window to fit the picture it is loading. You can sort the pictures into categories and add comments to each picture. The applet will show all of the categories in a select list, along with any comment included with the picture.

- **WebLog Manager Pro.** WebLog Manager Pro allows you to build a profile on search engine keywords, traffic, or Web hits. You can promote your site more effectively, understand whether a banner ad is working for you, and more. This Web site visitor tracking tool tells you where visitors come from, the search engine keywords used to get to your site, browser type, visitor country, visitor ISP host, and how often a particular visitor visits your site.

- **WinZip.** WinZip is *the* way to handle compressed (zipped) files, whether you get them from a friend or download them from the Internet. WinZip makes it painless to extract selected or all the files from a zipped file, create your own compressed files (including self-extracting files that anyone can decompress—even if they don't own WinZip), and a Wizard to walk you through the entire process.

GLOSSARY

A

Access. Access is a Microsoft database application.

Active Server Pages. An active server page is a special type of Web page that allows codes stored within it to be processed on a Web server. This allows for increased security and ease-of-use to programmers wishing to utilize specific features of the Web such as form processing, integration with a database, and so on.

AutoNumber field. An AutoNumber field is a type of field used with a database to automatically increment each record number. For example, as each new record is added, its record number increases by one.

B

Bookmark. A reference to a Web page stored within a browser application is referred to as a bookmark. Bookmarks are used to note locations to which the user wants to return in the future. They are generally available in other applications, such as Help files or word processing programs.

Browser. A browser is an application used to navigate the Web. Two typical browsers are Netscape Navigator and Microsoft Internet Explorer.

C

Clip art. A collection of graphics is often referred to as clip art. Clip art collections are included in many applications (including Microsoft Office) and are often, but not always, royalty free. Be sure to check the documentation for any clip art collection to determine whether you can use the clip art without restriction.

CRM. An abbreviation for Customer Relationship Management, CRM includes all practices that, in conjunction with general e-commerce principles, ensure a customer has a satisfying experience (at pre-, point of, and post-sale) when performing a business transaction on the Web.

Cyberspace. Cyberspace is a popular term used to denote the Web.

D

Database. A database is a special application, such as Microsoft Access, that is used to store and manipulate information. Dynamic Web pages integrate with databases so they can produce unique information depending on the specific user or condition.

Database Results Wizard. The Database Results Wizard is a special component within FrontPage that allows for easy integration of a Web page with an underlying database.

DHTML. An abbreviation for Dynamic Hypertext Markup Language, DHTML allows for additional functionality not supported or available with traditional HTML.

Domain name. The domain name indicates the location of a Web site. For example, in the URL http://www.microsoft.com, the domain name is microsoft.com.

DSN. DSN is an abbreviation for data source name. This is used to identify a database to a Web page, for example.

Dynamic Web page. As opposed to a static Web page, a dynamic Web page presents different information depending on variables (such as a specific visitor) set by the programmer of the Web page. Generally, these pages draw their information from an underlying database, such as Microsoft Access.

E

E-commerce. E-commerce is an abbreviation for electronic commerce, a term used to denote all procedures and practices for doing business on the Web.

E-mail. E-mail, an abbreviation for electronic mail, is rapidly becoming a medium of choice for quick communication between users who are in the same town, or in different parts of the world.

F

Form. In the context of this book, a form is a special element within a Web page that allows information to be collected about visitors to the page.

Form field. A specific element within a form, such as a one-line text box or radio button, is called a form field. Fields on a form allow you to gather information about visitors to a Web page.

Form validation. Form validation is a procedure used to ensure that the type of information entered into a form fits within specified parameters.

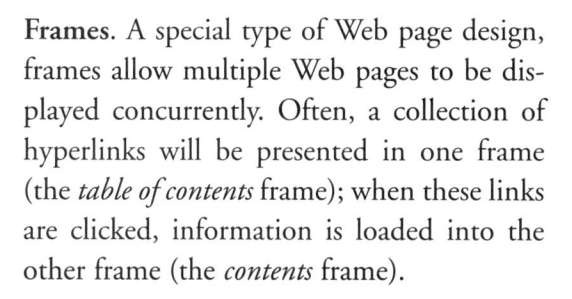

Frames. A special type of Web page design, frames allow multiple Web pages to be displayed concurrently. Often, a collection of hyperlinks will be presented in one frame (the *table of contents* frame); when these links are clicked, information is loaded into the other frame (the *contents* frame).

FrontPage. FrontPage is a Microsoft application used to design Web pages.

FrontPage Server Extensions. FrontPage Server Extensions are a special component of Microsoft FrontPage that, when loaded onto a Web server, allow increased functionality to users who construct Web pages in FrontPage.

FTP. FTP is an abbreviation for file transfer protocol—a method of transmitting files from one computer to another via the Web.

H

Hit counter. A hit counter is a special Web element used to record the number of visitors to a Web page.

Home page. A home page is the first page that loads when the URL for a Web site is entered into a browser.

HTML. An abbreviation for Hypertext Markup Language, HTML is the underlying source behind all Web pages.

HTTP. HTTP is an abbreviation for Hypertext Transfer Protocol.

Hyperlink. A hyperlink (sometimes referred to simply as a *link*) is a specially formatted text reference on a Web page that, when clicked, takes you to a different location on the Web.

I

Internet Server Provider. An ISP (*Internet Server Provider*) is an organization that provides both consumers and businesses with access to the Web.

Intranet. An Intranet is a closed version of the Internet used by organizations to provide their employees with the interface of the Web (that is, use of Web browsers, access to HTML pages, and so on), but without allowing access to individuals outside the organization.

J

JavaScript. A special Web programming language, JavaScript allows for increased functionality in Web pages.

O

ODBC. An abbreviation for Open Database Connectivity, ODBC is a popular method of allowing communication between databases and other applications.

P

Personal Web Server. Also referred to as PWS in this book, Personal Web Server is a compact, robust Web application that allows desktop computers to act as Web servers and thus serve files stored within them to users via the Web.

Plug-in. A plug-in is a special application that works in conjunction with a Web browser to allow additional features to function within a Web page. Typically, plug-ins allow extended audio, video, or other multimedia capabilities of the Web.

Primary Key. A primary key is one term for a special marker used within a database application to assign a unique value to each stored record.

S

Search engine. A search engine is a Web tool such as Yahoo!, which allows you to locate an item of interest (that is, a search term) on the Internet. The search engine, in turn, returns to you a list of links to the Web pages that contain the term.

SQL. An abbreviation for Structured Query Language, SQL is used to access information within a database in a variety of ways.

Static Web page. A Web page that is hard coded with information is considered to be a static Web page. In other words, a static Web page doesn't change unless the programmer/owner of the page physically changes the information.

T

Toolbar. A toolbar is a collection of related icons, menus, and so on within an application (such as Microsoft Word). Toolbars allow for quick access to specific features.

U

URL. URL is an abbreviation for Uniform Resource Locator, more commonly known as the address of a Web site. For example, the URL for Prima Publishing is http://www.primapub.com.

V

VBScript. VBScript is another type of special Web programming language. Unlike JavaScript, VBScript can only be executed with the Microsoft Internet Explorer Web browser, unless the VBScript is being executed on the server. In that case, rather than actually running the VBScript, the browser only receives the results of the code that is executed on the server.

W

Web Presence Provider. Similar to an Internet Service Provider, the WPP (*Web Presence Provider*) hosts your Web site on its servers so other people can access it via the Web.

Web server. A computer running special software (such as Microsoft Internet Information Server or Personal Web Server) is termed a Web server. The files on a Web server can be accessed by individuals via the Web.

WYSIWYG. WYSIWYG, a popular term pronounced "wiz-e-wig," is an acronym for "What You See Is What You Get." This term is used to describe applications that allow you to see within the application what the results will look like on the printed or Web page.

INDEX

1st Choice International Internet Services Web site, 267
1st Theme Factory for FrontPage (Entertainment), 301
1st Theme Factory for FrontPage (Series 1), 301
1st Theme Factory for FrontPage (Sports), 302
4004 Background Images and Sounds, 302

A

Access 2000, 22, 135, 271, 307
   database creation, 272–274
   Datasheet View, 283–284
   designing database, 134
   Query Wizard, 272
   table creation in Design View, 273–282
Access 2000 Fast and Easy, 271
Active Server Pages Network Web site, 267
Add Choice dialog box, 104
Add Criteria dialog box, 154–155
Add Field dialog box, 159–161
Add/Modify FTP Locations dialog box, 254
AddressBook table, 274–282
   deleting field, 287
   entering data, 284
   inserting field, 285–287
   modifying field data type, 288–290
Advanced Form Properties dialog box, 233–235

advertisements, 257
AKOS Web site, 267
Amazon.com home page, 184
Amazon.com Web site, 74
American Business Web Web site, 267
ASP (Active Server Pages), 118–120, 126, 132, 165, 200, 307
ASP 3 Fast & Easy Web Development, 120, 132, 165
.asp file extension, 200
automatic dial-up connection, disabling, 33–35, 60
AutoNumber field, 307

B

background in tables, 77
Ballard, Dugan, 192
BestPop CD Shop history, 192–193
BestPop database, 202–203
BestPop Web site, 238–239
   building themselves, 196–197
   catalog_search.asp page, 210–218
   construction options, 193–194
   cost estimates, 193
   customer feedback, 197
   databases, 201–205
   e-commerce features, 198
   general information, 197
   guestbook.asp page, 218–223

Index

BestPop Web site *(continued...)*
   guestbook_confirm.htm page, 223
   Home.htm page, 199–200
   homeleft.htm page, 200, 206
   home page design, 199–201
   homeright.asp page, 200
   ignoring design firm suggestions, 194–196
   insert_order.asp page, 236
   lack of business components, 194
   location.htm page, 206–210
   mailing_confirm.htm page, 223–225
   mailing_list.asp page, 223–225
   not listening to customer, 193
   online catalog search, 197
   order.asp page, 225–231
   Order page, 215
   order_status.htm page, 236–238
   order_status_results.asp page, 236–238
   overview, 197–201
   Place and Order hyperlink, 227
   place_order.asp page, 231–236
   related links, 198
   searching, 210–215
   search_results.asp page, 210–218
   third-party company control of, 194
BitShop.com Web site, 267
Blounkser, 302
bookmarks, 307
browsers, 307
business cards, 257
businesses, organizing process flow, 136–141
business intelligence, 136

C

catalog_search.asp page, 210–218
Catalog table, 146, 161, 202, 213–215, 233, 291, 293
CCC Webbs Web site, 267
CD-ROM (enclosed with this book)
   command buttons, 300
   Explore command button, 300
   Explore option, 301
   Help command button, 300
   Install command button, 300
   Install option, 300
   pop-up menu options, 300–301
   Prima License Agreement, 298
   software, 301–305
   user interface, 298–301
   View Help option, 301
   Windows 95/98/NT4/2000/Me, 297–298
CDShop database, 144
   Catalog table, 146, 215
   Comments table, 220
   database-driven Web page, 146–151
   tables, 149
CDShop.mdb file, 142, 161
Cell Properties command, 79, 82
Cell Properties dialog box, 77
centering text, 39
check box, 101–102
Check Box Properties dialog box, 101
Choose Theme dialog box, 70
Chrysler Web Web site, 184
clip art, 42–45, 307
Clip Art Gallery, 43–45
colors
   numeric values, 105
   text, 40
Comments table, 203, 220
computer consulting companies, 195
Comtrack Web site, 267
Concentric Web site, 267
confirmation pages, 225
container page, 89
Contains comparison, 213
content frame, 84
Control Panel, 33
Cool Edit 2000, 302

Index

Cool.htm page, 182–184
Corporate Presence Web, 75
   customizing, 71–72, 74
   home page, 71
   viewing in Web browser, 72
Corporate Presence Wizard, 67–71
Create Hyperlink dialog box, 108–109
Create New Data Source dialog box, 143
Create New Web dialog box, 60
Criteria dialog box, 154–155, 212, 229, 231
CRM (Customer Relationship Management), 6, 74, 307–308
customer relationship management, 136
customers
   e-mail, 181
   relevant order information, 8
   storing information, 7
Customers table, 203, 233
Customize Home Page, 71
customizing
   frame properties, 93–96
   Webs with wizards, 71–72, 74
CuteFTP, 253, 302
Cyberspace, 308

D

data, enabling with HTML, 9–10
database-driven Web page, 146–151
Database Results Properties command, 212, 229
Database Results Record Source command, 149
Database Results Wizard, 146, 154, 156, 226, 229, 231, 308
   Catalog table fields, 149
   CDShop data source, 148
   data display, 149
   grouping data, 149
   navigation buttons, 151
   search form, 152–157

Database Results Wizard command, 212–214
databases, 308
   accessing data, 141
   advanced integration, 158–163
   BestPop Web site, 201–205
   connecting with Web pages, 134
   creation of, 272–273
   Customers table, 135
   deleting information, 165
   designing, 18, 134
   DSN (data source name), 142–145
   inserting information, 158–163
   integrating with Web pages, 18
   keeping current, 8
   Orders table, 135
   preparing for Web pages, 142–157
   primary key field, 275–277
   Products table, 135
   queries, 290–293
   relational, 135–136
   search form, 151–157
   updating information, 165
Data length property, 212
Datasheet View, 283–284
Delete Rows command, 287
deleting
   field from table, 287
   table elements, 79
   tables, 82
Demo Web, 68–70
design
   drop-down menus, 11
   essentials, 11–13
   frames, 11
   general navigation scheme, 11
   special elements, 13, 15
   theme, 13
Design View, 283
   table creation, 273–282

Index

DHTML (Dynamic Hypertext Markup Language), 182, 308
DHTML effects, 181–184
DHTML toolbar, 183
Dial-up Connection dialog box, 33
dial-up networking connections, disabling, 33–35
disabling Windows automatic dial-up connection, 33–35
domain name, 244–245, 308
Drop-Down Menu Properties dialog box, 103–104
drop-down menus, 11–12, 103–104
Drop in by Word command, 183
DSN (data source name), 142–145, 308
dynamic forms, 132
dynamic Web pages, 7–8, 133–135, 308
dynamic Web sites, 9–10, 18, 118

E

e-commerce, 308
 considerations, 3–6
 enabling data with HTML, 9–10
 evolution, 6–10
Edit Hyperlink dialog box, 207, 216
electronic transactions, instantaneous speed of, 7–8
e-mail, 308
 about order, 8
 customers, 181
 integrating with FrontPage Webs, 178–180
e-mail addresses, 300
Exploit Submission Wizard, 257, 302
EZ Web Host Web site, 267

F

FastStats: Log File Analysis, 303
File, New, Page command, 85
File, New, Web command, 58, 67
File, New command, 97
File, Open command, 75
File, Open Web command, 251
File, Publish Web command, 248, 254
File, Recent, Files command, 76
File, Recent Webs command, 876
File, Save As command, 62, 87
File, Save command, 71, 94
File New Database dialog box, 273
files
 recently opened, 76
 Web-enabling, 30
finding domain name, 244–245
Flash 5 Fast & Easy Web Development, 184
Folders View, 37
FormA.htm page, 126, 171, 174
 changing radio button values, 128
 HTML tab, 124
Format, Dynamic HTML effects command, 183
formatting tables, 77
Formatting toolbar, 39, 43
FormB.asp page
 grouping radio buttons, 130
 HTML code changes, 129–130
 HTML tab, 128
 request.form, 130
 special information in HTML code, 124, 126
form collection, 126
form-processing Web pages, 124–131
Form Properties command, 123, 153, 159, 178, 212, 220, 233
Form Properties dialog box, 123, 153, 161, 178, 180, 220–221, 233
forms, 96–105, 308
 area of, 98
 browser testing of validation, 174
 check box, 101–102
 data range, 173
 determining required fields, 170–174
 drop-down menu, 103–104
 drop-down menu validation, 177
 dynamic, 132
 elements and form validation, 99
 field, 308

Index

field properties, 122
following function, 14
form elements, 98–105
   multiple, 99
   number of characters in field, 173
   one-line text box, 97, 100
   other element validation, 176–177
   processing, 98, 121–131
   properties, 123–124
   push button, 104–105
   radio button, 102
   radio button validation, 176–277
   Reset button, 105
   scrolling text box, 97, 100–101
   specific element data type, 172
   Submit button, 104–105, 174
   troubleshooting, 290
   validating, 170
   validation error, 174
FormTest file, 97
form validation, 99, 308
frame container, 199
frameleft.htm frame, 88, 91–92, 107
<frame name> tag, 91
Frame Properties command, 93
Frame Properties dialog box, 93–94
frameright.htm frame, 91
frames, 11–12, 309
   company name, 84
   content frame, 84
   customizing properties, 93–96
   naming, 88
   resizing, 93–94
   table of contents, 84
   Web browsers, 85
Frames page
   container page, 89
   creation of, 85
   HTML code, 89–92
   HTML tab, 93
   naming, 87

New Page buttons, 85
No Frames tab, 85
Normal tab, 93
operation of, 89–93
saving, 87–89
turning off border, 94–95
<frame> tag, 92
FrameTest.htm page, 87, 106–108, 112
   HTML tab, 89
   leftframe.htm frame, 111
frametop.htm frame, 91
FreeWebspace.net Web site, 267
FrontPage 2000, 9, 21, 309
   adding search feature to Web site, 184–186
   basics, 36–39
   Clip Art Gallery, 43–45
   Components, 47–51
   Corporate Presence Wizard, 67–71
   Database Results Wizard, 146
   DHTML effects, 182–184
   Folder List pane, 52
   Folders View, 37
   Font Color drop-down menu, 40
   Font drop-down menu, 40
   Formatting toolbar, 39
   forms, 96–105
   frames, 83–96
   hit counters, 47
   HTML view tab, 51
   hyperlinks, 106–112
   Hyperlinks View, 38
   inserting graphics, 41–47
   inserting information in database, 158–163
   Internet Explorer, 66
   JavaScript, 174
   Navigation View, 38
   Netscape Navigator, 66
   new Web page, 36
   No Frames tab, 92
   Page View, 36–37
   Picture toolbar, 45–47

Index

FrontPage 2000 *(continued...)*
    placing and formatting text, 39
    previewing Web pages, 50
    Preview tab, 50
    publishing Web site, 254–255
    recently opened files and Webs, 76
    Reporting View, 37
    saving Web pages, 51–52
    tables, 75–76
    Tasks View, 38
    themes, 70
    Web page creation, 39–52
    Web publishing features, 248–250
    wizards, 67–72
    WYSIWYG (what-you-see-is-what-you-get) interface, 119
FrontPage editor and Search Form element, 185
FrontPage Server Extensions, 32, 309
    publishing Web site with, 247–252
    publishing Web site without, 253–256
FrontPage Server Extensions folder, 32
FrontPage Web, 57
    accessing pages with Web browser, 65
    adding new pages, 61–62
    building, 57–66
    creation of, 58–61
    customizing with wizards, 71–72, 74
    integrating e-mail, 178–180
    location, 60
    naming, 58–61
    recently opened, 76
    storage location, 63
FTP (file transfer protocol), 309
FullName form element, 126

G

gathering and organizing information, 16–21
Get On The Web Internet Services Web site, 267
GifArt Clip Art Collection, 303
goals for Web site, 17

graphical hyperlinks, 111–112
graphics
    adding to tables, 80–83
    clip art, 42, 43–45
    designing your own, 42
    download times, 41
    inserting on Web page, 45
    modifying, 45
    obtaining, 42
    permission to use, 42
    previewing, 45
    tone set by, 41–42
guestbook.asp page, 218–223
guestbook_confirm.htm page, 223

H

HalfPrice Hosting Web site, 267
hit counters, 47, 309
Home.htm page, 65, 207
homeleft.htm page, 206
home pages, 3, 309
    creation of, 31
    location of, 60
    scrolling, 14
Home Page Wizard, 31
HosTek.com Web site, 267
The Hosting Company Web site, 268
hover buttons, 47
HTML (Hypertext Markup Language), 9–10, 119, 182, 309
HTML code, viewing, 51
HTTP (Hypertext Transfer Protocol), 309
Hyperlink Parameters dialog box, 216–217
Hyperlink Properties command, 207, 216–217
hyperlinks, 38, 92, 309
    adding unique identifier, 216–218
    graphical, 111–112
    testing in Web browser, 110–111
    text, 106–110
Hyperlinks View, 38

Index

I

IndoLinks Web site, 267
Infinities Web site, 268
information
    gathering and organizing, 16–21
    placement, 16–17
    as power, 136
Innerhost Web site, 268
Insert, Component, Search Form command, 185
Insert, Component command, 47
Insert, Database, Results command, 154
Insert, Form, One-Line Text Box command, 122
Insert, Form command, 97
Insert, Hyperlink command, 108, 112
Insert, Picture, Clip Art command, 111
Insert.asp page, 158, 161
insert_order.asp page, 236
Insert Rows command, 285
Insert Table dialog box, 76, 82
installing Personal Web Server, 27–35
Integer data type, 172
integrating databases with Web pages, 18
Internet Audio Mix, 303
Internet Explorer
    Cool.htm page, 183
    FrontPage, 66
    tables, 80
Internet Properties dialog box, 33
intranets, 27, 309
ISP (Internet Service Provider), 20, 309

J

JavaScript, 174, 309

L

Lamoureux, Jim, 192
leftframe.htm frame, 111
letterhead, 257
License, 300

links, 18
    See also hyperlinks
location.htm page, 206–210
Luxline Web site, 268

M

Macromedia Flash, 184
mailing_confirm.htm page, 223–225
mailing_list.asp page, 223–225
Mailing table, 203
major topics of discussion, 17
Marquee Properties dialog box, 48–49
marquees, 47–50
Microsoft Access Driver, 143
Microsoft Web site
    downloading Personal Web Server, 26
    FrontPage section, 247
MidWeb.net Web site, 268
Modify Criteria dialog box, 231
Modify Field dialog box, 222
modifying
    graphics, 45
    tables, 284–290
Modify Parameter dialog box, 217
monetary transactions, 258
More Options dialog box, 212, 229
multiple forms, 99
My Creations Clip Art Collection, 303

N

Name/Value Pair dialog box, 235
Navigation View, 38
NetCulture Web site, 268
NetData4 Web site, 268
Netscape Navigator
    Cool.htm page, 184
    FrontPage, 66
    tables, 80
NetStudio, 303–304
New Database Connection dialog box, 148

Index

New dialog box, 58–59, 97
New Page dialog box, 85
NewProducts.htm page, 108–109, 112
New Products hyperlink, 109
New Products page, 107–108
New Selections link, 84
New Web dialog box, 60, 67
No Constraints data type, 172
<noframes> tag, 92
notification of service, 138–139
Number data type, 172

O

ODBC (Open Database Connectivity), 309
ODBC Data Source Administrator dialog box, 143–144
ODBC Microsoft Access Setup dialog box, 143–144
one-line text box, 100
Open File dialog box, 63, 251
Open Web dialog box, 254
Options dialog box, 154
Options for Custom Form Handler dialog box, 123–124, 153–154, 212
Options for Saving Results of Form dialog box, 180
Options for Saving Results to Database dialog box, 159, 221–222
ORCS Web Inc. Web site, 268
order.asp page, 225–231
Order page, 215
orders and e-mail, 8
Orders table, 135
order_status.htm page, 236–238
order_status_results.asp page, 236–238
Ozelink Web site, 268

P

PacificNet Productions Web site, 268
PAC-Web Web site, 268
Page Load command, 183
Page Properties dialog box, 94

Page View, 36–37, 71
Paint Shop Pro, 304
Password, 304
permission to use graphics, 42
Personal Web Manager
   Advanced button, 121
   Publishing section, 59
Personal Web Server, 22, 310
   accessing FrontPage Web pages through, 65
   Advanced button, 31
   basic information about, 30
   component installation, 27–29
   customizing and editing directories, 31
   disabling Windows automatic dial-up connection, 33–35
   FrontPage 2000 server extensions, 32
   FrontPage Web in home directory, 59
   as full-fledged Web server, 30
   importance of, 26
   installing, 27–35
   intranets, 27
   Main button, 30
   obtaining, 25
   overview of features, 31
   Publish button, 30
   testing Web pages, 31
   verifying installation, 29–31
   Web Site button, 31
Picture toolbar, 45–47
Place and Order hyperlink, 227
place_order.asp page, 231–236
planning
   company demands, 20–21
   gathering and organizing information, 16–21
   logical, outline approach, 16
   major topics of discussion, 17
   ordering process, 16
   placing information, 16–17
   primary goal of Web site, 17
   Web site framework, 19
plug-ins, 13, 184, 310

Index

previewing
  graphics, 45
  Web pages, 50
Prima License Agreement, 298
primary goal of Web site, 17
primary key, 310
primary key field, 275–277
process flow
  bad Web design, 137–139
  in effective customer relationship management, 139
  notification of service, 138–139
  organizing, 136–141
  slow inventory update, 139
  successful Web design, 139–141
processing forms, 121–131
production Web sites, 205
product-oriented Web sites, 74
products, checked against currently available inventory, 7
Products table, 135
professional Web design, 138
Programs, Internet Explorer, Web Publishing Wizard command, 255
Programs, Microsoft FrontPage command, 36
Programs, Microsoft Office Tools, Server Extensions Administrator command, 32
promoting small business Web site, 256–258
promotional material, 258
publishing Web sites
  FrontPage, 254–255
  with FrontPage Server Extensions, 247–252
  selectively, 252
  Windows 98 Web Publishing Wizard, 255–256
  without FrontPage Server Extensions, 253–256
Publishing Wizard, 30
Publish Status report, 252
Publish Web dialog box, 248, 252, 254
Purp's World Graphics Clipart Collection, 304
push button, 104–105
Push Button Properties dialog box, 105

Q
queries, 272

R
radio button, 102
Radio Button Properties dialog box, 102, 176
Radio Button Validation dialog box, 171, 176–177
Readme files, 300
Register.com, 244–245
registering Web site name, 243–246
related subject links, 198
relational databases, 135–136
Reporting View, 37
reports, generating, 141
Reports, Publish Status command, 252
request.form, 126, 130
resizing
  frames, 93–94
  text, 40
RGM Webb Net Web site, 268
Run dialog box, 26

S
Save As dialog box, 51, 62, 87, 281
Save as Type drop-down menu, 124
Save Embedded Files dialog box, 51
saving
  frames pages, 87–89
  table of contents frame, 87–88
  Web pages, 51–52
scrolling text box, 97, 100–101
Scrolling Text Box Properties dialog box, 100
SearchA.htm page, 152, 156
SearchB.asp page, 154, 156
SearchCheck.htm page, 184, 186
search engines, 3, 310
search feature, 184–188
Search Form Properties dialog box, 185
search forms, 47, 151–157

search_results.asp page, 210–218
search results page, 154
Select Background Picture dialog box, 82
selectively publishing Web pages, 252
Server 101 Web site, 268
Settings, Control Panel command, 33
shop at home feature, 226–227
Signpost, 305
Simple Query Wizard, 290–293
site map, 19
slow inventory update, 139
SmallBiz Web, 75, 85
    ASP (Active Server Pages), 120–121
    FormA.htm page, 122, 171
    FormB.asp page, 124
    New Products page, 108
    processing forms, 121–124
    SearchCheck.htm page, 184
SmallBiz Web folder, 142
SpaceNet Web site, 268
special elements, 13, 15
Split Cells command, 80, 82
Split Cells dialog box, 80, 82
SQL (Structured Query Language), 272, 310
SQL Server, 202
Start, Settings, Control Panel command, 143
static Web sites, 7–10, 133, 310
storing customer information, 7
Submit-It Web site, 257

T

Table, Cell, Properties command, 79
Table, Delete Cells command, 82
Table, Delete command, 79
Table, Insert, Table command, 76, 82
Table, Properties, Cell command, 82
Table, Properties, Table command, 77
Table, Select, Cell command, 79
table of contents, 84
table of contents frame, 87–88, 200

Table Properties dialog box, 77
tables, 75–76
    adding text and graphics, 80–83
    Allow Zero Length property, 281
    background, 77
    blank fields, 279
    borders, 77
    cell alignment, 77
    cell padding, 77
    cell spacing, 77
    City field, 277
    Data type attribute, 280
    deleting, 82
    deleting elements, 79
    deleting field, 287
    Design View creation, 273–282
    editing, 79–80
    entering data in Datasheet View, 283–284
    field size, 278
    Field Size property, 280
    First Name field, 277
    formatting, 77
    ID field, 274–275
    inserting elements, 79
    inserting field, 285–287
    Internet Explorer, 80
    Last Name field, 277
    modifying, 284–290
    modifying field data type, 288–290
    Netscape, 80
    Phone Number field, 278
    planning, 282
    primary key, 282
    required fields, 279
    Required property, 281
    specific data types, 282
    splitting and merging cells, 79–80
    State field, 277
    Street Address field, 277
    Zip field, 278

Index

Tables, Insert command, 79
<TABLE> tag, 75
target audience, 140
Target Frame dialog box, 109–110, 207–208
Tasks View, 38, 71
Task/Upgrade Server Extensions command, 32
templates, 11
TestDatabase, 273–284
TestFrame page, 110
testing Web pages, 31
text
   adding to tables, 80–83
   centering, 39
   colors, 40
   fonts, 40
   FrontPage 2000 placement and formatting, 39–40
   resizing, 40
Text Box Properties dialog box, 100, 122, 171
Text Box Validation dialog box, 171–173
Text data type, 172
text files, 300
text hyperlinks, 106–110
themes, 70
title page, 200
toolbar, 310

U

URL (Uniform Resource Locator), 310
user interface
   left panel, 299
   resizing and closing, 298–299
   right panel, 299–300

V

validating forms, 170
VBScript, 310
Viewer, 305

W

Web address, 299–300
Web browsers
   accessing FrontPage Web pages, 65
   frames, 85
   not supporting frames, 92
   plug-ins, 13
   testing form validation, 174–176
   testing hyperlinks, 110–111
   testing Web sites in, 12
   viewing Corporate Presence Web, 72
Web design companies, 195
WebEnableSmallBusiness folder, 142
Web-enabling files, 30
Web hosting services, 265–268
WebLog Manager Pro, 305
Web pages
   connecting to database, 134
   database-driven, 146–151
   dynamic, 7–8, 133–135
   editing on Web server, 250–251
   form-processing, 124–131
   forms, 96–105
   frames, 83–96
   hyperlinks, 38, 106–112
   inserting graphics, 41–47
   inserting marquee, 48–50
   integrating databases with, 18
   multiple forms, 99
   navigational elements, 38
   new, 36
   organizing, 37
   placing and formatting text, 39
   preparing database for, 142–157
   previewing, 50
   saving, 51–52
   static, 7–8, 133
   storing, 57–66
   testing, 21–22, 31
The Web Power Web site, 268

Web servers, 21–22, 311
  ASP (Active Server Pages), 120
  editing pages on, 250–251
Web Settings dialog box, 148
Webshare folder, 63
Web Site Hosting Web site, 268
Web sites
  accessing all data in databases, 141
  accurate up-to-the-minute inventory information, 6
  basic information about company, 140
  cached pages, 252
  confirmation pages, 225
  content analysis, 37
  convenience of, 5
  CRM (Customer Relationship Management) strategy, 6
  current information, 20
  demands on company, 20–21
  design essentials, 11–13
  detailed information, 5
  domain name, 244–245
  dynamic, 118
  ease of access, 5
  ensuring validity, 21
  framework, 19
  generating reports, 141
  good navigation, 74
  good organization, 14
  hit counters, 47
  home page, 3
  hover buttons, 47
  information placement, 16–17
  as integrated business component, 117
  keeping customers informed, 75
  limited external assistance, 140–141
  links, 18
  major topics of discussion, 17
  marquees, 47
  outdated information, 118
  personalized experience, 74
  primary goals of, 17
  production, 205
  product-oriented, 74
  promoting, 256–258
  registering name, 243–246
  registering with search engines, 3
  related subject links, 198
  search feature, 184–188
  search forms, 47
  site map, 19
  target audience, 140
  tracking design tasks, 38
  updating general information, 140–141
  upgrading features, 20
  viewing hyperlinks, 38
Windows 95/98/NT4/2000/Me, 297–298
Windows 98 CD-ROM, downloading Personal Web Server, 26
Windows 98 Web Publishing Wizard, 255–256
Windows Dial-Up Connection dialog box, 60
Windows Explorer, 63
WinZip, 305
Wired Hosting Web site, 268
wizards and customizing webs, 71–72, 74
word of mouth, 258
World Wide Web, instantaneous speed of electronic transactions, 7–8
WPPs (Web Presence Providers), 179, 247, 310
Wwwroot folder, 63
WYSIWYG (What You See Is What You Get), 311
WYSIWYG (what-you-see-is-what-you-get) HTML editors, 9

Y

Yahoo!, 257
Yahoo! home page, 14

Looking for something to do this weekend?

Want to create your own Web page? Organize your finances? Upgrade your PC? It's time to put your weekends to work for you with PRIMA TECH's In a Weekend® series. Each book in the series is a practical, hands-on guide focused on helping you master the skills you need to achieve your goals. While you have the time, let our In a Weekend series show you how to make the most of it.

**Write Your Will
In a Weekend**
0-7615-2378-2
$24.99 U.S.

**Tune Up Your PC
In a Weekend**
0-7615-2451-7
$19.99 U.S. • $29.95 Can.

**Create Your First Mac
Web Page In a Weekend**
0-7615-2135-6
$24.99 U.S. • $37.95 Can.

**Create Your First Web Page
In a Weekend, 3rd Ed.**
0-7615-2482-7
$24.99 U.S. • $37.95 Can.

OTHER HOT TOPICS

**Build Your Home Theater
In a Weekend**
0-7615-2744-3
$24.99 U.S. • $37.95 Can.

**Create FrontPage 2000
Web Pages In a Weekend**
0-7615-1929-7
$24.99 U.S. • $37.95 Can.

**Increase Your Web Traffic
In a Weekend, 3rd Ed.**
0-7615-2313-8
$24.99 U.S. • $37.95 Can.

**Learn Access 97
In a Weekend**
0-7615-1379-5
$19.99 U.S. • $29.95 Can.

**Learn HTML
In a Weekend, Rev. Ed.**
0-7615-1800-2
$24.99 U.S. • $37.95 Can.

**Create Flash Pages
In a Weekend**
0-7615-2866-0
$24.99 U.S. • $37.95 Can.

**Electrify Your Web Site
In a Weekend**
0-7615-2505-X
$24.99 U.S. • $37.95 Can.

**Jumpstart Your Online
Job Search In a Weekend**
0-7615-2452-5
$24.99 U.S. • $37.95 Can.

**Learn Digital Photography
In a Weekend**
0-7615-1532-1
$24.99 U.S. • $37.95 Can.

**Set Up Your Home Office
In a Weekend**
0-7615-3054-1
$24.99 U.S. • $37.95 Can.

DO IT In a Weekend®

PRIMA TECH
A Division of Prima Publishing
www.prima-tech.com

**Call today to order!
1.800.632.8676, ext. 4444**

fast&easy™ web development

Getting Web developers up to speed

Less Time. Less Effort. More Development.

Don't spend your time leafing through lengthy manuals looking for the information you need. Spend it doing what you do best—Web development. Let PRIMA TECH's *fast & easy web development* series lead the way. Each book in this series contains step-by-step instructions and real screen shots to help you grasp concepts and master skills quickly and easily. Fast track your Web development skills with PRIMA TECH.

XHTML *Fast & Easy Web Development*
0-7615-2785-0 ■ CD Included
$24.99 U.S. ■ $37.95 Can.

Dreamweaver® *Fast & Easy Web Development*
0-7615-2905-5 ■ CD Included
$24.99 U.S. ■ $37.95 Can.

ASP 3 *Fast & Easy Web Development*
0-7615-2854-7 ■ CD Included
$24.99 U.S. ■ $37.95 Can.

CGI *Fast & Easy Web Development*
0-7615-2938-1 ■ CD Included
$24.99 U.S. ■ $37.95 Can.

ColdFusion® *Fast & Easy Web Development*
0-7615-3016-9 ■ CD Included
$24.99 U.S. ■ $37.95 Can.

Director® 8 and Lingo™ *Fast & Easy Web Development*
0-7615-3049-5 ■ CD Included
$24.99 U.S. ■ $37.95 Can.

Fireworks® *Fast & Easy Web Development*
0-7615-3082-7 ■ CD Included
$24.99 U.S. ■ $37.95 Can.

Flash™ X *Fast & Easy Web Development*
0-7615-2930-6 ■ CD Included
$24.99 U.S. ■ $37.95 Can.

Java™ 2 *Fast & Easy Web Development*
0-7615-3056-8 ■ CD Included
$24.99 U.S. ■ $37.95 Can.

PHP *Fast & Easy Web Development*
0-7615- 3055-x ■ CD Included
$24.99 U.S. ■ $37.95 Can.

PRIMA TECH
A Division of Prima Publishing
www.prima-tech.com

Call now to order!
1.800.632.8676, ext. 4444

License Agreement/Notice of Limited Warranty

By opening the sealed disc container in this book, you agree to the following terms and conditions. If, upon reading the following license agreement and notice of limited warranty, you cannot agree to the terms and conditions set forth, return the unused book with unopened disc to the place where you purchased it for a refund.

License:

The enclosed software is copyrighted by the copyright holder(s) indicated on the software disc. You are licensed to copy the software onto a single computer for use by a single concurrent user and to a backup disc. You may not reproduce, make copies, or distribute copies or rent or lease the software in whole or in part, except with written permission of the copyright holder(s). You may transfer the enclosed disc only together with this license, and only if you destroy all other copies of the software and the transferee agrees to the terms of the license. You may not decompile, reverse assemble, or reverse engineer the software.

Notice of Limited Warranty:

The enclosed disc is warranted by Prima Publishing to be free of physical defects in materials and workmanship for a period of sixty (60) days from end user's purchase of the book/disc combination. During the sixty-day term of the limited warranty, Prima will provide a replacement disc upon the return of a defective disc.

Limited Liability:

THE SOLE REMEDY FOR BREACH OF THIS LIMITED WARRANTY SHALL CONSIST ENTIRELY OF REPLACEMENT OF THE DEFECTIVE DISC. IN NO EVENT SHALL PRIMA OR THE AUTHORS BE LIABLE FOR ANY OTHER DAMAGES, INCLUDING LOSS OR CORRUPTION OF DATA, CHANGES IN THE FUNCTIONAL CHARACTERISTICS OF THE HARDWARE OR OPERATING SYSTEM, DELETERIOUS INTERACTION WITH OTHER SOFTWARE, OR ANY OTHER SPECIAL, INCIDENTAL, OR CONSEQUENTIAL DAMAGES THAT MAY ARISE, EVEN IF PRIMA AND/OR THE AUTHOR HAVE PREVIOUSLY BEEN NOTIFIED THAT THE POSSIBILITY OF SUCH DAMAGES EXISTS.

Disclaimer of Warranties:

PRIMA AND THE AUTHORS SPECIFICALLY DISCLAIM ANY AND ALL OTHER WARRANTIES, EITHER EXPRESS OR IMPLIED, INCLUDING WARRANTIES OF MERCHANTABILITY, SUITABILITY TO A PARTICULAR TASK OR PURPOSE, OR FREEDOM FROM ERRORS. SOME STATES DO NOT ALLOW FOR EXCLUSION OF IMPLIED WARRANTIES OR LIMITATION OF INCIDENTAL OR CONSEQUENTIAL DAMAGES, SO THESE LIMITATIONS MAY NOT APPLY TO YOU.

Other:

This Agreement is governed by the laws of the State of California without regard to choice of law principles. The United Convention of Contracts for the International Sale of Goods is specifically disclaimed. This Agreement constitutes the entire agreement between you and Prima Publishing regarding use of the software.